SOUL
MURDER

The Effects of Childhood
Abuse and Deprivation

LEONARD SHENGOLD, M.D.

YALE UNIVERSITY PRESS

New Haven & London

Published with assistance from the Mary Cady Tew Memorial Fund. Portions of
this book originally appeared in the *International Journal of Psycho-Analysis*.
Copyright © Institute of Psycho-Analysis. Other portions originally appeared in
the *Journal of the American Psychoanalytic Association*, *Psychoanalytic Study of
the Child*, and the *Psychoanalytic Quarterly*.

Designed by Richard Hendel
and set in Linotype Walbaum type by Tseng Information Systems, Inc.
Printed in the United States of America by Vail-Ballou Press, Binghamton, New York.

Library of Congress Cataloging-in-Publication Data
Shengold, Leonard.
Soul murder : the effects of childhood abuse and deprivation /
Leonard Shengold.
p.   cm.
Bibliography: p.
Includes index.
ISBN 0-300-04522-0 (alk. paper)
1. Adult child abuse victims—Mental health.   2. Psychoanalysis.
I. Title.   II. Title: Effects of childhood abuse and deprivation.
[DNLM: 1. Child Abuse—psychology.   2. Psychoanalytic
Interpretation. WA 320 S546s]
RC569.5.C55S54   1989
616.85'82—dc 19
DNLM/ DLC
for Library of Congress   89-5553
CIP

The paper in this book meets the guidelines for permanence and durability of
the Committee on Production Guidelines for Book Longevity of the Council on
Library Resources.

10   9   8   7   6   5   4   3   2

SOUL MURDER

The Effects of Childhood Abuse and Deprivation

To M., L. and L., N. and D.

CONTENTS

ACKNOWLEDGMENTS

In this book and in a previous one (Shengold 1988) I have published most of the ideas and discoveries that have been derived from my practice of psychoanalysis over the past thirty years. In my earlier book I thanked my patients and the teachers, family members, and friends who have instructed, influenced, and assisted me. Here I want again to acknowledge my indebtness to them and to add an expression of gratitude for the helpfulness and clear thinking of my two editors at Yale University Press, Gladys Topkis and Fred Kameny.

Too much and too little are qualities of experience. From the child's experiences we induce our theoretical psychoanalytic concepts of psychic energy and the "economic." Too much too-muchness we call trauma. Too much not-enoughness inhibits proper maturation. Child abuse means that the child has felt too much to bear; child deprivation means that the child has been exposed to too little to meet his or her needs. What the child's mind and body have been subjected to evokes discharge of body feeling and emotion; these in turn require defensive psychological measures against feeling—both discharge and defense are needed to avoid or lessen unbearable intensities. What comes from outside the body and mind in the form of stimulation operates in conjunction with constitutional givens and constitutional deficiencies (both can involve the all-important instinctual access to body feeling and emotions) to contribute to the normal and the pathological development of the structure and functioning of the mind.

The too-muchness of child abuse can be primarily sexual, as in being seduced or forced into sexual action and feeling. The overwhelming impact of the adult's sexuality and what it imposes on the child's relatively undeveloped physical and psychic capacity to function sexually and discharge sexual affect ensures that what can initially be pleasurable and promising to the child will produce overstimulation and pain. Psychologically, seduction can produce the same effect as outright rape (although the latter can result in greater physical damage). The frightening overstimulation inevitably leads to rage and an overwhelming mixture of sexual and aggressive feelings. If the abused child's experiences are primarily those stemming from aggressive attacks—being beaten and tormented—there is almost always a defensive sexualization of those experiences, which results in a similar sado-masochistic mixture of unbearable affect. To survive, the child must have enough gratification of the physical need for care and the psychological need to be wanted. The palpable absence of being cared about usually inhibits the developmental maturation of the mental structure and functioning needed to master intensities of affect. So for the developing child, deprivation can lead to the same traumatic and sado-masochistic imbalance as overstimulation. There are inescapable mixtures and alternations of overstimulation and neglect in everyone's development. These should be called child abuse and child deprivation only if "economic" conditions of intensity, duration, or both make for enough psychic damage that the result can be described as soul murder.

Soul murder is neither a diagnosis nor a condition. It is a dramatic term for circumstances that eventuate in crime—the deliberate attempt to eradicate or compromise the separate identity of another person.[1] The victims of soul murder remain in large part possessed by another, their souls in bondage to someone else. Thus Winston Smith at the end of *1984* loves the Big Brother who has taken over his mind. Torture and deprivation under conditions of complete dependency have elicited a terrible and terrifying combination of helplessness and rage —unbearable feelings that must be suppressed for the victim to survive. Brainwashing makes it possible to suppress what has happened and the terrible feelings evoked by the erased or discounted experiences. When it is necessary to retreat from feelings, good feelings as well as bad ones are compromised, and the victim's deepest feelings are invested primarily in the soul murderer (as Big Brother dominates the emotional universe of Winston Smith). Therefore murdering someone's soul means depriving the victim of the ability to feel joy and love as a separate person. In *1984* O'Brien says to Winston Smith: "You will be hollow. We will squeeze you empty, and then we shall fill you with ourselves" (p. 260).

Sexual abuse, emotional deprivation, physical and mental torture can eventuate in soul murder. Brainwashing keeps the condition of emotional bondage going. Children are the usual victims, for the child's almost complete physical and emotional dependence on adults easily makes possible tyranny and therefore child abuse; because he or she cannot escape from the tyrant-torturer, the child must submit to and identify with the abuser. ("The cut worm forgives the plough," Blake 1793, 96.) A consummated soul murder is a crime most often committed

1. Lionel Trilling wrote that the essence of morality is "making a willing suspension of disbelief in the selfhood of somebody else" (1955, p. 94).

by psychotic or psychopathic parents who treat the child as an extension of themselves or as an object with which to satisfy their desires. Lesser effects ensue from intermittent parental cruelty and indifference. I will try to demonstrate in my clinical examples something of what is done to effect soul murder and of how it comes about.

I cannot present a definitive exploration of child abuse and neglect, nor a solution for it. My case material will seem mild indeed to those dealing with battered and sexually assaulted children who turn up in police stations and hospital emergency rooms. I will describe people who were assaulted as children and have been scarred, but who have enough ego strength to maintain their psychological development and have summoned the considerable mental strength needed to present themselves as patients for psychoanalysis. The attempt to murder their souls was not completely successful. They are only a handful of people, but I would judge them representative of many others; I think my generalizations apply to many of the more disturbed victims too. But I have not studied any of the countless number who have ended up as derelicts, in madhouses, or in jails, or those who have not even survived an abused childhood.

I want to emphasize the complexity and the mystery involved in any attempt to connect pathological effects with specific causes. I stand against oversimplification, against reducing explanations just to external events or, conversely, just to intrapsychic forces. Children register in their minds, or at least are capable of registering the experiences of having been seduced or beaten, as well as fantasies of being seduced or beaten (based on universal inborn wishes). Psychological therapists are confronted with their patients' interrelated mental images of the world inside and of the world outside the self, which make up the individual's "representational world" (Sandler and Rosenblatt 1962)— the frontier at which patients interact with their therapists. Victims of attempts at soul murder find it very difficult to be responsible for their mental pictures of themselves, of others, and of the world around them. They often cannot properly register what they want and what they feel, or what they have done and what has been done to them.

Child abuse is the abuse of power. We do not have a coherent psychology of power; much is unknown. Soul murder is as old as human history, as old as the abuse of the helpless by the powerful in any group —which means as old as the family. But soul murder has a particular resonance with the twentieth century—with the world of Orwell's

1984—and a particular relevance to it. This is the century of the computer, the concentration camp, and the atomic bomb, of the presence of such destructive potential that all life on earth is threatened, and of a centralized power so monolithic and intrusive that it has been aimed at mastery over the individual's mind as well as body. This power has been implemented by twentieth-century discoveries in psychology and communications that have made brainwashing and mind control easily attained effects of terror and torture. Hitler and Stalin have proven that the strongest adults can be broken and deprived of their individuality and even of their humanity. That is one of the lessons of Orwell's *1984*—one that can also be learned from the lives of those who have grown up in the charge of crazy, cruel, and capricious parents, in the totalitarian family ambience that Randall Jarrell calls "one of God's concentration camps" (1963, p. 146).

In relation to both our external and our inner psychic lives, Freud viewed as all-important the influence of those first carriers of the environment and first objects of our instinctual drives, the parents: what they do, what they evoke in the child, how they are registered within the mind of the child and become part of its mental structure, how they are separated out to leave the child with its own individuality. For the developing infant, these gods of the nursery (or their caretaker substitutes) *are* the environment. They have power over the helpless, and they can easily get away with misrule and tyranny. They are also under a powerful unconscious compulsion to repeat the circumstances of their own childhood. We regularly find that abusers of children have been abused as children by their own parents. This is not heredity (although we cannot completely rule that out) but rather a passing down of a traumatic past from generation to generation. The sins of the father are laid upon the children—but not, as Freud has shown, upon innocent children. Children are easy to seduce because they want to be seduced. And we have learned that in the terrible circumstances of parents who do not love, are indifferent, or hate, children will turn to seduction, even to provocation to be beaten, to fulfill the imperative need for some parental attention. Those who have devised procedures for causing mental breakdown in inmates of prisons and concentration camps have resorted to a regimen of emotional deprivation and isolation, alternating with humiliation and torture. Child abuse is a consequence of our need for dependence and our innate sadism and masochism, and it enhances that sadism and masochism in its child victim.[2]

We find in our patients that they regularly identify with the aggressor. To identify means *to be* and *not to see* someone. It follows that when these people find their own victims they do not experience them as separate individuals—they do not empathize with them. The abused child's siblings, already subject to the primal displacement of murderous impulse from the parent to the intruding infant (this is the theme of the story of Cain and Abel), tend to be the first scapegoats of the abused child. Although individual variations may ensue, usually the hostility is eventually displaced onto people outside the family: underlings, especially those who play vague parental roles and yet are dependent—like servants, porters, waiters. This kind of hostility that denies the other's humanity is very often shifted onto those who are already the victims of persecution—the racially different, foreigners, "official" enemies, like the ever-changing warring opponents in *1984*. (These can all unconsciously stand for the denied and projected bad aspects of one's parent, self, and family.) Ultimately the compulsion to repeat a traumatic past focuses the rage of the former victims of attempted soul murder on children in general, and on their own children.[3] (As expected in psychic events, feelings of caring and concern, consisting of reaction formations against the hatred as well as genuine counterfeelings to it, can exist alongside it.)

What I have observed from my limited vantage point, as a psychoanalyst and psychotherapist in private practice who does some supervision of therapy with patients in clinics, confirms Freud's varied and complex

2. There is also a convincing sociological study of this in Colin Turnbull's *Mountain People* (1972), about an African tribe whose members humiliate and torment their children. The children grow up to be cruel to their own children in turn, to be uncaring of one another, and to abandon their old people.
3. In an autobiographical part of his short story "Three Years" (1895), Anton Chekhov writes of the emotions of his grown-up hero on revisiting his father's warehouse, where he was beaten daily (like Anton himself as a child in the family business of his own father): "Every little detail [in that warehouse] reminded him of the past, when he had been whipped and given plain, lenten food. He knew that boys were still whipped and punched in the nose until it bled, and that when these boys grew up they would do the punching" (p. 102). See also Daldin 1988.

views on psychic pathogenesis—views that would lead me to expect the infinite variety and complexity of the effects of child abuse and neglect. I know that the range of psychopathology that is encompassed, of diagnostic categories that are elicited, is broad and diverse. There are of course many combinations of effects. The most important determinant, overstimulation, involves power, or psychic economics. Too much neglect and too much torment and abuse (especially when these occur too early) interfere with development and functioning and can make for the blank slate of devastated psychic structure. The children may not physically survive the assaults, or they may later succumb to an inner need for annihilation analogous to that René Spitz (1945) found in his study of emotionally deprived infants who died after growing up in institutions. For the survivors of abuse and neglect, this self-destructive current develops into a strong, conscience-distorting need for punishment. It is all too easy to murder the souls as well as the bodies of children. There must be some minimum of care and some kind of acceptance from the parents for the child to survive.

What we do not know about child abuse and soul murder is probably more important than what we do, and in addition there is the mystery of greatly varying inherited gifts and ego strength: these enable some abused children to sustain more abuse and transcend it better than others.[4] Some of these children grow up impelled chiefly to contain rather than repeat the traumata, although differing proportions of both impulses will always be present. With faulty or inconstant defenses, with partially defective psychic structure (here again there is interplay with mysterious, in this case *negative*, "givens"), soul-murdered children can be or become psychotic, or psychopathic and criminal. Or, by using massive and primitive defenses (usually including denial and autohypnosis), they may be able to contain the terrifying, primarily murderous (sado-masochistic) charge of affect that they have been forced to bear. They have to pay a price for these defenses, but they can appear or really be neurotic. Some frequently can or even must function in an "as if" fashion: they act as if they were psychologically healthy, presenting a façade of normality that covers an essential hollowness of soul.

From my experience with patients and my reading about the lives of

4. See the work on so-called invulnerable children by C. James Anthony and others.

others, I know that one comes across the unexpected in these people. For example, alongside the scars and distortions produced by terrible childhoods there are some strengthening effects: some survivors appear to have derived from their experiences adaptive powers and talents that helped them survive. (I will be illustrating this with examples from my patients and from writers who have discussed their childhoods.) This enhancement of certain gifts is analogous to what has been observed in those who have survived wars and concentration camps. I have learned to be wary of generalizations about pathological limitations in people who were abused and neglected as children. But I have observed certain common pathological features, mostly based on specific consequences of prolonged or repeated abuse and neglect: the evocation of mur- der, cannibalism, and traumatic anxiety by the enforced and reactive overstimulation (frequently but not always marked by the eruption in analytic associations of cannibalistic creatures like the rat); the con- comitant imperative need for rescue from the unbearable intensities and defense against them; the need to take on the attributes of the tormentor and turn on other victims the abuse that was suffered.

Before further defining and describing soul murder I will present an instance of it. The childhood experiences of A., a superficially success- ful man, married and a father, deserve the label of soul murder. The soul murder was not completely successful: A.'s identity was warped and constricted, but it survived. There was no overt physical abuse on the part of the A.'s parents—the "crime" consisted of some cruelty toward him, but predominantly what made his childhood a hell was their indifference, their lack of loving care and empathy.

A. sought analysis because he was chronically and sometimes des- perately unhappy. His depression was intermixed with a smoldering hatred for his peers and superiors, especially at his work. He was afraid of retaliation, but it was the feeling of hatred itself that made him most anxious. Occasional outbursts of rage, like temper tantrums, were usually directed against his wife. "I have never been able to enjoy any- thing," he said with intense bitterness. Although his parents were very rich and had provided luxurious surroundings and the most expensive education, he had always felt deprived and cheated: "What father and mother did for me they did for themselves; they never bothered about what I wanted. They never even tried to find out what I wanted. They told me what I wanted." A. felt that his parents had not loved him or even liked him. "My parents despised their children; I despised my brothers; and I despised myself." He believed he had been stripped of the capacity for humor: "I can laugh only when I am drunk." Unfortunately, he was drunk all too frequently—his parents were alcoholics, and alcoholism was a family problem that had bridged generations. A.'s monotonous tone of accusatory complaint and his almost unchanging bitter, deadpan expression seemed to me to represent an unconscious challenge: "Just you *try* to like me!" He himself said: "People tolerate me because of my abilities, but I am simply not likable." His masochistic wife was registered as an exception to this rule, but as part of his despising himself he despised her for wanting him.

The story of A.'s childhood evoked for me F. Scott Fitzgerald's psychologically acute, much-quoted remark to Hemingway: "The very rich are different from you and me."[5] The special ambience of the mansions of A.'s childhood came from the contrast between his parents' visibly lavish fulfillment of material needs and their unawareness or frustration of emotional ones. He was brought up by servants in a nursery seldom visited by his father and mother even when they were at home—and they were frequently away, sometimes abroad. When in his parents' presence A. usually felt belittled and humiliated by them, especially in response to any show of emotion on his part. The family ideal was to be cool, witty, and physically distant. The habitual vicious teasing and sarcasm from both parents amounted to training A. to regard any empathic communication as a prelude to torment. It seemed consistent with adaptation to this background that he talked in a clipped monotone, like a machine.

A.'s mother had often told him that she had been looking for a strong man when she married his father. Indeed, the father tried to act the generalissimo at home and in his business. Both the family home and the country estate had the aura of a cavalry post, and the patient firmly believed that the parents' many horses received better care than the children. The servants in the stable were by and large kept on; those in the nursery were frequently and capriciously changed. The strong-willed parents seemed to agree only in their concern for horses and in their abusive treatment of their sons; they quarreled constantly and dramatically, especially when drunk. Stubborn and prolonged spitefulness abounded. The patient talked of family life in military metaphor—as a

5. Hemingway's cynical rejoinder, "Yes, they have more money," attests to his deficiency as a psychological novelist (see Trilling 1948, 214).

war with battles, retreats, campaigns. Although terrified by this, the boy was expected to express no feelings or complaints; he was reproached for not being grateful for his privileged life.

The parents of A. finally divorced when he was ten. The mother had always said that she wanted her son to be a strong man, like her own father, a professional army officer. The avowedly spartan character training the parents devised for their sons, marked by aloofness, nakedness, and the endurance of cold, was in confusing contrast to the self-indulgent life-style of the parents.[6]

Something of the current relationship of the depressed son with his mother was revealed by a birthday gift she sent to him shortly after she was told he had entered psychoanalysis. In a note accompanying the gift she said she was sorry to hear yet again about the weakness of his character, and the gift itself—a true "gift of Medea" (see Orgel and Shengold 1968)—was a set of pistols that had belonged to her father. It was apparent to me that this twentieth-century Hedda Gabler was telling her weak, deserting son to shoot himself. A. seemed to have some insight into his mother's motivation—he quoted a friend's comment that to give a pistol to a depressed man was not exactly a loving act. But this secondhand comment was superficially felt. The meaning of the pistols was overdetermined; A. talked more readily (yet with little feeling) about the paternal phallic symbolism of the pistols than about their destructive potential. Although he spoke of his mother's murderous intent when expanding on the quote from his friend, he essentially denied it. Medea too had sent her poisoned gift on the occasion of a threatened separation—a breaking of the symbiotic tie. Like Medea's victim, A. could not resist the magical promise of a present, even from an avowedly hostile witch. There had been many similar gifts in the past, but he could never keep from an insistent, almost delusional anticipation that this time the gift and therefore the giver would turn out to be good (this is characteristic of soul-murder victims). He found himself drawn to playing with the pistols.

A.'s father was a tyrannical, paranoid loner who quarreled with and alienated everyone. With both parents drinking so heavily, the silent

6. I feel that these parents were two of "those who have been maltreated in childhood [and] have an almost uncanny ability to find and to marry someone with a similar background and similar ideas about child rearing" (Steele 1976, 14).

and embittered home atmosphere could suddenly be transformed by violence. The parents' verbal abuse could become physical assault, and sometimes the parental battles would end in turbulent and exhibitionistic sex within view of the terrified children. (See Silber 1974, 1977, on alcoholism and parental abuse.) Sometimes the parents would then disappear for weeks.

Overstimulation was not A.'s main complaint about his childhood. He remembered suffering most from intense emotional deprivation, and this he immediately transferred onto the analytic situation: "Nobody cared, and you don't care!" Being the object of his parents' sarcasm and witnessing their sex and violence at least provided some sort of contact. What was worst was the emotional abandonment and the misery of feeling alone, uncared for, and helpless to do anything about it. He had turned off his feelings because feeling nothing was better than feeling panic and pain. Now A. was distressed by his inability to respond lovingly to his wife and children.

Any nurse or governess to whom A. became too attached was soon dismissed. He learned to hide his feelings toward the servants and was able through craft to maintain two meaningful relationships, with a cook and a gardener. These two substitute parents seemed genuinely concerned about him and actually listened to him. Unfortunately the gardener's caring was partly spoiled by the sexual interest that he took in A. after the boy became pubescent. A. found the man's sexual advances frightening and disgusting, but for a while he submitted to being masturbated because he craved the emotional warmth. And he was able to discontinue the sex without breaking the relationship. It became obvious in the analysis that he had been greatly threatened by the intensity of his unconscious passive cravings. Both parents insisted that he be "manly," and his strong temptation to accuse and betray the beloved gardener to his father was a torment to the boy. It came as a relief to be sent away to boarding school.

A characteristic of this family's habits (one frequently found mutatis mutandis in the families of many soul-murder patients that I have observed) was the enforced emotional isolation of the immediate family group. To preserve the myth that the parents' ways are not pathogenic and sometimes bizarre, the family members have to keep away from others. In A.'s family there were many houseguests, generally at drunken weekend parties, but there was a constant turnover and those who were repeaters paid little attention to the children. There was no extended family, no literal or figurative aunts or uncles to act as substitute parents. (Most importantly for A., the two servants I mentioned did fulfill this function.) The children's friends were not permitted to visit the family homes, and A.'s parents discouraged their children from visiting the homes of their schoolmates. In the other homes they might have gained some perspective on their own domestic soul-murder atmosphere by viewing and sharing more relaxed, loving family relationships, and in late adolescence and beyond A. did to some extent gain such a perspective. This avoidance of other families and parents can be encouraged and enforced by the soul-murdering parents consciously, unconsciously, or both. At some point the need to keep away is usually taken over by the child victim. To see from others' lives that one's life and parents might have been different can provide some hope for the future, for a change for the better; unfortunately there is usually alongside this hopeful feeling a preponderant pain and danger. To be able to make comparisons and attain a sense of proportion and perspective threatens the denial necessary for the soul-murder victim to keep the delusion of having good parents, and intense destructive impulses against the bad parent might be felt. As this was becoming clear in A.'s analysis, he said to me plaintively, "You don't understand that a real honest look at other families would lead to the total destruction of my family." He was terrified of the murderous rage in his walled-off fantasy life; to him, fully feeling this rage meant that change brought the prospect of unsustainable loss, even if the change promised something better.

Perhaps the acme of the recurrent, agonizing combination of overwhelming promise and cruel frustration came at Christmas. Every year a huge tree was beautifully decorated and presents were piled underneath. There was great stir in the house, which was filled with guests, and a showy but exciting ritual of opening the presents on Christmas morning. On Christmas day the boy was permitted to play with the expensive toys he had received. But the next morning he had to help his father repack the toys in their boxes: they were to be given away, every one, to the "poor children." How he hated those poor children! Of course he hated them instead of his father; they were nasty vermin like his younger brothers. A. usually remembered the past as if he were an only child, so intense was the hatred displaced from the parents onto the siblings. No cooperation or community of feeling as fellow victims was possible for these brothers in the face of their mutual, murderous, malignant envy.[7]

Christmas left the boy feeling wicked, guilty, and depressed. His father must be good—he was doing Christ's work by giving to the poor. A.'s conviction that his father was benevolent meant a complete suppression of rage toward him and a nonregistration of what had happened. The rage was untenable, and the absolute need to suppress it and be left with at least a potentially good and giving parent made for brainwashing. The cruelty of the giving and then taking away was denied; the boy identified with the aggressor, his conscience taking over his father's inhumanity. He, the boy, was unworthy, and he accepted as valid his father's professed charitable and character-building motives. He idealized his tormentor and suppressed the torment. As Christmas again approached he would remember what had happened to last year's toys, but the insistent hope that this time things would be different would return (and need turned this hope into delusional promise). He was effectively deprived of his feelings, memory, and identity and became his parents' creature: the Good Boy, a pseudo-identity marked by mechanical dutifulness and a cheerless, loveless existence. The brainwashing, involving denial, emotional isolation, and autohypnotic states, became a continuous internalized process, and this made for a chronic soulless façade. Underneath lurked murder and suicide; yet A. functioned and he achieved.

I am fond of meandering designs; this book proceeds more by association than by orderly progression, and some motifs recur throughout. I begin with a more comprehensive picture of soul murder and other examples of it and go on to examine brainwashing and its consequences. I say something about the difficulty of definitively establishing past occurrences, then investigate the play *Oedipus Rex*, which depicts primal soul-murdering parents (phenomena found in the play are paralleled in some of my patients). George Orwell's *1984* provides material about soul murder throughout this book, and there is a chapter specifically

7. The turning on the fellow victim was like that depicted by Orwell in *1984* as the final crushing of Winston Smith's humanity and identity, when he displaces the cannibalistic rage aroused by his torturers onto his lover Julia (see chapter 5).

examining Orwell's life and his last novel. Another recurrent theme, one linked with Orwell, is the frequency with which some victims of child abuse use the image of the rat—an animal that evokes intense anxiety and murderous, cannibalistic impulses; I offer clinical and literary examples. I also investigate what Orwell describes as a concomitant of brainwashing—the use of autohypnosis. There follow presentations of attempts at soul murder in the lives and some of the works of Dickens, Chekhov, and Kipling; these are juxtaposed with the story of a patient who had incest with his mother. The literary and clinical presentations support the surprising finding that the damaging traumata can also contribute to the strengths and talents of the suffering victim. Finally, I have some observations (which have more general valence too) on these patients' need for insight and perspective, and some comments on the technique and course of analytic treatment used with them.

1

Aspects of Soul Murder

A mother drags a reluctant, whimpering child along a street. The mother, her face convulsed with rage, mouth twitching, stops suddenly and brutally slaps the child across the face. The little girl falls down and the mother begins to kick her. Is the mother psychotic? Is she a drug addict? What will happen to the child of such a mother, *if* the child survives to grow up? (When the observer advanced toward the two, instinctively starting to "rescue" the child, the mother looked up at him with an unforgettable, menacing grin and brandished her fist over the child's head.) And if the child grows up, will she in turn kick her own child?[1]

Some of the stories that patients tell about their parents and childhood could make the psychiatrist weep: my father beat us so badly he broke bones; my mother put lye in my halfwit brother's oatmeal; my mother kept the bedroom door open when she brought men home for sex; my stepfather took baths with me and taught me to suck him off, and when I told my mother she slapped me and called me a liar. Sometimes the accusations do not primarily concern beatings and sexual abuse but hatred and mental torture; or they are about complete indifference, neglect, and desertion. They present parents who are psychotic or psychopathic or alcoholic. Love and empathy are described as never or only intermittently present—cold indifference or destructive hatred

1. "If one's early life was unfortunately beset by neglect and abuse, then one is likely to repeat it, and treat one's offspring as one was treated" (Steele 1976, 14; compare Greenacre 1960 and Shengold 1967, which stress the *compulsion* to repeat the traumatic past).

reigns. Often one hears of a kind of brainwashing, a cultivation of denial by the parents that makes the child doubt the evidence of his or her own senses and memory. It is not easy to peer into these pictures of childhood hell, especially if the psychological worker thinks of the millions of abused and deprived who never seek out therapy and end up in misery and destitution, in prisons and madhouses. And the listener is often inclined to seek a defense against the terrible intensity of these stories of helpless children under the tyranny of monstrous parents, sometimes by doubting the "truth" of what has been told. And what is truth? Can the observer be sure that what has been recounted has actually happened?

Freud believed that destructiveness and the abuse of power are part of our inherited biological nature, flowing from our bodies to our minds in the form of instinctual drives. He viewed our attempts at civilization, at transcending our murderous, polymorphous perverse, and incestuous human nature, as heroic and tragic—capable at best of achieving a partial success, a compromise that leaves us inherently neurotic, with a discontent that can easily regress to hatred and misery (Freud 1930).

Freud did not begin with this pessimistic, universal view of neurosis. He was a child of the rationalistic, scientific second half of the nineteenth century. His first theory of psychic pathogenesis centered on child abuse, viewed as a trauma with tragic consequences. Neurotics, he said, suffer from reminiscences of overstimulating events in childhood. He wrote to his friend Fliess in 1896 that hysteria is the result not of heredity (as the psychiatric thinking then current would have it) but of "seduction by the father" (Freud, 1892–99, p. 239). Psychoneurotics told Freud that they had been sexually assaulted as children by parents, older siblings, or other adults. Later, after listening further to his patients and after his own self-analysis, Freud concluded that not all the stories of seduction he had been told were true, and so discovered the role of fantasy in human motivation. In his theory a psychic life of fantasy, in large part unconscious, developed in the course of transforming instinctual drives and body feelings. As a Lamarckian he believed that some fantasies might even be part of phylogenetic inheritance. Freud described these primal fantasies, involving sex and murder (such as the oedipus complex), as expressing the motivating instinctual forces of the mind. He never minimized the role of the environment or of traumatic intrusion and interference in pathogenesis. He was aware of the past and continuing actuality of "seduction by the father" for some of his patients. But Freud's ideas of universal drives, of unconscious conflict and fantasy, led him to the conviction that neurosis not only affects "them," the sick patients, but is inherent in "us"—to be human is to be neurotic.

Differentiating fantasy from memory to determine if an event really occurred is never easy and sometimes impossible. Memory and fantasy are always intertwined. Yet we depend on a good enough ability to differentiate the two in the present, and this capacity for "reality testing" is acquired in the course of childhood development. To feel that we have an identity, we must know (or at least feel that we know) what is and was "real"; we must trust at least some of our memories if not most of them and be able to set them apart from our conscious fantasies. Yet it is characteristic of the victims of soul murder that they have lost the ability to make these differentiations. Erasing history by cultivating denial is essential to the brainwashing that is an inevitable part of psychic murder, resulting all too often in what Nietzsche called the worst form of slavery: that of the slave who has lost the knowledge of being a slave. No one has documented this better than George Orwell in *1984*. (Chapter 5 deals with Orwell's appreciation of how complicated this denial is.)

I assume that actual overwhelming *experiences* in a child's development of seduction, rape, and beatings by parents have a different, more profound destructive and pathogenic effect than do the fantasies of such experiences that inevitably arise in the psychic elaboration of the child's sexual and aggressive impulses. It seems less controversial to see as potentially destructive and pathogenic the experiences of early deprivation of *care* and deprivation of *caring* (the latter is subtler but equally devastating). There ought not to be disagreement that experiences have greater pathogenicity than do fantasies.[2] The crucial clinical problem is to know how experiences of overstimulation and deprivation influence the motivating fantasies of an individual (Fliess 1956, xvii). And how do those motivating fantasies relate to an individual's impulses, actions, and experiences?

Soul murder is my dramatic designation for a certain category of traumatic experience: instances of repetitive and chronic overstimulation, alternating with emotional deprivation, that are deliberately

2. The clinical writings of some Kleinian theorists (not all) occasionally give the impression that the child's actual experiences hardly matter.

brought about by another individual.[3] The term does not define a clinical entity; it applies more to pathogenic circumstances than to specific effects.

History of the Term "Soul Murder"

The phrase "soul murder" should be familiar to psychoanalytic readers because of its use by the paranoic judge Daniel Paul Schreber, whose *Memoirs* (1903) were the subject of one of Freud's case histories (1911). The earliest use I have found is in *Kaspar Hauser: Beispiel eines Verbrecherens am Seelenleben des Menschen* (*Kaspar Hauser: An Instance of a Crime against the Life of the Soul of Man*), a popular book by Anselm von Feuerbach (1832). The first English translation of the book has an even longer sub-title summarizing the story: *Kaspar Hauser: An Account of an Individual Kept in a Dungeon, Separated from All Communication with the World, from Early Childhood to about the Age of Seventeen.* The case of Kaspar was a *cause célèbre* in his time. Imprisoned in a dark cellar, he had been cut off from all human contact except for an occasional glimpse of his jailer (whom he called "the Man who was always there"). When Kaspar was turned loose he was discovered wandering in the streets of Nuremberg, at seventeen more a baby than a man. Here are details of an eyewitness account:

> He appeared neither to know nor to suspect where he was. He betrayed neither fear, nor astonishment, nor confusion; he rather showed an almost brutish dullness . . . his tears and whimpering, while he was always pointing to his tottering feet [he seemed not to know how to walk correctly], and his awkward, and, at the same time, childish demeanour, soon excited the compassion of all present . . . his whole conduct . . . seemed to be that of a child scarcely two or three years old, with the body of a young man. (Von Feuerbach, 1832, 3–4)

Kaspar had to be taught to speak and walk properly, to learn the difference between the organic and the inorganic. He showed an intense,

3. "Deliberately" should be interpreted loosely; the therapist's inability to empathize with some psychotics makes responsibility for their actions undeterminable.

passionate wish to learn and displayed unusual powers (he could distinguish colors in the dark, for example). Kaspar seemed asexual and incapable of anger; he showed no indignation at "the Man who was always there." It was as if some instinctual energy had been extinguished. When von Feuerbach expressed surprise that Kaspar "should wish to return to that abominably bad man, [Kaspar] replied with mild indignation, 'Man not bad, man me no bad done'" (1832, pp. 71–72). There proved no way of making up for the emotional deficits, and after a period of wonderful intellectual promise (the observers talked of genius) Kaspar, his mind unprepared emotionally to grasp how much he had been deprived of, gradually regressed into a kind of obsessive-compulsive automaton. (This is marvelously portrayed in Werner Herzog's film on Kaspar Hauser, 1974.) His pathetic story (which led to romantic speculation that he was of royal blood) and the excitement of his education and subsequent murder were followed by thousands of readers in the newspapers of Europe. Von Feuerbach, who befriended Kaspar and helped care for him, wrote indignantly about Kaspar's imprisonment and "the cruel withholding from him of . . . all the means of mental development and culture—the unnatural detention of a human soul in a state of irrational animality." Even after his release at Nuremberg, Kaspar was subject to states of hypnosis and stuporous sleep.

Having been sunk during the whole of the earlier part of his life in animal sleep, [Kaspar] has passed through this extensive and beautiful part of it, without having lived through it. His existence was, during all this time, similar to that of a person really dead: in having slept through his youthful years, they have passed by him, without his having had them in his possession; because he was rendered unable to become conscious of their existence. This chasm, which crime has torn in his life, cannot any more be filled up; that time, in which he omitted to live, can never be brought back, that it may be lived through; that juvenility, which fled while his soul was asleep, can never be overtaken. How long soever he may live, he must for ever remain a man without childhood, and boyhood, a monstrous being, who, contrary to the usual course of nature, only began to live in the middle of his life. Inasmuch as all the earlier part of his life was thus taken from him, he may be said to have been the subject of a partial *soul-murder* . . . the life of a human soul was mutilated at its commencement. (1832, pp. 52, 56–57; my italics)

Feuerbach was a distinguished judge and legal scholar, and his work may very well have been read by his fellow jurist Schreber.[4]

In 1887 Strindberg gave the title "Soul Murder" to an article on Ibsen's *Rosmersholm*. He said that instances of actual murder were decreasing in the Western world, but that soul (or psychic) murder, which he defined as taking away a person's reason for living, was on the increase. This concept obsessed Strindberg, who was at that time illustrating it in his great play *The Father* (see Jacobs 1969). Soul murder was a repetitive theme of Ibsen, who uses the term directly in his play *John Gabriel Borkman* (1896) when Ella Rentheim says to the title character: "You are guilty of a double murder—the murder of your own soul, and mine" (Meyer, trans., p. 268). In the play Ibsen speaks of soul murder as a "mysterious" sin mentioned in the Bible "for which there is no forgiveness" (Archer, trans., p. 246), and as "killing the instinct for love" (Paulson, trans., p. 334), "killing the love-life in a human soul" (Archer, trans., p. 246), and murdering "love in a human being" (Meyer, trans., p. 269).

Ibsen and Strindberg wrote mainly about the destruction of the souls of adults within the arena of the family, the familiar territory of the psychological therapist. The capacity to destroy a soul hinges entirely on having another human being in one's power, and this confrontation of the powerful and the helplessly dependent is inherent in childhood. Because this conflict is inevitable no matter what efforts we make to minimize its effects, institutionalized soul murder too, like individual soul murder, has always been with us and always will be. Human history is as full of instances of psychic murder as it is of physical murder. The totalitarian soul murder of our recent past is described in books like Koestler's *Darkness at Noon* and Orwell's *1984*, in many of Hannah Arendt's works, and in the memoirs of Nadezhda Mandelstam and many other victims of Stalin and the Nazis.

In individuals, psychic murder is founded on the relations between hostile, cruel, indifferent, psychotic, or psychopathic parents and the child prisoners in their charge. Kipling has dealt with this in his fiction;

---

4. I am grateful to Jeffrey Masson for directing me to von Feuerbach's book. For a full account of the soul murder of Kaspar Hauser see Shengold 1988.

so has Dickens (see chapters 10 and 12).[5] Children can be broken much more easily than adults, and the effect on them of torture, hatred, seduction, and rape—or even of indifference and withholding love and care—is usually the devastating one of developmental arrest, for their souls, their psychological structure and functioning, are still forming (see the important work of David Freedman, 1969, 1971, 1975; Freedman and Brown, 1968).

Schreber and Soul Murder

Schreber (1903) furnished elaborate, paranoid variations on fantasies he called *soul murder;* these can supply some unconscious reverberations of the term's meaning. Complementing Ibsen's characterization of soul murder as "mysterious," Schreber presents the concept as inherently vague, saying that he can present only "hints" at a definition (p. 58). He alludes to a pact with the devil (invoking *Faust, Manfred,* Weber's *Freischütz*); one person absorbs the life of another. Schreber connects soul murder with his psychiatrist, the father figure Professor Flechsig, "or one of his forebears" (p. 58), but ultimately it is God, the Father in Heaven, who is accused of lacking empathy, the power to know what it was like to be a child and His son (as Niederland convincingly shows, Schreber's father could have been similarly accused): "*A fundamental misunderstanding* obtained, however, which has since run like a red thread through my entire life. It is based upon the fact that, *within the Order of the World, God did not really understand the living human being.* . . . He dealt only with corpses" (1903, p. 75; Schreber's italics). This is Schreber's allusive, bitter, reproachful cri de coeur about his father.

According to Schreber, in soul murder the victim's identity, including the sexual identity, is lost. Schreber writes about the *violation* as well as

5. More recent fictional depictions of soul murder can be found in Christina Stead's *Man Who Loved Children* and Henry Roth's *Call It Sleep.* Here is Randall Jarrell's epitome of Stead's depiction of brainwashing, from his introduction to Stead's book (Louie is a little girl who feels her life is a misery and her home a torture chamber; Sam is her tormenting father): "Sam [wakes up Louie] and asks her what she's dreaming just so as to be able to make her dream something different; and then tells her that not every little girl is lucky enough to have a Sam to wake her up" (Jarrell 1965, pp. xx–xxi).

the *murder* of souls. The sexual meaning of soul murder for Schreber is apparent from the breaks in the text of the *Memoirs* made by the original publishers, who eliminated first a passage and then the better part of the third chapter describing soul murder. Of the deleted section Schreber writes: "The content of Chapters I and II was a necessary preliminary to what follows. What could so far only partially be put up as axiomatic, will now be proved as far as at all possible" (1902, p. 61). The entire remaining portion of the crucial Chapter III follows: "I will first consider some events concerning *other members of my family*, which may possibly in some way be related to the presumed soul murder; these are all more or less mysterious, and can hardly be explained in the light of usual experience" (Schreber's italics). The deletion is then announced by the publisher's notice: "The further content of this chapter is omitted as unfit for publication" (p. 61). The censorship (pp. 58, 61) undoubtedly occurred because the soul murder was sexual (and from what Schreber underlines, apparently incestuous). But some specific sexual implications were left in. Freud points out the connections in the text between Schreber's accusations of soul murder and of forced masturbation and homosexuality. Schreber himself writes:

> A plot was laid against me . . . the purpose of which was to hand me over to another human being [the celestially transformed Dr. Flechsig] . . . in such a way that my soul was handed over to him, but my body—transformed into a female body and . . . left to that human being for sexual misuse . . . All attempts at committing soul murder, at unmanning me for purposes *contrary to the Order of the World* (that is to say for the sexual satisfaction of a human being), and later at destruction of my reason, have failed. (pp. 75, 58; my italics)

Here intimations of castration and homosexuality were coupled with an assault on Schreber's reason.

This attack on the power of rational thought is expressed in Schreber's "vagueness" about the whole topic. We know from Orwell's *1984* of the confusion and split registration in thinking (Orwell calls it *doublethink*)[6] that are both the effects of brainwashing and the means by which the torturer's hold is maintained. The victim must not be able

---

6. Orwell on doublethink: "to hold simultaneously two opinions which cancelled out, knowing them to be contradictory and believing both" (1949, p. 215).

to reason about what has happened, must not be able to know. Schreber gives an example of doublethink about soul murder in a footnote to the passage about "unmanning" quoted above. To his declaration that the attempt at soul murder made against him was evil and "contrary to the Order of the World," Schreber adds a completely contradictory statement: his feminization may prove to be "in consonance to the Order of the World" and may unite him with God (p. 58).

Freud interpreted that Schreber was casting his father in the role of God-devil. Schreber himself identified with the God-devil father as soul murderer: "I, myself, have been 'represented' as the one who had committed soul murder" (p. 55). Niederland's work on the crazy and inhuman child-rearing ideas and practices of Schreber's father has supplied the environmental genesis for the soul murder (see Niederland 1959a, 1959b, 1960, 1963). Niederland presents Schreber as a child manipulated as a "thing," with no evidence of empathy from the parents. He seems to have been purposely, systematically, and righteously deprived of his own will and of his capacity for pleasure and joy. Certainly these are among the accusations the paranoid adult Schreber brings against his persecutors.

The righteousness and religiosity of parents like the elder Schreber (as presented by Niederland) can undermine the child's ability to register and hate what the parents have done. If the victim is in the tormentor's absolute power, the child can turn for rescue and relief only to the tormentor, making for an intense need to see the torturer as good and right and to identify with the torturer; where this need is reinforced by a parental claim to godlike, benevolent parental rightness "consonant with the Order of the World," the child *must* lose all knowledge of what has happened and responsibility for how he or she has been made to feel; this means that any sense of a separate identity is compromised. The child submits to and becomes like the righteous parent.

The effects of massive trauma and of deprivation on the development of the child have been studied extensively by analysts. Ferenczi's paper "On the Confusion of Tongues between Adults and the Child" (1933) is a pioneer effort full of clinical value concerning the incidence and effects of the sexual abuse of children. Spitz (1945, 1946a, 1946b, 1964) and Greenacre (1960, 1968) focus on the earliest years. In a series of papers on child abuse and the "battered child syndrome," Brandt Steele (1970, 1976, 1977) and his colleagues (Steele et al. 1962, Steele and Pollock 1968) have concentrated on trauma during the child's first

three years. My own clinical material deals chiefly with traumata after the age of three. Fliess (1956, 1961, 1973) has written with great clinical insight on the effects and frequency of sexual abuse of children; his unfortunately extreme views on the ubiquity of actual seduction for neurosogenesis have been coarsened and oversimplified (eliminating fantasy altogether) by Masson (1984).

Of course a touch of soul murder can be an everyday affair. Every life contains occasions when one is the victim or the perpetrator of an assault on a person's right to a separate identity and a full range of human responses. Few people are without at least moments of beastliness. We are all capable of behavior so bad that we find it necessary not to register what has been said or done. To repeat one of Freud's favorite quotations from Nietzsche: " 'I did that,' says my memory. 'I could not have done that,' says my pride, and remains inexorable. Eventually— the memory yields" (Nietzsche 1886, 451).

Of course a few isolated incidents of parental abuse cannot be called psychic murder; to deform a soul takes chronic and repetitive abuse. Nietzsche's all-too-human confession and accusation takes on sinister connotations only if we transpose it into a statement by a soul murderer, for the victim's assumption of some form of the malefactor's nonregistration of what has happened is essential to the brainwashing that sustains soul murder (on "gaslighting" see Calef and Weinshel 1981). The denying parent transmits denial to the child. Brainwashing is inherent in psychic murder. That is what makes the difficult but crucial ability to differentiate between fantasy and reality a burning issue for each individual who has been subject to overwhelming trauma.

2

Brainwashing and the Defensive Consequences of Psychic Murder

Soul, or psychic, murder involves trauma imposed from the world outside the mind that is so overwhelming that the mental apparatus is flooded with feeling. The same overstimulated state can result as a reaction to great deprivation. The terrifying too-muchness requires massive and mind-distorting defensive operations for the child to continue to think and feel and live. The child's sense of identity (that is, the emotional maintenance of the mental images of his or her self) is threatened. Our identity depends initially on good parental care and good parental caring—on the transmitted feeling that it is good that we are there. The little girl kicked by her mother cannot turn to the mother for physical or psychological rescue. Yet to whom else can she turn? How can she deal by herself with the pain, fear, humiliation, and above all the rage? We know that when overwhelmed by feeling, people can react by fainting or with the more adaptive defense of shutting off all emotion, often by using autohypnosis (see Fliess 1953; Dickes 1965; Shengold 1967; and chapter 8, below).

Everyone needs to evolve defenses against overstimulation. A development of defensive systems starts with the inborn physiological barrier against stimuli and develops into the complicated and interlocking psychic series of mechanisms of defense and defensive character structure of later childhood. There is a burgeoning of defensive functioning dur-

ing the so-called anal-sadistic period of development (from about one year of age to three and a half years), which I have described elsewhere (Shengold 1985, 1987) as "anal-narcissistic defensiveness." Here part of the mind functions as a kind of emotional counterpart to the anal sphincter, supplying control by shutting down feeling. After the subsequent, oedipal phase of development and transformation, the mind forms a massive repressive barrier that initiates the so-called period of latency (where the force of the instinctual drives is calmed). These defensive operations are necessary for the development of thinking and the consolidation of a separate identity. Because so much of the defense is related to anality, we are all left with a variable proportion of anally related obsessive-compulsive defenses, character traits, and symptoms. These obsessive propensities become part of a defensive mental structure that effects some necessary distancing of the primal intensities of our earliest life, permitting us to say no to the urgency of our instinctual drives and accept the inevitable frustrations imposed by the human condition. Our primal drives and narcissistic claims must be partly given up for us to become human. Like Adam and Eve, we must lose the promise of the glory of Eden—in part to escape the hell of the overstimulation brought on by the intensity and inevitable frustrations of our drives (especially aggression). In situations of crisis and trauma, these developmental defensive efforts guard us from within as once our parents guarded us from without. But if the traumatic crises are recurrent or chronic, ordinary defenses will not suffice and regression to early, massive, "anal-narcissistic defenses" (which used to blank out primal feelings) will also become chronic. What happens to the child subjected to soul murder is so terrible, so overwhelming, and usually so recurrent that the child must not feel it and cannot register it, and resorts to a massive isolation of feeling, which is maintained by brainwashing (a mixture of confusion, denial, and identifying with the aggressor). A hypnotic living deadness, a state of existing "as if" one were there, is often the result of chronic early overstimulation or deprivation. As Ferenczi (1933) put it, "The [abused] child changes into a mechanical obedient automaton" (p. 163; this is what happened to Kaspar Hauser). But the automaton has murder within.

After a period of inherent infantile resistance to overstimulation, infants are vulnerable to too-muchness coming from within or without the body. What ensures survival through this dangerous period when the mind and a separate identity are starting to form is the care of a mothering figure. Spitz has observed that the child who has scant emotional care may not even survive.

I have stated that the child who is tormented by a parent must frequently call on that same parent for help and rescue. The other parent is only too often weak or absent, or is at least an unconscious abettor of the tormentor: "A parent's propensity for abuse is commonly supported by a corresponding tendency in the spouse . . . thus the abuse or neglect of offspring can often be an unconscious collusion or cooperation between the parents, even though only one of them is the active agent" (Steele 1976, 14). If the child must turn to the very parent who inflicts abuse and who is felt as bad for relief of the distress that the parent has caused, then the child must break with what has been experienced and out of a desperate need for rescue, must register the parent, *delusionally,* as good. Only the mental image of a good parent who will rescue can help the child deal with the terrifying intensity of fear and rage that is the effect of the tormenting experiences. The alternative—to maintain the overwhelming stimulation and bad parental image—means annihilation of identity, of the feeling of the self. So the bad has to be registered as good. This is a mind-splitting or mind-fragmenting operation. To survive, such children must keep in some compartment of their minds the delusion of good parents and the delusive promise that all the terror, pain, and hate will be transformed into love. These need not be psychotic delusions—neurotic delusions are frequent enough. The mysterious compulsion to repeat traumatic experiences (here the compulsion to provoke parental abuse) can be understood partly as the child's need to affirm in action that the next time the contact will bring love instead of hate. The desperate need to hold on to the *promise* of the good and loving parent is the source of the greatest resistance to the therapist's efforts to undo the delusion. Interpretations of "objective" reality threaten to effect the loss of the mental image of the "good" parent, thereby restoring the danger of annihilation and its attendant traumatic anxiety. The child's mind is split into contradictory fragments to separate the bad from the good (Ferenczi 1933, 165). I am describing not schizophrenia (although in psychotic children a more destructive fragmentation of the mind can also occur in response to trauma) but the establishment of isolated divisions of the mind in which contradictory images of the self and of the parents are never permitted to coalesce. This compartmentalized "vertical splitting" transcends diagnostic categories. Feeling and thinking are compromised; registration of what has happened and what is happening is divided into "compartments" and therefore is inadequate. Orwell describes this in *1984*: brainwashing is used to enforce the delusion that Big Brother is good. Orwell's "doublethink" is a system of vertical mind-splits that makes it possible to believe that two plus two equals five:

> To know and not to know, to be conscious of complete truthfulness while telling carefully constructed lies, to hold simultaneously two opinions which cancelled out, knowing them to be contradictory and believing both . . . to forget whatever it is necessary to forget, then to draw it back into the memory again at the moment it was needed, and then promptly to forget it again, and above all to apply the same process to the process itself . . . consciously to induce unconsciousness, and then once again to become unconscious of the act of hypnosis you had just performed. (1949, p. 36; note that Orwell knows about the use of autohypnosis in brainwashing)

With the attainment of "doublethink" (imposed by the need for rescue during psychological torture), Winston Smith can go on to identify with his tormentor and to "love Big Brother."

It is easy for an adult to become a Big Brother and to crush a child's joy in life, to attempt to "murder his soul." This was a crime for which Dostoyevski could not forgive himself, his parents, or God:[1]

> This poor child of five was subjected to every possible torture by [her] cultivated parents. They beat her, thrashed her, kicked her for no reason till her body was one bruise. Then, they went to greater refinements of cruelty—shut her up all night in the cold and frost in a privy, and because she didn't ask to be taken up at night . . . they smeared her face with excrement and forced her to eat it, and it was her mother, her mother did this. And that mother could sleep, hearing the groans of the poor child locked up in that vile place at night! *A little creature, who can't understand what's done to her,* in the dark and cold of that vile place, beats her little aching

1. As Freud mentions in his work *Dostoyevsky and Parricide* (1928), there has been much speculation, derived from the initially deleted section "Stavrogin's Confession" of *The Possessed*, that Dostoyevski himself might have sexually abused a little girl.

breast with her tiny fist and weeps her bloody meek unresentful tears begging dear, kind God to protect her! (Dostoyevski 1880, 286)

Since the child "can't understand what's done to her," her mind is unable to deal with, to work over, what is not understood and what may not even be allowed to register. It is this inhibition of the ego's power to remember and test reality that makes soul murder so effective as a continuing force. The absolute need for good mothering makes the child believe in the promise that her parents and "dear, kind God" will be good and rescue her, and to believe that she herself must be bad. The moral facts get confused along with the realistic ones—the child can take on the guilt for what the parents do, guilt that the righteous, god-quoting parents may feel only briefly, if at all.[2] (The tyrant becomes god for the crushed victim.) After a sexual attack on a child, "the harsh behaviour of the adult partner tormented and made angry by his remorse renders *the child* still more conscious of his own guilt and still more ashamed. Almost always the perpetrator behaves as though nothing had happened, and consoles himself with the thought: 'Oh, it is only a child, he does not know anything, he will forget it all.' Not infrequently after such events, the seducer becomes over-moralistic or religious and endeavours to save the *soul* of the child by severity" (Ferenczi 1933, 162–163; my italics).

Like Ferenczi, Steele (1976) studied the abusing parents; he states that they were themselves abused as children and quotes their justifications, adding: "These . . . examples show how deeply embedded the pattern of abuse can be and also indicate the strong sense of rightness, if not righteousness, with which behavior learned from parents can be repeated" (p. 15). Idealization of the offending parent leads to enhancement of the child's unconscious need for punishment and to intense masochism (see Berliner 1940; Fliess 1956). Later in life these children, in a compulsion to repeat, masochistically provoke their parents or turn to other people who are tormentors in the continuing delusive expectation that this time they will be loved. This makes for a pattern

2. There are still many Victorian households that recall that of Schreber; and the defensive denial of the behavior of (for example) alcoholic, abusive parents would provide a widespread modern equivalent that would have the same effect: of projecting guilt onto the child even in a superficially different moral and religious atmosphere.

of sadomasochistic relationships. The child's defensive need to "keep" the parent, even to merge with the parent, is often complemented by the disturbed parent's need to prevent individuation and hold on to the child, who is regarded as a need-fulfilling adjunct or even as part of the parent's self-image (Mahler and Furer 1968). Submitting to and becoming part of the tormentor can alternate with a more total identification with the tormentor, or function alongside such an identification. Ferenczi speaks of two ways of forming identificatory imagos: "anxiety-ridden identification" and "introjection of the . . . aggressor" (1933, p. 163). Identification with the aggressor enables the former victim to follow the compulsion to repeat, playing the active, sadistic, parental role. This too can be motivated in part by the delusive wish to make the bad parent good: "I'll be father and do it, and *this time* it will be good." The child's contradictory mental splits, or fragments of impulse and identity—reflecting the confusion between victim and tormentor, good and bad—were noted by Ferenczi, who also indicated the brainwashing (without using that term) that prevents synthesis: "When the child recovers from [the adult's sexual] attack, he feels enormously confused, in fact, split—innocent and culpable at the same time—and the confidence in the testimony of his own senses is broken" (1933, p. 162).

A Prototypical Instance: The Squashed Fruit

A male patient described the following as a "typical event": The father entered the dining room where the table was set for the family meal. Beside each plate was a fresh piece of fruit—the dessert. The man made a complete round of the table, stopping at every chair to reach out and squeeze to a pulp every piece of fruit except his own. The older children and the intimidated mother, used to such happenings, said nothing. But the youngest, a five-year-old boy, cried when he saw the mangled banana at his plate. The father then turned on him viciously, demanding that he be quiet—how dare he make such a fuss about a banana?

I want to emphasize the terrible confusion the boy was left with. What had happened? Who was to blame? Was father bad, or was the boy himself bad? Mother and the others had not reacted as he had—why *did* he make that fuss about the banana? The father, so confident of his greatness and rightness (like the parents of Dostoyevski's poor little girl), must be good. But how could that be? (The five-year-old boy's castration anxiety, caused by his oedipal wishes, was surely mobilized by his father's crushing his banana; this compounded his reaction and made him even more readily assume the guilt his father had shown no evidence of feeling.)

Need enforced the preservation in the child's mind of a delusional place in which the father must be good and right, the boy bad and wrong. Yet some registration that the father was bad was made somewhere, as it were in another compartment. (One patient said: "I am not a human being—I live in compartments.") These mental compartments are walled off and their contents cannot be blended; this is part of the defensive isolation brought about by brainwashing. The child is motivated with compulsive force to avoid bringing the contradictory pictures together; the rage associated with the bad, which can overwhelm and destroy, must be kept away from the needed mental image of the good parent, but the rage remains. The boy learned early to cover it over with indifference, with dullness—but underneath, the anger festered: to kill father or be killed by him, or to become the bad father and crush those around him. The murderous rage terrified him. The continuing subjection to his father's terrifying cruelty evoked a vicious cycle: the more the anger was suppressed (and his father saw to it that no angry manifestations went unpunished), the greater was the feeling of danger from it. The boy's unconscious became a murderous cauldron; murder aimed at his father and himself was compartmentalized and usually disconnected from consciousness. It was occasionally felt in relation to scapegoats—creatures more helpless and passive than he was (his father reduced people to the impersonal, so why shouldn't he?). Frequently these creatures were female.

To be able to contain all this, the boy needed first to establish what was happening to him. A more realistic, less masochistic mother might have helped him do this—at least identify that something bad had happened (a necessary first step toward understanding the father's destructiveness). But only a woman who was herself brainwashed could have stayed with this father. As it turned out, the boy was not completely crushed (unlike his banana). He did not fully accept his father's unspoken order not to know and not to feel. Some isolated registration occurred, and in the long course of work that included the murderous business being transferred onto the analyst, the patient and analyst were able to erode the walls of the mental compartment that contained the emotional imprint of his memories. The patient gradually became responsible for his knowledge of his father's character and how he had identified with him. He had to feel the murder and the cruelty both in his father and in himself. The analysis progressed so that he was able to give up his autohypnosis; the feelings released thereby made emotional conviction possible, so that knowledge could be more than intellectual and provisional. (Only when knowing involves a free range of feeling is brainwashing undone, and inauthentic "as if" living given over.) Within the structure provided by the patient's conviction about the past and especially about his father, the intense rage, without disappearing, became increasingly tolerable. The contents of the mental compartments became subject to a synthesis of emotions and ideas (although the tendency to compartmentalize was not given up completely). The patient could own what he felt and what had happened to him. Avoiding denial and tolerating rage were achieved together; his ego and superego were slowly modified.

Consider the effect on the five-year-old boy's unfolding sexuality of the incident I have described as typical and recurrent. It was a household in which castration was in the air, as Niederland said of Schreber's. At the height of his oedipal development, the boy was driven to compete with a demonic father powerful enough to mold the reality of the family world to match his paranoid grandiosity and establish himself as a domestic Hitler presiding over docile subjects. Mother was a broken yet worshipful victim. Compelled to register his father's cruelty as good and right, the boy could not adequately identify with his antagonism toward his father and come to terms with it. The prospect might seem dim that this boy would be able to transcend his involvement with his parents' overwhelmingly sadomasochistic relationship and the need to become his father's passive, broken, worshipful victim (renouncing his masculinity as well as his identity). Yet somehow this boy acquired some ability to work and love—even, after his analysis, to love women.

3

Did It Really Happen?

An Assault on Truth, Historical and Narrative

"Did it really happen?" is a burning question for the victim of soul murder. If the answer is "no" or "I don't know," the parent is spared. If the answer is "yes, I know," the former child victim can begin to separate and achieve independence from the soul murderer.

Man lives by metaphor; his mind is a poetry-making organ (Trilling 1940) and a myth-making and history-making organ. Once past infancy, we have an intense need for psychic synthesis, continuity, and causality. We weave our memories into narrative, from which we construct our identities, despite our faulty registration of what goes on around us and within us. What goes on within and without our minds may be ultimately unknowable; yet sanity and survival depend on comparatively accurate registration of the outer and inner worlds. However relativistic and inadequate our senses and memory, there is a reality out there and there are absolutes. There was a past, however imperfectly we have registered it and however impossible it is for us to communicate it or recapture it completely. This contradictory dilemma is part of the human condition. Each human being spins a personal narrative, and yet we bear the burden of the inexorability of the past, or as the Arabs say of "what is written."

Freud taught us that the instinctual drives and laws of the unconscious mind can be equally inexorable. But he also showed us the need for acquiring the reality principle.

In the eighteenth century, George Berkeley made an extremist contribution to the lively debate then current on ancient philosophical inquiries: What can we know of reality? Is the universe matter, idea, or both? Berkeley insisted that our perceptions and ideas have an existence independent of matter—nothing exists beyond the mind and its ideas. Samuel Johnson, that champion of common sense (perhaps expressing his disgust at metaphysics), kicked a stone, saying, "I refute Berkeley *thus*." Of course Berkeley cannot really be refuted by experience; we cannot ultimately know reality. Yet I am convinced that the psychoanalyst must subscribe to Johnson's imperfect working assumption without dismissing Berkeley. "Truth such as is necessary to the regulation of life, is always to be found where it is honestly sought" (Johnson, quoted in Bate 1975, p. 316). However unsatisfactory and vague this is (what is truth?), the psychoanalyst, as an "honest seeker," must adopt something as approximate as this as a working goal, must try to seek it out.

There is a current controversy in psychoanalysis (with extremist positions worthy of Berkeley) that seems evocative of the eighteenth-century epistemological ferment. On one side is Masson (1984) and his oversimplified "assault on truth," which denies the pathogenic power of fantasies. His book ascribes the mind's idea of what has happened almost completely to the registration and effect of "actual" traumata —a view that downgrades the power of the "poetry-making" organ and denies its nature. Pushing in the opposite direction is Berkeley's psychoanalytic descendant, Spence (1982), who mounts his own assault on historical truth and idealizes "narrative truth." For him the *recherche du temps perdu*, the search for the "real" past, should be abandoned—the making of a narrative is all. The analyst's task is to be a superior novelist of the psyche. For every patient the answer to the question "Did it really happen?" is a matter of concern, but for the victim of soul murder it is always a burning question, often crucially important to the victim's ability to master the past and answer it.

Had Oscar Wilde's Lady Bracknell turned her formidable curiosity toward psychoanalysis, her inquisition of Jack Worthing in *The Importance of Being Earnest* might have been as follows:

Lady B. I have always been of the opinion that a man who desires to [be a psychoanalyst] should know everything or nothing [about the past]. Which do you know?
Jack [here played by Spence]. I know nothing, Lady Bracknell.
(Wilde 1896, 359).

In contrast, Masson's tone implies that he knows everything; he has the certainty one seldom hears from the psychoanalyst. For the most part the psychoanalyst learns from patients how little he knows; but some certainties are gathered and some patterns of thought and feeling so insistent that here and there the analyst can say, "I know this truth about my patient; here I am certain." Every human being must know something between everything and nothing.

Spence attacks the scientific foundations of psychoanalytic work with extreme answers to the ancient philosophical question "What do we know?" Like Jack Worthing, Spence answers that we psychoanalysts know nothing, that our patients know nothing, that all of us can know only nothing. He tells us that there is no real free association and that even the attempt at it is ineffectual and counter to good analytic results; that our patients cannot communicate in words the pictures and other sensory impressions in their minds; that we cannot really listen with free-floating attention and (again) that it is counterproductive even to try; that our transcribing of what goes on with the patient is unreliable and "probably some indeterminate mixture of what was said and how it was constructed" (p. 193); that our interpretations are determined by our own fantasies and shaped by our own shared, idiosyncratic generalizations, our "underlying preparatory beliefs" (p. 286); that "this view of the psychoanalytic enterprise, with its emphasis on narrative truth, raises serious questions about how we go about constructing a general theory" (p. 296). "Seen in this light," Spence himself tells us, "the impossible profession becomes even more so" (p. 294). What is left to such a poor, bare, forked analyst?

We are in an alienated universe with Spence, as mysterious and disordered as Beckett's, and with the world within the mind portrayed as equally unknowable. And yet we get little of Beckett's nihilism or even of Freud's healthier pessimism. Spence manages to sound hopeful and even cheerful at the end of his devastating critique.

It is a critique that all should consider seriously. For beginning analysts it can be a healthily cautionary and reassuring lesson in humility, for experienced ones a proper plea for modesty and a reproach of absolutist tendencies. Following Freud's cognizant example, we analysts must be aware that we also operate somewhere in between knowing nothing and knowing everything. We must be able to tolerate uncertainty and mystery, and yet be capable of conviction and transient sureness; so eventually must our patients. It can be said of analysts (as E. M. Forster says of one of his characters) that they must work with and are "cursed with the Primal curse, which is not the knowledge of good and evil, but the knowledge of good-and-evil" (quoted in Trilling 1943, p. 13). Similarly, they must work with the knowledge of certainty-and-doubt, and if their own analysis has succeeded for them, their patients too will be able to live and work with good-and-evil, with certainly-and-doubt. Counter to Spence and Masson, I believe patient and analyst must strive for both narrative and historical truth—falling back on narrative when the historical recedes, but a narrative supplied whenever possible by the patient, not by the analyst.

Spence outlines the inadequacies of Freud's archeological metaphor for the recovery of the past in psychoanalysis (this is right) and then goes so far as to deprive it of all validity (this is wrong). I will try to furnish a different although related metaphor, also inadequate.

Our minds are like vast, neglected historical museums—here barely lit, there flooded with radiance—filled for the most part with figures of our selves and our important "others" from every period of our past. Some are immobile like statues or idols; others resemble figures in a science fiction wax museum threatening to dissolve suddenly into mobility under the hot glare of our emotion-laden, self-observing presence, or even to become galvanized into a cinematic re-presentation of past events, shown over and over and not always in the same way. The distinct personas change their ages, costumes, even their sex. Despite these changes (which are reversible), most figures usually manage to retain their identity. Between the visible areas of display of the standing and rushing figures are so many places of darkness. Certain scenes turn up repeatedly—sometimes seemingly fixed in stone, sometimes in mobile drama with endless, inverting variations. Freud, reacting to Fliess's "discovery" of bisexuality, wrote to him: "Now for bisexuality! . . . I am accustoming myself to the idea of regarding every sexual act as a process in which four persons are involved" (Freud 1887–1902, p. 289).

Freud's "four" is pitifully inadequate. One's identity is a multidimensional web, consisting of myriad introjected images from early childhood of one's parents, modified by later editions of them and their successors. These images are in all states of transformation into pictures of one's former and present selves, and of coalescence with these pictures. These composite, time-transcending, kaleidoscopic images are somehow held together by the synthesizing structure of our minds, our cinematic historical museums. My inadequate metaphor attempts to evoke this complicated dynamism, which wavers between transient organization and near chaos. It is a dynamism that furnishes us with transformed and adulterated fragments of what we search for, and despite the inherent difficulties and even ultimate impossibility of more than scant success, of what we *ought* to search for and try to refine: historical truth.

Spence insists that psychoanalysis should not be viewed as a discovery of what is and was there for the patient (that is, of the archeological fragments in the museum); encountering the past becomes instead creation. We are to supply a coherent narrative for our patient's life. We are not to see the figure in the carpet but to conceive it ourselves: "We can create truth by statement" (p. 177)—an astonishing "statement" indeed. We create truth by supplying connections, make those connections memorable by devising aesthetic form and manner of statement, make the construct "plausible" (a key word for Spence). And to what end? For a satisfying "narrative fit" (p. 179) that will effect conviction and change. Spence portrays the analyst (properly in his view) as shaping the evidence, creating the connections with interpretations, "[defining] the dream [or it could be the symptom, or any psychic event] in a particular way that the patient is likely to remember [in order to] create a new cluster of ideas" (p. 178).

Spence enthusiastically presents the ideal of attractive and effectual "narrative fit." Gone is the inexorability of the Unconscious as well as the inevitability of the past. Spence implies that the psychoanalyst needs only Wit, if not Piety, and is to ignore the historical and create narrative truth: "Once stated, it becomes partially true, as it is repeated and extended, it becomes familiar; and as its familiarity adds to its plausibility, it becomes completely true" (p. 177). This quotation has Orwellian overtones: the analyst can "create" the past with artful connections. And as Orwell says: "After all, how do we know that two and two make four? Or that the force of gravity works: *Or that the past is unchangeable?* If both the past and the external world exist only in the mind, and if the mind itself is controllable—what then?" (1949, p. 80; my italics).

Here is a description of the totalitarian doctrine "Ingsoc":

The mutability of the past is the central tenet of Ingsoc. Past events, it is argued, have no objective existence, but survive only in written records and in human memories. The past is whatever the records and the memories agree upon. And since the Party [read the soul-murdering parent, or the analyst who can play the role of Big Brother] is in full control of all the records, and in equally full control of the minds of its members [read the victims of soul murder, or the patients of the analyst-as-Big Brother], it follows that the past is whatever the Party chooses to make it. It also follows that though the past is alterable, it never has been altered in any specific instance. For when it has been recreated in whatever shape is needed at the moment, then this new version *is* the past, and no different past can ever have existed. (1949, pp. 214–215)

And finally:

"Who controls the past," ran the Party slogan, "controls the future: who controls the present controls the past." And yet the past, though of its nature alterable, never had been altered. Whatever was true now was true from everlasting to everlasting. It was quite simple. All that was needed was a series of victories over your own memory. "Reality control," they called it; . . . "doublethink." (1949, pp. 35–36)

The rat-torture session at the end of *1984* that finally breaks Winston Smith can be read simultaneously as reflecting the totalitarian techniques of mind control (specifically the misuse of psychiatry and psychiatric theory by Stalin) and as a projection onto history (that fits) of the brainwashing of the child by the soul-murdering adult.[1]

Masson (1984) believes in a kind of exclusive traumatic pathogenesis: neurotics become mentally ill only if they have actually been seduced as children. Masson sees Freud's discovery of the power of unconscious fantasies as retreating from and even denying Freud's initial belief that neurosis was a result of "seduction by the father." This belief was based on stories told to Freud by his patients, and at the beginning of his

1. It is unfair to unload all this on the shoulders of Spence; brainwashing is clearly not his intention, but it does follow if his prescriptions are carried to their ultimate conclusions. The primal parent's power to impose doublethink is transferred onto the analyst, whom the soul-murder patient will inevitably regard as evil; and analysts who do not know this will fail their patients if they do not do their best to pursue the ultimate although perhaps unreachable reality of historical truth.

self-analysis he thought it confirmed in his own case. Masson charges (erroneously) that Freud abandoned the seduction theory. What Freud did was question the universality of seduction as a neurosogenic factor and supplement it with his assumption of universal fantasies of being seduced—an assumption that led Freud to see the importance of the Oedipus complex.

In a review of Masson's book *The Assault on Truth: Freud's Suppression of the Seduction Theory* (1984) and of Janet Malcolm's book about Masson, *In the Freud Archives* (1984), Charles Hanly (1987) comments on Masson's charges, and counters by quoting Freud's statements on the seduction of children as fantasy and as reality. Hanly's assumption is like mine, and contrary to what Malcolm implies it is a common one among practicing psychoanalysts—that it does make a difference whether something actually happened, but that this does not deny the pathogenic power of fantasy:

> Freud never suppressed the seduction theory. He amended it, to make it correspond with the facts, and he brought it into relationship with the discovery of infantile sexuality and its potential for pathogenesis. It is Masson who, through a biased selection of textual references, . . . suppresses for his readers the fact of Freud's continued recognition of the sexual seduction of children. For example, Masson quotes only a part of Freud's (1905) clear statement concerning internal and external factors in the aetiology of neurosis and manages interpretively to distort even this part. The complete statement [of Freud's] follows:
>> The reappearance of sexual activity is determined by internal causes and external contingencies. . . . I shall have to speak presently of the internal causes; great and lasting importance attaches at this period to the accidental *external* contingencies. In the foreground we find the effects of seduction, which treats a child as a sexual object and teaches him, in highly emotional circumstances, how to obtain satisfaction from his genital zones, a satisfaction which he is then usually obliged to repeat again and again by masturbation. An influence of this kind may originate either from adults or from other children. I cannot admit that in my paper on "The Aetiology of Hysteria" (1896) I exaggerated the frequency or importance of that influence, though I did not then know that persons who remain normal

may have had the same experiences in their childhood, and
though I consequently overrated the importance of seduction in
comparison with the factors of sexual constitution and development. Obviously seduction is not required in order to arouse a
child's sexual life; that can also come about spontaneously from
internal causes. (p. 190)

One need only ask oneself how Freud could have found out that
an adult may be normal despite having been sexually seduced in
childhood, to know that Freud continued to credit as true histories
of sexual seductions told to him, and did not automatically consider them to be phantasies. The complete passage makes it clear
that if Freud had had any wish to suppress the seduction theory he
would not have insisted as he does in 1905 that the eighteen patients of "The Aetiology of Hysteria" had told him true accounts of
having been seduced in childhood. Instead, he would have claimed
that their stories were historically false and only psychologically
true—i.e. that they were phantasies. (Hanly 1987, 517; Hanly's
italics)

Hanly adds three later quotations from Freud to document further
Freud's continuing awareness of the importance of actual childhood
sexual traumata:

Phantasies of being seduced are of particular interest, because *so
often* they are not phantasies but real memories. (1916–17, p. 370;
my italics)

Actual seduction, too, is common enough . . . (1931, p. 232)

A girl who was made the object of a sexual seduction in her early
childhood may direct her later sexual life so as to provoke constantly similar attacks. (1939, pp. 75–76)

An Analogy

A clinical situation analogous to that of a patient who has been seduced
as a child is presented by one who has seduced or been seduced by a
therapist. An analyst who has practiced long enough to see several such
cases will be painfully aware of how much contrast these unfortunate

people have with the great majority of previously treated patients, who have all had a *fantasy* of seduction involving their therapists. Having had the actual sexual experience does not necessarily make one patient sicker than another who has only transferred onto the therapist the fantasy of sexual contact without acting out or repeating it; but the analyst who treats such a patient later will palpably sense the distinct quality conferred by the actual experience, and will feel its effect in the intensity of the patient's distrust, the corruptibility of the patient's superego, the depth of the expectation of repetition—and in other resistances that affect the viability of future treatment. In most of these cases (leaving out the very sickest patients) there is not much doubt on the victim's part as to whether the seduction actually did happen—it has full memory quality. This is in contrast to the child who is the victim of seduction and abuse by corrupt, betraying adult caretakers. Trying to define what can be known and remembered about these seemingly historical events, trying to get the patient to differentiate memory from fantasy, is part of what must be done in the therapy to undo the brainwashing inherent to soul murder. With some patients this is a relatively straightforward task if not an easy one; with others it can approach the impossible. In my experience, being able to define the limits of certainty in the attempt to answer the question "did it really happen?" almost always helps the patient; this has been true even in those sad instances where the patient has had to conclude, and therefore know, only that he or she simply can never know.

The Parent as Sphinx

A study of the vicissitudes of the relationship of Oedipus and his mother-wife, Jocasta (as portrayed in the myth directly and as the Sphinx), provides a parallel to the fate and character of children whose souls or separate identities have been murdered by overstimulation and seduction on the part of parents or parental figures.

Van der Sterren (1952) indicates the hostility between son and mother in *Oedipus Rex*. I feel there remain unexplored implications and un-emphasized intensities about the mother-son hostility. Many authors, some of them psychoanalysts, have pointed to the analogy between Jo-casta and the monstrous Sphinx that figures in the Oedipus legend. Here is the telling statement of Kanzer (1950): "The action of the play, as a whole, is a repetitious depiction of the duel between Oedipus and the Sphinx. In the presence of her true form, the mother, he again carries on a remorseless inquiry into his origin . . . [when] the riddle of his birth is solved, then Jocasta kills herself, as had the Sphinx" (pp. 564–565). Kanzer equates the brooches of Jocasta, with which Oedipus blinds himself, with the talons of the Sphinx. He states that the Sphinx in the legend, who has been destroyed before the play by Sophocles begins and whose destruction has led Oedipus to the throne and given him the right to marry the queen, connotes both the erotic, incestuous drives toward Jocasta and (especially) the anxiety and aggression of the "preoedipal," early relationship with the mother.

The Sphinx is a monster with the head and breasts of a woman, the body of a lion, the wings of an eagle. The name literally means "strangler" (compare the word *sphincter*); she would throttle and devour those who could not read her riddle. Sophocles calls her "the Dog-faced Witch" (Watling, trans., p. 36) and "the She-devil, the Claw-foot Lady" (p. 59). She has been held to represent the imago of the "terrible mother" (Jung 1938), the phallic mother (Rank 1912), a depiction of both parents in intercourse (Roheim 1934; Reik 1951). Freud (1928) states simply that the Sphinx is "the monster who symbolizes the *father*" (p. 188; my italics).

A patient whom I will call C., when recalling childhood seductions by his psychotic mother, would describe her terrifying transformation into a monster, "like Dr. Jekyll and Mr. Hyde" (note the alteration and therefore confusion of gender). His mother's facial expression would change completely—she would suddenly "stare through" him with no sign of recognition; her face would become a feral mask while she gnashed her teeth wildly. Sometimes baring and offering her breast, she would use her finger as a penetrative organ to invade the child's anus. This was the most frequent of the many bizarre seductions carried out by this mother from the child's third year to his sixth. It was also this sphinxlike mother who through repeated and full exhibition of her genitals gave her son a frightening initiation into the "mystery of the origin of children," as Freud reads the riddle of the Sphinx.

I believe the Sphinx represents what I call the primal parent; Freud, always more ready to spare the mother, talked of the frightening and tyrannical head of the primal horde: the primal father, the phylogenetic *UrVater*, in *Totem and Taboo* (1913). But our ontogenetic history begins not with primal mother or father but with parent.[1] Fliess (1956) writes of the "archaic, aggressive parent" in describing the inner picture of the superego derived from the parents. This destructive figure emerges in ontogenetic development as the bad, cannibalistic mother of the oral-sadistic stage. Cannibalistically penetrative by way of tooth

1. Freud (1923) refers to the identification with the father in speaking of primary identifications: "The first and most important identification of all . . . a direct and immediate identification [that] takes place earlier than any object cathexis." But in a footnote he amends this: "Perhaps it would be safer to say 'with the parents' for before a child has arrived at definite knowledge of the difference between the sexes, the missing penis [that is, before the child has solved the riddle of the Sphinx], it does not distinguish in value between its father and its mother" (p. 31).

and claw, the imago develops into the phallic, penetrative parent—first mother, then father—toward whom the negative oedipus complex becomes activated in the male.

The phylogenetic primal parent has been described as terrifying and violent (Freud 1913), intent on torturing and killing (Freud 1913; Fliess 1956), cannibalistic (Freud 1913), mendacious (Fliess 1956): "Most pertinent . . . is the fact that the archaic parent shows in projection [of the patient's superego onto the analyst] the same unvarying traits: the intent of torturing and killing, mendacity and lack of humor" (Fliess 1956, 39). This figure is omnipresent in the child's development, entering into superego formation, blatantly emergent in pathologic states like depression and paranoia. In present-day reality, the archaic figure can be approximated by a psychotic or psychopathic parent whose defused instincts can in relation to the child bring into play the intent to torture, kill, and devour (something close to "a pure culture of the death instinct"). This is the specter I found in the street when I saw a mother viciously kicking her child: the parent as soul murderer.

The encounter of Oedipus with the Sphinx can represent various phases of the preoedipal parent-child relationship, but most connotations underline the confrontation at the oral-sadistic stage. In terms of object relations theory, this takes place before the child's separation and individuation (Mahler). It is during the cannibalistic second oral stage (Abraham) that the infant's state of mind, characterized by Freud as "I am the breast, the breast is part of me" (1938, p. 299), develops toward the establishment of ego and body ego by way of primary and secondary identifications, so that the child can conceive of the breast: " 'I have it'—that is, 'I am not it' " (Freud 1938, 299). It is as if the ego is to be carved out of "the future 'object' . . . with the teeth" (Fliess 1956, 101); the aggressive drive derivatives become clinically manifest at the time of the second oral stage. It is necessary for the child to direct this onslaught of cannibalistic hostility outwards, away from the child's own body; this requires the help of a "good enough" mother-child relationship (see Mahler, Pine, and Bergman 1975, 47). The deflection of aggression from the infant's own body, together with secondary narcissistic cathexis of the body, are needed for the developing introjective and projective mechanisms that lead to normal identification with the mother and eventually to the child's separation from the mother.

In at least four papers (1905, 1908, 1909, 1925) Freud interprets the riddle of the Sphinx—with different degrees of certainty: "The riddle of where babies come from . . . this in a distorted form which can easily be rectified is the same riddle that was propounded by the Theban Sphinx" (1905, p. 195). A later statement of Freud's is less positive. He says of little Hans: "He was faced with the great riddle of where babies come from, which is *perhaps* the first problem to engage a child's mental powers, and of which the riddle of the Theban Sphinx is *possibly* no more than a distorted version" (1909, p. 133; my italics). By 1925 certainty has returned: "The riddle of the Sphinx—that is, the question of where babies come from" (p. 37). This interpretation has been amplified by several analysts (Roheim 1934; Kanzer 1950) who have held that the figure of the Sphinx indicates the parents in intercourse, citing the monster's ambiguities of form, sex, and genitals as well as the changing number of limbs in the riddle. I think Freud's meaning can be further supplemented, yet without bringing the riddle's solution to an aesthetically satisfactory conclusion.

Locomotion

Mahler and Gosliner (1955) describe the "symbiotically overanxious psychotic mother": "The mother's hitherto doting attitude changes abruptly at the advent of the separation-individuation phase [that is, with locomotion]. . . . It is the maturational growth of locomotion which exposes the infant to the important experience of deliberate and active body separation from and reunion with the mother" (pp. 201, 195). It follows then that it is the child's standing up and walking away, out of the symbiotic unit, that these potentially soul-murdering mothers cannot tolerate. With this in mind, here is the riddle of the Sphinx: "What being, with only one voice, has sometimes two feet, sometimes three, sometimes four, *and is weakest when it has the most?*" Oedipus's solution: "Man—because he crawls on all fours as an infant, stands firmly on his two feet as a youth, and leans on his staff in his old age" (Graves 1955, 10; my italics).

The entire riddle is about locomotion—the ability to move away from the mother—and in answering it Oedipus establishes his separate identity and manhood. Instead of suffering the fate of the defeated challenger—being devoured by the monster (thus reestablishing the symbiosis)—the victorious Oedipus watches the Sphinx hurl herself to her death; the child is rid of the symbiotic incubus. Thomas de Quincey recognized that Oedipus was himself the subject of the riddle and its solution. He suggested that instead of answering "Man," Oedipus might have said: "Oedipus, for who so weak at birth as the abandoned infant with feet pinned together, who so powerful and upright at noon, and who so in need of assistance in his last blind years?" (see also Kouretas 1963). Sophocles has his chorus say of Oedipus: "He slew the maiden with crooked talons who sang darkly [the Sphinx]. *He arose for our land as a tower* against death. And from that time, Oedipus, thou hast been called our king" (p. 47; my italics; all translations are by Jebb unless otherwise indicated). For this great deed Oedipus was awarded the city and his mother—symbol and thing symbolized—which meant he could now have his mother and need no longer be part of her. With this heroic step the child's developmental transition away from symbiosis becomes possible. Normal identification and an object relationship with the separated mother allows the child to move from the preoedipal relationship with the mother to the oedipal. We are all Oedipus and must all destroy the Sphinx.

The Character of Jocasta

The Sphinx is to be understood as a disguised depiction of Jocasta, specifically Jocasta as primal parent, as a soul murderer. Jocasta is also directly portrayed as a primal parent in the play, in a way that is hidden not by Sophocles but by the reader's own reluctance, paralleling that of Oedipus, to admit that this kind of mother can really exist. The main revelation of the mother's hostility toward the son was noted by Van der Sterren (1952). Sophocles artfully has Oedipus go step by step toward the final, terrible uncovering of his fate. Just before it is irrevocably clear who he is and who his mother is, he confronts the herdsman who had been given the infant child of Laius and Jocasta to abandon to its death. The herdsman is evasive about who was responsible, then says:

> *Herdsman.* . . . but thy lady within [Jocasta] could best say how these things are.
> *Oedipus.* How? She gave it to thee?
> *Herdman.* Yea, O King.
> *Oedipus.* For what end?

Herdman. That I should make away with it.

Oedipus. Her own child, the wretch! (p. 46; Campbell translates
the last line as "And could a mother's heart be steeled to this?"

With this revelation, Oedipus simultaneously discovers his parricide
and incest and his parents' murderous hostility toward him (what affects
him most is his mother's). In other words, he discovers his oedipal
and preoedipal involvement with his mother and father. It is to be remembered that the pinning together of the infant's ankles resulted in
a lifelong deformity for Oedipus. One can say that his ability to rise
up and walk away was compromised, and the potential effect on his
identity is marked by his very name, Oedipus (that is, Clubfoot).

Mendacity has been described as a characteristic of the "primal parent." Van der Sterren does not point out that before the herdsman's
revelation about her, Jocasta has lied. She evades her own responsibility for the infant's abandonment, specifically blaming her former
husband:

Jocasta. And the child's birth was not three days past when Laius
pinned its ankles together and had it thrown, by others' hands,
on a trackless mountain. (p. 29)

This lie is crucial in understanding the character of Jocasta. The urgency of the difference to Oedipus between his mother's hostility to
him as an infant and his father's is shown in a scene with the messenger from Corinth that also precedes the one with the herdsman quoted
above. Oedipus is told by the messenger (who has come to announce
the death of Oedipus's supposed father in Corinth) that he is not really
of the royal house of Corinth but had been given to the messenger by
the herdsman as an infant, ankles pinned together. Oedipus passionately responds: "Oh for the gods' love, was the deed my mother's or my
father's—speak!" (p. 41). A similar wish to spare the mother was seen
in a patient who dreamed of himself as the victim of two dissimilar carnivorous animals (put together they would have made a kind of sphinx),
which he associated with his mother and father. The animal that represented his father was depicted as biting the patient, while the equally
ferocious and menacing one associated with the mother only looked
on. The dream reversed the historic reality, in which it was the overtly
psychotic mother who had seduced and attacked the child, again with
the face of a wild animal. (This mother had once tried to feed a caustic
poison to her child.) The dream followed memories brought up in the

psychiatric treatment; it represented a wish that it had been the more dispensable father rather than the mother who had done "the deed" (Laius and not Jocasta).

In the early part of the play Jocasta repeatedly wants to deny, pretend, not know what is to be revealed. This involves her in what to the Greeks was impiety. After reciting the supposedly unfulfilled prediction that Laius would be murdered by his son, she derides such prophecies: "A fig for divination. After this, I would not walk across the road for any of it" (Watling, trans., p. 49). This is met with horror by the chorus, to whom it means the scorning of divine and human natural order: "Who walks his own high handed way, disdaining true righteousness and holy ornament; who falsely wins, all sacred things profaning; shall he escape his doomed pride's punishment?" (Watling, trans., p. 50). "If such deeds as these are honored," the chorus asks after Jocasta's impiety, "why should I dance and sing?" (Fergusson 1953, 44).

Immediately after, in a scene of terrible irony, Jocasta, scorner of prophecies and oracles, comes on the stage with incense and offerings to lay on the altar of the gods and prays to Apollo for deliverance from fear (see Kitto 1955). Her show of certainty can no longer be maintained. When denial is not possible and she knows before Oedipus does that he is her son, she cannot face the truth with him and rushes off to take her own life, again traumatically abandoning her son. This too takes place before the herdsman reveals to Oedipus that it was Jocasta who gave him over to be killed; it is not only incest but infanticide that she cannot own.

The final encounter between mother and son occurs after Oedipus learns the full truth and is offstage (like all climactic violent action in Greek tragedy). What happens represents a preoedipal, sadomasochistic encounter with the mother, and also a primal scene expressed in regressive, sadistic terms. A witness reports:

> For with a shriek Oedipus burst in . . . on him, as he rushed around, our eyes were set. To and fro he went, asking us to give him a *sword*, asking where he should find the wife who was no wife but a mother whose *womb* had borne alike himself and his children. And, in his frenzy, a power above man was his guide; for 'twas none of us mortals who were nigh. And with a dread shriek, as though some one beckoned him on, he sprang at the double doors, and from their sockets *forced* the bending bolts, and rushed into the room. (p. 49; my italics)

After this sadistic penetration into the room where Jocasta has hanged herself, Oedipus sees her body. The mother, reduced to her sexual parts, is attacked with cannibalistic fury. Again Oedipus confronts the Sphinx, directly and by way of identification. Jocasta's suicide diverts his murderous intent. He turns the cannibalistic impulse inward and uses her brooches to blind himself: "For he tore from her raiment the golden brooches wherewith she was decked, and lifted them, and smote full on his own eye-balls" (p. 49).

The condemnation of the mother (and her genitals) and the rage toward them are expressed symbolically in Oedipus's apostrophe to the trifurcation of the road, where he had killed the old man who had tried to thrust him out of the path—the old man who has turned out to be his father, Laius: "For now I am found evil and of evil birth. O ye three roads, and thou *secret glen*—thou *coppice and narrow way* where three paths met—*Ye who drank from my hands that father's blood* which was my own, —remember ye, perchance, what deeds I wrought for you to see,—and then, when I came hither, what fresh deeds I went on to do?" (pp. 53–54; my italics)

Abraham (1923) held the trifurcation of the road as the symbol of the maternal genitals, the place of traffic with the father and the son. (This interpretation is certainly reinforced by the words "secret glen" and "coppice and narrow way.") In the speech, the mother's genitals become charged with oral-sadistic libido and drink blood. The "place where three paths meet" is called on to witness the past, "the deeds I wrought for you to see." This is after Oedipus has destroyed his own sight, has symbolically castrated himself. (Eyes are related to testicles symbolically and etymologically—note the German *Eier* (egg) and *Auge* (eye) —and *testicles* literally means "little witnesses.") I have stated that part of soul murder is the consequence of seduced children taking on the guilt of the seducing parent (Ferenczi 1925; Fliess 1953). By assuming the adult's lies and denial, the children renounce their own ability to see what is and has been. They cease being reliable witnesses to the past and to present repetitions of the past.

Denial of the Primal Parent: Oedipus at Colonus

As I have noted, the riddle of the Sphinx involves at one level the developmental separation from the Sphinx-mother. At first the infant crawls on all fours, then with full individuation stands and can walk away on two legs, and finally, approaching full circle, hobbles with a cane, bent and about to fall to earth to reunite, remerge with the mother. The last part of this cycle is dealt with by Sophocles in *Oedipus at Colonus*, where Oedipus has fulfilled the prophecy of Teiresias that evokes the Sphinx's riddle: "A blind man, he who now hath sight, a beggar, who now is rich, he shall make his way to a strange land, *feeling the ground before him with his staff*" (p. 19; my italics).

Oedipus Rex clarifies the further vicissitudes of the mother-son relationship that are portrayed in *Oedipus at Colonus*. Just before the herdsman's final revelation, which implies both preoedipal and oedipal traffic with the mother, Jocasta rushes from the scene. Oedipus attributes her leaving to pride of blood—she does not want to be married to someone who might have been born a slave: "Go someone, fetch me the herdsman hither, and leave yon woman to glory in her princely stock" (p. 42).

Anger at what he assumes to be his deserting wife's snobbery and prejudice seems a strange reaction from a man on the brink of knowing who he is and what he has done. Why should he turn aside from the fears and passions involved in his quest? The diversion of hatred turns out to serve as a grandiose denial, of his own guilt but first of all of that of his mother, who has again just abandoned him. He accomplishes this denial by devaluing Jocasta and claiming another mother, in a speech that I have found rings true in my understanding of patients who have had incestuous contact: "Yon woman [Jocasta] . . . thinks shame of my base source. *But I, who hold myself son of Fortune that gives good*, will not be dishonored—*She* is the mother from whom I sprung. . . . Such being my lineage, never more can I prove false to it, or spare to search out the secret of my birth" (p. 42; my italics). This magnificent pride in being a son of Fortune is yet another note of almost unbearable irony, for Fortune is about to deal Oedipus the most terrible blow. Yet it is exactly this other mother—the good mother wished for and insisted on —to whom Oedipus returns in *Oedipus at Colonus*.

Bowlby, Robertson, and Rosenbluth (1952) describe a similar split of the mental representation of the mother in a two-year-old patient who had suffered traumatic separation from her mother. The image of the real mother was swamped and obliterated by two contradictory mental pictures: one of the idealized, wholly satisfying mother the child so badly needed and desired (that is, Fortune), and, alongside, that of a wholly frustrating, hated mother who had deserted the child and caused such torment (the Sphinx). On reunion after separation, the normal two-year-old often has difficulty recognizing the real mother —that is, identifying either of the contradictory, emotionally extreme bad and good images with the real mother. With the primal parent —the soul-murdering parent—who has subjected the child to unbearable stimulation, the child's bad parental imago is more powerful, and as we have seen the need is even greater for the idealized, "good" mother to offer comfort and restore the child's sense of being. This idealized mother is Oedipus's Fortune, who then so cruelly uses him. This, however, is denied, and in Sophocles' last play Oedipus returns as a child of Fortune to his preordained, sacred resting place, his mother's womb. Mother-wife and son-husband are reunited in the guiltless eternal peace of the baby at the breast, the undisturbed narcissism of early orality.

At the beginning of the play Oedipus—blind, very old, and leaning on his daughter Antigone (his "staff," as in the riddle and Teiresias' prophecy)—approaches a "sacred place" at Colonus, near Athens: "The place is sacred to all seeming—thickset with laurel, olive, vine, and in its heart, a feathered choir of nightingales makes music" (p. 61). The poetic, symbolic evocation is of the maternal genitals, the sacred place where "birds" perform. We learn that it is "not lawful to tread" on this ground (p. 62). It is dedicated to the Eumenides, "the daughters of Earth and darkness" (p. 62), whom Oedipus invokes as "Queens of dread aspect" (p. 64) and "Daughters of primeval Darkness" (p. 65); here we return to the Sphinx. Apollo had prophesied that after many years Oedipus would find rest where he would come upon this "seat of the Awful Goddesses" (p. 64). It turns out that none may dwell in this "seat" but Oedipus. His death and burial there (reunion with the mother) would bless the land. And it is in Sophocles' mother-city, Athens, that Oedipus is to find rest. Oedipus is finally taken off by a god to his final resting place, a "sacred tomb [where] . . . no one should draw nigh" (p. 122); this is out of sight of the audience, as in the climactic scene from the earlier play in which Oedipus confronted his dead mother. Oedipus returns in apotheosis to the maternal womb. (Sophocles himself was born at Colonus.) Again he is the magnificent child of Fortune (incest is the privilege of the gods). Oedipus has transcendentally triumphed over the enormity of his sins and his suffering.

And yet we see more in *Oedipus at Colonus* of the destructive effects of both the mother-Sphinx's depredations and the incest. The outcast has undergone a characterological regression since the end of *Oedipus Rex*. Trilling describes him at the beginning of the later play: "His quickness to anger has not diminished, and now his rage is directed toward his two sons because they have permitted him to continue in the exile to which he had doomed himself. He is bitter at his fate and he insists on his blamelessness [in contrast to *Oedipus Rex*, written thirty years earlier]—he is not, it is plain, an endearing person" (1967, p. 42). Hadas (1950) notes the difference in Sophocles' outlook in the two plays: "Oedipus' disclaimer of guilt in *Oedipus at Colonus* when he had acknowledged guilt in the earlier *Oedipus Rex* showed that the Sophists had done their work [in influencing Sophocles' thought about human responsibility]" (pp. 84–85).

In the earlier play, part of Oedipus's greatness lies in his accepting his own responsibility as well as blaming the gods for what has happened to him. When asked by the Chorus why he has blinded himself, he gives a complex reply: "Apollo, friends, Apollo was he that brought these my woes, my sore, sore woes, to pass, but the hand that struck the eyes was none save mine" (p. 51). In the later play Oedipus strikes a note of almost querulous insistence on his guiltlessness: "I have suffered misery, strangers,—suffered it through unwitting deeds, and of those acts—be Heaven my witness!—no part was of my own choice" (p. 80). An identification with the denying Jocasta is apparent.

Another effect of soul murder is seen in the outbreak of Oedipus's impatient, cannibalistic rage. This had led to the killing of Laius and in the earlier play was evoked by brother and father figures like Creon and (especially) Teiresias, the blind prophet who personifies Oedipus's fate but whom Oedipus taunts so cruelly.[2] Where were you, Oedipus asks

2. "The action of the play . . . nothing other than the process of revealing, with cunning delays and ever-mounting excitement . . . that Oedipus himself is the murderer of Laius . . . [and] the son of the murdered man and Jocasta . . . can be likened to the work of a psychoanalysis" (Freud 1900, 261–262). If this is so, how familiar are the reproaches of Oedipus against the truth-teller Teiresias to the reproaches of the analysand against the analyst, and how similar the reasons for these reproaches: "What, basest of the base, for thou wouldest anger a very stone—wilt thou never speak out? Can nothing touch thee? Wilt thou never make an end?" (p. 15). Here speaks the angry, frustrated analysand to whom the silent analyst has not given a solution that would spare the patient and the patient's parents. The analyst then tells the unwelcome truth and gives

Teiresias, when the Sphinx was devastating the land? You, the seer, were blind, "until I came—I, ignorant Oedipus came—and stopped the Riddler's mouth" (Watling, trans., p. 37). Note the passive, cannibalistic expression here while Oedipus is making a vicious (sphinxlike) verbal attack (that is, an oral attack) on a blind old man, the semblance of his future self.

The identification with the oral-sadistic mother is at its fullest with Oedipus's cursing of his sons. His sons had not interceded when he was banished from Thebes; now they have quarreled, and the elder, Polyneices, about to make war on his brother, Eteocles, at Thebes, has come to get his father's blessing, which oracles have told will give victory to the side that obtains it. Oedipus reviles him, praying that his sons will kill each other:

> And thou—begone, abhorred of me and unfathered! Begone thou vilest of the vile, and with thee take these my curses which I call down on thee—never to vanquish the land of thy race, no, nor ever return to hill-girt Argos, but by a kindred hand to die, and slay him by whom thou hast been driven out. Such is my prayer; and I call the paternal darkness of dread Tartarus to take thee unto another home—I call the spirits of this place—I call the Destroying God —who hath set that dreadful hatred in you twain. Go—with these words in thy ears. (p. 110)

Here Oedipus, like his parents, willfully abandons his sons to death. To paraphrase Oedipus's reference to the mother who had given over her infant to be killed, "And could a father's heart be steeled to this?"

Polyneices, rightly taking these curses as a death warrant for himself and his brother, says farewell to his sisters and goes. Earlier in the play, King Theseus of Athens had been warned by Oedipus that sheltering him (the exiled parricide) would bring on strife between Thebes (ruled by Oedipus's sons) and Athens. The gift the blind old man has to bestow —to bless the place of interment—will bring about a war over his body. Because of this expectation, Oedipus looks forward to a time "when my slumbering and buried corpse, cold in death, *shall one day drink [my*

---

the interpretation that causes such pain: "Thou art maimed in ear, and in wit, and in eye . . . a scheming juggler is this, a tricky quack, who hath eyes only for his gains, but in his art is blind!" (p. 17). Stripped of archaic language, these are everyday expressions of what we call in our jargon "negative transference."

sons'] warm blood, if Zeus is still Zeus, and Phoebus, the son of Zeus, speaks true" (p. 84). Like the mother-Sphinx, like the primal parent Kronos, Oedipus too will eat his children. The imagery in this speech is similar to that which Oedipus used in describing the trifurcation of the road (symbol of the maternal genitals), which "drank from my hands that father's blood which was mine own," further underlining the identification with the cannibalistic mother.

Psychotic Seductive Parents and the Fruit of Incest

After he has blinded himself, Oedipus takes the guilt of his actions on himself and exonerates his mother: "I know not with what eyes I could e'en have looked on my father, when I came to the place of the dead, aye, or on my miserable mother, since against both I have sinned such sins as *strangling* could not punish" (p. 53; my italics). Because "sphinx" literally means "strangler," Oedipus is showing the need for punishment at the hands of the Sphinx as well as expressing the regressive wish to be swallowed by the preoedipal mother. Later in the play, with great bitterness, he again condemns his parents, asking to be cast out of the city: "Suffer me to abide on the hills, where yonder is Cithaeron, famed as mine,—which my mother and sire, while they lived, set for my appointed tomb.—that so I may die by their decree who sought to slay me" (p. 55). In *Oedipus at Colonus* Oedipus holds both himself and his parents guiltless. It is Fate or Fortune that is responsible (and presumably evil). Yet Oedipus has the promise of final reunion with the good mother Fortune contained in Apollo's prophecy about the sacredness of his grave and the magical result of his interment. (These moral attitudes are full of contradictions and doublethink.)

I have seen this combination in patients who have had incestuous contact: feeling oneself the privileged and entitled child of Fortune (in part because of having transgressed the sternest human proscription, having like the gods committed parricide and lived in incest), and yet feeling the need for punishment (banishment, blindness, castration, annihilation). I will later present the case of a man who had intercourse with his mother during his adolescence (see chapter 9). The two patients whom I am about to describe (studied in analysis as adults) had been seduced by their mothers in other ways as small children. They seem to have certain common characteristics traceable to the incestuous contact and to have passed through some of the vicissitudes of Oedipus's struggles.

Patient B.

B. would have been shocked to hear me say that his soul had been murdered; he was however aware that much of the time he lived an "as if" life. Chronic denial was not quite efficient enough to spare him intermittent consciousness of the emotional shallowness of his existence. He had considered acting as a career, not because he was especially talented but because being on stage as a character made him feel so comfortable. In his analysis he was struggling to acknowledge fully and give up perverse impulses and actions that we found to have derived from childhood seductions by his psychotic mother. In a session he talked about a girl he had taken out. He had felt it would have been easy to seduce her but had no real desire to do so. "I'm a handsome guy and she really likes me," he said. That he did not feel desire displeased him, "so," he said, "I kissed her just to deny my homosexuality." (This was typical of the intellectualized distancing of his feelings; he was not a homosexual, although he had strong homosexual impulses.)

B. would become excited less by women's bodies than by the desire to have them do sexual things to him, as his mother had done when he was a child. This had come to his mind when he was kissing the young woman. That night he dreamed—only a speech in the dream was remembered: "Everything goes for you, B." The associations in his analytic hour led to a number of meanings of this phrase, which, because it was spoken, turned out to be predominantly about superego attitudes (see Fliess 1953):

1. Everything goes your way. It is arranged that you will achieve whatever you desire. Sexually, everything, the whole world, any man, any woman, "goes for" you and will do whatever you want. You are entitled to everything. (*Everything* and *the world* ultimately meant mother.)

2. You can get away with everything, you can do anything you desire (like his mother, who did unspeakable and forbidden things that were then declared never to have happened). You are above all laws and yet . . .

3. Everything goes for you to track you down and destroy you as you deserve. You will and should be crushed and annihilated.

B. showed a combination of psychopathic tendencies (mainly thinly disguised sadistic impulses that he blandly indulged with a narcissistic droit du seigneur—a conviction of his own rightness and goodness no matter what) and a strong unconscious need for punishment, together with an essential feeling of lack of identity and hollowness. These contradictory trends were integrated with the aid of characterologic lying (conscious and unconscious), rationalizing, and dishonest doubting, so that he seemed like a moral chameleon; he could have been a disciple of Orwell's Big Brother. But he was very far from sharing Oedipus's unflinching determination to continue toward the truth; this was the chief obstacle to the first part of his analysis. His lying involved a version of doublethink in which he could be intellectually aware of what he was doing, and yet essentially denied it all the same. This transcended the familiar isolation seen in the obsessive-compulsive character (aspects of which were also present in B.). B.'s attitude toward the truth was in identification with his psychotic mother. In identifying with a psychotic parent, the neurotic may try to approximate the psychotic's ability to abolish reality by decree. As I have described above, this is often accomplished by a severe, stubborn, and almost bizarre isolation of fact and feeling, and splits in awareness that amount to a kind of vertical ego splitting (compartmentalization). These defenses operate against intensity of feeling and can supply the personality with the characteristic denying, double-faced surface that evokes *1984*.

Patient C.

This clinical excerpt also features a dream which consisted of words. In this instance they were seen and read in a newspaper headline: "Always Mr. C., Again Mr. C." Reading this in the dream made the patient feel good: "too good, as with a cloying sweetness." Here again, the associations led to both promise and punishment. Before the dream, C. had been looking at a clipping about himself from a second-rate trade paper, with a mixture of pleasure and shame. He was ashamed that something that meant so little could please him so much. This gifted and most ambitious person had always had intense daydreams about being greatly talented and famous. In the past, the need for punishment had asserted itself whenever he approached fulfillment, and despite considerable success he felt he had suffered a series of self-induced failures. *Always* and *again* in the dream led him in his associations to the past opportunities he had missed, the repeated promise and disappointment: always and again great success, everyone will love you, glory and magnificence; always and again failure, no one loves you, humiliation and punishment. His being called "Mister" in the dream reminded the patient of a stage in his training that had resulted in self-provoked failure, during which he was sarcastically called "Mister" in allusion to his lack of status. Grownups are called "Mister," but C.'s father was always addressed by his title, "Professor," which the patient's "Mister" could not rival.

The sense of cloying sweetness in the dream, of "too good," led C. to the falsely insisted on "good" character of the mother that was disappearing with amnesia removal, and to the initial pleasure of the seductive experiences at her hands, which preceded a terrifying overstimulation that was too much to bear. The newspaper is symbolic—paper, derived from wood and material, symbolizes woman and mother (Freud 1915–16, pp. 159–160)—and the opening of a newspaper and its perusal represent C.'s conflict-filled, scoptophilic, terrified "enjoyment" of his mother's spread thighs and genitals during her exhibitionistic displays. Having, owning, and becoming the mother were brought up in the analysis at the time of the dream. C., like B., had an almost delusional conviction that come what may he would be loved and granted success by Fortune, despite his repeated failures. It would all work out to be good *the next time*. (This is the cry of the soul-murdered, who are subject to the compulsion to repeat the traumatic past.) C.'s dream had brought up, again and always, simultaneous and alternative promises of glory and punishment.

Trilling wrote of the apotheosis of the blind and exiled Oedipus at Colonus: "By divine agency he is carried off from earth to live as a demigod. This end is not granted Oedipus in compensation for his suffering, but in recognition of some power of his nature that approaches the divine. We are left to ponder how it is that this cursed man became a blessing and why this guilty man should have been so supremely rewarded" (1967, p. 42). This prepares us for some contradictory findings in those who have suffered from attempts to murder their souls, especially when incestuous contact has been involved.

The Superego

"If, as theory has it, an identification occurs after the model of canni-balistic incorporation, its result is that the parent has become deposited in some part of the ego (in the wider sense of the term). One is, conse-quently, prepared to recognize him in the adult patient as a constituent part of a morbid ego and the nucleus of a morbid superego" (Fliess 1956, 90). To be subject to experiences imbued with cannibalistic feel-ing at the hands of parents would seem likely to intensify the morbidity of such identifications.

> Someone who has been damaged by and has identified with a psychotic parent . . . becomes the object of defused aggression (maltreated and beaten almost within an inch of his life), and of a perverse sexuality that hardly knows an incest barrier (is seduced in the most bizarre ways by the parent, and at his or her instiga-tion, by others). Among the damages one may single out one as perhaps the severest: it appears as though the child takes over all of the feelings of guilt over incest that the parent *should have had*, but being psychotic, *did not*. This promotes an excessive uncon-scious need for punishment, of which Freud has said that "it sets the most stringent limitations to our therapeutic endeavor." (Fliess 1956, xvii–xviii; italics in original)

The identification with the psychotic in both ego and superego en-sures the reversibility of roles. It is therefore not a surprise that in both patients B. and C. there were contradictory, simultaneous, or alternat-ing superego-ego relationships: a sadistic superego with a masochistic ego (expressed in the need for punishment, as Fliess implies in what I have just quoted), and alongside this the compliant superego that allows the rampant ego fulfillment of every impulse (manifested in an atti-tude of total entitlement). With a precipitate of the sadistic, seductive parent in both ego and superego, the superego can appear to be both too harsh and almost nonexistent. In these shifting, contradictory, and conflict-ridden superego-ego relationships, the parent-child confron-tation and its consummation in incestuous contact and identification can be reenacted. And so can the triumph over the third figure in the oedipal triangle and punishment by that figure (with both B. and C. this would be the father). As in the Oedipus legend, the oedipus complex is pervaded by preoedipal feelings. Contradictory but predominantly destructive effects on identity and "soul" are implicit in these terrible psychic dynamics.

Contradictory superego attitudes can be traced to both father and mother in the two cases cited. With both patients, the fathers had really been deprived of their relationship to the sons—in part because of their passive natures, but even more because the hatred in the sons, which stemmed from (preoedipal) overstimulation by the mother, was tremendously enhanced by the hostile oedipal rivalry and parricidal wishes that inevitably accompany incestuous contact with the mother. The father is defeated and eliminated, yet also personifies the retaliatory force that is submitted to, by way of the need for punishment. (These weak fathers were hated because they were not powerful enough to rescue their sons from the mothers; in fantasy they were endowed with strength and submitted to—this was then transferred onto other men, with masochistic and homosexual implications.) In these cases involving a psychotic mother as the soul murderer, the genuinely destructive bad mother was blended with the phylogenetic primal parent (or at least that imago's destructive aspects). The latter always supplements the prohibiting father of ontogenetic development. I have been examining the figure of Jocasta and have therefore stressed the primal parent as personified by the psychotic, sadistic, seductive mother in relation to a male child victim. The bisexual and treacherous Laius could also furnish a prototype of the primal parent.[3] I have found that patients who have been attacked and traumatically seduced as children by psychotic and psychopathic fathers have mutatis mutandis shown similar effects (with variations depending on the sex of the child).

The shifting and contradictory superego described above was demonstrated in B., who was not an overt homosexual, by a kind of public performance that is frequently indulged in by homosexuals (in whom it can also conceivably stem from childhood seduction): compulsive sexual activities in public toilets, subway trains, and parks, which can express and "play with" the wish to be caught and punished, and simultaneously assert that one can get away with anything. B., for whom "everything goes," was given to surreptitious masturbation when in professional group meetings. If caught, this would have meant humili-

3. Laius has also been linked to the Sphinx; see the illustration from a Greek vase in Kouretas's article of 1963, which shows a phallic sphinx in "homosexual" contact with its male victim.

ating disgrace, but his narcissistic insistence on his entitlement and invulnerability ("I am the child of Fortune who gives good") was not to be resisted. Simultaneous identification with the mother and subjection to her was being publicly reenacted, defying the father-authorities and yet provoking castigation.

Rage and Traumatic Anxiety as a
Result of Overstimulation

These patients had experienced true traumatic anxiety as a result of being seduced by their psychotic parents. During these experiences the overwhelming stimulation threatened the intactness of the physiological and psychological barrier to stimuli. The threat to psychic structure and its possible destruction are expressed through rage, and that rage of the victim is complemented by the angry destructive impulses that are part of identification with the parent-aggressor.

C. demonstrated the active repetition of the cannibalistic impulses that had previously been experienced passively. He showed two layers of hostility toward his mother. The more superficial one was conscious, expressed at first directly and then through the transference. His mother was described as unloving and frustrating, though vaguely good. The patient said she had never given him enough of the care and the things he had wanted. Some of the deprivations and frustrations that he "remembered" from childhood with a burning hatred turned out to be fabricated, others greatly exaggerated. In the course of the analysis, with the remembering of the mother's seductions (especially their initial part, which was exciting and pleasurable), this hatred could be traced to the child's reaction to the mother's having stopped these activities and returned to the father. She had provoked and stimulated him, then given him up. This intensity of rage was frequently expressed toward the analyst, usually by way of spiteful acting out: if the analyst would not continue the seductions, someone else could be found. (Except for sporadic outbursts, this was all experienced at the distance provided by the patient's characteristic "anal narcissistic defenses"; see Shengold 1986). Later in the analysis, after the patient had reacted negatively to success, and his need for punishment had been repeatedly reenacted and interpreted with effect, he was able to approach the deeper layer of his rage at his mother. This was done with the greatest difficulty, as expressed in the cry of Oedipus, "And could a mother's

heart be steeled to this?" The rage accompanied memories of the subsequent part of the seductions, during which C. became overstimulated
to the point of feeling that somehow he would explode, a state accompanied by overwhelming (traumatic) anxiety. He had apparently almost
fainted and had the expectation that he would just cease to be. With
these memories the rage against the mother broke out in its cannibalistic intensity: "I wish I had a scissors, a knife—I would slash her cheeks,
I could carve out the mark of Cain on her face."[4] Anger of such frightening extremity had rarely been felt, but it had occasionally surfaced
in "accidents" in which the patient's anger had been turned onto himself. He had expressed it very infrequently toward others, usually in an
attenuated, nonphysical way. In the analysis, he began to feel and voice
anger toward the analyst—finally, without provocatively acting it out
to evoke punishment.

During this time C. talked about a shoe fetishist who was wont to
put a man's shoe between the legs of his lover. He next expressed a
wish to be the analyst's passive anal partner, then said with a sudden
anger, "I would like to throw *my* shoe at *you*. I would like to take a
spiky, high-heeled shoe and gouge your eyes out." The shift to the
female shoe and its penetrative high heel made the analyst think of
identification with the phallic mother; the patient associated to the
wish to lie between his mother's thighs and use his penis on her. What
followed was a wish to penetrate the analyst anally with the female
high heel. He was aware that this meant the penis: historically it represented the invading finger of the mother during her seduction of
him in childhood; phylogenetically it was the primal parent's destructive penetrative organ—the claws of the Sphinx. The analyst was used
first to represent the penetrative phallic mother, then the child who is

4. The mark of Cain, which the patient was wont to say belonged on *his* forehead, turned out in the analysis to refer to the "impression" of the mother's
pubic hair and genitals, into which his face had been pressed, apparently while
the mother had had orgasm. In the Bible, the mark of Cain has the contradictory superego meanings that I have attributed to the victims of psychic murder:
(1) It is the mark of punishment of the primal murderer, to whom God says in
language that resembles that of Oedipus to his son Eteocles, "And now art thou
cursed from the earth, which hath opened her mouth to receive thy brother's
blood from thy hand [Genesis 4:10]. . . . a fugitive and a vagabond shalt thou
be in the earth [Genesis 4:12]"; (2) And yet it is also the mark of God's special
protection (that is, Fortune's): "And the Lord set a mark upon Cain, lest any
finding him should kill him [Genesis 4:15]."

penetrated, with the patient becoming the aggressor who will penetrate the "parent" through the eyes with the destructive maternal phallus. (Thus Oedipus, subject and object, put out his eyes with his mother's brooches, the claws of the Sphinx.) C. then shifted part-objects from the analyst's eyes to the analyst's anus. Next he reversed this, returning to the wish to be anally entered, and said, again expressing the cannibalistic fury of the overstimulation involved in his impulses: "If you touched me in that way, I would shatter glass over your head, I would tear the flesh off your face with my nails."

Patient B. had been seduced by his mother for a number of years after the age of three. The sexual contact included his mother's rubbing and sucking at his genitals and putting her finger into his anus. The seductions mobilized not only the child's passive responsiveness but also intense, positive oedipal wishes that were not fulfillable. He had correspondingly intense castration fears; these were augmented by his repeated and unequivocal views of his mother's genitals: "I have seen my mother's vagina many times."

The excitement involved in the sexual contacts, with sexual stimulation in between them furnished by the mother's exhibitionism, brought about overstimulation, traumatic anxiety, and rage. The overstimulation, especially in response to the mother's digital penetration of the anus, brought the boy to intimations of ego dissolution. Generally speaking, a child's sexual excitement in relation to an adult's cannot result in any kind of balanced mutuality; it is simply too much for the child, whose psychosexual organization is not capable of adequate discharge in orgasm. The wish for, need for, discharge is expressed through the child's fainting or sometimes by a loss of sphincter control (usually urethral), but a full release cannot be achieved. It appears that the wish for discharge can be transformed into a wish for a passive, penetrative experience, explosive or implosive—perhaps a kind of anal orgasm. This also might threaten to shatter the ego, but one can speculate that the child's organism might be better able to approximate it. At any rate, the wish for an explosive penetration, even a castrative penetration, can be mobilized to end the torment of prolonged and finally unbearable forepleasure.[5] The wish for anal explosion can

5. This complex of overstimulation and anal regression is similar to that found in children who have suffered traumatic enema experiences. In both instances the child's basic body ego—defensive mastery, furnished by the control of the anal sphincter, is compromised.

leave its mark on subsequent sexual experiences; because the wish involves castration and ego dissolution, it does not represent any kind of satisfactory solution. Another patient, for example, in recalling his excitement at being seduced as a child, expressed the wish to be "fucked to death" anally—to be castrated and explosively ground out of existence in order to end the unbearable overstimulation. In fact he had had many homosexual experiences, in some of which he had been anally penetrated, but these were always under carefully chosen and controlled conditions. Despite the opportunities, he had always avoided the really sadistic older pederast he so much craved. He both desired and feared a passive explosive experience.

The Good and the Bad Mother

The mind's picture of the good mother basically represents the mother into whom the infant can dissolve to furnish the timeless peace of the first oral stage, a regressive symbiosis with mother and breast (we theorize) that carries the individual back before the oral-cannibalistic phase of the libido. Sleep, conceived of psychologically, without considering its somatic physiology, supplies a needed restorative function that shows us the continued presence throughout life of this kind of regression.

Developmentally, the increased oral-sadistic impulses in the second half of the first year of life are also defended against regressively, by some kind of calling upon and merging with the incompletely differentiated mental image of the mother. In the course of development, aggression must be directed outward, away from the child's body. The inevitable frustrations brought about by the mother are needed to help establish, by way of projection, the initially bad "not me" that is to develop into an external object (this is part of the establishment of a separate self). Hoffer (1950a, 1950b) tried to understand why infants passing through the early developmental stage that is characterized by oral sadism do not bite themselves—why the aggression is turned outward. He cited the pain barrier (also called the stimulus barrier), existing at birth and from about the third month of life onward reinforced by the gradual beginning development of the body ego, which is basic to the psychic ego: "Progressive libidinization of the infantile body and growth of the body ego can only be assumed if self-destructive drives are either dealt with within the body or directed elsewhere outside it. The fact that there is an increase of motor activity from the second half of the first year onwards supports the second assumption." (This motor activity is the beginning of the liberating locomotion that is the heart of the riddle of the Sphinx.) "It is primarily the pain barrier which protects the infant against his destructive instinct turning against his own self. In addition is the process of *libidinization* of the body [leading to] . . . increase of primary narcissism [which] forms a second protective barrier. This occurs in the oral sadistic stage" (1950b, p. 22; my italics).

Mahler has written of the need for an affectionate, caring mother (not just her mental image) to furnish through body contact the progressive libidinization of the infant's body surfaces, and to provide the deeper sensory and motor experiences basic to body ego and eventual psychic ego formation. It is particularly the oral sadistic pressures from within that potentially endanger the infant's body integrity at around the age of six months (see Mahler and Elkisch 1959). To survive, the infant must therefore have maternal presence and care in the first half-year of life. In discussing anxiety development in infants, Spitz (1950) states that if the mother goes away when the child is nine months old this is especially grievous, because at that time the mother is simultaneously a libidinal object and a complementary part of the infant's immature ego: "The loss of the object is therefore a diminution of the ego at this age and is as severe a narcissistic trauma as a loss of a large part of the body. . . . Anxiety is the affect evoked in the threatening occurrence of such a representation loss . . . [The danger is that] the ego will be swamped by uncontrollable stimuli with which it cannot deal. It is the threat of the breakthrough of the protective shield against stimuli in analogy of its prototype in the trauma of birth" (pp. 141, 143). The actual good mother and the partly internalized, inadequately differentiated image of the good mother (the mental representation of the good mother blended with the self) are desperately needed to help the infant master the threat of this early access of oral sadistic impulses.

In a study of the failure of individuation of psychotic children, Mahler (1955) points out the influence of symbiotic, parasitic mothers who like the Sphinx cannot bear the child's ability to get away from them physically (by locomotion) and emotionally (with an ultimate separate identity); they need to continue overprotection and are "an engulfing threat detrimental to the child's normal enjoyment and individuation from his second year of life on" (p. 201). Another kind of symbiotic, parasitic mother cannot endure the loss of "the hitherto vegetative appendage [and] has to slough him off abruptly" (p. 201). But of course, "These children are not to be thought of as normal children in whom a psychotic process is induced by an emotionally disturbing mother" (p. 201).

Mahler was describing psychotic children whose identity had never been established. My clinical material concerns nonpsychotic children, influenced, seduced, and abused by psychopathic and psychotic parents who induce a regression to oral sadism after the child's individuation has been established. The overwhelmingly stimulating experiences of the child threaten to break through the protective shield against stimuli, and as a defensive measure, a partial reestablishment of the symbiotic relation is needed to deal with the terrible too-muchness. This means the child partially regresses toward the narcissistic period of less differentiated development, where the child still needs some kind of mental image of a good mother to help keep the stimulus barrier intact and ward off complete ego disintegration.

If the soul murderer is the mother, the very person who makes the child her object of attack has to be called on to get rid of the unbearable sensations and affect. This involves partial, regressive, symbiotic use of the image of the good mother as ego auxiliary, and also an identification with the aggressor—in other words, what is fostered is identification with both the good mother and the bad. Consciously, however, the bad mother is denied, in an effort to distance the overwhelming trauma. These patients need a good mother so desperately that they insist on aspects of the mother's goodness. If these were really present (and at least some need-fulfilling functions must of course have been provided for the child to have survived) they are stretched and pieced together into a confabulated good mother and held on to with delusional persistence. (I have found this to be so even in the rare instances where the actual mother is accused—usually of minor obfuscating offenses—and criticized; in such cases it turns out that the soul-murdered patients are paying a superficial lip service that disguises a quasi-delusion involving a good mother and a child of Fortune.)

For example, C. was struggling late in his analysis with an acknowledgment of his mother's sadism in the childhood seductions. At this time he was subjected to a sudden, unprovoked reversal of fortune. He at first dealt with this realistically, but in one session, after expressing great anger toward the analyst, he went on to talk of a sudden, quasi-religious feeling. After a statement that he did not believe in God, C. added that in spite of this he had started to feel as if his reversals were only a preparation for a future of greater triumph: "I have the feeling somehow that it all might be part of God's plan." (Compare Oedipus's "I am the son of Fortune who gives good.") In his retreat from his anger at his mother and his analyst, he was insisting that even his adversities had to be seen as part of a larger scheme in which his good parent, God, would ultimately show beneficence. When I interpreted that he wanted somehow, desperately to excuse and explain away what he had remembered about his mother, C. began to weep. He recalled how during his first years at school, after the seductions, he would rush home for lunch with desperate eagerness and ring the bell, hardly able to delay seeing his "good, loving" mother. With great bitterness and conscious irony he described the loving feeling that was simulated between them as being "sticky and gooey—my sweet, fat mommy and her little apple pie," thus evoking incidentally the passive, cannibalistic relation of the victim to the Sphinx.

The anger at the analyst that preceded the interpretation and the insight amounted to an attempt to attribute the blows of fortune to the bad analyst. This involved splitting off the image of the bad mother and projecting it onto someone else, a process that had begun with the patient's father, to whom he had attributed all sorts of evil intent. The delusion of the good mother is regularly accompanied by the delusion about the bad analyst (who takes the part of Teiresias). The undoing of these delusions has important technical implications. This patient, late in the analysis, was able to relinquish the delusion about the bad analyst rather easily (although it was not completely banished), as a more trusting, positive "object-relationship" had been established. As he remembered truly ("with great bitterness"), he was able to give up the identification with his mother, to see her rather than be her.

B. had not had a good mother, but with a similar delusional intensity he insisted that he had. In the course of his analysis, when a partial lifting of repression brought up memories of the sexual traffic with his mother, a negative therapeutic reaction invariably followed, marked by identification with the lying, deceitful mother. This was accompanied and in fact evidenced by an insistence on his mother's good character. Here too evil was projected, narcissistically and quasi-delusionally, rather than transferred onto the analyst. The patient would himself become sadistic and repudiate the truth in many ways. That is, with the access of oral sadistic stimuli (as the past memories of overstimulation became conscious), identification with the mother brought about a partial symbiotic reestablishment: the patient became the mother to keep his ego intact. (Again, one sees here the incompatibility of seeing the mother and being the mother.) While insisting that his mother was good, he maintained that somehow the things he remembered could not have happened, although at the same time he knew very well that they had. (The analyst was merely an onlooker in all this.) At these times of denial B. would literally grind and gnash his teeth, just as the mother had done in her sadistic attacks. Thus the identification was continually reestablished with any approach to a reenactment of the original oral sadistic relation of victim and invader between child and parent. The patient would often act out his mother's role and choose his own victim. Her deceitfulness and mendacity were continued in these relationships. He would never face up to his abuse of his love partners, which was sometimes outrageous. It would always appear to the patient that he was actually good and that his cruelties either had a higher purpose or simply could not have happened. So skillful was he that these views were shared by the carefully chosen masochistic lover, as well as by any casual observer. They were explained away and deprived of meaning, much as his psychotic mother had waved away reality. B.'s continual obsessive rationalizations, and his suppressions and isolations culminating in denial, severely compromised his sense of identity. He once dreamed he was a man without a passport in a foreign country. He regarded himself as hollow and without convictions. There had indeed been a partial psychic murder. At times the entire force of his character was devoted to the protective falsification and therefore retention of the traumatic relationship and the identification with his mother.

I have stressed a somewhat neglected view of the Oedipus myth as exemplified in Sophocles' plays: the preoedipal relationship to the mother-Sphinx—the primal parent. This stress is not intended to minimize the oedipal connotations of the Sophoclean dramas, which like all art on the very highest level are an encyclopedia of creative psychological insight. Using Jocasta-Sphinx as the imago of the bad primal parent, I have compared aspects of the character of the son-husband, Oedipus, to those of children seduced and abused by psychotic and psychopathic parents. I feel the myth and the clinical material are mutually enriching.

Freud's parallel of the unfolding drama of *Oedipus Rex* to the course of a psychoanalysis helps one to understand the therapeutic effects of that treatment on B. and C. Each patient achieved the following:

1. Eventually, a *partial* ability to see, know, and stand for the still terrible truth—particularly the truth about his parent's psychosis and incestuous, destructive intent. This meant a modification of the super-ego's contradictions and distortions (ameliorating the insistence on being a "son of Fortune" and the unconscious need for punishment exemplified in Oedipus's blinding himself).

2. The diminished use of massive isolation and other defensive mechanisms based on a need to approximate the psychotic parent's ability to ignore and deny reality (for Oedipus this would have meant giving up his identification with mendacious, denying Jocasta).

3. More tolerance of the characteristic rage to which victims of soul murder are subject (recall Oedipus's ungovernable temper, his "tragic flaw"). The rage is there both through identification with the murderous, cannibalistic aggressor (the Sphinx) and as the legacy of over-whelmingly stimulating traumata. Like the "anal rage" described by Ruth Mack Brunswick, this affect involves the feeling that one is both subject and object of destructive, angry forces.

The effect of the psychoanalysis is similar to that of Oedipus's solving the Sphinx's riddle: to get rid of the invading intrapsychic monster—that is, to undo or at least ameliorate the damaging identification with the soul-destroying parent. For B. and C., this meant not only helping them to free themselves from the mother as incestuous object (Jocasta) but also from the mother as destructive, symbiotic partner (the Sphinx). Oedipus too is freed: first by causing the death of the mother-Sphinx, finally by knowing and acknowledging the full truth personified by the analyst figure, the seer Teiresias (see Abrams 1981). But Oedipus remains crippled and blind until his death and apotheosis. Similarly, my patients, despite marked improvement (like Oedipus, they established an identity by being able to walk away from the bad, primal parent-Sphinx), showed indelible effects that the traumatic incestuous experiences had left on their characters—the attenuated marks of soul murder.

Instances of soul murder like these cases of a psychotic parent having seduced a child are apt to evoke compassion in the analyst. Although this is natural, it must not be allowed to interfere with amnesia removal, reconstruction, or both, or with the general technical management of the analysis. The latter still requires what Freud somewhat unfortunately called "surgical coolness." The poet's case is very different. What prompts Ivan Karamazov to "give God back his entrance ticket" to the universe is his knowledge of the "unavenged suffering" of tortured children. And Sophocles has his chorus cry: "When such things are done, what man shall contrive to shield his soul from the shafts of the God? When such deeds are held in honour, why should I honour the Gods in the dance?" (D. Grene, trans.).

5

Soul Murder, Rats, and 1984

Aside from his schoolboy experiences, one cannot present George Orwell as a victim of child abuse. Orwell was reticent about his earliest years and his family, but there is no evidence of any extraordinary neglect or cruelty in his first eight years. He tells us only that he was unhappy, lonely, and felt unlovable. Analysts are familiar with how little reliance can be placed on the initial, conscious memories of the patient's self and parents in childhood, and some of us are sadly aware of how even the best psychoanalyses leave us with at most a palimpsest of the past: a bit of certainty and a lot of doubt. We cannot expect to establish objective past reality, although we do our best to approach it. And of course Orwell was not an analytic patient; one cannot conceive of psychoanalysis even being considered by this man, who apparently confided in no one. I make use of Orwell because whatever the "facts" of his actual experiences, he portrays with such vividness what it felt like and feels like to be an abused child—to feel helpless, inadequate, and guilty in a world one never made.

I will begin with a sketch of a patient, D., who had been seduced as a child and who feared and was fascinated by rats. I will be using this clinical material to make parallels with George Orwell's life and especially with the view of the world he presented in *1984*, a primer on soul murder.

Patient D.

A young man in analysis for several years complained of having difficulty with his memory and of disruptions in his thinking that interfered with his professional achievements. Despite his complaints, his achievements were considerable. D. was very intelligent, but at his work he seemed always to promote dissension, controversy, and ultimately punishment or even dismissal. He seemed unaware of his provocation of authority figures. D. lived a life of disconnected and largely unacknowledged sadomasochistic fantasy, which he occasionally expressed in action that he quickly disavowed. So much was disavowed that his functioning sometimes suffered because of a discontinuity in his memory; this affected his sense of identity, and he had little awareness of himself as a child—only dim feelings about a little person with his name who seemed like somebody else. D. insisted on the façade of being regarded as the decent, helpful, kindly, but feckless friend of the family—of so many families. His specialty was compulsively and successfully seducing the wives of his "good friends." This was part of a secret life that he covered over by competent impersonation. D. had been engaged for many years to a masochistic young woman who worshiped him and whom he treated very badly. He seemed to despise her for loving him, yet felt he needed her dependable affirmation of his "lovability."

D.'s painful, although intermittent, awareness of not being able to be responsible for what he was feeling and doing was connected by the analyst with the patient's deepening memories of having been given as a child repeated, overstimulating enemas by his mother. She appeared to have had very little interest in him, but much fascination with his anus and bowel habits. The enemas always went beyond what he could stand. More pleasurable were the occasions of having his anus wiped by her—a habit that continued even after he started going to school. (The anally fixated D. was a "rat person" [see chapters 6 and 7] who frequently associated to rodents and had a specific fantasy of rats crawling up his anus.) In the early phases of analysis, D. described his childhood with few specific memories but generally thought of it as quite happy. During one session when he seemed to be integrating past and present more than was usual, he commented with poignancy, "It is sad. I am not really a whole person. I live in compartments, in fragments." The analyst said, stressing the defense, "In disconnected fragments."

Some time after this, D. reported an incident he had never told anyone about. As a teenager he had been a babysitter for an infant female relative. Once he had exposed his erect penis and tried to get the baby to play with it and suck on it. He was unsure of the baby's age but thought she was too young to know what was going on. He "really didn't think anything had really happened," but with his memory defects he of course could not expect to know this for sure. He was however sure of one thing: that the girl in her adolescence had become a promiscuous delinquent had nothing to do with his attempt at seduction. When the analyst (who was not feeling kindly that day) asked him how he could be certain, D. became furious. He characteristically wanted to treat this vaguely recalled sin as if he were telling it in confession (his family was Catholic). He had reported it; he gave himself absolution; it was over and should no longer matter. He did not want to connect the incident, even speculatively, with the past or present—neither with the former little girl nor with his analyst (for it had current transference implications). What had happened must have no consequences that might threaten his self-esteem.[1]

After this session came a series of provocative actions. It was as if D. were trying to show by example some of the terrible intensity of accusation and hatred connected with his sexual excitement about children, intensity that he could not responsibly feel or connect with his mother, his analyst, or himself. His behavior seemed to be a reaction to the confession of his crime, designed to evoke punishment while simultaneously expressing anger. The punishments came mostly at work, although he obviously wanted to provoke the analyst to be the spanker and enema giver. His main victim and scapegoat was his fiancée. Using the excuse of financial pressure (which unconsciously represented an urgent anal impulse), he sold a treasured heirloom that had been given to her by her beloved mother. He had extorted his fiancée's permission for this, but when he had sold the heirloom and returned to the apartment he shared with her, she burst into tears. "I knew I had been a son of a bitch," he said. "I knew I should be feeling sorry for her. She truly is a good person. But I hated her for *reproaching* me with her weeping. She's so goddam *helpless;* she can't even yell at me. And—I don't want to tell you this—when I saw her crying that way, I got an erection." "As you got an erection with the 'helpless' baby," I added. "That has nothing to do with this! You make me sound like a monster! . . . Listen to me screaming, as if I were a woman. I can't even be properly angry with you. It's all a show!"

D., the "son of a bitch" (he would also frequently call himself a "rat"),

---

1. He had also succeeded in repeating the past in an attentuated way in relation to the analyst. He had provoked me by his defensive disavowal into putting an "unkind" and critical pressure on him to be responsible.

was struggling with feminine identifications—an identification with the "monster . . . woman," the bad mother of his childhood, as well as with the seduced child and with his fiancée as victim. But he was not able to be responsibly aware that this was going on. His terror of his suppressed and isolated feelings made much of his life into a dramatic simulation: he lived *as if* he were involved. After he had gained some insight, D. described himself, echoing T. S. Eliot, as a hollow man, a stuffed man. (He associated to the straw-stuffed Scarecrow who in one of L. Frank Baum's books about the land of Oz carried mice in his straw.)

Eric Blair

Little is known of Orwell's earliest childhood. He wrote an autobiographical essay, "Such, Such Were the Joys" (1947), about his experiences between the ages of eight and eleven in boarding school (St. Cyprian's). Eight was a crucial, vulnerable age for the boy Eric Blair (Orwell's given name). He was sent to school just after his father had returned to the family after four years in India. The absence had deprived the boy of the opportunity for masculine identification. With his father's return, Eric was displaced as the "man" in the family (he had two sisters), which was a blow to his narcissism. Shortly after came the exile to boarding school, which must have further enhanced both his oedipal conflicts and their concomitant preoedipal antecedents. The boy was accepted at the school on partial scholarship as one likely to win prizes. This gave him a sense of demeaning obligation that he felt was used by the headmistress for emotional blackmail. He was a bed wetter, which led to further and repeated humiliations by the couple who ran the school. Many aspects of *1984*, including brainwashing, are implicit in the way Orwell depicts his experiences at this school (see West 1958). And "Such, Such Were the Joys" was written at the same time that he was working on *1984*. "Your home might be far from perfect, but at least it was a place ruled by love rather than by fear . . . At eight years old you were suddenly taken out of this warm nest and flung into a world of force and fraud and secrecy, like a goldfish into a tank full of pike" (1947, p. 23).

Although his friend and schoolmate Cyril Connolly called "Such, Such Were the Joys" the "key to [Orwell's] formation" (see Crick 1980,

67), others have questioned the centrality of the school experiences, and other schoolmates have cast doubt on the objective facts as presented. This brings in the complicated relation between fantasy and reality (see chapter 4, above). Orwell has written of how the adult remembered the child's feelings. The headmaster's wife, who bullied and shamed Orwell and who is portrayed as having made him doubt his own perceptions and feel that he was guilty and bad, may or may not have deserved to be a prototype of Big Brother in the novel, but I have no doubt that Orwell considered her to be so.

In most families with a soul-murdering parent, the other parent is an unconscious colluder,[2] a fellow victim, or both. (Where this is not so, the situation is less "totalitarian," and the trauma tends to be less devastating—the child has someone else to turn to.) When one parent can tyrannize, the need for a loving and rescuing authority is so intense that the child must break with the registration of what he or she has suffered, and establish within the mind (delusionally) the existence of a loving parent who will care and who really must be right. Like the broken Winston Smith at the end of *1984*, the child loves Big Brother. (In the adult, there may be a good deal of intellectual awareness of what the parent is like, but the delusion of goodness continues underneath

2. Here is an instance of "family collusion" from the memoirs of Lucy Boston (1979), an English writer born in 1895. The author describes herself reaching puberty. Her mother, then a widow, never mentioned sex to her but started to treat her with suspicion, "seeing evil where none was" (p. 81). The mother interfered with an innocent friendship with a very nice boy whom the mother suddenly characterized as "dangerous." In contrast, the girl was encouraged to stay with her aunt and uncle. Lucy describes her uncle as having an air of "rolling self-confidence and gusto. He had the twinkling little eyes of a porker. They now took notice of me. After a few displeasing signals of his intentions, he one day caught me on the landing and carried me fighting like a bull-calf into a bedroom where he flung me onto the bed and his twenty stone on top of me. From this extremity I was rescued by one of his sons calling his father to order. The old man was not put out of countenance. 'Ah, well. All right, my boy.' Neither man seemed to think it out of the ordinary. A few days later when Mother wished to send me with a message to her sister, I refused to go, saying Uncle was too dangerous. He wouldn't let me alone. 'Nonsense, you silly child,' she replied. 'It's only Uncle's way.' This was her side of the family and therefore perfectly conformable. But she was right—it was Uncle's way, and there was to be no help from her" (p. 81).

and surfaces when needed.) The child takes on the guilt for the abuse, turning inward the murderous feeling that is evoked by the traumata. The actuality of torment intensifies what is a usual vicissitude of hatred toward a needed parent. The child denies what has happened, sometimes but not always with orders from the tormentor. The parent is right and good; the child must be wrong and bad. I repeat these sequelae of soul murder because they are so movingly presented in Orwell's essay and in his prophetic novel.

Shortly after arriving at school, Orwell began to wet his bed. This was felt to be criminal, and even though the child had no control over the symptom, he felt the authorities were right. He was threatened with beating, and when the symptom continued the threat was carried out. The headmaster had "already taken a bone-handled riding crop out of the cupboard, but it was part of the punishment of reporting yourself that you had to proclaim your offense with your own lips. When I had said my say, he read me a short but pompous lecture . . . He had a habit of continuing his lecture while he flogged you, and I remember the words, 'you dir-ty lit-tle boy' keeping time with the blows" (1947, pp. 3–4).

The beating did not hurt much, which made the boy smile. (The boy's masochistic provocation, similar to my patient's, can be seen here.) Therefore the beating was repeated:

> This time Sim laid on in real earnest. He continued for a length of time that frightened and astonished me—about five minutes, it seemed—ending up by breaking the riding crop. The bone handle went flying across the room.
>
> "Look what you've made me do!" he said furiously, holding up the broken crop . . . The second beating had not hurt very much either. Fright and shame had anesthetised me. I was crying partly because I felt that this was expected of me, partly from genuine repentance, but partly also because of a deeper grief which is peculiar to childhood . . . a sense of desolate loneliness and helplessness, of being locked up not only in a hostile world but in a world of good and evil where the rules were such that it was actually not possible for me to keep them. . . . I had a conviction of sin and folly and weakness, such as I do not remember to have felt before . . . [Another result] is that I accepted the broken riding crop as my own crime. I can still recall my feeling as I saw the handle lying on the carpet—the feeling of having done an ill-bred, clumsy thing,

and ruined an expensive object. *I* had broken it: so Sim told me, and so I believed. This acceptance of guilt lay unnoticed in my memory for twenty or thirty years. (pp. 4–6; Orwell's italics)

The abused child takes on the guilt that the self-righteous parent so often lacks.

Here is Winston Smith's response to being tortured beyond his endurance. The tormentor, O'Brien, has been holding up four fingers and insisting that Winston see five. With enough pain, Winston gives in. He loses consciousness and recovers to find O'Brien holding him. "For a moment he clung to O'Brien like a baby, curiously comforted by the heavy arm round his shoulders. He had the feeling that O'Brien was his protector, that the pain was something that came from outside, from some other source, and that it was O'Brien that would save him from it" (1949, p. 254). O'Brien correctly predicts the result of the brainwashing he is administering. It is a description chillingly appropriate to my patient D.: "Never again will you be capable of ordinary human feeling. Everything will be dead inside you. Never again will you be capable of love, or friendship, or joy of living, or laughter, or curiosity, or courage, or integrity. You will be hollow [patient D. called himself a "hollow man"]. We shall squeeze you empty, and then we shall fill you with ourselves" (pp. 259–260).

Orwell shows that Winston Smith has been forced by torture both to identify with the tormentor and to cultivate denial—the erasing of what has happened, the abolition of the past; this has become a principle of government: "All history was a palimpsest, scraped clean and reinscribed exactly as often as was necessary" (p. 41). "If the Party could thrust its hand into the past and say of this or that event, it never happened—that surely was more terrifying than mere torture and death" (p. 35).

D.'s Denial

I recall the interferences with D.'s thinking of which he complained. In one session, during a period when D. was attempting to recall his enema experiences and his wish to be wiped by his mother, he became restless, turned on his side on the couch, and said that he felt as if he were going to be goosed. I suggested that he was feeling anal excitement. "I don't know what you mean by 'anal excitement,'" D.

responded. I pointed out that he had told me he liked to have his anus played with by a particular woman. "I wouldn't call that excitement," he rejoined. Since I was aware that D. frequently wanted to argue (that is, to be contacted, scolded) instead of registering and becoming responsible for the subject of the argument, I left the exchange at that. During the next session, D. reported that on the previous night he had for the first time masturbated while stimulating his anus. Several weeks later, again while talking about enemas but this time stressing how unpleasant he thought they had been (he was speculating rather than remembering), he started to wriggle on the couch and again turned on his side, presenting his behind. I interpreted that his body seemed to be remembering better than his mind and was perhaps expressing the anal pain and anal excitement that he seemed unable to feel. "What is this anal excitement business?" he exclaimed. "I have no idea what you mean by anal excitement." I reminded him of the anal masturbation that had occurred a few weeks back. "Oh that," he said, "What doe. that mean? It only happened once."

In *1984* Orwell describes this power of denial, of being able to split one's responsible awareness ("It is like trying to write on water," Freud is alleged to have said of how one patient dealt with his interpretations), as part of the principle of doublethink:

> To know and not to know, to be conscious of complete truthfulness while telling carefully constructed lies, to hold simultaneously two opinions which cancelled out, knowing them to be contradictory and believing both . . . to forget, then to draw it back into the memory again at the moment when it was needed, and then promptly to forget it again, and above all to apply the same process to the process itself . . . consciously to induce unconsciousness, and then once again to become unconscious of the act of *hypnosis* you had just performed. Even to understand the word "doublethink" involved the use of doublethink. (1949, p. 36; my italics)

Orwell mentions hypnosis, and the passage is relevant to the autohypnosis so often used by victims of soul murder to effect nonregistration and denial (see chapter 8). Therapeutically, the patient needs to become aware of using doublethink and autohypnosis, and, harder still, to become responsible for using them.

Anal Defense

It is necessary for the patient to get away from the torment of overstimulation and the rage and murderousness it brings forth by identifying
with the tormentor and turning the rage on the self and on others. I conceive of what happens defensively as a regression to the so-called anal-
sadistic period of development (between the ages of 18 months and
42 months), during which the child usually evolves defenses against
a burgeoning aggressive drive; this regression may also be conceived
of as an enhancement of the anal-sadistic period and eventually as a
fixation on it. The regression is of course partial and subject to great
individual variation. I have called what makes it necessary "anal defensiveness," central to which is an idea of Robert Fliess's: he conceived of
the unconscious involvement of the anal sphincter in the defensive task
of mastering the basically aggressive destructive feelings we are born
with (he calls these *primal*, or *archaic*, affects): "It is often as though
the anal sphincter were charged with the mastery of regressive and
archaic affect, intrinsic to whatever phase of development, because it
is the strongest [sphincter]; and as though the ego chose anal-erotic
elaboration upon instinctual strivings of whatever nature as the most
reliable means of preserving its organization" (1956, p. 124).

This implies that becoming able to control the anal sphincter (a momentous developmental achievement) has its psychic counterpart in
the control of aggressively charged emotion (that is, murderous emotion). There is a primitive kind of shutting off of feeling as well as a
primitive kind of letting go of feeling. We all require some amount of
obsessive-compulsive defensive structuring (which implies anal defensive structuring)—the developmental conversion of impulse and action
into thought—and the kind of emotional sphincter control that goes
along with the possibility of isolating feeling from idea. Optimally, this
obsessive-compulsive scaffolding is not so constrictive as to prohibit
subsequent emotional development toward the capacity to care about
and love others; this is a goal that severe obsessive-compulsive characters with anal fixations (such as D.) do not achieve. We all have to
master hate, but those who have been abused as children have more
hate to master than most, and they frequently do not have the needed
help of a loving parent. What results can be a massive recourse to
obsessive-compulsive defenses, to anal mechanisms, symptoms, and

erogeneity.[3] The overuse of the emotional sphincter makes for a kind of anal-sadistic universe with all the contradictions that this entails. Repression, isolation, and excessive emotional control (which can result in a kind of zombie existence) can be found alongside outbursts of intense, hate-filled sadism and masochism (sometimes covered over, as in D., by a very different "as if" façade of "normality"). In *1984* the enforced, docile conformity coexists with perpetual war and daily hate sessions. In our patients there are myriad combinations of these contradictions, which usually subsist unsynthesized, side by side, in fragments or compartments, and result in the confusing variety of clinical pictures we find.

Before toilet training anal consciousness is cloacal consciousness, and control of the urethral sphincter plays its important but lesser part in asserting a kind of instinctual defensive mastery alongside control of the anal sphincter. Urethral control is usually attained first. Bed-wetting, a frequent response in children subjected to neglect or overstimulation (and a cry for help from them—Orwell illustrates both), means an unconscious relinquishment of urethral control. This probably involves a regression that enhances the anal organization and defensive need for the anal sphincter; here is one explanation for the terror that accompanies loss of the sphincter's integrity for bed wetters like Orwell. This would underlie Orwell's fear of rats (and Winston Smith's): as in the florid fantasies of Freud's Rat Man, these animals are endowed with the power of penetrating the body by eating through sphincters.

3. A specific instance for Orwell occurred when he was hospitalized in his early thirties for pneumonia. His sister Avril reported "the nurse telling her that when Eric had been delirious, he had talked incessantly about money: one of the obsessions of his life emerging, as it were, from the unconscious and demanding to be heard . . . 'We reassured him that everything was all right, and he needn't worry about money. But it turned out that it wasn't actually his situation in life as regards money that he was worrying about, it was actual cash —he felt that he wanted cash sort of under his pillow'" (Stansky and Abrahams 1980, 47). Orwell was regressing to anal defensiveness at a time when his life was in danger—holding on with his anal sphincter to try to keep control (see Shengold 1988).

Rats

The most devastating effect on children of psychic or soul murder is the suppression of the joy in life that depends on having been cared for, and on being able to care about another human being. In *1984* this is finally effected by torture: Winston Smith is faced by O'Brien (who has found out that rats are Smith's worst fear) with the prospect of a cage of starving rats being lowered onto his face. Orwell more than once described his childhood as unhappy; it contained "quite unnecessary torments" (1948, p. 415). He had a "complex about being an ugly and smelly child" (that is, a rat; see Crick 1980, 56), and he seems to have been preoccupied with rodents even before his stay at preparatory school. During his first term at St. Cyprian's he wrote home: "I am very sorry to hear we had those beastly freaks of smelly white mice back. I hope these arnt *smelly one* [*sic*]. If they arnt, I shall like them" (Crick 1980, 64; my italics).

Orwell's obsession with rats was lifelong. A comrade said that when Orwell fought in the Spanish Civil War, "he was more concerned with rats [in the trenches] than with bullets" (Crick 1980, 325). His ambivalence was compounded by identification, for he himself had been the "smelly one." He wrote: "A child's belief in its own shortcomings is not much influenced by facts. I believed, for example, that I 'smelt' " (Orwell 1947, 37). Some of the ambivalent obsession had turned to action by the time he was seventeen,[4] when he wrote to a friend who was a dedicated hunter:

4. There is some evidence of at least an unconscious wish to bring about contact with what he would in his fiction call "the worst thing in the world" (1948, p. 286): Orwell appeared to be indifferent to how he dressed. He was equally unconcerned about where he lived, as long as he could be left alone and his room was large with a lot of light so that he could write. In practice this carelessness meant that he was sometimes surrounded by dirt and disorder. Janet Gimson, a twenty-one-year-old medical student, had a room in the same house where Orwell boarded in 1935 when he was in his early thirties: "Janet tended to be censorious where cleanliness and neatness were concerned; in those respects Eric's room simply would not pass. She thought it then and remembers it still as "filthy." He seems to have been a firm believer in the principle of "sweep it under the carpet" or "move it out of sight." The result of the latter was that forgotten, half-finished boxes of biscuits grew old at the back of the cup-

I have bought one of those big cage-rat traps. This place is overrun with rats. It is rather good sport to catch a rat & then let it out & shoot it as it runs. If it gets away I think one ought to let it go & not chase it. If they are threshing the corn while you are there, I should advise you to go—it is well worth it. The rats come out in dozens. It is also rather sport to go at night to a cornstack with an acetylene bicycle lamp & you can dazzle the rats that are running along the side & whack at them—or shoot them with a rifle. (Buddicom 1974, 110–111)[5]

Crick (1980) comments on this letter: "Thus Blair bought the cage that eventually was thrust at the face of Winston Smith in *Nineteen Eighty-Four*. And the rat seems to be the devil to be striven against in a child's own created world of domestic animals" (p. 130). This apt observation ignores the devil in the child himself. The letter shows Orwell's identification with the rat as killer as well as with the rat as victim. His delight in the slaughter is made even more chilling by the matter-of-fact prose of the description. Murderous wishes are projected onto the rat; then by killing it one can kill the bad impulses.

Contradictions are the stuff of life; they abound in adolescence and are inherent to anality. This letter was written at a time when young Orwell was becoming passionately involved in resisting authority and in ideas about class antagonism. There was an ambivalent, intellectualized identification with the lower classes (who had rodentlike connotations for him). Orwell said he had been brought up to believe that "the lower classes smell" (1937, p. 129), as he believed he had as a child. Of Orwell's preoccupation with bad odors, Crick writes: "From his earliest days he grew to associate smell with oppression" (1980, 64).

Readers of *Homage to Catalonia* (1938) will remember the frequent, hateful references to rats in the front lines near Madrid: "rats, rats, rats, rats as big as cats" (p. 78; see also pp. 83, 102, 106). One passage strongly resembles the letter quoted above: "In the barn where we waited . . . the place was alive with rats. The filthy brutes came swarm-

---

board and were taken over by mice—at night Janet could hear them rustling about; and after Eric moved from Parliament Hill the next summer, she and [the landlady] discovered a family of mice nesting in an extra blanket he had tossed out of sight on the floor of the closet" (Stansky and Abrahams 1980, 96).
5. Compare Marcel Proust's sadistic feelings and practices in relation to rats (see Shengold 1988).

ing out of the ground on every side. If there is one thing I hate more than another it is a rat running over me in the darkness. However, I had the satisfaction of catching one of them a good punch that sent him flying" (1938, p. 83). The prose has improved, but the man revealed here does not seem much changed from the boy of seventeen.

Isolation: Contradictions and "Compartments"

There are many contradictory descriptions by others of Orwell's behavior and personality. He showed different aspects of himself to different people; this seemed a conscious policy. Orwell's biographers cannot do more than sketch and speculate about the inner man—what it felt like to be Orwell. He was secretive and solitary, and he never wanted his biography to be written. His characteristic role in life, primarily defensive, was that of the observer, detached from pain and emotional involvement. (D. resembled him in this.) In so many situations in his life he was the "odd man out," apart from the crowd and against the establishment. V. S. Pritchett perceptively describes Orwell's masochistic isolation: "Tall and bony, the face lined with pain, eyes that stared out of their caves, he looked far away over one's head, as if seeking more discomfort and new indignations" (quoted in Stansky and Abrahams 1980, 284).

Orwell had acquaintances and friends, but he avoided bringing together those who did not already know one another. Like D., Orwell kept parts of his life "in compartments."[6] He made adaptive use of his detachment: even as a child he was determined to become a "famous author" (see Buddicom 1974, 389), and his compulsive need to be the observer became the vantage point for the journalism, essays, and fiction that finally emerged. I feel that he used his strong will and persistent determination to force himself away from some hated and feared part of his nature—probably these were primarily his sadistic and dominating impulses. He remained able to fight and did so liter-

6. One of the women Orwell dated before he married Eileen O'Shaughnessy wrote to Stansky and Abrahams (1980): "He compartmentalized his women friends so much that one only met one's predecessors or successors by accident, mostly elsewhere than with him" (p. 99). The "compartmentalization" was also a way of dealing with his male friends.

ally, and with conspicuous courage, in the Spanish Civil War. He is described as characteristically aloof and unruffled in crises, even under fire (perhaps especially so).

When Orwell was about thirty he published his first book, under his pseudonym, and began to forge a new public identity: Eric Blair became George Orwell, the author bent on evolving a simple and honest prose, the fighter for truth and justice, or, more important, against lies and oppression. (We can speculate that his complex personality contained Big Brother and O'Brien as well as Winston Smith.) Chekhov wrote of having had to "squeeze the serf out of [himself], drop by drop" (see chapter 11), and George Orwell must have made a similar effort; both men come through in their writing as truly moral and virtuous.[7]

Orwell's essay "Why I Write" (1946) documents his obsessional character defenses and their creative transformation:

> From a very early age, perhaps the age of five or six, I knew that when I grew up I should be a writer . . . I was the middle child of three, but there was a gap of five years on either side, and I barely saw my father before I was eight. For this and other reasons I was somewhat lonely, and I soon developed disagreeable mannerisms which made me unpopular throughout my schooldays. I had the lonely child's habit of making up stories and holding conversations with imaginary persons, and I think from the very start my literary ambitions were mixed up with the feeling of being isolated and undervalued. I knew that I had a facility with words and a power of facing unpleasant facts, and I felt that this created a sort of private world in which I could get my own back for my failure in everyday life. [Together with early writings, I started] carrying out a literary exercise of a quite different kind: this was the making up of a continuous "story" about myself, a sort of diary existing only in the mind. I believe this is a common habit of children and adolescents

---

7. Like Chekhov, similarly elusive and emotionally aloof (though more gregarious), Orwell was liked and even loved by his friends. And Orwell did his effective best to be a good and devoted father to his adopted son (see Fyvel 1981). Both men were enigmatic personalities. Trilling (1955a) wrote of Orwell's work: "What matters most of all is our sense of the man who tells the truth" (p. 226); this is equally applicable to Chekhov, whose greater gifts made it possible for him to present life and people more richly than Orwell. (Both authors are in such contrast to D., who made lying into a way of living.)

. . . my "story" [became] a . . . description of what I was doing and the things I saw. For minutes at a time this kind of thing would be running through my head: "He pushed the door open and entered the room. A yellow beam of sunlight, filtering through the muslin curtains, slanted on to the table, where a matchbox, half open, lay beside the inkpot. With his right hand in his pocket he moved across to the window . . . etc., etc. This habit continued till I was about twenty-five, right through my non-literary years. (1946, pp. 309–311)

Even if the adult was exaggerating in retrospect, one feels that the essential truth is told here. A split of this magnitude between the observing ego and the experiencing ego (a *vertical* split) is not "a common habit of children and adolescents"; nor is it ordinary to be able to turn it to adaptive, creative use. (Note that when Orwell started to write for publication, the "split" receded.) The strength and pervasiveness of his isolative defenses do resemble what is found in those who have to ward off the overstimulation and rage that are the results of child abuse (as with D., who used means different from those of Orwell to attain his emotional detachment). It must have helped Orwell in his life that he was able to deal with the rat imago in his fiction. His artistic success, which came late in his career, helped too, but a need for failure persisted to the end.[8]

8. Orwell and Chekhov both died in their mid-forties of tuberculosis that had been denied and deliberately neglected—unconsciously cultivated. As a young man—during the years after he lived as a destitute tramp to write *Down and Out in Paris and London* (1933), Orwell refused to wear a topcoat, even in winter. This was in the face of his history of lung illnesses, and despite warnings and pleas from his friends that he take better care of himself. "The result was predictable. In the middle of [one] December, while out on his motor bike, he was caught in an icy rainstorm, got thoroughly drenched, and came down with a terrible chill . . . [he was] blue with cold . . . the chill developed into pneumonia; with his weak chest his condition worsened perceptibly; and . . . he was transferred to the Uxbridge Cottage Hospital, just up from the school [where he was teaching]. He was terribly ill; in fact it was thought almost certain that he would die . . . but by the time [his mother and sister] arrived in Uxbridge, the crisis had passed and the chances of his recovery had notably improved" (Stansky and Abrahams 1980, 46–47).

1984

1984 is about a world full of bad smells and sadism and infested with rats. O'Brien says to Winston Smith: "The thing that is in Room 101 is the worst thing in the world. In your case . . . the worst thing in the world happens to be rats . . . Do you remember . . . the moment of panic that used to occur in your dreams? . . . There was something terrible on the other side of [a] wall . . . It was the rats that were on the other side of the wall" (pp. 286–287). O'Brien then shows Smith a cage containing starving rats, fixed to a mask about to be lowered onto Smith's face. " 'The rat,' said O'Brien, still addressing his invisible audience, 'although a rodent, is carnivorous' " (p. 289).

Earlier in the book, before the lovers Winston and Julia are arrested (to make love without permission is to act against the State), Winston expresses the inevitability of their being forced to confess under torture: " 'I don't mean confessing. Confession is not betrayal. What you say or do doesn't matter; *only feelings matter.* If they could make me stop loving you—that would be the real betrayal.' She thought it over. 'They can't do that . . . They can't get inside you' " (p. 167; my italics).

But getting inside body and soul is just what the soul-murdering parent can do. And it is exactly the ability to feel that is so vulnerable to ruin and mutilation, especially the ability to feel love. It follows that when being threatened by the ravenous rats, Winston feels he can evade them only by betraying the only person (beside the lost mother of his childhood) he has ever loved:

> The cage was nearer; it was closing in . . . Suddenly the foul musty odor of the brutes struck his nostrils. There was a violent convulsion of nausea inside him, and he almost lost consciousness . . . For an instant he was insane, a screaming animal. Yet he came out of the blackness clutching an idea. There was one and only one way to save himself. He must interpose another human being, the *body* of another human being, between himself and the rats . . . Winston could see the whiskers and the yellow tail. Again the black panic took hold of him . . . 'It was a common punishment in Imperial China.' said O'Brien . . . And he was shouting frantically over and over: 'Do it to Julia! Do it to Julia! Not me! Julia! Not me! I don't care what you do to her. Tear her face off, strip her to the bones. Not me! Julia! Not me!' (pp. 288–289; Orwell's italics)

The feelings are of cannibalistic intensity. Winston Smith has *become* the cannibalistic rat. Child abuse makes for child abusers. Soul murder makes for soul murderers.

But this reality must be denied to preserve inner pictures of a loving parent and a loving self—the loving breast and the beloved child. D., who after some analysis came to characterize himself as a "closet Nazi," whose fiancée's tears left him dry-eyed but full of hate-filled sexual excitement, would weep copiously at sentimental movies and plays, especially when parenthood was being celebrated. And here is the final emotional state of Winston Smith: "He gazed up at the enormous face. Forty years it had taken him to learn what kind of smile was hidden behind the dark mustache. O cruel, needless misunderstanding! O stubborn, self-willed exile from *the loving breast*! Two gin-scented tears trickled down the side of his nose. But it was alright, the struggle was finished. He had won the victory over himself. He loved Big Brother" (1949, p. 300; my italics).

CHAPTER

6

Rat People

The compulsion to repeat dominates the lives of people who have been seduced or beaten by psychotic and psychopathic parents. I have stressed the importance for these people of fixation on the cannibalistic level of libido development and regression to it, with concomitant maldevelopment and regression of the ego and superego. Overstimulation continues to be a central problem in the lives of these people, and therefore also in their analytic transferences.

The clinical conditions I have been describing as the effects of soul murder sometimes appear in combination with a preoccupation with rats. In chapter 5 I characterize patient D. as a rat person. Obviously not all soul murder victims are rat people, and whether all people who are preoccupied with toothed creatures and rodents have suffered actual overstimulating experiences as children must also be subject to doubt. But such a preoccupation, evidenced by the frequent appearance of rats in analytic associations, should alert the observer to the possibility of soul murder. All the rat people I describe in this book were victims of soul murder, and my generalizations about them are applicable to other victims.

I view the image of the rat as a kind of hallmark indicating cannibalistic impulses and the presence of too-muchness (having had to bear the unbearable), and I will try to illustrate this in the clinical material of this chapter and in works of literature other than Orwell's *1984*. The rat is one of the principal symbolic mental images (imagos) of cannibalism —probably by virtue of the impact on the human mind of the rat's propensity for murdering and devouring members of its own species, of its omnivorous destructiveness, and perhaps above all of its remarkable teeth. On reviewing Freud's case of the Rat Man (1909), one sees that the rat can stand for subject or object of any stage of libidinal development but is particularly associated with eating and being eaten and with anal erogeneity.

Rats, Cannibalism, and Overstimulation

A literary quotation that connects rats, oral sadism, and overstimulation comes from the novel *Torture Garden* (1899) by Octave Mirbeau, which I believe to be the source of the story that obsessed Freud's famous patient known in psychoanalytic circles as the Rat Man (Freud 1909). This story, the Rat Man told Freud, was related to him by the sadistic Captain N., who " 'had *read* of a specially horrible punishment used in the East . . . the criminal was tied up . . . a pot was turned upside down on his buttocks . . . some *rats* were put into it . . . and they . . .'—he got up again and was showing every sign of horror and resistance—'*bored their way in* . . .'—'into his anus,' I [Freud] helped him out"(Freud 1909,166; the Rat Man is speaking and the hesitations are his; italics in original).[1]

The difficulty of saying "into his anus" is demonstrated by its not being specifically stated in Mirbeau's story either. I think this evasion marks the special resistance evoked by the cannibalistic vulnerability of the anal zone and especially the anal sphincter. The psychological importance of the anal sphincter has to do with its resonance in the body ego's and subsequently the psychic ego's control of intense, early (primal), drive-derived affects and body-feelings (see Shengold 1985). In my clinical experience, the anal and perianal area of erogeneity seems to be the principal intrapsychic site for the overwhelming stimulation (experienced as being eaten into and eaten up) that can lead to ego dissolution.

Torture Garden was published in Paris in 1899, seven years before the Rat Man's encounter with Captain N. During those years the book was widely read in Europe and acquired notoriety for being pornographic; it is, however, the work of a serious artist (see Wilson 1950).

1. Freud's "help" is cited by Kanzer (1952) as evidence of his countertransference. He verbally performs a penetration.

The book's climactic episode is about a rat torture; the Garden is in China ("the East"), the torturer is Chinese, and the heroine, Clara, obsessed by torture, asks him:

"What is this torture of the rat? . . . Can you describe it to us?" [The torturer answers:] "You take a condemned man, charming lady, a condemned man, or anybody else . . . you take a man, as young and strong as possible, whose muscles are quite resistant; in virtue of this principle: the more strength, the more struggle—and the more struggle, the more pain! Good! You undress him. Good! And when he is stark naked . . . Yes, milady? You make him kneel, his back bent, on the earth, where you fasten him with chains . . . Good! I don't know if I'm making myself understood? Then in a big pot, whose bottom is pierced with a little hole . . . a flowerpot, milady . . . you place a very fat rat whom it's wise to have deprived of nourishment for a couple of days,[2] to excite its ferocity. And this pot, inhabited by this rat, you apply hermetically, like an enormous cupping-glass, to the back of the condemned by means of stout thongs attached to a leather girdle about the loins. Ah ha! Now the plot thickens!" He looked maliciously at [her] out of the corners of his lowered lids, to judge the effect his words were producing. "And then?" said Clara, simply. "Then, milady, you introduce into the little hole into the pot . . . guess what!" "How should I know?" The good fellow rubbed his hands, smiled horribly, and then continued: "You introduce an iron rod, heated red hot at the fire of a forge . . . and when the iron rod is introduced, what happens? Ah, ha ha! Imagine what must happen, milady . . ." "Oh, come on, you

2. In the version that the Rat Man told to Freud one rat becomes "some rats." We do not know if this is his distortion or Captain N.'s. (According to Freud's notes [p. 291], the Rat Man at one point remembered Captain N.'s mentioning two rats.) What does this multiplication signify? There are many possible meanings, in two categories: defensive (for example, obfuscation) and revelatory (for example, *some* could connote *two* [female symbol] or *three* [male symbol]; the two categories can also coexist). According to one defensive meaning, the one rat is the biting phallus from which one must keep away. The Rat Man speaks of both "the rat punishment" and "the punishment of the rats" but when the rat becomes singular it is clearly phallic: "When he was wishing Constanze the rats he felt a rat gnawing at his own anus and had a visual image of it" (Freud 1909, 308).

old gossip!" . . . "A little patience, milady . . . Well, you introduce into the pot's hole, an iron rod, heated red-hot at the fire of a forge. The rat tries to escape the burning of the rod and its dazzling light. It goes mad, cuts capers, leaps and bounds, runs around the walls of the pot, crawls and gallops over the man's flesh, which it first tickles and then tears with its nails and bites with its sharp teeth, seeking an exit through the torn and bleeding skin. But there is no exit. During the first frenzied moments, the rat can find none. And the iron rod, handled cleverly and slowly, still draws near the rat, threatens it, scorches its fur. What do you think of this for a beginning?" (pp. 191–193)

At the beginning of the torturer's narrative there are many hesitations, similar to those in the Rat Man's concise retelling. For the Rat Man whose predominant involvement is with the passive victim, these interstices are simultaneously attempts at isolation and a supplying of holes to be penetrated. (Freud responded to this when he interjected the words "into his anus".) For the torturer, who boasts that he invented the torture of the rat, the making of interrupting "holes" is predominantly in the service of tormenting the impatient Clara. Once arrived at the nearly climactic penetration of the "pot's hole" by the phallic, red-hot iron rod, the torturer's narration becomes an unimpeded gush. This is peristaltic language, the halts and rushes in the service of overexcited passion. The torturer's description continues:

"Its great merit lies in the fact that you must know how to prolong this initial operation as much as possible, for the laws of physiology teach us that there is nothing more horrible to the human flesh than the combination of tickling and biting. It may even happen that the victim goes mad from it. He howls and struggles; his body . . . heaves and contorts, shaken by agonizing shudders. But his limbs are firmly held by the chains, and the pot, by the thongs. And the movements of the condemned man only augment the rat's fury, to which the intoxication of blood is often added. It's sublime, milady!" "And then?" said Clara . . . "Finally . . . for I see you're anxious to know the climax of this wonderful and jolly story; finally . . . threatened by the glowing rod and thanks to the excitation of a few well-chosen burns, the rat ends by finding an exit, milady. Ah ha ha! "How horrible!" exclaimed Clara. "Ah, you see . . . I'm proud of the interest you take in my torture. But wait! [With Clara's increasing impatience, the Torturer has resumed his hesitations.] The rat penetrates the man's body, widening with claws and teeth the opening he madly digs, as in the earth. And he croaks, stifled, at the same time that the victim who, after a half-hour of ineffable, incomparable torture, ends by succumbing to a hemorrhage . . . when it isn't from too much suffering . . . or even the congestion caused by a frightful insanity. In all cases, milady, and whatever the final cause of this death . . . you can be sure it's extremely beautiful!" (pp. 193–194)

The anal erotism and oral and anal sadomasochism that are associated with the obsessions of the Rat Man are set forth here, as are the connotations of overstimulation and cannibalism.[3] First the rat is overstimulated with the red-hot iron rod (the danger throughout is that of a penetrative, mainly anal invasion by a phallus equipped with flesh-destroying, flesh-eating power). The rat "goes mad" and tears and bites at the man's flesh, finally making a cannibalistic anal penetration after unbearably overstimulating the victim with the "prolonged" and "horrible . . . combination of tickling and biting". Both rat and victim are trapped and helpless in the face of increasing torment. Both are overstimulated and die. The basic story of the victim's being eaten and anally penetrated by the rat is also present in displacement in relation to the glowing rod and the rat (here as victim); symbolically, it is presented through the heated iron rod and the flowerpot with the hole in its bottom; in attenuation the theme is repeated by way of the torturer's teasing method of telling his story to the enthralled, overexcited, impatient Clara.[4]

The Rat as Carrier of the Tooth

The words *rat* and *rodent* are derived from the Latin *rodere:* to gnaw, consume. Related roots are *radere* (Latin), to scratch, and *radona* (Sanskrit), tooth.

3. The Rat Man told Freud of having a dream in 1906 involving Oriental torture —before the meeting with Captain N.
4. Robert Fliess (1956) calls impatience "the cannibalistic affect" (p. 107). Mirbeau describes in an earlier part of *Torture Garden* Clara's fascinated curiosity about details of literal cannibalism (pp. 92–100).

The rat imago appears as a leading motif in the study of oral sadistic and masochistic phenomena (tooth phenomena).[5] The rat is a tooth carrier, endowed with the power to creep back and forth from level to level of libidinal development, from one erogenous zone to another, biting and being bitten. It is among the most common of many imagos that are first of all cannibalistic: carriers of the destructive tooth. These include the wolf, snake, and spider, which are found in nature, and the monstrous sphinx, vampire, and werewolf. These are biting, sucking, tearing, devouring creatures.[6]

The rat is a very ancient animal. Remains of rats and men have been found together in fossils of the Pliocene and Pleistocene periods (Zinsser 1934). There are no references to rats as such in classical or biblical literature; for Greeks and Hebrews, the term for *mouse* was used to indicate both kinds of animal.[7] Herodotus mentions field mice, and according to Zinsser (1934): "in ancient Palestine, the Jews considered all seven mouse varieties . . . unclean, and as unsuited for human nourishment as were pigs" (p. 191). The special designation for the rat was adopted in European languages only after the great invasions from Asia by the black rat in the twelfth and thirteenth centuries. The black rat probably exterminated the prevailing indigenous rats and brought with it the devastating medieval plagues.[8] The brown rat, *mus norvegi-*

5. Lewin (1950) refers to the regression seen in pharmacothymic stupors: "The wish to be eaten sometimes makes its appearance starkly in the delirious hallucination of menacing animals, large and small" (p 123). Rats are especially common in the hallucinations of delirium tremens.

6. "We get to look upon the child's fear of being devoured, or cut up, or torn to pieces . . . as a regular component of its mental life. And we know that the man-eating wolf . . . and all the evil monsters out of myths and fairy stories flourish and exert their unconscious influence in the phantasy of each individual child" (Klein 1933, 268).

7. Some patients make no differentiation between mice and rats; more frequently, the mouse has more benevolent (or less destructive) connotations. For example, it is used as a symbol of pubic hair and in some languages as a term of affection. Often the mouse is the rat-as-victim for example in the Witch's song in act 3 of Humperdinck's *Hansel und Gretel*: "Kommt kleine Mäuslein, kommt in mein Häuslein" (Come little mousie, come into my housie); see also the clinical example below.

8. Encyclopedia Britannica, 14th ed., s.v. "rat."

cus, swept over Europe in the early eighteenth century and in its turn killed off the black rat in most parts of the world.

The resemblance between men and rats has often been pointed out, usually in connection with their adaptability, their success as species in proliferating and occupying territory, and their similar intraspecific destructive competitiveness. Lorenz (1963) notes "the collective aggression of one community [of rats] against another" (p. 134) as a model of what now threatens mankind. Both creatures demonstrate murderous aggressiveness within the species: "The gradual, relentless progressive extermination of the black rat by the brown has no parallel in nature so close as that of the similar extermination of one race of man by another" (Zinsser 1934). "There are other similarities: the difficulties of combatting the most successful biological opponent to man, the brown rat, lies chiefly in the fact that the rat operates basically with the same methods as those of man, by transmission of experience and its dissemination within the close community" (Lorenz 1963, 137).

The rat is usually described in literature as evil and is detested; it persecutes and is persecuted. "Rats are, indeed," wrote the mild-mannered Charles Lamb (1799), "the most despised and contemptible parts of God's earth. I killed a rat the other day by punching him to pieces and I feel a weight of blood on me to this hour" (p. 41). The series of quotations that follows illustrates the rat's connection with overstimulation and cannibalism.

The rat is destructive, voracious, omnivorous:

> By the fourteenth century [the rat] was well enough established in Northern Europe that rat-transmitted *Pasteurella pestis,* the organism causing bubonic plague, managed to kill some 25 million people, more than a quarter of the European population, during the Black Death (McLaughlin 1978, 124). Rat-borne diseases have resulted in the deaths of more people during the last 5000 years than the combined casualties of the wars taking place over those years (Barker 1951, 114). Most rats kill birds or animals for their flesh and blood; others simply have a lust for killing (Mills 1959). Their diet is omnivorous; they eat anything, including human flesh . . . when driven by hunger they are so ravenous that neglected babies have been killed and eaten by them . . . [There are] a few cases of able-bodied men who have suffered a like fate when attacked by hordes of rats (*Encyclopaedia Americana* 1957, vol. 23).

It eats anything that lets it, and—like man—devours its own kind, under stress. (Zinsser 1935, p. 195)

The rat is fecund so that if left unchecked it can overwhelm other species:

The terrible rate at which the rat increases explains the slow process of extermination, despite the vast sums expended. It has been calculated that two rats, if left unchecked, would in the course of three to four years multiply into 20 millions. (Protheroe 1940) They are able to breed at three to four months and can produce up to seven litters a year, each containing 6 to 22 young. (*Encyclopaedia Britannica* 1985, vol. 9, p. 950) By 1910, Norway rats outnumbered humans.

The rat is especially ferocious and destructive toward its own kind:

They change into horrible brutes as soon as they encounter members of any other society of their own species . . . what rats do when a member of a strange rat-clan enters their territory . . . is one of the most horrible and repulsive things which can be observed in animals . . . with their eyes bulging from their sockets, their hair standing on end, the rats set out on the rat hunt. They are so angry that if two of them meet they bite each other . . . [The strange rat] is slowly torn to pieces by its fellows. Only rarely does one see an animal in such desperation and panic, so conscious of the inevitability of a terrible death, as a rat which is about to be slain by rats. It ceases to defend itself. (Lorenz 1963, p. 139)

(This description of the "rat hunt" notes both the sadistic fury and the terrified masochistic submission that can be evoked by the rat.)

The rat, like all rodents, has amazing teeth:

[They] have a set of fierce looking gnawing teeth . . . [these] incisors sharpen themselves to chisel-like points as they are used. The owner gradually grinds down these teeth with incessant gnawing, but they never wear out. A rodent's incisors continue to grow as the fingernails of people do. (Hegner 1942) The rat's incisors grow at the rate of five inches a year. (Mills 1959)

The rat must not lose an incisor or his teeth can cause his death:

Should a member of this group have the misfortune to break a chisel tooth, he is often doomed to death. The broken tooth fails to meet the tooth opposite; both teeth grow unhindered. Since they are no longer ground off against each other, they grow wildly, sometimes circling the victim's face, locking his jaws, and causing starvation. (Hegner 1942)

The rat is continuously teething:

The incisors grow, calcify and erupt continuously throughout the life of the animal. (Shour and Masser 1949)

The rat is a fit object on which to project cannibalism. It is particularly linked with anal erogeneity because of its association with dirt and disease. Man has had to deal continually with the rat because of its omnipresence, destructiveness, and great fecundity; the last has made the rat's extermination necessary but ineffectual. The problem of the continual increase in the number of rats, emphasized by the historical invasions of rats on a grand scale (with accompanying cataclysmic, deadly plagues), makes the rat particularly suited to represent, by allusion, overstimulation (too-muchness). And cannibalism is invoked. The linkage of rats, teeth, and biting is evidenced by folklore from all parts of the world (see below). As for the rat's remarkable teeth, one may say, paraphrasing Freud, that they must use them to bite others or they will literally bite themselves.

Meanings of the Rat to the Rat Man

The Rat Man came to Freud complaining about an obsession and compulsive actions that had begun when he was on military maneuvers, after the sadistic Captain N. told him about the rat punishment. On the same occasion the Captain had said something about paying back money that was owed to a third person. The violent symptomatic reaction that followed was analyzed by Freud: "In the short interval between the captain's story and the request . . . to pay back the money, rats had acquired a series of symbolic meanings, to which, during the period that followed, fresh ones were continually being added" (p. 213). Rats, Freud said, are associated with anal eroticism. They are connected with dirt (feces, money), infection (venereal disease), and cruelty and sadism. Rats mean teeth and biting and cannibalism (the Rat Man felt that a rat was feeding off his father's corpse). There is a condensation of meanings from the oral sadistic and anal sadistic developmental phases. Most rat phenomena of the Rat Man (and of other rat people too) can be schematically conceived of in terms used by Fliess (1956): the erogeneity involved (where the bodily excitement is) is anal, but the libido is oral sadistic (the energy of the instinctual drives is seen as derived from the latter half of the oral developmental period and possessing certain qualities of it). The instinctual aim is destructive and ultimately cannibalistic; if turned against the self, the aim is to be destroyed and eaten, and anal erogeneity implies that the anal region is the site for destruction.

The rat was equated by the Rat Man with the penis, especially in relation to anal (anal sadistic) intercourse. Here phallic power is equated with cannibalistic penetration: the penis has teeth and can bite (for example, the rat was linked by the Rat Man with syphilis, which eats into the body). Not only is the rat as a phallic symbol destructive (as are such symbols as the knife, spear, club, and gun) in contrast to more benign phallic symbols such as the stick, necktie, umbrella, and balloon, but it is also specifically cannibalistic.

Like the penis (the little one) rats can represent children, but these are dirty, biting, raging children. As vermin, rats can symbolize unwanted siblings or unwanted children who evoke rage.[9]

The law of talion applies to rats—if they bite, they can be bitten: "But rats cannot be sharp-toothed, greedy and dirty with impunity; they are cruelly persecuted and mercilessly put to death by men" (Freud 1909, p. 216). If the rat equals the penis, destructivity toward the rat involves castration. If the rat equals the child, destructivity toward the rat involves child murder.

I want to underline the ubiquitous oral sadism and masochism in all these meanings that Freud and his patient attach to rats: rats bite into the anus; the rat-penis has teeth; rat-children bite and are bitten. The

9. As in *The Pied Piper of Hamelin* or in Ibsen's play *Little Eyolf.* Eyolf is an unwanted child, like Oedipus crippled by his parents' selfishness. He is covertly resented by both parents, regarded as a guilt-producing sibling rather than as their child. He bites at his parents' consciences like a rat, and is finally lured to his death by the Rat Wife, a mysterious old lady, the embodiment of death wishes toward unwanted creatures, who had introduced herself prophetically by asking, "I humbly beg pardon—but are your worships troubled with any gnawing things in your house . . . for it would be such a pleasure to me to rid your worships' house of them?" (1894, p. 19). Many of the ambiguous meanings of the rat for the Rat Man can also be found in Ibsen's play.

basic fantasy of castration is the biting off of the penis; intercourse is a biting into the cloaca.

The rat can represent subject or object, part-subject or part-object; that is, it can refer to oneself or to another, or to part of oneself or part of another. The Rat Man, "a nasty little wretch who was apt to bite people when he was in a rage" (p. 216), was also subject to the rat: he remembered being "fearfully punished" (p. 216) by his father at the age of three or four "because he had bitten someone" (p. 206), and this he had taken as a castration threat. The father, here playing the role of rat as persecutor, is in the fantasy of the adult Rat Man eventually eaten by a rat, in his grave. Father, mother,[10] and analyst can all be rats who bite and are bitten.

Implicit in Freud's clinical material and explicit in the rat torture is the association of overstimulation and rage with rats.

Clinical Material: Patients' Experiences of Overstimulation

The rat people discussed in this section suffered experiences of over-stimulation when they were children that made them victims of soul murder. The traumata endured included sexual seduction by an adult (frequently a parent), often involving penetration or defloration; re-peated, extensive exposure to adult exhibitionism, especially to the primal scene; and being beaten often and severely. These events had occurred at the beginning of the phallic phase of development or dur-ing it (ages three to six). In these patients, one has the sense of dealing with recurrent themes in their analytic and therapeutic associations irrespective of their diagnoses. These themes are sounded repeatedly by patient after patient.

Much of the patients' material (fantasies, dreams, phobias) involves a cannibalistic animal, frequently the rat. Unlike the Rat Man, most of these patients do not talk of mice and rats constantly. Rats appear in the material as derivative expressions of activated cannibalistic im-pulses, usually in relation to anal erogeneity. some patients grind and gnash their teeth like rodents (often during sleep). The rat imago is both subject and object, with the ambiguity and multiplicity of mean-

10. "The real objects behind those imaginary terrifying figures (evoking can-nibalism) are the child's own parents, and those dreadful shapes . . . reflect the features of its father and mother" (Klein 1933, 268).

ing that can be seen in the case of the Rat Man; this involves both an identification with the rat as torturer and a relationship to the rat as victim.

Because of the compulsion to repeat, traumata in childhood lead to reenactments—usually with people not originally involved (see Greenacre 1960). As with other victims of soul murder, one finds that most frequently a really traumatic experience is avoided by identification with the aggressor, as the once passive and masochistic child now appears in the role of active sadist: rat-victim becomes rat-torturer. The terrifying wish for the passive role is great, and passivity is allowed under carefully controlled conditions, or in circumstances making for attenuation. The frightening passive wishes, usually involving anal erogeneity, come out strongly in the fairly safe repetition circumstances of the analysis, with the analyst appearing as the rat-torturer who is to be made into the rat-victim. The adult maintains the chronic state of overstimulation, partly by repeating the original traumata in conjunction with others, partly by continuing relations with the original, overstimulating soul murderer and, most important, by identifying with the soul murderer.

The effects of the traumata, defenses, symptoms, and fantasies, and the means the child took to try to deal with them, are also subject to the unconscious compulsion to repeat. For example, it would seem that a child subjected to repeated seduction by an adult cannot discharge the resulting state of chronic overstimulation, because most children are incapable of orgasm (Kramer 1954). The child may faint (I have seen one patient, unfortunately insufficiently studied, who continued to do this into adult life), or attempt to obtain discharge by urinating or defecating. According to Fliess (1956), urination is a regular method for releasing cannibalistic impulses. (I have found this true for defecation, too.) Ferenczi (1915) describes how urination can calm the distressed and frightened (that is, overstimulated) child, and says this may be because "it provides for the child a *sudden* relief" (p. 317; my italics).[11] Like all who have been overstimulated, like the victims of soul murder, these rat people are particularly afraid that nothing is going to happen

11. Often attacks on the child begin with a sudden change in the adult assaulter and end with equal suddenness. The child frequently fears and expects abrupt shifts in mood followed by a sudden onslaught. One musical patient broke into a cold sweat when hearing the words "And suddenly" in the *Messiah* of Handel or in Bach's *Christmas Oratorio*.

—that they will be left in a state of terrible overexcitation. This makes the analytic requirement for frustration of action and gratification more difficult for them. For example, once a transference neurosis has been established the analyst's vacation, which arouses feelings of being left, is often experienced as almost intolerable. Also, in life and in analytic transference, the unbearable feelings of overstimulation frequently lead to rage of a cannibalistic intensity.

Even after past traumata are brought out of repression by hard analytic work, the patient attempts to treat them as never having happened (see chapter 2), and this denial is especially needed if the seduction or beating was at the hands of a parent. The great need not to know what has happened is often supplemented by a direct order from the seducer (the psychic murderer) not to tell about it. The not knowing is accomplished by massive isolation, transient ego splits ("She is naughty, I am good," said one nonpsychotic patient about herself),[12] and chronic autohypnotic states. Frequently a combination of these is present, with a resultant (partial) impairment of intellectual functioning that remains in part instinctualized (Keiser 1962). The brainwashing that creates denial implies a compromised identity.

The stories of rat people again show that when the seducer or torturer is a parent, the child victim usually can seek rescue and the fulfillment of basic needs only from the person who has brought about the child's distress. This is poignantly presented in Orwell's *1984* when Winston Smith, tortured by rats, ends up loving Big Brother. In patients one finds a similar delusional insistence on the goodness of the destructive parent who is "loved." This is not only to deny the terrible experiences: the tormented, overstimulated child desperately needs a loving parent ("Who else would have buttered my bread?" was one patient's explanation of why she could never inform on her seducing mother). Most urgent is that loss of the parent leaves the child in danger of being pushed beyond the stimulus barrier toward ego dissolution; the loss of the parent is felt as unbearable.

12. These vertical ego splits are often denoted by the patient's switching from the first to the second or third person; this also involves defensive generalization. An example: "I felt very excited about the size of his penis. I said to myself, 'You are not interested in that. Only homosexuals are interested in penis size. They get excited by other men's penises. One sometimes has thoughts like that, but they go away.'" In the course of his last four sentences, the patient's "I" also went away.

Parents, especially if they have assaulted their children during acute psychotic episodes, are experienced as lost during the abusive attacks; they are transformed by their loss of emotional control. The patients often describe what happened in terms of a feral alteration ("Suddenly [again!] mother would become a wild beast"), usually into a cannibalistic creature (especially rat, wolf, or tiger; sphinx, witch, werewolf, or vampire). Many myths and stories about these creatures involve transformations. The good parent becomes a destructive, alien presence who does not recognize the child's identity or kinship; the child is treated as a need-fulfilling part-object, an extension of the parent's own body that can be discarded after use. The child denies loss of the good parent who must be there to make everything all right, and insists on the parent's goodness. A loving parent is desperately needed and must be fabricated by delusion. Like poor Winston Smith, the children can turn only to their tormentor for rescue: "[Winston Smith] opened his eyes and looked up gratefully at O'Brien . . . He had never loved [O'Brien] so deeply as at this moment, and not merely because he had stopped the pain . . . O'Brien had tortured him to the edge of lunacy, and in a little while, it was certain, he would send him to his death. It made no difference. In some sense that went deeper than friendship, they were intimates" (Orwell 1948, 256).

The intimate relation of O'Brien to his victim is illuminated by a remark of Freud to Fliess about the confessions of those supposedly possessed by the devil that were extracted under torture during the Inquisition. He traced back to their seduction as children by adults, by parents; the torture and torment, the leading questions and compliant answers of inquisitor and accused: "Thus victim and torturer alike recall their earliest youth" (Freud 1887–1902, 188).

The presence of another, healthier parent, so important as a source of identification for the healthier aspects of the patient, does not help the child if (as is often the case) that parent either does not know or must deny what is going on with the soul-murdering spouse. The brainwashing that is produced by the child's denial of the overstimulating experiences easily develops into characterological lying (often most pronounced on an unconscious level, and involving lying to oneself). Lying makes easier the experiences that are repetitive of the traumata. Paradoxically, the insistent need for a protective parent becomes part of the motivation for repeating the traumatic events, in the delusional insistence that "this next time it won't be allowed to happen."

Soul murder means damage to the child's conscience (see chapter 4): a severity evidenced by a strong, unconscious need for punishment coexists or alternates with an overpermissiveness that allows for psychopathological behavior in identification with the parent, who is frequently psychotic and usually (at least intermittently) psychopathic. If the seducer-torturer is not a parent, the effect is similar but diluted (see chapter 12 on Kipling, below).[13]

As in Freud's cases of the Rat Man and Wolf Man, one finds in the associations of these patients the regressive expression of oedipal conflicts in oral sadistic terms. In addition to this, I emphasize the actual state of overstimulation and its characteristic rage—the experience of feeling passive and having active cannibalistic strivings.[14]

Clinical Material

PATIENT E.

Over a few previous sessions E., a young male homosexual whose symptoms included a phobia of mice and rats, had fully remembered having been pressed against the genitals of his psychotic mother when he was a child, apparently while she had an orgasm. This had begun with the mother exposing herself to the five-year-old boy, using her hands to open her vagina fully, so that the shock of castration was especially great. E. began the next session as follows:

> I don't want to ferret around in the past today like yesterday. Ferret is a kind of rat, I think. You know I hate rats; once one fell into a

13. See Klein (1948) on the effects on the superegos of children seduced by adults, and Simmel (1944) on the "multiple superegos" created in children seduced by parents, as seen in alcoholics.

14. "The idea of being devoured by the father is typical age-old childhood material. It has familiar parallels in mythology (e.g. the myth of Kronos) and in the animal kingdom. Analytic observation shows that the idea of being devoured by the father gives expression, in a form that has undergone regressive degradation, to a passive, tender impulse to be loved by him in a genital erotic sense. Is it, moreover, a question merely of the replacement of the psychical representative by a regressive form of expression or is it a question of a genuine regressive degradation of the genitally-directed impulse in the id?" (Freud 1926, 105). Freud felt that the latter description applies to the Wolf Man. I think it is also true of my patients whose fantasy life means regressing to the cannibalistic *experience* of overstimulation and fixating on it.

wastebasket, and I had to call someone else to throw it out—as if I were a woman. Rats bite; I think of their teeth, as if one would bite into the base of my penis. Fur—one touch, and I can't stand it. They burrow. I think of the strawberry color of my mother's genitals; I think of rubbing against it, like against a rat's muzzle . . . I can't stand it [the patient seems most anxious and writhes on the couch]—her spread white thighs—punish me! Fuck me to death!

This is said as the patient is working through the experience he has brought out of repression. The state of overstimulation is characteristic, although the terrible intensity has been brought out by the memory. E. would go to an older homosexual who would slowly and discreetly stimulate E.'s genitals "for hours", teasing and tormenting him and keeping him from orgasm, which he would finally achieve, as he could not in childhood.

The cannibalistic animal is present. The rat stands for the maternal *vagina dentata* connected with the experience the patient has just remembered, and for the mother's penetrating finger that gave anal stimulation during other sexual assaults in childhood. The mother has and is the rat, and by way of primal scene observations is also subject to the rat, which stands for the invading father and his penis. E. himself, despite his passive longings, usually played the role of the sadistic rat. He was characteristically sarcastic and coldly masterful toward the men he picked up and with whom he played the active role sexually. He was always seeking but never allowing himself to find a sadistic older man to "fuck him to death" anally. This meant simultaneously repeating the childhood experience with his mother and obtaining a castrative punishment by his father. He was most afraid of this destructive wish involving both parents, sensing (probably rightly) that it would bring on intimations of ego dissolution, and so had always avoided the compelling but terrifying experience.

E. was very intelligent, yet his intellectual functioning and identity were impaired by his inability to hold to a conviction for any length of time. Everything had to be made hypothetical in the service of denying and not knowing about the incestuous contact with his "good" mother. This effect of soul murder was revealed in the analysis in the great difficulty and shame with which the patient told me of his oral-anal sexual activities. These intimacies, routine in his homosexual contacts (this was before the era of AIDS), evoked the greatest transference resistance as he began to fantasize about me. This was because of an even deeper repression resistance: the mother was the original object, and the past must not be remembered. He told me at this time of how without knowing why he did it he was wont to whisper into the ear of his dog, who came into his bed to lick his face in the morning, "We have a secret." He consciously identified with the dog, which seemed to him to represent predominantly an orally and anally excited child. At the same time he was literally repeating his mother's words from the past sexual scenes. Before his analysis he used to masturbate in the presence of the dog, not allowing himself to acknowledge fully that he wanted and was excited by the dog's looking on. He was thus repeating the past, but he could not know the past, consummate the knowledge of it. This confusion and contradiction spilled over into his working life, where he found it necessary to borrow the convictions of others; this was done "secretly"—that is, without any acknowledgment to his "leader," whom often he would later let down and betray.

One aspect of E.'s intellectual malfunctioning was that he had trouble reading "good" books, although he could easily read mystery stories, popular novels, and especially magazines and newspapers; I have found this to be characteristic of reading difficulties in such patients. "Good" books seem particularly charged (as symbols) with incestuous meaning. E. as an adolescent frequently had erections when reading in public libraries—he associated the open book with his mother's spread thighs. He said, "I have difficulty only when I really respect what I'm reading and want to know and remember what I have read." He would usually read the beginning and then the end of a worthwhile book, but not the middle, revealing the castration anxiety he felt when dealing with his mother in this symbolic and allusive form that repeated past experiences. Another patient (also a rat person) found himself completely unable to read the hardcover edition of a classic novel that had been assigned in a college course. He had no trouble when he found a used, underlined (that is, dirty) paperback edition of the book. As might be guessed, he suffered from a compulsion to split his affection and sexuality in what is often called the madonna-whore complex.

PATIENT F.

A young woman had been repeatedly overstimulated sexually as a child by her mother. Under the pretext of guarding against or treating a supposed infection in the child, the mother would regularly "clean out" the girl's vagina. This was but the most frequent of many seductive contacts. The rather gentle rubbing the mother performed was not described as frightening or cruel; it became cannibalistic and expressible in rat imagery because of the teasing, mounting excitement that evoked an unbearable need for discharge—a need the child could not fulfill. Although children (particularly girls) may be capable of some kind of orgastic experiences, these do not appear to effect an adequate discharge of the overstimulation evoked in prepubescents by an adult's sexual excitement and seductive contact.

During the session preceding the one I will deal with at length, F. had told me of her feeling of revulsion on seeing "a swollen, foul-smelling rat." She had seen it when in the company of a person she characterized as "looking like a vampire," with teeth that "gleam like a rodent's." She continued: "I feel as if *I* am rotten and swollen somehow, with vaginal and rectal odors—as if I were that rat."

In the waiting room before the next session, F. had a fantasy of performing fellatio on the analyst: "I pictured it, but I had no real sexual feeling about it." This showed her characteristic isolation of affect, which she maintained in part by autohypnotic states. "I felt like sinking into a trance," she said, and then reported this dream: "Our positions were reversed. I was sitting and you were lying down. As you talked, I turned into a sphinx. I couldn't control my mouth. It kept opening and closing, like a lion's." Associations led to a telephone conversation that she had had with her mother before going to sleep the preceding night. She had been "ferociously angry" with her mother and felt like telling her she never wanted to see her again (that is, she wanted to lose control of her mouth and do something destructive with it). She had not told her mother anything of the kind, realizing that it was not true that she did not want to see her and sensing that she really wanted to provoke her mother to a retaliatory verbal attack (to bite her back). I interpreted, "That would have intensified things, while it would have appeared, falsely, that you wanted to be rid of her." F. agreed. The falseness consisted of her fooling herself—a kind of dishonesty that had made her unaware that her consistent rebelliousness was a disguise for the symbiotic relationship with her mother.

When F. was dreaming, she had felt like ripping and tearing with her teeth, and in the session now began to feel this way again (the autohypnosis was lifting). "I feel my mouth; it is the only part of me that feels fully alive"—the oral excitement was being experienced. I interpreted that her fantasy in the waiting room of fellatio was apparently connected with an impulse to bite my penis. "Yes, I have a feeling as if my two front upper teeth were very large and were stiffening my upper lip, making it immobile, *like a rodent's.*" Here F. had become the rat. Then she commented on a noise in the room: "It sounds as if you are moving in your chair. I feel as if you are writhing." Then, after a pause: "*You* said writhing," and she realized she had made a slip of the tongue —she had meant to say, "*I* said writhing." (The slip of the tongue is a "doing something wrong with the mouth." See Yazmajian 1966.) I responded that it was she who had the desire to writhe and that twice, directly and in the slip, she had tried to attribute it to me (the dream had reversed historical roles and made me, the parent figure, the object of a cannibalistic attack). The interpretation seemed valid—F. started to feel her overexcitement. She went on to tell me about her sadistic sexual teasing: making men writhe, or trying to. The reversal of roles in the dream represents F.'s characteristic attempt to become the Sphinx (devouring, bisexual) or an oral sadistic castrative animal like the rat. In the dream the analyst is the victim. F.'s overstimulated state, evaded at the beginning of the session by hypnosis, came out as she associated to the dream, so that finally she was able to become aware that it was she who felt like writhing. As the feelings began to flow, there was as usual a reciprocal lifting of the hypnotic defensive state.

As a child, F. had repeatedly teased male dogs. She was taking the role of the overstimulating adult who whether man or woman is always endowed with a penetrative, cannibalistic phallus. She would stroke the dog's penis to erection, but, if she could help it, not enough to let him ejaculate. She would also get the dog excited by letting him sniff her genital area (and sometimes lick it, paralleling the mother's "cleaning her out"). She was especially gratified if the dog would get so excited by the smelling that he would ejaculate onto the floor, without his penis being touched. Making the male ejaculate with a humiliating loss of control meant conquering and castrating him. As an adult, F. repeated the performance with susceptible men.[15] Sensing the nature of her ex-

---

15. Three of the patients discussed in this book, one man and two women, had fantasies of a man ejaculating without being touched, having been overstimulated by teasing. The male patient would carry out the passive role in his fantasy while "masturbating" by lying on his back and, without touching it, pushing

citement, one man asked her early in his relationship with her, "Do you want me to tease you?" She complained of him: "He touches [my clitoris] and lets me subside, not letting me quite reach climax. It goes on and on, so I feel tortured for want of satisfaction." But predominantly it was F., a present-day version of Mirbeau's Clara, who teased in many ways, all leaving the man in a state of overexcitation. She almost always had an orgasm, or at least sadistic satisfaction, but seldom allowed her partner to climax, or made him, like the dog, ejaculate onto the floor without having his penis touched. She would also tease him by "lightly touching and rubbing" his penis, again preventing him from coming to orgasm, like the dogs from her childhood. She had fantasies of "tormenting men sexually to the point of unbearable sensations—so that the man would go into an *arc de cercle* with the torment."

Autohypnosis

In addition to F.'s portrayal in her dream of the analyst as the victim of a cannibalistic attack that was revealed in her associations, she assigned to him a contrasting role of causing her to change into a sphinx under his hypnotic control. I quote from the dream as F. wrote it out after the session: "I was watching and listening to you. You were saying, among other things, that I was a sphinx. As you spoke I became conscious of my arms which projected from my shoulders like the forelegs of a lion . . . [there was] a growing feeling that my arms had paws and claws. As you continued speaking the feeling of being a man-eating animal grew . . . I felt that your voice was bringing out my true nature and activity. I felt like biting." Here the analyst became the overstimulating parent, making the patient into a ferocious, man-eating animal by arousing the rage of overstimulation. The session had begun with F.'s feeling she

---

his penis up "against the air" (see chapter 8). Among its other meanings were those of anal movement and sensation, and an unconscious identification with the passive, feminine position—paralleling the role that this woman patient (F.) assigned to her victim-dog (an anal creature). The male patient was also unable to bear the stimulation and usually had to ejaculate by using his hand vigorously. Thus the passive role seemed to predominate up to a point, then the active—although there was throughout a split that enabled him to impersonate both partners in fantasied anal intercourse (the air was associated to farting).

was "in a trance"; she was in a state of autohypnosis characteristically used to evade her sexual excitement.[16]

One of F.'s associations to the sphinx was Baudelaire's poem *La Beauté*, in which beauty is personified as a stone sphinx: "I reign in the azure like a sphinx beyond all understanding (*Je trône dans l'azur comme un sphinx incompris*) against which poets hurl and bruise themselves." It is to these poets that the sphinxlike Beauty refers when she says, "to hypnotize my enslaved lovers" (*pour fasciner mes dociles amants*). F.'s love affairs involved a continual kind of playacting intended to fascinate and hypnotize her lovers, most of them masochistic. Being subject to autohypnotic states was characteristic; this had become clear in the course of her analysis. Hypnosis was used not only as a defense to deal with the erogeneity, excitement, and rage involved in her predominantly sadomasochistic fantasies, but also to bring about in attenuation repetitions of the past traumata. She could do with others and to others what had previously been done to her, and in addition to the defense of identifying with the past aggressor could more successfully evade the approach to overstimulation by using autohypnosis. The defensive use of hypnosis seems most important, but hypnosis can also provide gratification without responsibility in service of the compulsion to repeat past traumatic experiences; this prompts me to use the term *hypnotic facilitation* to complement what Fliess calls hypnotic evasion —the pair constituting a kind of symptomatic state (see chapter 8).

At another time, F. remarked that before going to bed she "was so sexually excited I was beside myself." (I omit material that shows the anal erogeneity aroused, except to report that she was afraid she would lose control and soil the sheets.) She dreamed that a favorite dog from childhood had been caught by a frightening, evil man, who "demanded that my dog submit to an immediate rape by members of his family and held him immobile and exposed—as though they might even take him sexually while he was being so held . . . at this point, my ability to see what was happening disappeared, and I understood that the dog was partially or wholly eaten by the family."

16. Most of the patients cited in this chapter were subject to autohypnotic states; I believe that if I had known about hypnotic defense at the beginning of my practice I would have found it in all of them. I think it is a universal human defense phenomenon, but its frequency of use, depth, and pervasiveness are greater in victims of soul murder. This is the subject of chapter 8.

While telling the last part of this dream of impatient sexual urgency, F. said that she felt "great relief at the speed and completeness with which the dog's suffering was ended." Before this, during the narration of most of the dream, she had felt as if she would "lose control and urinate in a broad stream the entire contents of my body." This represented an attempt to pass off the overstimulation involved in the rape scene, this time by urination. The wish-fear was for an explosive discharge that is really cloacal—the discharge would end an unbearable forepleasure. At the same time such a discharge involves the terrifying feeling of losing sphincter control, and its incipient evocation of ego dissolution (see Shengold 1988; F. had also been subjected to traumatic enemas as a child). The feeling of relief about "the speed and completeness with which the dog's suffering was ended" refers not only to the need for discharge but to F.'s penis envy, which for her was definitely colored by cannibalistic impulse (biting off the penis).

Both male and female children who have been overstimulated tend to see the adult penis as an organ that can effectively discharge cannibalistic overexcitation and can bite. The mothers in these cases seem always to be predominantly phallic mothers for the children—mothers who have or who have stolen the paternal penis. These patients frequently have fantasies of *penis dentatus* as well as of *vagina dentata*. F. identified with the phallic adult who can have orgasm, or tried to, with her body as a phallus. The wish for an explosive discharge that can relieve the painful tension and destroy the object also means the possibility of ego dissolution (emptying out "the whole body contents") and must of course be defended against. The wish lives on, in nonpsychotic patients, through introversion in their fantasies, and in some instances these explosive fantasies are enacted in attenuation, or under carefully controlled conditions.

Ego Regression and Ego Splits in Rat People

Freud used the case of the Rat Man to describe the dynamic antecedents and the symptoms and defenses of obsessive-compulsive neurosis. I have stressed the intensity and massiveness of the isolating defenses used by people who were subjected to soul murder—defenses needed to split off and contain their traumatic, overstimulating experiences. In the case of the Rat Man Freud described two kinds of isolation. There is disconnection between idea and idea, which is one mechanism that can bring about the more defensively fundamental disconnection between thought and affect. "Repression is effected not by means of amnesia but by a severance of causal connexions brought about by a withdrawal of affect. These repressed connexions appear to persist in some kind of shadowy form . . . and they are thus transferred, in a process of projection, into the external world, where they bear witness to what has been effaced from consciousness" (1909, pp. 231–232; my italics).

The disconnection between thoughts can also be accomplished by "inserting a time interval" between them (Freud 1909, 246). Where such isolation is massive and intense, as with the victims of soul murder I am calling rat people, vertical splits occur in the mental apparatus, making possible those mental processes that Orwell calls doublethink (and his definition includes the use of autohypnosis). Doublethink was conditioned, in part by the use of rat-torture, onto the victim and hero of *1984*. Freud says the Rat Man "went on to say that he would like to speak of a criminal act, whose author he did not recognize as himself, though he quite clearly recollected committing it." The Rat Man then paraphrases to Freud the saying of Nietzsche quoted above (see chapter 1): " 'I did this,' says my Memory. 'I cannot have done this,' says my Pride and remains inexorable. In the end—Memory yields' " (Freud 1901, 184). But for the Rat Man, "yielding" still leaves the memory in the "shadowy" form described by Freud, and he goes on to relate this to Freud. The shadowy memories make for two kinds of knowing: "For he knows [things] in that he has not forgotten them, but he does not know them in that he is unaware of their significance" (1909, p. 196).

The result of this is an "as if" knowing, and for some people this can involve an as if part of their personality—small, considerable, or predominant. "I certainly act as if I love my husband and children," one woman remarked, "but I really can't feel it." Freud describes this in a way that shows the centrality of feelings for "owning" one's convictions and characteristics. (For me this implies the crucial clinical and human importance of some theoretical concept of drive energy —what Freud called economic considerations—that is implicit in our emotions.) "[The Rat Man] could not help believing in the premonitory power of dreams, for he had several remarkable experiences to prove it. Consciously he does not really believe in it (the two views exist side by side, *but the critical one is sterile*)" (1909, p. 268; my italics). Freud gives another example in his early work *Studies on Hysteria* (1893–95), quoting the following dialogue between himself and his patient Miss

Lucy R. Freud had asked about her relationship with her employer. (He knew that an unconscious incestuous attachment was involved, though she did not.)

> [*Freud:*] But if you knew you loved your employer, why didn't you tell me?
>
> [*Lucy R.:*] I didn't know—or rather I didn't want to know. I wanted to drive it out of my mind and not think of it again, and latterly I believed I had succeeded. (1894, p. 117)

In a footnote apparently written somewhat later, Freud adds, "I have never managed to give a better description than this of *the strange state of mind* in which one knows and does not know of a thing at the same time. It is clearly impossible to understand it unless one has been in such a state oneself" (1894, p. 117; my italics). The "strange state of mind" is for me an alteration of consciousness. This predominantly defensive autohypnosis is universally used (we have all "been in such a state" ourselves) and is such a striking feature of those who have had to ward off soul murder.

Freud goes on to tell about the "very remarkable experience of this sort" that he himself had once had (p. 117), ending with a memorable metaphoric phrase appropriate to the future discoverer of the oedipus complex, to Oedipus himself, and to everyone: "I was afflicted by that *blindness of the seeing eye* which is so astonishing in the attitude of mothers to their daughters, husbands to their wives and rulers to their favourites" (p. 117; my italics). For Freud, this was an occasional, exceptional experience, but for the victim of soul murder and for rat people it represents a kind of thinking that can dominate their mind and their world—as it does in *1984*, where doublethink is aimed at abolishing the *memories* of the past. (In chapter 5 I describe "compartmentalization" in patient D. and in Orwell himself.)

By means of isolation and autohypnosis, vertical splits of the ego take place. A major one is inherent in the intense isolation of affect—the split between the cognitive ego and the experiencing ego (see Shuren 1967; Shuren's formulation is based on clinical material similar to mine). A functioning of the ego necessary for the subjective feeling of identity, the ability to feel what is there to be felt,[17] is disrupted by this split; the

---

17. The complete absence of the split is seen in Walt Whitman's well-known affirmation of identity when one takes his statements in reverse order: "I am the Man; I suffered; I was there" (1855, p. 76).

personality is compartmentalized in vertical splits of the ego (like the Rat Man's), usually not completely but in a partial and "shadowy" fashion (mentioned by Freud). It is "as if" there are provisional and alternating personas that can take over with slight alterations of consciousness. Freud twice describes the compartmentalization in the Rat Man. In the published case history he notes his

> impression that [the Rat Man] had, as it were, disintegrated into three personalities: into one unconscious personality, that is to say, and into two preconscious ones between which his consciousness could oscillate. His unconscious comprised those of his impulses which had been suppressed at an early age and which might be described as passionate and evil impulses. In his normal state he was kind, cheerful and sensible—an enlightened and superior kind of person—while in his third *psychological organization* he paid homage to superstition and asceticism. Thus he was able to have two different creeds and two different outlooks upon life. (1909, p. 248; my italics)

This is more succinctly put, without the "topographical" explanation, in the case record not meant for publication: "He is made up of three personalities—one humourous and normal, another ascetic and religious and a third immoral and perverse" (p. 278). In my patients "hypnoid states," alterations of consciousness, and autohypnosis keep separate these "psychological organizations," between which these people can shift. This disrupts the consummation of feeling what is there to be felt (preconsciously) that is ordinarily taken for granted. For example, a patient says: "I know that I hate you and I want to bite off your penis but that part of me is wrapped in cellophane." When the patient is fully "awake" (the hypnotic wrapping dissolved), these feelings can be acknowledged: the patient can know experientially that she hates. When analysis works for such people, the autohypnotic symptomatology is given up, and the synthetic function of an ego really able to know and own feelings is free to blend the disparate "personalities" and contradictory trends.

Teeth and Teething

I have presented the rat as a psychological image that derives much of its emotional power from being the carrier of the tooth: the rat as biter. There is much folklore connecting rats, mice, and teeth. As will be seen, these rodents are portrayed as having a special relationship to the losing of teeth. I mention this here to underline the impact of the rodent's amazing teeth on human psychology, where these teeth figure as an element in the external world that is used to express what is going on in the individual's mind and body. The teeth have acquired a symbolic significance in the Freudian sense: become a part of our cultural inheritance (and as Freud would have us add, our phylogenetic inheritance).

In describing the second oral state of libido development, Abraham (1924) points out that the development of the teeth coincides with an influx of sadism:

> Undoubtedly the teeth are the first instruments with which the child can do damage to the outer world. For they are already effective at a time when the hands can at most only assist their activity by seizing and keeping hold of the object . . . the teeth are the only organs [small children] possess that are sufficiently hard to be able to injure objects around them. One has only to look at children to see how intense the impulse to bite is. This is the stage in which the cannibalistic impulses predominate. (p. 451)[18]

Abraham quotes a comment of van Ophuijsen, who believes "that certain neurotic phenomena are due to a regression to the age when teeth were being formed" (1924, p. 451). Despite much that has been written on biting and oral sadism, the phenomenon of teething has since been strangely neglected in psychoanalytic literature. An exception is an article of Kucera (1959), which points out that pleasure in sucking is interfered with by teething, and that this intensifies the sadistic effect on the infant of the coming in of the teeth. Kucera notes further that the "*experience* which is regularly provoked during teeth eruption can be looked upon as the key situation for the origin of primary masochism, as its physiological organic foundation" (p. 289; my italics). Without going into the moot question of the origin of primary masochism, I will deal with the *experience* of teething, and its experiential link with aggressive phenomena.

18. Painful teething usually takes place between the ages of six months and eighteen months. This fits in with Abraham's timing. Teething accompanies all the stages of libido development, however: the last baby teeth to come in, the second molars, usually erupt in the first half of the third year. The permanent teeth begin to come in when the child is about six (Spock 1957).

As the teeth painfully force their way through the mucosa of the gum, infants can be said to bite themselves (and experience being bitten) before they can bite anything or anyone else; this occurs both during and of course after the eruption of the tooth. Tooth eruption produces the experience of being simultaneously the subject and object of biting for the owner of the tooth and surrounding mucosa. One cannot of course empathize with the infant, for the ego at the initial time of teething is in a rudimentary state, with incomplete differentiation of subject and object, of inside and outside. As part of the development of body ego and ego, this differentiation is taking place during the time of teething, which corresponds in our theory to the oral sadistic phase of libido development. During this phase the infant has to deal with an instinctual access of aggression, which must be modified by libido, and of primal affects (see Fliess 1956; Shengold 1988). To deal with the frustration of need satisfaction and with overstimulation, a loving mother is needed to counteract the danger of a breakthrough of the stimulus barrier at the time the aggressive instinct is burgeoning (see Hoffer 1950; Mahler 1952). Active discharge of the aggressive drive takes place by way of the teeth and the body musculature—by biting and eventually by locomotion. Passive oral masochism is also experienced in the body (registering therefore in the forming body ego that is fundamental to the psychic ego), in part by way of the teeth and their adjacent mucosa. The phylogenetic significance of the teeth and the teething experience is probably much greater than the ontogenetic. A look at animal life with evolution in mind, or at what Tennyson calls "nature red in tooth and claw," certainly suggests this. (The continuously teething rat may also epitomize a primal, common ancestor for man.) I do not know that children have been sufficiently "observed" teething. The change of what has hitherto been predominantly a pleasure-giving erogenous zone to a source of tension and unpleasure, at a time when the ego is beginning to coalesce, may be very significant. Perhaps we have avoided its significance because of primal anxieties and concomitant resistances.

Cannibalistic Wishes, Infantile Experiences, and Teething

Teething might furnish an ontogenetic root for the subjective reality of the cannibalistic act. The existence of the act is questioned by Fliess

(1956), who says that the second oral phase is the only phase of libido development when direct instinctual gratification is denied. Although children do not discharge their oral impulses by eating flesh from the breast, they do bite themselves when they are teething, and the breast when they have teeth. Most analysts would agree that autocannibalism stems from the time when the mother's breast is still regarded as part of the body ego of the child—a time when "The breast is a part of me —I am the breast" (Freud 1938, 299). Lewin (1950) pointed out that the infant's wish to be devoured is not based on direct infant observation but is "a heuristic fiction . . . a construction based on inference" (p. 104). Klein (1933) asserted that the fear of being eaten is experienced during the first year of life, and that this is due to the projection of active oral sadistic wishes onto the parent. Simmel (1944) spoke of cannibalistic fears and wishes as associated with the infant's identification with food. The food that is incorporated becomes a part of the baby's ego, and the baby might be considered as eating itself. About the baby at the breast during this period, alternately chewing at its fingers and toes, "one may say, with licence, that it indulges thereby in an act of autocannibalism" (Lewin 1950, 107). I would ask the same license for my formulation that teething involves autocannibalism; it supplements rather than supplants the other constructions.

Teething as a Physiological Prototype of Projection

Teething also provides an experience of discharge of painful tension in the infant's first year (with an experiencing ego present):

> Fell sorrow's tooth doth never rankle more
> Than when it bites but lanceth not the sore
> (*Richard II*, 1.3.301–302)

But when the tooth actually breaks through the mucosa of the gum, tension is discharged and the sore is lanced.[19] Perhaps this experience conditions some of the fantasies of explosive cannibalistic penetration,

19. There is at least one instance in literature in which rats deliver the victim from a traumatic and unendurable situation (that is, they discharge tension): rats bite through the ropes to release the prisoner in Poe's story *The Pit and the Pendulum*. I am grateful to Mark Kanzer for pointing this out.

passive and active, that one finds in patients who have undergone experiences of overstimulation, and who compulsively and repetitively crave a discharge of tension, as if they were addicts. They seek out any kind of destructive penetration as a means of getting rid of the overstimulation. (One recalls the patient who wanted to be "fucked to death" to discharge his terrible, overstimulated state.)

After tooth eruption, the infant can bite others as well as bite itself. Aggression can be turned outward and also projected onto the environment, so that a tension felt within becomes "outside" and "other." The eruption of the tooth is a physiological prototype, especially meaningful for what starts out as a body ego, like a material projection onto the environment. When the psychic capacity for projection becomes possible, not only can the tooth be used against others, but others can be endowed with it by the mind. Freud (1920) said of internal stimuli (like the drive representatives of oral masochism): "There is a tendency to treat them as though they were acting, not from the inside, but from the outside, so that it may be possible to bring the shield against stimuli into operation as a means of defence against them. This is the origin of projection" (p. 29). The eruption of the teeth may make for an experiential impetus for this early defensive operation.

Teeth and Castration Anxiety

There is much in the psychoanalytic literature about teeth and the phallic phase of libido development—for example, tooth dreams interpreted as referring to masturbation (Freud 1900). These tooth phenomena usually involve the falling out of the teeth rather than their eruption and invoke castration anxiety. I believe it is also because the teeth can connote the terrors of oral destruction as well that they can evoke the "surprise . . . [of] strong resistance" pointed out by Freud (1900, p. 385). Freud is referring mainly to castration anxiety. The developmentally earlier danger situations that give rise to preoedipal anxiety are connected with the tooth experience that precedes the falling out of teeth: the biting and being bitten associated with tooth eruption. The two levels of anxiety can of course coalesce: Fliess (1956) wondered whether castration is not at its most frightening level conceived of as effected through biting.

The phenomena related to teething have also been surrounded by a surprising "strong resistance," and not only by psychoanalysts whose very few contributions I have already mentioned. The fact of physiologically painful teething, familiar to any parent, had been minimized and even denied by generations of dentists and pediatricians (see Kucera 1959).

The Object Endowed with a Tooth

Fliess (1956) has pointed out how oral sadistic libido is regularly discharged in subsequent stages of libido development in situations both normal and pathological, so that any erogenic zone can be infused with cannibalistic libido. Any combination of a sudden access of defused aggression and ego regression involves an impending loss of control of the instinctual access, and means a return to traumatic, passive, cannibalistic terror if it goes far enough. In relation to the anal stage, for example, the Rat Man's terror concerns the rat biting its way into his body through his anus. (This threatens to undo the power of the anal sphincter, so much needed for the anal defensive foundation of feelings of control; see Shengold 1988.) I have reviewed the many meanings of the rat for the Rat Man: the animal is above all the carrier of the tooth and thus gains its full terrifying power. This is illustrated by Abraham (1922) in his explication of another symbol that can be endowed with a tooth, the spider. Abraham implicitly stratifies the symbolic meanings of the spider, with each added statement bringing in more terrifying connotations. The spider symbolizes the destructive phallic mother. It also symbolizes her destructive phallus, which can castrate. Abraham quotes Nunberg, who says that the spider sucks blood, and finally Freud, who adds that some female spiders devour their mates after sex: they eat cannibalistically and so castrate by biting. The symbol for the phallic mother becomes terrifying when the phallus is endowed with teeth that can castrate and devour.

The tooth equips, accompanies, and is the prototype for penetrative, devouring objects at any stage of libidinal development, and in relation to any erogenic body zone that discharges oral sadistic libido. Differentiated objects that can be tooth carriers include: the penetrative, castrating phallus of the parent (father or phallic mother) and the fecal mass of the second anal stage that is clearly "not me". The fecal stick that is simultaneously me and not me and the breast-mouth are the earlier, not completely differentiated subject-objects that can be charged with cannibalistic libido. So both subject and object, self and other, can be equipped with teeth. The fantasies can take many forms, involving erogenous zones that are part object and part subject: breast with teeth, vagina dentata, *rectum dentatum, urethra dentata* (Keiser 1954), phallus equipped with a mouth (Fliess 1965). "The mouth of this [second oral] stage is transferable on to all subsequent dominant erogenic zones" (Fliess 1956, 86). Subject, object, and erogenous zone can all be represented by cannibalistic creatures like the rat, which will appear in analysis in the associations of patients who have had traumatic overstimulating experiences, who have been subject to attempts at soul murder.

Material from Myths and Folklore Illustrating the Endowment of Objects with a Tooth

Many myths show the connections among the teeth, the projection of cannibalistic aggression, and mice and rats.

> Thus in many parts of the world it is customary to put extracted teeth in some place where they will be found by a mouse or a rat, in the hope that through the sympathy which continues to exist between them and their former owner, his other teeth may acquire the same firmness and excellence as the teeth of these rodents. In Germany it is said to be almost a universal maxim that when you have a tooth taken out, you should insert it in a mouse's hole. To do so with a child's milk tooth . . . will prevent the child from having toothache. (Frazer 1890, 31–32)

Lewis (1958) quote folklore about mice and rats and the loss of teeth from Russia, Germany, Costa Rica, Oceania, and Polish Jews. Frazer has examples from Jews, Germans, Sinhalese, and Americans.

In this folklore the tooth is projected upon the rodent (literally), as in earlier development aggression is projected upon the mother to form the bad mother and bad "not me." To put it genetically, the breast is endowed with teeth: this is the basic meaning of the rat (into whose hole the lost tooth is to be inserted). The bad, toothed breast is a projected part of the self at first, invested with narcissistic libido—part self, part object. After the establishment of object relations and a sense of self, the danger of being eaten and the sources of overstimulation are felt clearly as coming from outside. This is eventually evidenced by the castration fear of the oedipal period; expressed and disguised in regressive terms, this fear has an important role in these myths about losing teeth. The parent will not castrate the child if the child loses the penetrative tooth that can symbolize the penis, or has it knocked out (as in puberty initiation rites). At a more regressive level, these myths are about refraining from biting to avoid being bitten: the rat has the tooth, not I.

CHAPTER

7

Clinical and Literary Examples of Rat People

The rat imago is used repetitively by some patients who have been overstimulated and continue to be; beside themselves with rage and frustration, they long for a discharge to escape the traumatic state of too-muchness. I have described some of the concomitant ego and superego regressions of soul-murder victims as part of the reaction to trauma. These victims, rat people included, are quick to feel ill used, to blame and accuse others, to project their rage; this can give their feelings and thoughts a paranoid cast, hidden and latent or strikingly overt. An alternative that can coexist is intense masochism.

Dostoyevski's *Notes from Underground* (1864) captures the atmosphere of the lives of rat people. The Underground Man characterizes himself repeatedly as a "mouse" (he is predominantly masochistic, but his sadism is a constant presence) who lives "underground" in a cloacal rat hole. He gnashes his teeth and longs to bite, suffers from toothache and finally has come to enjoy it, and in language evoking the rat biting himself claims to enjoy turning sadism into masochism: "I got to the point of feeling a sort of secret abnormal, despicable enjoyment in returning home to my corner on some disgusting Petersburg night, acutely conscious that that day I had committed a loathesome action again, that what was done could never be undone, and secretly, *inwardly gnawing, gnawing at myself for it, tearing and consuming myself* till at last the bitterness turned into a sort of shameful accursed sweetness, and at last—into positive real enjoyment! Yes, into enjoyment, into enjoyment!" (pp. 132–133; my italics). There is a paranoid potential, with masochistic coloring: "I, for instance, have a great deal of *amour propre*. I am as suspicious and prone to take offense as a humpback or a dwarf" (p. 133).

The Underground Man vents and courts spite—the mouse has identified with the rat, has been endowed with the tooth and bites himself: "I am a spiteful man. I am an unattractive man. I believe my liver is diseased . . . I refuse to consult a doctor from spite . . . I am perfectly well aware that I cannot 'pay out' the doctors by not consulting them; I know better than any one that by all this I am only injuring myself and no one else. But still, if I don't consult a doctor it is from spite. My liver is bad, well—let it get worse!" (p. 129). Later the man describes himself in the third person, his "I" split-off: "There in its nasty, stinking underground home our insulted, crushed and ridiculed mouse promptly becomes absorbed in cold, malignant and, above all, everlasting spite" (p. 135).

We see in the Underground Man that these vertical ego splits are not only transient, as above, but amount to conflicting personalities, as with the Rat Man: "When petitioners would come to me [he has his petty place in the shabby, corrupt, "dirty" government bureaucracy] . . . I used to grind my teeth at them, and felt intense enjoyment when I succeeded in making anybody unhappy." The man then says he is conscious of not being a spiteful man basically and that he wants to be loved, and he describes his contradictory, typically reversible attitudes. "I was lying when I said just now that I was a spiteful official. I was lying from spite. I was simply amusing myself with the petitioners . . . and in reality I never would become spiteful. I was conscious every moment in myself of many, very many elements absolutely opposite to that. I felt them positively swarming in myself, these opposite elements" (p. 130). Later are set forth the concomitant lack of identity and inability to love, the common residues of soul murder: "Even in my underground dreams I did not imagine love except as a struggle. I began it always with hatred and ended it with moral subjugation, and afterwards I never knew what to do with the subjugated object" (p. 218).

The Underground Man himself is predominantly the poor "mouse," "the subjugated object," although he confesses to having tormented and rejected (while still "loving") the mousy young girl Liza—after getting her to love him. He disavows the genuine, warm, loving feelings he has had for Liza by telling her: "I was laughing at you! I had been insulted just before, at dinner, by the fellows who came that evening before me. I came to you, meaning to thrash one of them, an officer; but I didn't succeed, I didn't find him; I had to avenge the insult on someone to get back my own again; you turned up, I vented my spleen on you and laughed at you. I had been humiliated, so I wanted to humiliate; I had been treated like a rag so I wanted to show my power" (p. 215).

The victim's identification with the soul murderer is here expressed by the Underground Man, who shows his rodent identification in his preoccupation with his teeth:

> Even in toothache there is enjoyment . . . The enjoyment of the sufferer finds expression in . . . moans . . . they express the consciousness that you have no enemy to punish, but that you have pain; the consciousness that . . . you are in complete slavery to your teeth; that if someone wishes it, your teeth will leave off aching, and if he does not, they will go on aching another three months; and that finally, if you are still contumacious and still protest, all that is left you for your own gratification is to thrash yourself or beat your wall with your fist as hard as you can, and absolutely nothing more. Well, these mortal insults, these jeers on the part of someone unknown, end at least in an enjoyment which sometimes reaches the highest degree of voluptuousness. (pp. 137–138)

In the terms of the folklore reviewed above, here the tooth has been inserted into the mouse's hole. I have found no better evocation of the rat person than this description of passionate rage and frustration transmuted into a blend of paranoid and masochistic feeling.

Patient G.

G., a young woman, was both a soul murder victim and a rat person. She came to analysis complaining of pervasive feelings of worthlessness— her reaction to what she called her "bad" sexual impulses, which were sadomasochistic and accompanied by rage. There was much angry, accusatory, paranoid affect, generally confined to fantasy or verbal rumination. If enacted, these angry, accusatory feelings were first converted masochistically and directed at the patient herself; in this she resembled the Underground Man. G.'s sadomasochistic impulses were ruthlessly suppressed in sexual interaction, but at times the excitement was overwhelming and she felt compelled to masturbate. Her rage was rarely experienced, although she was almost always aware it was there; this recalls the Rat Man's "anal defensiveness," knowing and yet affectively not knowing. In turning rage on herself G. could act the role of a martyr and provoke people to treat her as one. Although her cruel impulses were conscious and were manifestly sexual in her masturbatory fantasies, they had no real significance for her. They were divided off from her "official" personality, and G. was generally regarded, with good reason, as a gentle and kind person (again, like the Rat Man). When apt to feel rage and sexual excitement, instead G. would usually go into an autohypnotic state and often would provoke trouble. Sometimes she took a masochistic role, as when she "found herself" inviting a strange and suspicious-looking man into her apartment simply because he had rung her bell. Sometimes she would do or more often say something sadistic, but the sadism was almost always denied or at least disguised. (When a close friend, fearful of rejection, confessed to G. her homosexuality, G. was devastated *afterward* by the dismissive cruelty of her own response.) In the analysis G. was constantly inviting and expecting rage and sexual attack, but this was blocked off from her responsible awareness by her hypnoid states. What happened when she was "wrapped in cotton wool," as G. put it, did not count. It became clear that in her altered states of consciousness she wanted to be raped. This meant wishing a repetition of experiences from childhood with her sadistic and seductive father—a true soul murderer. The autohypnosis effectively deprived G. of identity when she was the subject of her repeated, overstimulated states. As the analysis proceeded and this began to become clear, G. talked of herself as having two personalities (as with the Rat Man these were in addition to her surface personality), which she called the rat and the mouse. To be the mouse meant to be the little girl victim of her cruel father. As the mouse she craved to have something violent and sexual done to her to end the traumatic overexcitement and provide a discharge. Her rat personality was especially disowned. As the rat she was aware of the wish to bite and revenge herself—specifically she wanted to castrate by biting, to bite off the penis of the person who was overstimulating her. One day she talked of her excitement on seeing Marlowe's *Edward II*, a play about a homosexual king who is killed onstage, in this production by having a red-hot poker shoved up his anus.[1] G. wanted this done to herself; she wanted to do it to the analyst. In this retaliatory, sadomasochistic "primal scene" version of the murder of Edward II are some of the elements of the rat torture of *Torture Garden*: the red-hot poker, the anal penetration that kills. G. projected herself into the scene in her role as the rat—the possessor of the poker, unconsciously equated with the deadly "toothed" penis that the child feels has the power to discharge tormenting over-stimulation. As a little girl she had often sat on her father's lap and felt his erection against her bottom. She was compelled to repeat this in fantasy: to crave both being the victim (the mouse) and also to reverse roles, to become the rat and do it to "the king."

In subsequent analytic work G. was eventually able to remember with emotion and body feelings. Owning her feelings and memories then made it possible to integrate the mouse and rat personas and thus undo much of their power.

Patient H.

H., a young, Jewish man, told his analyst that while in the waiting room he had walked to the window. Another patient, a woman, was then behind him; he had wanted to stare at her but did not. (It had been established many times that for H. women in the waiting room were objects of incestuous desire: they belonged to the analyst.) As he looked out the window far down at the street below, H. fantasized that the woman behind him would say, "Don't jump—fall!" As H. reported this he felt it as a kind of joke, but not a funny one. At the window he had in fact experienced a momentary impulse to jump. After telling me this he went into a resistant, autohypnotic state, almost falling asleep on the couch. On emerging from this state he said: "I suddenly think

---

1. As Marlowe wrote it, his murderer crushes Edward (like a rat?) with a table; the murderer is then stabbed and thrown into a ditch, like a rat. The staged version was not without historical foundation, however. Edward II was murdered at Berkeley Castle. There were no marks found on his body, and "John Trevisa, who was a child living in the little town of Berkeley at the time, later translated Higden's account of [Edward's] reign in his *Polychronicon*, and interpolated the information that Edward was killed 'with a hoote broche putte thro the secret place posterialle'" (Johnson 1906, p. viii).

of a story I read. It was about one of Freud's patients he called the Rat Man. Hungarians or Ukrainians put some rats upside down on his buttocks . . . God! . . . how cruel! . . . but . . . the story . . . excited me [the patient was replicating the pauses of the Rat Man and of the torturer in *Torture Garden*!]. I felt that maybe if I could get away with it, I would do it."

At this point in the analysis H. had not acknowledged his own, predominantly passive anal cravings. Although the ambiguity of "I would do it" allows for an interpretation of his being the rat victim, he consciously meant that he would have liked to administer the rat torture to someone else—perhaps the woman behind him in the waiting room or to the analyst behind him in the consulting room. It was the woman behind him who in his fantasy had wanted him to fall (symbolically, to become a woman), and I assumed it was the arousal of anal excitement with the fantasy of a destructive penetration that had brought on his hypnosis.

H. had distorted the "Oriental torture" mentioned in the case of the Rat Man and connected it to Eastern Europe. In his associations Hungarians and Ukrainians were anti-Semitic torturers who might have persecuted his own ancestors. But H. himself had a Hungarian name and was a Jewish anti-Semite; the hated analyst behind him was also perceived as Jewish. His anal excitement had both active and passive aspects. He went on to talk of his traumatic experiences as the recipient in childhood of his mother's enemas.

Being both a Jew and an anti-Semite was typical of the splits in H.'s personality. Like patient G. he was generally regarded as a kind and good-natured person, and thought of himself as such most of the time. He too was subject to altered states of consciousness that protected him against having to acknowledge his own wishes and body feelings while allowing for repetitions of the past experiences on which these were based. He too performed and suffered cruelties that he usually refused to recognize.

One day, at a high point in the analysis, H. felt great anger toward me, and to his shock this anger was accompanied by fully acknowledged anal excitement. The next day he came in disturbed and hypnotic; with no mention of the previous session, he went on to talk of his anger toward the whole world. His hypnoid state deepened, and he actually went to sleep and had a dream on the couch. He dreamed that his stepmother was standing beside him. He woke, told me the dream, and became very upset at his continuing "sleepiness" (autohypnosis). Then he said: "Now I remember yesterday's session, but it is so vague. The man who had those feelings in his anus is someone else." Later in the session, after long silences, I asked him to associate to dreaming about his stepmother. H. asked in consternation: "What dream? What stepmother?" He had completely suppressed the dream of ten minutes before. As he remembered it he said poignantly, "My God! How bizarre! I'm not a person. I exist in pieces!"

Overstimulation and Fantasies of Clitoral Urinary Discharge

PATIENT J.

This young woman had been subject as a small child to repeated primal scene experiences and other sexual traumata. J. felt chronically overexcited sexually and engaged in frequent sexual activity, mainly involving masturbation because intercourse rarely brought orgasm. The clitoral orgasm of masturbation also left her dissatisfied. The feelings of unfulfillment intensified when analysis brought with it a revival of the infantile situation: I was seen as the exhibitionistic, seductive father. J.'s overexcitement often led to fits of rage, temper tantrums of cannibalistic intensity. During a period of excited anger at me, she dreamed of being "swallowed whole by a monstrous pelican." J. associated to stories she had been told of her biting her mother's breast, so that nursing had to be discontinued. She herself was what King Lear called a "pelican daughter," wanting to feast on her parent's blood and flesh (it was believed in Shakespeare's time that pelicans feed their young with their own blood).[2]

2. Lear is on the heath in the great storm—a fury of too-muchness projected onto the environment in this play about the relationship of fathers and children that is so full of cannibalistic imagery and feeling. Lear says of Edgar, disguised as the almost naked "poor Tom": "Nothing could have subdued Nature / To such a lowness but his unkind daughters. / Is it the fashion that discarded fathers / Should have thus little mercy on their flesh? / Judicious punishment! T'was this flesh begot / Those pelican daughters" (*King Lear*, III. 4. 72–77). J.'s identification with the father who had "little mercy" on her flesh is only partly outlined in my clinical material.

Any emotional or physical approach to her sadistic parent, or to someone else who consciously or unconsciously stood for him, or to the analyst on whom he had been transferred, brought with it for J. "an unbearable rage that terrifies me."

The time just before my vacation was particularly difficult for J., because it represented a repetition of being left in a state of unbearable sexual excitement as a child. (There is almost always an element of this in every analytic patient, but for those who have been seduced as children, being abandoned in overstimulated frustration is a torment.) The following is from a session just before my summer vacation:

> I was lying in bed in a state of great sexual excitement. I hadn't been able to read or think all day. [This thinking inhibition occurred intermittently whenever she felt this kind of sexual arousal.] I began to fantasize nightmare figures. The central terrifying figure was an octopus: appendages and a mouth that devours. Also there were reptiles, prehistoric monsters, things that were coiled up and could spread out and do harm and strangle. [The sphinx is a strangler.] Then I had the fantasy of being forced to perform fellatio.

The fantasy frightened J., and yet she felt so excited that she "had to" masturbate. She was very much afraid that her masturbation would awaken her roommate, and yet "at the same time I felt *supremely* confident it wouldn't." (This is an example of an unconscious need for punishment and a simultaneous, psychopathic insistence on being able to act without being found out or punished—another vertical ego split.) In these circumstances, the supreme confidence (recalling Oedipus) was false and quasi-delusional, and represented an identification with a psychopathic parent.

The associations to J.'s fantasy led to primal scene "observations" of her parents in mutual oral-genital contact, with a close view of her father's penis. These were undoubtedly distorted in memory and transformed by fantasy (with such details historical and narrative truth are often hard to separate). After J. told me of this memory (for so did she consider it), her desire to perform fellatio was reawakened. She felt a great sexual too-muchness and said: "I have a bursting clitoral erection. I feel that if I could urinate it would make some of the excitement go away. If only the clitoris could ejaculate!"

J. wanted the "bursting" clitoris to function like her father's penis. She often urinated when left in excitement after intercourse, but, "It doesn't work well. As a child I held in my urine to the last possible moment in order to try and get a feeling of enormous relief afterwards." (Here is the rat person's need for an explosive discharge.) At the next session J. said: "Last night I was looking at my own pubic hair. It suddenly came to me that the nightmare images resembled pubic hair, seen close up." Then J. remembered her father standing at the side of her crib in the parental bedroom, standing naked with "his penis and pubic hair sort of sticking through the bars. I feel that I wanted to suck it." The desire for fellatio and fear of it were both very great. In J.'s fantasy, the octopus (which can bite) stood for her father's penis and pubic hair ("appendages and mouth"). This was a fantasy of *penis dentatus* similar to that attached to the mythological Medusa. That Gorgon, whose head and hair of snakes have an evocative resemblance to the reptiles and octopus of J.'s nightmare fantasy, is said to stand for the phallic mother by Freud and by Abraham (when writing about the octopuslike imago of the spider).[3]

J. seemed to have linked her memories, or fantasies, of the primal scene predominantly with oral impulses. This bears out the observation of Lewin (1950) about the frequent conjunction of primal scene and oral "analytic material." He tries to explain that the observed genital excitement of the adult is usually communicated to the child "in the language of the child's oral experiences . . . reciprocal cannibalism . . . or reciprocal sucking" (p. 117). The oral triad of wishes (to sleep, to eat, to be eaten) is reactivated, he says and he gives great weight to the disturbance of the primal scene stimuli by the child's sleep. In subsequent development the "language of the child's oral experiences" is of course supplemented by the language of his anal and phallic experiences. Primal scene traumata that follow the earliest registration of what goes on outside the self always invoke anality (and anal "analytic material"), for anality is basic to defensive operations of the body ego (see Shengold 1985, 1988). Although it is not well illustrated here this was true of J. too, and the phallic reverberations are obvious in the material.

3. I think this material shows that phallic *parent* would be more correct. What starts as an undifferentiated mental representation of the actual mothering figure gets transferred inevitably in the course of development to an actual fathering figure.

Revenge Fantasies of Cannibalistic Castration

J. told me the following "exciting" fantasy, which she quite rightly called a "revenge" fantasy: it reverses the roles of tantalizing father and overstimulated, helpless child: "Naked men are chained to the wall. A belly dancer is performing in front of them so that they have erections and have to ejaculate. This is so humiliating for them." The ejaculation here meant castration. J. often had fantasies of herself as Salome, dancing to tantalize Herod so that she could have the head of John the Baptist. The castration wish is obvious.[4] Castration in J.'s fantasy meant causing a loss of potency and control, similar to the loss of control over semen seen in sufferers from ejaculatio praecox (this loss of control resembles urination).

J. went on to tell me of another revenge fantasy similar to some told to me by patient F. (see chapter 6), who wanted to make men writhe. J. had read of a Japanese prostitute who made men ejaculate by brushing their penises lightly with a very fine camel-hair brush. To J. this meant torture by tantalization (both J. and F. were akin to *Torture Garden*'s Clara) and represented a repetition of childhood experiences. These were originally overwhelming, but in J.'s fantasies they were weakened and fractioned to become tormented "teasing," and with the child having identified with the aggressor and now taking the parental role of active tormentor.

Overstimulation and Cannibalistic Anal Rage

PATIENT K.

K. was a male homosexual who had slept in his mother's bed from the age of three (when his father died) to past his puberty. He had the usual double knowledge about this. At first he "confessed" it, without detail and with mock seriousness ("as if it were about someone else," he said later). When the analysis was further along and he was expected to be responsible for his memories (and he expected himself to be responsible for them), K. attempted pitiful, desperate denials: every boy in the

4. For confirmation of the cannibalistic connotations here see in the final scene of Oscar Wilde's famous *Salomé* (1894) the soliloquy beginning, "Ah, I have kissed your mouth, Iokanaan."

part of the country he came from slept with his mother, and it had no meaning. Such statements K. himself could not accept intellectually, but they showed how little the previous confessions about his mother meant to him.

The danger of reexperiencing the affects of the past necessitated K.'s defect in "knowing"; he had a general inability to consummate knowledge. K. worked in an intellectual field, but his performance had never been as good as his intelligence promised. The emotions involved in sleeping with his mother had to do with traumatic overstimulation; what bothered him most was his intense rage. But K. was also subject to both positive and negative oedipal strivings, felt as well as expressed on the regressive oral and anal sadistic levels where the incest and the murder of the Oedipus legend come together as cannibalistic penetration. Also, K.'s mother was the main object for both the positive and the negative oedipal impulses, and both sets of impulses of course involve murder as well as sexual intercourse.

As the analysis proceeded, the transference of feelings onto the analyst threatened to revive the overwhelming incestuous excitement. In his homosexual escapades, K. had worked out ways of reexperiencing the past without bringing about a direct return of the terrifying overstimulation. Thus the homosexual actions that he could carry out with little anxiety (but with impaired pleasure) were terrifying when fantasied in relation to the analyst upon whom the incestuous object (mainly the phallic mother) had been transferred. In one session K. reported having picked up a sailor. While he was performing anal intercourse on the sailor,

> He told me stories of a man with a fabulously big penis that went down to the knees. The sailor said, "I like to be screwed by a man with a big cock." My penis was inside him then, although I wasn't feeling much, and I said, "well, you've got the biggest thing *I* have inside you except a broom handle." I was angry, and felt like really using a broom handle and ramming it up him. Ugh! I think of that being done to me. I have a feeling of horror—I was excited by his story of the man with a fantastically big penis. I think of the time I said I was raped—I wasn't really, though. Broomstick makes me think of *witch*, and *rats*. You know I'm awfully afraid of rats. At fourteen, I felt horror at seeing rats in our storeroom. Once I jumped up and came down on one; I must have hurt him terribly,

because there was a crunch—he screamed and I jumped again. I felt sorry and I wanted to help it [note the defensive change of gender] but it was gone. Once when I was eight, I got so angry that I threw a block of wood and hit my mother on the forehead. She bled . . . now I picture my mother in the bathroom. I walk in on her there.

K. had been cared for mostly by his father until the father died; after K.'s birth his mother had gone to work. The phallic, bisexual witch with a broomstick can stand for either parent. The flow of association from the sailor story to the rat and then to the mother rightly denotes the mother as the principal phallic and cannibalistic parent (witch, rat). Historically, she had been the source of the experiences of sexual overstimulation. (K.'s sick and weak father figured mainly as the frighteningly vulnerable one—the rat you can jump on and feel sorry for.) But the mother was also the bleeding rat victim whom K. wanted to enter as he had seen his father do (in his associations "to walk in on her in the bathroom"). K. identified with his mother in taking both an active, masculine and a passive, feminine role in homosexual intercourse; he both was and submitted to the sadistic mother type in his sexual and emotional relationships. K.'s passivity predominated; he was one of those who long for anal rape and are terrified of it. His love relationships seemed fixed in a pattern: his sadistic lover would lie, tease, and become unfaithful, then gradually withdraw from the affair, leaving the patient in a state of excitement and fury. K. felt repeatedly that only the current, forsaking lover could bring fulfillment (which no lover had ever been able to do—as in Proust, only the unavailable was idealized). K.'s compulsive and repetitive masochistic object choice (repeating the soul murder of his childhood in attenuation) made him one of those unfortunates who follow one of Samuel Butler's characteristically twisted quotations (here he was having fun, but serious fun, with Tennyson): " 'Tis better to have loved and lost, than never to have lost at all" (1885, p. 370).

After being separated from his lovers, K. would begin a frantic period of promiscuous sexual activity with anonymous pickups, like the sailor. But here there was even less satisfaction. He would sometimes masturbate many times in succession, feeling a desperate need to discharge the excitement adequately—a need he could not fulfill.

Alongside the feeling of intolerable overstimulation was murderous rage. K. was afraid that he might lose control and kill his lover during their quarrels, although he had never physically hurt anyone. In the session quoted from above, the rage was felt toward the sailor when K. thought that his penis was being belittled. This had again made him the small boy, in bed with his mother, who could not compete with the big-penised man whose place he had taken. The rage was felt as a desire to destroy the object by way of a tearing anal penetration (as in the Captain's story in the case of the Rat Man), to "really" use the broomstick. This kind of anger was terrifying, partly because K. would also feel himself a helpless victim of his own rage, and partly because the rage turned outward threatened to annihilate the psychic image of his mother, the original and much needed soul murderer. To keep both the overstimulation and the rage in check, K. used massive isolation of his feelings at a terrible price—the price of his own identity. (This kind of isolation is what I have called anal narcissistic defense: using the mind as a kind of anal sphincter to control or even eliminate feeling. See Shengold 1985) K. lived a hollow, "as if" life, simulating love, friendship, and joy. He was "filled" by the soul-murdering aggressor, his lifelong submission to his mother engraved into his conscience. And like the broken Winston Smith, he not only loved sadistic Big Brothers but had to see the world falsely, through their eyes. Orwell's epitome of brainwashing's effect on the knowledge of truth held for this patient: if Big Brother said so, "two plus two equals five." K. in his promiscuous pursuits and in his relationship with lovers was always driven by the insistent expectation of achieving satisfaction and love. He had never achieved this expectation and knew it was false, but K.'s mother had told him she loved him and promised that her love would make him happy, and that had to be true—clearly K. made use of doublethink.

Overstimulation, the affective storm center of the traumatic situation and of automatic anxiety, comes under the sway of the repetition compulsion in patients who have undergone traumatic experiences. It is found, frequently in disguise and dilution, to be at the root of the psychopathology of soul murder. Because I feel that traumatic overstimulation involves a passive, cannibalistic experience, I have tried to demonstrate this in soul murder victims and rat people. The cannibalism can appear in analytic material in symbolism or allusion, through a cannibalistic animal like the rat. More basic evidence for it are compulsive and repetitive experiences of cannibalistic rage, and the expectation of being the object of cannibalistic attack. This unbearable rage of overstimulation is similar to the "anal rage" described by Bruns-wick,[5] which would be part of everyone's repertory of response, but it has a terrible urgency and power in these victims of soul murder (recall what was said by the homosexual patient C., described in chapter 4, who wanted the analyst to "fuck" him: "If you . . . touch me, . . . I would tear the flesh off your face with my nails"). The anal area has an erogeneity that is so frequently invested with oral sadistic libido. There are probably phylogenetic reasons as well as ontogenetic ones for the anal region to be a route par excellence for cannibalistic attack. One very important consideration I have dealt with at length elsewhere (Shengold 1985, 1988). According to this hypothesis, an elaboration of an idea of R. Fliess (1956), the anal sphincter, anal erogeneity, and anal mechanisms of defense are a vital part of the defensive system of the body ego and the developing one of the psychic ego, and these defensive systems are designed to preserve bodily and psychic integrity.

Any strong bodily excitement derived from internal instinctual access and evoked and enhanced by external stimulation can intensify for a child, and spread to become traumatic overstimulation and an ap-proach to ego dissolution. K.'s mother had habitually fondled and "kissed" his genitals. Pleasurable repetitions of this kind of sexual contact with his homosexual partners were daily occurrences, but the wishful fantasy of the analyst's touching his penis induced a reaction from childhood similar to that Brunswick describes in some children anally overstimulated by enemas: "The child reacts with a tempestu-ous although helpless outburst of rage which can only be likened to orgasm" (1940, p. 273). It would be better to speak of an attempt at or-gasm, for none of the approximations available to the child seems able to bring effective relief—the anal rage certainly does not. This rage derived from feeling too much when unable to do anything about it is terrifying. Another patient, L., recalled that as a child he would reach a frightened agreement with his mother as to the amount of water that would be administered in one of his frequent enemas. "Count to thirty,"

5. "In the nursery one can observe that during the anal period [of development] any stimulation of the anal zone (or in the course of an adult analysis, any stimulation of anal mechanisms or material) may cause a violent outburst of rage" (Brunswick 1940, 273). This involves overstimulation, and the rage is of cannibalistic intensity. Paranoid thinking frequently accompanies this rage, indicating the need to project the rage outside the mind and the self.

the mother would say. But when thirty had been reached, it was always "just three or four more more," then "just a few more," and so on until the child was beside himself. The "helpless rage," automatic anxiety, and painful overstimulation would then be partially passed off with the explosive anal discharge of the enema water. There was also a definite pleasurable element in the anal feelings, especially at the beginning (before the overstimulation). L. once dreamed of being "goosed by two men"—two men are a symbol of the mother according to Fliess (1961). The anal feeling was experienced fully in the dream. "An intolerable pain was felt from my anus all the way through to my penis. I couldn't stand it . . . Yet there was something exquisite about it. I could have killed those men who goosed me."[6] He ground his teeth as he said this.

The model for an outburst of cannibalistic rage past infancy is a severe temper tantrum. Cannibalistic rage, "tempestuous," as Brunswick says, and making the subject feel "helpless," results in an experience of psychic splitting: feeling oneself not only actively furious but subject to the fury and threatened by it. The rage evoked by soul murder experiences brings about and expresses in subsequent repetitions this simultaneous identification with the sadistic, enraged aggressor, and the helpless, terrified reaction of the victim. The regressive intensity of this "splitting" threatens to dissolve boundaries between the self and the other. In the fury, urges to rend flesh and kill accompany feelings of being torn apart and overwhelmed. Like the rat, the patient bites and is bitten. (The seemingly easy psychic availability of the rat imago means that all soul-murder victims have the potential to become rat people.)

Projected Overstimulation, Rage, and Paranoia

As can be seen in my clinical material, one way of dealing with the experience of overstimulation is to project onto the analyst (or someone

6. The danger of the goosing was not so much its evocation of passive homosexuality per se but its power to repeat traumatic anal overstimulation from childhood. (I reiterate that there is a special threat posed by any intensity of feeling that psychically threatens to compromise the functioning of the anal sphincter so needed for body ego defense. As one patient said, "Fucking means murder," and on that primitive level anal fucking is meant.)

else) the role of rat torturer—a role frequently denied in relation to the actual adult overstimulator from childhood. This projection makes for the paranoid, quasi-delusional feeling evidenced in relation to the analyst that all these patients showed at one time or another. With some of them it was occasional, with others it had become a part of their character.[7] The proto-paranoid projection could be expressed as follows in the oral sadistic language of overstimulation: "It is not *I* who want to bite you, it is *you* who want to bite me." Working with these patients can give some insight into the transformation of "I love him" to "I hate him," later followed by "he hates me," seen so regularly in paranoids (see Freud 1911).[8]

C., the homosexual patient who wanted to be anally penetrated by his analyst but then felt that after "one touch" he would tear apart the analyst and himself, was also terrified of loving feelings toward him. We know that to the one with paranoid feelings the "loved" person represents an incestuous object-choice. For the abused child, loving feeling means providing the emotional opening for the abuser (either the parent or one identified with the parent) that leads in unconscious expectation to a danger of being traumatically flooded with sensation and intimations of ego disintegration. The defensive transformation from loving feeling to "I hate him" that follows represents an attempt to maintain ego identity. Because of the ego regression that occurs in these people and because soul murder is usually committed by one parent and not both, one parent usually pushes the other out of the picture emotionally. Both aspects of the Oedipus complex are concentrated on the one parent who has been the abuser and is needed to be the rescuer. To love the person who stands for the soul-murdering parent acquires the meanings of castrating or being castrated by, killing or being killed by, the "loving" contact ("One touch and . . ."). The victim must repudiate the contact that would bring overstimulation and the ego dissolution

7. I see this tendency as an exaggerated, universal one. I definitely do not feel that soul-murder victims, who can vary so despite common defensive characteristics, should categorically be put in the grab-basket of "borderline" diagnoses, which to me is not useful (see chapter 14).
8. "In persecutory paranoia the patient fends off an excessively strong homosexual attachment to some particular person in a special way; and as a result this person whom he loved most becomes a persecutor, against whom the patient directs an often dangerous aggressiveness" (Freud 1923, 43).

of the past, that would threaten to destroy the mental image of the parent as much-needed rescuer (perhaps this is the hardest of all). So the object is distanced with an externalized hatred: I hate him; he is causing me this impossible feeling; he is eating me up. To hate the parent substitute is to try to project away and repudiate the desired, terrifying contact. A compromise that brings about the return of the repressed is reached with "he hates me," for the hated object is ever-present, like the rat ready to invade and attack. But the former soul-murder victim no longer feels open for the attack, and direct contact is avoided. Having been abused as a child can furnish the "kernel of truth," of historic truth, that Freud said is present in paranoid delusions. As is frequently so for paranoid people, the abused child's needed parent is spared, and displaced onto another who becomes the persecutor (the parental imago within is projected).

Patient C., for example, started one analytic session in a state of cannibalistic rage. During the session this became connected with experiences of overstimulation involving incestuous contact with his mother —his head pressed between her legs after she had been exhibitionistically masturbating. C.'s associations began to flow readily, the rage was no longer felt toward the analyst, and, what was rare and difficult for C., he felt grateful toward the analyst. At the end of the hour, as C. was about to leave, his voice was full of tears and affection as he said, "I love you." He then got up from the couch, walked toward the door, which involved turning his back to the analyst, and suddenly (this was a repetitive motif) turned around transformed. That he was feeling "too much" was evident in his tremulousness and facial contortions. Finally, again in the rage that had started the session, he shouted, "I hate you"; it sounded as if this had been torn out of his throat. The heartfelt "I love you" had again left him open to traumatic overstimulation (anal attack) and the immediate transposition to "I hate you" occurred. (This of course also accomplished a defensive shift from the mother, whose loss was threatened by the recovery of memory, to the more easily dispensable analyst.) After this session C. developed a paranoid attitude. He reported the next day that after the analytic hour, he had felt I was like a hypnotist who was putting sexual thoughts into his mind. This sequence of feelings—love, hate, projection—was observed many times in the course of the analysis.

These patients spoke and thought in the language of cannibalism. In their rage they felt an actual remnant of an experience that evoked feelings of eating and being eaten, and intimations of ego dissolution (a nightmare version of Lewin's oral triad). There were other cannibalistic traces: the gnashing and grinding of teeth, fantasies of torment and being tormented, terrible impatience, and the drive for sadistic and masochistic activity.

Despite its enormous destructiveness and seeming inexterminability as a species, the rat is a small creature, and individual rats are easily caught and destroyed. Despite their impulses these patients were not violent or destructive people in action—perhaps partly because their strong unconscious need for punishment ensured that they would turn their aggression predominantly inward, against themselves. The sparing of the object, of the other, was effected primarily to preserve the parent, Big Brother, who was needed for rescue and whose guilt was taken on by the child victim. But other, current "scapegoat" objects were attacked, at least in thought, speech, and impulse, and in fantasy destroyed.[9] When these rat people acted destructively toward others it was in an oblique and diluted fashion. Above all they teased: they freely dispensed mental torture, but only played with physical torture. Here differences in psychic structure of course count. I worried that one of my rat patients (not described in this book), who had once been diagnosed by another analyst as schizophrenic, might lose control and actually harm someone else physically, but this never occurred in the many years the patient was followed. Transference fantasies left no doubt that each of these patients wanted to tear the analyst apart with his or her teeth. Yet as the analyst also stood for the desperately needed parent, he had to be spared. (Only with the working over and eventual integration of the past that successful analysis can give could the murderous impulses toward the analyst really be acknowledged.) This terrible ambivalence characterizes the overwhelming "galloping" transferences with which rat people frequently start their analyses. An alternative start is one of overwhelming, stubborn initial resistance—of massive defense against the transference. All victims of soul murder start out with "too much" to bear. They expect suddenly to be betrayed and traumatized again. They crave the explosive action that will end

9. See Winston Smith's speech quoted in chapter 5: "Do it to Julia! . . . Not me!"

overstimulation, are terrified of it, and do not want to be responsible for it. On entering therapy they are immediately and intensely set up to relive the traumata of childhood. They must defend themselves against the compulsion to repeat.

The ability to contain the overstimulation without being completely overwhelmed makes for a seeming similarity in these patients. For *rat people* as well as *soul murder* are designations that transcend diagnostic categories. Those who are psychotic (surely not uncommon if there is a psychotic parent) would either break down repeatedly or be able somehow, by ego-distorting defenses, to keep together the predetermined "lines of cleavage" (Freud 1933, 59) in their psychic structure. Whether they are psychotic or neurotic (as my patients were), what characterizes rat people is the development of ponderous characterologic defenses, specifically of a chronic, powerful combination of emotional isolation and denial that can make for unauthentic, hollow, "as if" functioning. Ego regression and distortion are present, but at least in my patients the resultant ego was still able to provide strong defenses against the preoedipal, aggression-laden drives. So much energy is directed to defense that the ability to love, work, and be creative is compromised. But the mystery of creative gifts and talents, and the adaptive potential of vertical ego splits, did enable some of the rat people to achieve widely varied kinds of success. I have tried to demonstrate in the clinical excerpts from the cases of these rat people the typical themes found in victims of soul murder: an extraordinary power of disassociation from feeling and experience; autohypnotic states; compromised identity, with vertical ego splitting allowing for phenomena analagous to the doublethink and crimestop of Orwell's *1984*; a paranoid potentiality (if you can't trust your parents, whom can you trust?); superego defenses with simultaneous overpermissiveness and a strong unconscious need for punishment ("to repudiate morality while laying claim to it" [Orwell 1949, 36]). In disguise or nakedly present is a submission to a cruel morality; some massive place in the mind is dedicated to denial in the service of protecting and preserving the soul-murdering parent.

What happened to these patients as children was so terrible that it could not be borne. The experiences of terrible overstimulation made for a kind of life that was like existence in a concentration camp (hence the easy analogy to *1984*). Survival was possible, but only under the conditions of denial of reality and distortion of identity. A special need for denial should alert the analyst not only to the possibility of a very disturbed and regressive ego, but also to the possibility that the patient is one of those who have lived through too much.

8

Autohypnosis

Hypnotic Evasion, Autohypnotic Vigilance, and Hypnotic Facilitation

Psychoanalysis has dealt with alterations in consciousness and hypnosis since its beginning. As a cathartic technique it first involved the therapeutic use of hypnosis, and it developed from a theoretical basis that stressed "hypnoid states" (see Freud and Breuer, 1893–95). There has never been any doubt that there occur altered states of consciousness in hypnotic forms and autohypnosis,[1] but psychoanalysts have not worked out an aesthetically and scientifically satisfactory integrated understanding of their nature.

Hypnosis can be defined as an artificially induced state resembling sleep and characterized by greatly increased suggestibility toward the hypnotizer. It can proceed to various depths, from superficial to deep. These "degrees" of hypnosis also characterize autohypnosis.

The analyst quickly becomes familiar with the phenomenon of hypnosis through hearing requests to be hypnotized from his patients. This passive turning toward the parent figure-analyst ranges in meaning from a longing for symbiotic merger to a desire for sexual submission in intercourse.

I am convinced from my work with patients that conditions of autohypnosis are part of ordinary mental functioning—part of the everyday

---

1. I will not attempt the much-needed classification and description of altered states of consciousness.

range of states of consciousness between deep sleep and full, wide-awake alertness (see Lewin 1950, 1955). It seems however sensible to view as pathological the overuse, prolonged intensity, or excessive duration of autohypnosis. Such pathological use of autohypnosis occurs regularly in victims of soul murder.

Freud expanded Bernheim's theory that hypnotic phenomena are based on the universal susceptibility to suggestion. For Freud (1921) suggestibility was fundamentally the transference onto the hypnotist of an infantile sexual tie. Ferenczi had been the first to hypothecate this; in 1909 he stressed the transference of very early erotic, *masochistic* drives and feelings directed toward the parent to account for the subject's susceptibility to the hypnotist's commands.[2] Transference is obvious in an act of hypnosis performed by a hypnotist on a subject. It is present but hidden in what appears to be "spontaneous" autohypnosis.

Freud believed in a phylogenetic origin for the tendency to be hypnotized. The hypnotist's technique evokes in the subject a predisposition toward compliance to the parent that has survived in the unconscious from the early history of the human family (from the postulated time of the primal horde). This archaic subservience to the primal father (primal parent is a better term) is revived in the course of the individual's development. What is reawakened is "the idea of a paramount and dangerous personality, towards whom only a passive-masochistic attitude is possible, to whom one's will has to be surrendered" (1921, p. 127).

Fliess (1953) observes that by means of the technique of manual "passes" and verbal suggestions, the hypnotist arouses the subject's erogeneity, and uses this sexual excitement to establish a particular kind of transference—a transference that precipitates an identification. This is enhanced by the repeated suggestion to go to sleep delivered by the hypnotist in an authoritative but somnolent tone—it sounds as if the hypnotist were going to sleep. Freud formulates that the hypnotized person identifies by incorporating and depositing the hypnotist as part of the superego. With the exception of the tie with the hypnotist, all contact with the outside world is cut off, and the hypnotist who has taken over some of the functions of the superego can now abolish reality

2. Ferenczi described two kinds of hypnosis: one coaxing and soothing, which he considered modeled on the loving mother lulling the child to sleep (mother hypnosis); the other, threatening, is derived from the father (father hypnosis).

testing. In autohypnosis, of course, the continuing presence of the mental representation of the hypnotist as part of the superego can similarly effect denial from within. (See Weinshel 1986 on the superego's role in reality testing.)

Defensiveness or Mendacity?

Freud observes that there is something pretended and gamelike about hypnosis because its power is really based on the phylogenetic subjection to the primal father. Fliess adds that the hypnotist's command to sleep is pretended—neither the hypnotist who sounds sleepy nor the subject really goes to sleep. This reflects for Fliess the dangerous deceptiveness of the primal parent. According to Freud, "Some knowledge that in spite of everything hypnosis is only a game, a deceptive renewal of these old [primal horde] impressions, may, however, remain behind and take care that there is a resistance against any too serious consequences of the suspension of the will in hypnosis" (1921, p. 127). It has been frequently noticed that these resistances to morally offensive hypnotic suggestions occur despite complete suggestive compliance in other respects; here the "game" has a benevolent effect, preserving the self-protective power of the conscience.

In contrast, for those who have experienced effective soul murder, the encounter with the primal parent-sphinx has resulted in an identification of such *continuing* power that the moral resistance of the conscience has been severely compromised. For them, the gamelike or pretense quality has an effect that is not benevolent but preponderantly malignant and destructive (that is, dangerously deceptive), and the universal tendency to autohypnosis (subjection to the Sphinx deposited within the mind) is enhanced.[3] Schreber defined the term soul murder

3. In a series of publications, Rangell has focused on the functioning of the superego in conflicts centering on what he calls "the syndrome of the compromise of integrity" (see Rangell 1974, 1976, 1980). He sees: "[these] syndromes resulting from the compromise of identity [as] *endogenous to human life* . . . [they] are as diffuse in behaviour and their *ingredients*, as *ubiquitous* in unconscious mentation as are the ingredients which will result in neurosis" (1974, p. 7; my italics). Rangell describes as follows the syndrome of the compromise of identity (which incidentally resembles Orwell's doublethink): "A combined

by analogy with hypnosis: "A person's nervous system [is] influenced by another's to the extent of imprisoning his will power, such as occurs during hypnosis; in order to stress forcefully that this was a malpractice it was called 'soul murder' " (MacAlpine and Hunter 1955, 35).

Lewin (1955) depicts "the analytic situation [as] an altered hypnotic situation, as the analytic hour is an altered hypnotic session" (p. 169), and he enjoins us to be aware of "the ratio between sleep and waking in the analytic patient" (1955, p. 198). He portrays the analyst as the waker or arouser, who sometimes also soothes (puts the analysand to sleep a little). A range of states of consciousness in the analyst as well as in the patient is described as normal by McLaughlin (1975). Fliess (1953) describes the subtlety of the autohypnotic phenomena that occur in analysis. The analysand, instead of associating freely, can escape into a first degree of hypnosis that can go unnoticed by both patient and analyst. This makes for a kind of contact that precludes responsibility for what is said and felt; it amounts, says Fliess, to "hypnotic evasion."

A regressive shift away from full, clear consciousness can principally serve either the ego's need to defend against drive tensions or its need to further their discharge. (An example of the latter would be the approach to a loss of consciousness at the moment of orgasm.) In performing either a primarily defensive or a primarily releasing function, shifts in states of consciousness are carrying out the basic psychic tasks we assign to the ego—the mediation between the drive representations of the id and those of the external world, the screening out and letting through of instinctual drive representations. Fliess (1953) and Dickes (1965) stress the defensive use of autohypnosis against libidinal and aggressive impulse (Fliess's *hypnotic evasion*). Stein (1965) clearly describes shifts in consciousness as defensive in relation to trauma. In a paper (1967) I note autohypnotic phenomena that transcend the defensive function, and use the term *hypnotic facilitation*. Gill and Brenman (1959) mention "the appearance of vivid and intense outbursts of feeling" (p. 48) occuring during hypnosis, and describe it as a frequently noted phenomenon. I will not try to bring up to date Dickes's excellent review of the literature on shifts of consciousness.

---

mechanism of distortion, denial, rationalization, *deception of the self and others* [which] bridges across [the] unconscious, preconscious and conscious" (1974, p. 9; my italics). I believe that autohypnosis is one of the endogenous, ubiquitous ingredients that supplies part of the mechanism for the "syndrome."

Autohypnotic Vigilance

A young woman, M., who as a child of five had been seduced by an adult man, was subject to repetitive, contradictory symptomatic states that involved alterations of consciousness. During these periods of perceptible autohypnosis, there was a simultaneous shutting off of emotion and perception and a hypersensitive seeking and awareness of certain signals that to M. meant the possible reliving of the trauma from childhood. She could at the same moment both block out and be hyperaware of inner reality, outer reality, or both. Sometimes this manifested itself by her insisting on the figure while ignoring the ground; sometimes by being overconcerned with the surroundings but neglecting the central, meaningful event. She was therefore both an expert witness, even a sensitive detective preternaturally alert to clues, and a completely unreliable observer. Her predominantly good character included transient paranoid suspiciousness and masochistic, guilt-ridden self-doubt. Sometimes simultaneously and sometimes alternately she played the roles of Cassandra and of that unfortunate woman's disbelieving audience.

M. reported one day that she had left the previous analytic session feeling "sleepy and out of things." She had been in a characteristic hypnoid state: "I didn't even know how to open the door or whether to leave it open; it was as if I weren't quite there, and I had no awareness of you or of leaving your office. And yet when I went out into the waiting room, I heard the sound of a man urinating from the bathroom. I am sure it was a man—from the sound. And before that, as I was closing the door, you had a phone call and I heard the change in your voice. You weren't talking to a patient, but to someone you didn't want to hear from."

M. was as usual right. I was by this time familiar with her not knowing what was going on and her concurrent, uncanny accuracy about perceptual details. The patient whom I had seen just after her on the previous day had been a man; he reported to me that he had urinated before coming into his session. Just as M. was closing the door to my office, I had received a telephone call from an insurance salesman, and although the young woman could only have heard me say "hello" and perhaps "no," I had *not* welcomed the call. Despite the patient's alteration of consciousness, her perceptions had been accurate and registered almost instantaneously.

As a child of five, M. was seduced to perform fellatio after she opened a bathroom door on a man who was urinating. His anger at the intruder ("someone you didn't want to hear from") turned to sexual excitement, and he started to masturbate. The girl especially remembered the sound of his excited breathing. She was "fascinated—as if hypnotized" by this exhibition and was easily induced to suck on the man's penis. When M. first reported this incident she had not yet remembered the terrifying overstimulation and shock that ended this initially tolerable and even pleasurable contact. Despite the terror, the sexual encounter was repeated several times. The man was a relative, a father-substitute who lived for a time in the large family house; part of his duty was looking after the children.

In later life M.'s autohypnosis blocked the sexual excitement that could have resulted from perceptions unconsciously linked to the memory of the earlier seductions. At the same time the hypnosis was compatible with a concentrated hypercathexis of perceptory signals and perhaps even enhanced it; that is, there was a *hypnotic vigilance*. M. often listened intently for sounds of the analyst's breathing and was aware of nuances of change. These would evoke a "sleepy feeling," or increase it if it were already present, and she would often say something like, "I am aware of the breathing, but now it's almost as if you aren't even there."

I believe this is an instance of a symptomatic state that is not uncommon: simultaneous hypnotic evasion and hypnotic facilitation. The alteration of consciousness as M. left the session both warded off and repeated the past (see Fliess 1953; Dickes 1965; Shengold 1967). The hypercathected listening and watchfulness also functioned dually; for defense against derivatives of instinctual drive (here, voyeuristic excitement) and for their discharge. For M. to be seduced while she was hypnotized meant that she was passive and therefore not responsible for what had happened and what was happening. (Like all soul-murder victims I have studied, M. had to spare the aggressor and take on the guilt for the seductions; this had in time become the mainstay of her masochistic character.) The excited beginning of the seduction was easier to repeat than was the subsequent terror, overstimulation, and rage. Ultimately, it was the overwhelming fear associated with M.'s rage—a rage that could reach the pitch of wanting to bite and kill—that was evaded by the hypnosis. The analysis clearly brought out the evolution of the wish to suck the penis into the wish to bite it off—

castration by biting followed by the expectation of terrible retaliation. (There was an even deeper fear of the sheer annihilative intensity of her rage—a more primal reaction to overstimulation.) The alteration in consciousness also served to keep out of conscious awareness the incestuous object of M.'s feelings (the fantasied parent in the guise of the actual seducer). There was a compulsion to repeat the past traumatic events, and the expectation of repetition made for a characteristic alertness to signals (for M., especially auditory signals) as part of a generalized watchfulness that was compatible with autohypnosis.

I have frequently found hypnotic facilitation to account for part of the significance of autohypnotic phenomena. Hypnosis allows for the attainment of a forbidden satisfaction without responsibility for it; the latter is at least the conscious intention. This is marvelously illustrated in a short story by Balzac, "The Venial Sin" (one of his *Droll Stories*), in which a boy is seduced by a woman who pretends she is asleep. I will return to this story.

Hypnotic Facilitation: Patient N.

Balzac's story was mentioned to me by N., who in the course of the analysis recognized something of himself in it. Although in his thirties, N. still lived with his seductive and psychotic mother, who did everything she could to keep her son from moving out. During the analysis he remembered that as a child he had been seduced by his mother in a variety of bizarre ways, which included her playing with and sucking on his penis, but usually centered on her manual invasion of his anus, frequently in connection with extended enema rituals. He simultaneously identified with his mother and was tied to her as a sexual object—in disguised fantasy. His sexual experiences, casual and joyless, were exclusively with women. N.'s masturbatory fantasies were sometimes homosexual and sometimes heterosexual. (This involved being and having his mother; of course he was not initially conscious of this.) But N.'s masturbation usually could culminate in orgasm only if he lapsed into an altered state of awareness that strongly resembled the first stage of hypnosis.

It was many (seemingly unproductive) years into the analysis before he acknowledged the autohypnotic states. Unlike most of the soul-murder victims I have seen, N. had been quite aware of these states and accused himself of "deceptiveness" for not having told his analyst about them before. Indeed, he went on to describe the masturbation performed under autohypnosis as being "[full of] fraudulence. It involves pretending that it is happening to me rather than that I am doing it to myself. [N. was *actively* reproducing predominantly *passive* traumatic experiences.] And when I do it I feel *half-asleep* [these are the same words used by Shakespeare's Desdemona: see note 4, below], so in effect I have no responsibility for it, I feel in a fog about the whole thing." The pleasure of his orgasm when N. was "half-asleep" was compromised: "It's not satisfactory because it is done under a ruse— it's too sudden and too short and I feel immediately discontented with it. It's different from the fuller feeling I get when I'm wide awake and know that I am masturbating." Here hypnotic evasion and facilitation coexisted, and the sexual discharge that related to forbidden impulses was allowed to occur but in a compromised way.

In the middle phase of his analysis, N. had become involved with intense sexual feelings about his analyst, feelings that were transferred mainly from the psychotic, "phallic" mother of his childhood whose contacts he was remembering. These feelings were being worked out as he was also communicating first the existence and then the extent of his autohypnosis. He discovered that the full feeling of erogeneity could abolish the hypnosis: "Last night I was standing near a kiosk. Why did I use that foreign term—I think it's *French*—instead of newsstand? I became aware I was in hypnosis and I was staring at a TV magazine with a picture of a good-looking doctor from a soap opera on the cover. The headline said, 'Everybody's *Son* the Doctor.' I realized the sexual excitement about him. I got an erection and that snapped me out of the hypnosis." N.'s fantasy was of fellatio (in slang, "French" sex—actually both the French word *kiosque* and the English *kiosk* are derived from a Turkish word, and Turkey was associated with N.'s mother's family) and directed at his own doctor-parent, but he was simultaneously in fantasy the parent performing fellatio on the "son."

During this period N. had a dream. He started a session as follows:

I feel sleepy. As I was coming in I thought, if I'm sleepy, I can't get sexually excited. I had an orgasm last night, but I guess I'm still in heat because all week I have tried not to masturbate. When I went to bed last night, I felt hypnotic [M. had by now adopted the analyst's term]. I had the thought, "If I'm half-asleep, I'm not responsible." So I started to masturbate, but didn't finish. I remember hoping that a wet dream would finish it off for me. Then, after the dream, which wasn't a wet one, I did masturbate when I was still half-asleep. I woke from the dream with an erection. Here's the dream:

I was to be analyzed with a different analyst. There was a couch or a stretcher. [N. had on the previous day visited a relative who had been hospitalized after suffering some rectal bleeding; he had found him in a hallway lying on a stretcher.] The analysis was to take place in the open air. I had the thought, "This is like being analyzed by a friend." I then woke with an erection.

N. then associated: "I don't really want another analyst, but I don't want to have these sexual feelings about you. 'The open air'—it reminds me of what I told you about masturbating 'against the air.' "

N. had an unusual masturbatory practice involving trying to have an ejaculation without using his hands, lying on his back, moving his penis up and down, as he put it, "against the air." (Here N. revealed his characteristic preconscious mendaciousness when dealing with his conflicted sexuality: because masturbation is defined as manual self-stimulation, not using his hands meant that what he was doing did not have to count as masturbation.) A variation was moving his pelvis and penis up against a sheet or blanket ("material" symbolizing mother). These experiences, which never did culminate in ejaculation without his resorting finally to manipulation, involved movements of his hips and buttocks that induced anal feelings and excitement. Frequently there was also the conscious fantasy of visualizing a woman's body, especially her behind. The seductive "air" represented the active partner who was to bring the passive patient (identified with the woman and her cloacal parts) to climax. N. associated the "open air" with "being blown." The phantomlike, invisible, "airy" presence was also a kind of denial of the past reality of his mother's having "blown" him. These masturbatory experiences reproduced a teasing, overstimulating sexual contact evoking phallic but especially anal excitement; a repetition of the incestuous contact from childhood, when N. could not ejaculate and satisfactorily discharge the anal and genital overexcitement. As an adult, the increasing unpleasure of the overstimulation would finally make manual stimulation mandatory, and the resultant orgasm would "break" the fantasy; N. could then "wake up." The orgasm was a relief, but always a disappointment.

At the beginning of the session, N. was chiefly evading his own passive anal excitement—his wish to be the person with the bloody anus on
a stretcher. Even more distant was the murderous rage at the enforced
passivity; this rage was associated with the wish to get rid of the analyst.
In the course of his associations N. talked of having pictured before the
dream "a kind of prostitute I once picked up. I had intercourse with
her, but it was no good. I was left with the vivid image of her lifting up
her knees onto her chest. I was revolted and disgusted by the sight of
her anus and the dirtiness around it, a brown, discolored area. I never
wanted to see her again." N. then told me that for the last few months
he had worn pajamas to bed instead of his dirty underwear, which was
usually slightly stained by feces. The slight staining was due to "continuous sweating" around his anus, which he attributed in part to the
habitual, periodic "steeling" of his perineal muscles, which alternated
with their relaxation. This unconscious anal play (which resembled the
perianal movements in his masturbating "against the air") made for
a rather constant need to evade the concomitant anal excitement, and
this defensive requirement seemed to go along with the almost continuous intensity of his autohypnosis. (For N. the hypnotic evasion also
seemed to be a chief mechanism for his impressive, characteristic defensive ability to isolate both his emotions—including rage and vague
paranoid feelings—and his responsibility for his actions. Clearly, this
was also an anal ability; see Shengold 1988.)

Several days before the dream N.'s apartment had been robbed (his
"room" entered, an anal invasion). When going out to his analysis,
he had left his keys in his mailbox, denoting the apartment to which
the keys belonged. Also, he had left behind his wallet, full of recently
counted bills, on the table in his room "in open view" (symbolizing
his anus and rectum "in the open air"). N. realized that he had invited the theft. During the session in which he recounted his dream
of "open-air" analysis, he suddenly interjected, "Now I realize that I
was in hypnosis when I left my keys in my mailbox." The analyst was
the one he had unconsciously invited to penetrate his "room," and N.
was unconsciously acting out the role of the dirty, "anal" prostitute.
(The roles were reversible: it was he who paid the analyst.) N.'s "hypnoid state" had facilitated the theft but defended him against the body
feelings and emotions associated with what he was reenacting.

During this period of the analysis N. also told me about the story
by Balzac that he found particularly exciting and had often read while

masturbating. Although the story is about what is described as a simulation of sleep ("deceptiveness") and not necessarily about a true hypnotic state, it illustrates the symptomatic nature of alterations of consciousness, which range from mild hypnosis to deep sleep. (Before this session N. had not been responsibly aware that the story of the seduction of a boy represented a repetition of his own past.)

"The Venial Sin"

In Balzac's tale, a young woman, Blanche, virginal and knowing nothing about sex, is married to an impotent old man. When she realizes that he cannot father a child, she consults her confessor; he tells her the story of Sainte Lidoire, who

> went to sleep terribly soundly one very hot day with one leg here and the other there and very little on and a young man full of evil came up and very slyly filled her with child and as the saint was utterly ignorant that this wicked thing had been done to her she was very surprised indeed after some time to have to take to childbed. She had thought the swelling of her pouch must be some serious ailment. Now, Ste. Lidoire did penance as for a mere venial sin, since she had had no pleasure from the wicked act, as the evil man himself bore out, for at the gallows when the noose was round his neck, he declared that the saint never even budged.
>
> "Oh, Father," said Blanche, "you may be sure I shall not budge any more than Ste. Lidoire did." (pp. 53–54)

Blanche decides to seduce a young page of fourteen. She does this by pretending to be asleep as he reads to her, sitting at her feet and looking up at her lap. There is much hesitation—Blanche finds it necessary to say to the page with her eyes closed, "Go on René . . . I am asleep, you know" (p. 59). The page then realizes her intention:

> that very same evening . . . [René the page] went seeking and, finding Blanche asleep, forthwith made her dreams very lovely ones. So thoroughly indeed did he ravish that which agonized her, and with such good husbandry did he sow his baby seed that there was really enough left over to have made a couple more, when suddenly the dear woman squeezed her page by the head, crushed him to her, and cried: "Oh, René, you woke me up!"

True enough, no sleep could have survived that onslaught, and Blanche and René together concluded that the saints must sleep very soundly indeed. (1832, p. 59)

Blanche experienced a kind of healthy, erotic hyperawareness that is in contrast to the defensive and punitive dimming of pleasure of N. and qualitatively different from the defensive vigilance of M. The mendaciousness (of the primal parent) inherent to the hypnotic state is present in Balzac's story. The young woman, an adult, blames the "sin" on the fourteen-year-old page (child)—*she* was "asleep": "Come now, René! Do you realize that while I have only committed venial sins, because I was asleep, you have got mortal sins on your conscience?" (p. 60). Despite the sunny, Rabelaisian comic tone, the soul murderer's shifting of guilt onto the child is clearly evoked here. In the story, the defensive hypnotic evasion is the predominant motivation; but the alleged shift in consciousness is used to facilitate the "discharge of libido." When Blanche's old husband refuses to believe that "the page could get in [your hole] without waking you" (p. 63), she replies: "Of course I felt it, and nicely too, but, you see, as you never taught me what it was, I thought I was only dreaming" (p. 63).

Freud (1899) wrote to Fliess about a contrasting example, a story told to him that seems to involve a true hypnotic state:

An important and wealthy man (a bank director), aged about sixty, came to see me and entertained me with the peculiarities of a young girl with whom he has a *liaison*. I threw out the guess that she was probably quite anaesthetic. On the contrary, she has from four to six orgasms during a single coitus. *But—at the very first approach she is seized with a tremor and immediately afterwards falls into a pathological sleep; while she is in this she talks as though she was in hypnosis, carries out post hypnotic suggestions, and has complete amnesia for the whole condition.* He is going to marry her off, and she will certainly be anaesthetic with her husband. The old gentlemen, through the possibility of being identified with the powerful father of her childhood, evidently has the effect of being able to set free the libido attached to her phantasies. Instructive! (pp. 277–278; my italics)

The libido was "set free" and the multiple orgasms achieved only with use of the simultaneously defensive and facilitating state of "hypnosis."

A Clinical Example of Defensive and Facilitating Autohypnosis

Once M., the vigilant hypnotic, had failed to pay her bill at the end of the month, which was unusual for her. Then the analyst had to cancel several sessions without prior notice because of illness—a most unusual occurrence in the analysis. When the analysis was resumed, M. came into the office, and instead of handing the analyst a check in her usual fashion—tentatively, passively, almost dropping it—she thrust it out at him aggressively. On the couch, she began:

> I felt like shoving the money at you, and yet I was so glad to see you. I was worried when your phone service called [another unexpected and unwelcome telephone call] to say you were not going to be here. I thought either you were sick or *someone had died*. But you looked so nice at the door; you looked like you had just had a haircut, like a little child all dressed up for his birthday. It made me feel good to see you.
>
> Analyst: You felt good *and bad* to see me.
>
> Patient: Why did you say that? I only had good feelings towards you. [long silence] Where did you get the bad feelings from?
>
> Analyst: What about your "shoving the money at me"?
>
> Patient: *Oh, as I was listening to you just now I felt as if I were falling asleep.* And at first I didn't know what you were talking about. I forgot that I had said that to you. How strange!
>
> Analyst: It does seem strange that you have to go to sleep to keep from hearing me repeat what you were able to say to me seemingly with full awareness.
>
> Patient: Well what *I* say isn't so meaningful; when you say it, it counts.

This patient was characteristically most threatened by her destructive impulses (oral and anal) and their resultant "bad" feelings. In thrusting the money at the analyst, she was reversing her passivity in relation to the man from her childhood who had thrust his erect penis out for her to suck. The incident from the past was connected with a destructive fury that terrified her; such fury could castrate and kill, and this proved to be what most demanded hypnotic defense—feeling "as if I were falling asleep".[4] The anger is suppressed, the positive side of her

4. Dickes (1965) pointed out a similar instance of hypnosis being called sleep in Shakespeare's *Othello*. Desdemona is reacting to the devastating verbal (oral)

ambivalence is stressed, the analyst looks "so nice." This idealization is the reactive disguise for a devaluation—the analyst is reduced to a birthday child with a haircut (presumably the younger brother whose birth displaced her as the family's center of attention; she had wanted more than his hair cut off). When the analyst underlines her "bad" aggressive feelings ("someone had died"), she greets this with an isolating silence. When he reminds her of her aggressive "thrusting" action, she resorts to hypnosis to cancel out both the responsibility for the impulse and (especially) the potential for experiencing in feeling the terrible intensities involved. Finally, she gives a wise explanation of why the analyst's repetition of her words affects her more than her initial confession of the "shoving" impulse. (M. is not aware that the repeating is an erotic "rubbing.") She has made the analyst responsible for what she feels and what she says; his verbal repetition is an oral invasive thrust (like the phone call and the interpretations); these invasions evoke the past trauma and must be evaded by autohypnosis. And simultaneously, the hypnosis furnishes an absence (a blank space also supplied by her protracted silence), which could facilitate a repetition of the sexual assault of the past. After the session M. realized and later reported that she had wanted to suck the analyst's penis when she first saw him at the door. It took much more analysis for her to become responsibly conscious, to "own," that she also wanted to bite and swallow it. (For more about M. see chapter 14.)

Autohypnosis in both its defensive and facilitating effects works in the service of denial: what is allowed to happen does not count. It is regularly employed by the soul-murder victim to spare the soul murderer and to repeat the childhood trauma, directly and in attenuation.

---

attack of the half-crazed, jealous Othello, which culminates with his ironic: "I cry you mercy then: / I took you for that cunning whore of Venice / That married with Othello (IV.2. 88–90). When Othello leaves and Emilia asks Desdemona, "How do you, my good lady?" she replies, "*Faith, half asleep*" (my italics; compare patient N.). The "Faith" shows the denial of the betrayal, and the "half asleep" screens out the oral rage of the black man (the father in the dark), primarily in an attempt to deny what had just happened; secondarily it dilutes Desdemona's own *reactive* rage. For my patient M., getting away from her own potentially murderous anger ("someone had died") seemed to be the main motive for the autohypnosis; she was also denying the aggressiveness she attributed to the analyst, who had previously handed her the bill, invaded her by means of the telephone call (an oral and aural penetration), and betrayed her by disappearing.

The original traumata of ten occurred under conditions that evoked autohypnosis; the altered state of consciousness then reappears whenever the traumatized subject is obeying an unconscious compulsion to repeat the past events.[5] Because autohypnosis is often there without the patient's awareness, it must be anticipated and looked for by the therapist. The inherent, concomitant evasion of responsibility for what is being said, thought, and felt makes autohypnosis a formidable, resistance to analysis in any patient, and if not recognized an insurmountable one. Autohypnosis affects reality testing by both ego and superego (see Weinshel 1986). Where hypnotic alterations of consciousness exist to an extensive degree, it may be evidence of brainwashing—or, in Orwell's terms, of enforced doublethink. Autohypnosis can operate as part of the mechanism for the isolating, mind-splitting defenses involved in what psychoanalysts call *denial*: the nonregistration or blanking out of what is happening and what has happened. And where doublethink and autohypnosis flourish, one should look out for soul murder.

Countertransference, Counteridentification, and Autohypnosis

"Anal defensiveness" involves a panoply of defenses evolved during the anal phase of psychic development that culminates with the individual's power to reduce anything that is meaningful to "shit"—to the nominal,

---

5. After completing most of this book I read the English translation published in 1988 of Ferenczi's clinical diary (Ferenczi 1932). In these private notes Ferenczi foreshadowed much that I have written about the effects of sexual abuse on the child victim, as he did in the paper of 1933 from which I have quoted above. In the diary Ferenczi specifically deals with autohypnotic states (termed by him "trance"; see pp. 29, 30, 55) that occur during as well as after the child's traumatic seduction or rape by an adult. He also describes defensive vertical splits in the ego (called "fragmentation," pp. 38–42, as well as "splits," pp. 62, 63), and massive emotional isolation that I characterize as the result of anal narcissistic regression (Ferenczi writes of states of "not-being or not-wanting-to-be," p. 40, and, of "giving up the ghost," which is more regressive p. 39). Whatever doubts one has concerning some of Ferenczi's generalizations about pathogenesis and technique, his clinical descriptions are convincing and most valuable.

the degraded, the undifferentiated. Part of the defensive effect is accomplished by means of shifts of consciousness and autohypnosis. Dr. Brian Robertson reports:

Very early in my analytic career, I took into analysis a young married woman (a mother with two young daughters). She had sought help originally over a rather mild, though persistent, depression and for fears that she would harm her children. Of note is that she had no conscious recollection of what turned out to have been her horrendous childhood and seemed the product of a rather conventional middle-class home. One fact did stand out. Her mother had been a psychiatric patient who had had a number of admissions to various hospitals for a paranoid illness. I felt the patient to be suffering from depression, secondary to guilt over persistent oedipal conflicts linked to incestuous wishes toward a rather seductive father.

Soon after she entered psychoanalytic treatment I found myself, after about ten minutes or so of each session, rapidly losing my concentration and becoming sleepy. This happened persistently and with a shocking (I felt as I realized it) regularity. In retrospect, of course, I see that she made use of a particular manner of speech, in a particular tone, the droning "peculiar, expressionless hypnotic tone" to which Shengold referred. In my self-analysis, after many vicissitudes, I was able to associate to a particular nursing assistant on my ward—at that time I was in charge of an admitting ward in a local mental hospital—whose nickname amongst the staff was "Mother." She was so named because of her well-known talent for handling very severely disturbed and aggressive psychotic patients without recourse to undue medication or physical restraint. Recalling the psychotic illness of my patient's mother, I wondered aloud as to whether, when she was a child, she had ever had to comfort or soothe her mother. Indeed, this *had* been a major activity of her childhood. We then began to explore the story of a childhood of terrible abuse, the details of which and their psychic ramifications occupied the bulk of the analysis, especially as manifested in the transference. My patient on the couch had been (with the transference) in the presence of a murderous, extremely dangerous, cunning and psychotic "analyst-mother." Unconsciously it was kill or be killed, and the hypnotic drone of her voice (coupled with her associations, that were a form of defensive—dissociative and isolating—list making) protected her from her murderous rage toward me as the analyst-mother, and represented an attempt to soothe me. At the same time she effectively "murdered" my ability to analyze. [This last observation implicitly recognizes the presence of "hypnotic facilitation" as well as of "hypnotic evasion."] As a child, she had had a closet in her bedroom to which she would retreat, often in fear of her life. This closet also symbolized a secret place, the container within her that both kept her alive, and kept her psychotic mother out. It goes without saying that she had kept herself in an intrapsychic version of that closet, isolated from others and from her reactions to them, to ward off a world that for her remained both psychotic and murderous. Only her children had been allowed to break through, fortunately, causing her to seek treatment. (italics in original)[6]

The walling in of that defensive "closet" (the mental compartment so familiar to students of obsessional mechanisms, and so massively isolated in soul-murder victims) was accomplished in large part by autohypnosis. And, Robertson tells us, the hypnosis was transmitted to the analyst. I have found in supervising analysts and in my own cases that this kind of "putting the analyst to sleep" happens much more frequently than has been written about. As I have stated, the hypnotic defense is universal. We all have had recourse to shifts in consciousness to ward off the traumatic. The murderous confrontation between parent and child that constitutes soul murder is the source of the deepest resistance—and not only in the patient who has been involved; the analyst too must be aware of how difficult it is to face and to own feelings of intense hostility toward the parent and from the parent. Here the preoedipal and oedipal terrors merge: the oedipus complex is about patricide and matricide as well as about incest.

6. Dr. Brian Robertson has given me permission to quote some of his remarks on autohypnosis made in Montreal at a meeting of the Canadian Psychoanalytic Society in 1985 when he discussed one of my papers on "anal defensiveness" (Shengold 1985).

CHAPTER

9

A Case of Incest between Mother
and Adolescent Son

This chapter is a metaphorical bridge of speculation that connects mystery to mystery, the known with the unknown. My bridge is like a single plank that requires the support of others to form a firm foundation. I am presenting a case history of an interrupted analysis. The patient ran off before a natural termination or even the consolidation of the analytic work could be achieved. I treated him very early in my career; my records are inadequate; my skill was probably also inadequate. The justification for presenting and publishing this case history is that its rarity makes it a potential bridge to three areas about which there is much to learn: (1) incestuous action, its causes and consequences; (2) the impact on the adolescent of consummated incest; and (3) the effect of soul murder of the child on the adolescent's sexuality and incest barrier.

The metaphor of the bridge is relevant to incest in adolescence. Anna Freud views adolescence as a "bridge between the diffuse infantile and the genitally centered adult sexuality" (1958, p. 138). And there is something inherently incestuous about the bridge as a symbol, according to Ferenczi (1921a, b) and Sigmund Freud (1933), who felt that the bridge symbolizes the male genital, the father's penis, which can be observed by the child as connecting the father to the mother in the primal scene. The bridge is often associated with water, a symbol of birth. For the child of either sex, acquiring the paternal phallus would provide the bridge that could bring the child back to the mother and her womb. Freud (1933) pointed out that the bridge can denote any kind of transition in life and that its use as a symbol has a special rela-

tion to birth and death. Birth, death, and incest all involve going back
to the mother's womb. As D. H. Lawrence wrote after the death of his
mother:

> My little love, my darling,
> You were a doorway to me:
> You let me out of the confines
> Into this strange countrie
> Where people are crowded like thistles,
> Yet are shapely and comely to see.
>
> My little love, my dearest,
> Twice you have issued me,
> Once from your womb, sweet mother,
> Once from your soul, to be
> Free of all fears my darling,
> Of each heart's entrance free.
>
> And so, my love, my mother,
> I shall always be true to you.
> Twice I am born, my dearest:
> To life and to death, in you;
> And this is the life hereafter
> Wherein I am true. (1913, pp. 83–84)

The poet sees his mother as both the liberator and the confiner of his
soul and his sexual identity. Her body is the child's bridge to the other
worlds, the worlds before birth and after death. The title of Lawrence's
poem "The Virgin Mother" shows the symbiosis: the Son and Virgin
Mother are fused as in a pietà. The poem ends:

> Is the last word now uttered?
> Is the farewell said?
> Spare me the strength to leave you
> Now you are dead.
> I must go, but my *soul* lies helpless
> Beside your bed. (pp. 84–85; my italics)

For those who like Lawrence are incestuously bound, even the loss of
the mother's body through death is not enough to set their souls free.

It was from the vantage point of the son in analysis many years later
that the story I am telling of incest between mother and adolescent

son was remembered and reconstructed ("reassembled" is Isay's happy choice of word; see Isay 1975, 536). Little has been written about the reconstructions of adolescence from the analysis of an adult (1975, p. 536), and even less about cases of incest between mother and adolescent son. I do not know of a psychoanalytic study of such incest, and even published accounts of therapy or casual observatiion are scarce, with the son-partner usually described as psychotic or very near it (see Wahl 1960); my patient was neurotic, like virtually all of us. Peter Blos (1965) wondered about the contrast between the "almost nonexistent mother/son incest during the adolescent years . . . [and] the relatively frequent occurrence of father/daughter incest" (p. 153).

First mystery: why should this be so? Is it because most psychiatrists are male and deeply resist uncovering or publishing anything about the fulfillment of the male's characteristic, forbidden oedipal wish? I surely cannot dismiss this resistance, because I have felt its power. It has been a struggle to think about and write this patient's story, and the reader will have noted the apologetic tone with which I began it. On several occasions when a male colleague asked me what I was working on, one of us eventually noticed that the conversation had unaccountably shifted to the subject of father-daughter incest. I believe nonetheless that incest between mother and adolescent son is rare, and that there are psychological reasons for this, having to do with the primal importance of the mother for the child of either sex (the shadow of the preoedipal becoming attached to the oedipal mother), and, more specifically and more speculatively, the special forbiddenness of the wish to impregnate the mother. (I feel that more horror is provoked in both sexes by the son's impregnation of the mother than by the father's impregnation of the daughter; more of this later.) As for incestuous contact between parent and prepubescent child, where the child would usually take the passive role and where there be no question of impregnation, my guess is that there is no statistically significant difference between the incidence of contact with boys and the incidence of contact with girls. Incest in adolescence, although often following earlier incest in individual cases, is a qualitatively different phenomenon. The physiological maturation that makes orgasm and impregnation possible brings concomitant psychological changes (including a burgeoning of sexual and specifically oedipal fantasy). What before evoked inevitable overstimulation (as in the case histories given so far) can after puberty be dealt with by discharge; this potentiality can also make containment of excitement easier. Although relief has become attainable in adolescence (most frequently of course through masturbation), still the physiological increase in excitement can occasionally or even frequently make for the feeling of too-muchness. Children who have been the victims of soul murder, either through direct seduction or by a turning toward sexualization to try to hold on to the abusive and negligent parent, have already experienced sexual too-muchness before puberty. And for them, the possibility of orgastic discharge brings a much needed promise of relief. Unfortunately, the forbiddenness of the murderous and incestuous intensities sometimes inhibits use of the potentiality for what should be a healthy, at least transient, alleviation. For the boy, the potential use of the phallic bridge to the mother makes possible a specific kind of reversal from passivity to activity; but this feeling of activity also increases his sense of responsibility, his castration anxiety, and his guilt.

Freud presented the concept of the oedipus complex as the core of normal and of neurotic psychological development. He described the sexual and initially incestuous drive as occurring in two waves: one forming and developing over the first five or six years of life, followed by a latent period and then by a reprise of earlier development, accompanied this time by the somatic and psychological changes of puberty. The adolescent has the task of transcending the destructive preoedipal quality of the incestuous wishes and of loosening the incestuous connections by turning away from the parents to other emotional and sexual partners. Yet we know how powerfully the oedipal wishes continue to function throughout life. This has been well described with clinical material from the analysis of middle-aged parents by Rangell (1955, 1970): "The Oedipus complex has a continuous and dynamic line of development, from its earliest origin through various phases in the life of man, and the described phenomena are but stages in this continual moving stream. By no means is it an event which plays a tumultuous but rather short-lived role limited to the phallic scene of the play of life, but it is rather a constantly reappearing character which comes across the stage in new and changing roles progressing with the ages of man" (1970, p. 332).[1]

1. This statement is consistent with Abrams's concept of "oedipal phase organization" (1978, p. 398): a developmental transformation that entails not only a phase of instinctual conflict and potential pathogenesis but also positive

Before he formulated the oedipus complex, Freud had based his for-
mulations of mental illness on incestuous actions (see chapter 1). He
later doubted some of his patients' stories of seduction, and with re-
inforcement from his self-analysis discovered that universal fantasies
of being seduced are part of childhood sexuality; this led him to for-
mulate the oedipus complex. Viewing the "innumerable peculiarities
of the erotic life of human beings" (1905, p. 239), he saw that both
wish and deed contribute to psychopathology: "Psychoanalytic investigation shows, however, how intensely the individual struggles with the
temptation to incest during his period of growth and how frequently
the barrier is transgressed in fantasy *and even in reality*" (Freud 1905,
p. 225; my italics). Freud added this note to the *Three Essays* in 1915—
Dr. Masson take note!

There is indeed a return to the primacy of incestuous action in *Totem
and Taboo* (1913), but the acts of incest and father murder are trans-
posed back to racial prehistory. (One can speculate that Freud's motivation was in part defensive.) Freud's "bungled action" (1901, 177) of
putting the wrong medicine in the eye of a ninety-year-old lady in-
directly brought in his own incestuous wish toward "the old woman"
(p. 177). This was accomplished by way of his thoughts toward a young
male patient, who had a dream that to Freud obviously referred to
intercourse with the patient's mother. In a footnote, Freud mentioned
Jocasta's disclaimer in *Oedipus Rex* about mother-son incest:

> Nor need this mother-marrying bother you;
> Many a man has dreamt as much. Such things
> Must be forgotten if life is to be endured.
>   (Watling, trans., p. 52)

Freud commented: "The strange fact that the [Oedipus] legend finds
nothing objectionable in Queen Jocasta's age seemed to me to fit in
well with the conclusion that in being in love with one's own mother
one is *never* concerned with her as she is in the present but with her
youthful mnemic image carried over from one's childhood" (p. 178;
my italics). The "never" is too strong—a denial or negation in what
is an uncharacteristically absolute statement by Freud. Freud's defensive need (in 1901) would seem to have been in the service of denying

———
achievements—integration and synthesis of object relations, balance of libidinal and aggressive drive, and ego and superego maturation (see Abrams 1977).

any current possibility of the deed, and Freud here is unconsciously reinforcing reductive denial of the act by the "old woman" Jocasta to the dream-wish. (Freud's old mother was still alive and well.)

Freud accounted for the inborn nature, as he conceived of it, of both the oedipus complex and the barrier against incest by using the prehistoric incestuous and parricidal deeds postulated in *Totem and Taboo* (he believed in the Lamarckian theory of the inheritance of acquired characteristics). He ended the book with a quote from Goethe (*Faust*, 1.3), which without scanting the basic pathogenic power of fantasies and drives can still be applied to the pathological development of some individuals, especially the victims of child abuse and soul murder: "Im Anfang war die Tat" (In the beginning was the Deed; Freud 1913, 161).

The not infrequent occurrence of actual incest involving preadolescent children has been pointed out by many analysts, most notably Ferenczi (1933) and more recently Fliess (1956, 1961, 1973). Masson (1984) has made it the subject of current controversy. Other relevant studies by analysts and psychiatrists include Bender and Blau (1977), Steele and Pollock (1968), Steele (1976), Katan (1973), Rosenfeld et al. (1977), and Masson and Masson (1978).

The primary determinant of the failure of the incest barrier would appear to be the pathology of the parent, who is usually extremely disturbed, compelled to repeat his or her own incestuous past in relation to the child, or both. Whatever natural barriers to incest may exist for children, my view from analyses of adults who were or were *not* seduced as children leads me to doubt that these barriers are strong enough for most children to be able to resist insistent parental seductiveness. The child's wishes are inevitably present, and the intensity of the individual child's sexual provocation is a secondary factor precipitating incest (see Abraham 1907). Sometimes there is an inherent defect making for an excessive sexual drive in a child; often, emotionally deprived children hungry for any kind of contact become seductive and overrespond to sexual signals. These intrapsychic factors in the child would interact with parental pathology. Some published studies have suggested that incestuous contact may have had some good effect on traumatically deprived children (alongside the undoubted destructive results), in that it supplies some human warmth in an otherwise emotionally desolate or primarily hostile environmental matrix (see Rosenfeld et al. 1977). Such "warmth" is obviously not necessarily a benefit: Katan (1973) pointed out how early sexual events prevent the fusion of aggression with libido, and in earlier chapters I have described other, most destructive effects. There is mystery here: is too-muchness better than nothing? Is the sexualization of the craving for human contact that can lead to incest and perversion a healthier turn than the arrest of emotional and sexual development? Can one draw valid general conclusions about these questions from the story of a few individuals? I know too little to answer. Clinically one sees that too often what starts out as the craving for love ends up in traumatic and crippling overstimulation for the child. The terrible price that incestuous action extracts from the child is much more familiar to us than any benefits involved.

Therapists treating boys in early puberty describe how angry and threatened the boys feel by the "seductiveness" of their mothers, and these are mothers who are not overtly incestuous. The awareness of the mother's sexuality evokes in the young adolescent boy the fears associated with both the oedipal and the preoedipal mothers (as described in Blos 1965). The boy's anger and fear (often expressed by distancing—keeping away or even running away from the mother) mark a heightening of the incest barrier at the time when castration anxiety is increasing along with the sexual drive. What is the effect on the adolescent boy of a literally seductive mother? Is the terror that accompanies incestuous fantasy and the approach to incest inevitably less in reality than the terror connected with the act itself? Are there circumstances in which the incestuous action can make for less danger, or for different dangers that can represent a kind of ameliorating adaptation to earlier traumata? I present another mystery: my patient's intercourse with his mother during adolescence appears to have had some considerable good effect on him, alongside the damage and devastation one would expect.[2]

The price to be paid evokes the most famous case of consummated mother-son incest—that described in the legend of Oedipus and in Sophocles' great play. The unwanted baby son is crippled by the neglect and malice of his parents and given away to be killed (see chapter 4). In Sophocles' play the mother is blamed more than the father for the preoedipal trauma—although many who have written about the play ignore this. Oedipus returns as a man to kill his father, unwittingly.

2. A similar good effect is portrayed in Louis Malle's film of 1971 *Le Souffle au Cœur* (Murmur of the Heart), about an adolescent boy who has sex with his mother. In the film, intimations of concomitant damage are suppressed.

He solves the riddle and causes the death of the Sphinx—the primal parent, the preoedipal mother. For this he becomes king, marries his mother, and when he discovers what he has done punishes himself: by taking on all the guilt of his parents, blinding himself, and going into exile. But he is also rewarded by the gods with wisdom, and his death is a kind of apotheosis. I repeat the story because I intend to derive parallels with the fate of my patient.

Freud's first recorded dynamic generalization about incest is a statement in a letter to Fliess of 12 June 1897: "Thus incest is antisocial—civilization consists in this progressive renunciation . . . Contrariwise the 'super-man' " (1950, p. 257). Oedipus was a king, and incest in myth and history was regarded as the privilege of the gods and royalty; but even those historical rulers who indulged in it claimed the status of divinity (like the Egyptian pharoahs, the Inca rulers, and insane Roman emperors), and usually only brother-sister incest was involved. Each culture has a father-god like Zeus, who raped his mother, Rhea, and married his sister, Hera (see Graves 1955, 53). This father-god lies in wait with his thunderbolts for those mortals who, like my patient, aspire to emulate him and become a "super-man."

The Case History

A man in his mid-thirties, married and a father, came for analysis because he was depressed and unhappy. (He did not mention Zeus but said, "It is as if there were a black cloud hanging over me and I'm waiting to be struck by lightning.") He felt that something in his character prevented him from achieving success. Actually he had a fine professional reputation and had always been able to support his family, but his modest demeanor concealed intense ambition—he wanted spectacular success—and in trying to become rich and famous he had provoked a series of rejections and failures. The pattern was that he would get into trouble as he approached an important achievement, or just after he had consolidated one.

He was a tall, slim, but strong-looking man with rugged good looks and an athletic presence. He dressed in casual clothes that gave him the aggressively masculine aura of a cigarette advertisement, with a rumpled, cowboy look that was rather unusual in the business world of Manhattan. Yet at times during the first interview, the expression around his eyes would become that of a passive and suffering child, quite in contrast to his predominantly macho appearance.

He spoke of his marriage as "good," but with faint enthusiasm. He talked about his wife with emotional distance and complained of her "frigidity." His own sexual functioning was marked by good mechanical performance, but there was a sense of dimmed pleasure with intercourse, and his occasional masturbation was often more satisfying.

The analysis began with great resistance; there was covert hostile and competitive feeling toward the analyst manifested by a passive stubborn provocative attitude. There were long periods of silence punctuated by intermittent bursts of self-deprecation. He seemed to dread scolding and punishment and yet to court them. His fear of my anger and his own was intense. Gradually he became more comfortable with the depth of his distrust of me, and the story of his childhood and adolescence emerged. I will condense years of treatment and present the story consecutively.

The mental illness of the patient's mother had dominated the family. She was frequently "depressed"—a slow, burning rage would occasionally burst out against her husband with a violence that would terrify him and the children. They were intimidated by her brooding silences (here was one source of the patient's anticipatory thunder-and-lightning metaphor). There were periods of relative calm and even some seeming contentment on the mother's part, but usually there was smoldering war between the parents. The father, "a weak man in a strong man's body," reacted mainly by absenting himself and working out of town. He too was occasionally abusive and could bully the children, but turned passive and ineffectual whenever the mother was subject to one of her fits of rage. In spite of the intermittent turmoil and terror, there were happy periods, and the boy felt that both parents cared about him, although his father kept him at an emotional remove. He was clearly his mother's favorite child, but not his father's.

He was the mother's first-born, and she had wanted a girl. This was puzzling, because she did not seem to like girls. She refused to have her son's hair cut, so that it grew out in long ringlets, and he was induced and then forced for years to wear homemade outfits that resembled dresses. This feminization was the subject of battles between the parents. Indeed, the son had believed that his mother's chief motivation in keeping him in skirts was to spite his father; this view, valid enough, minimized that he himself was also the object of her spite.

The mother fed her son well but like many a soul-murdering parent was obsessed by his bowel functions, insisting on wiping his anus until he was old enough to go to school. There was a regimen of stool inspection and frequent enemas. The feelings that this anal stimulation involved for the boy—ultimately revealed as great excitement and great rage—were initially not available; the "events" were remembered in emotional isolation. But there had been overstimulation, and a fixation on anal excitement had developed.

The boy hated to wear the enforced girl's costume as soon as he became aware of how different it made him look from the other boys. When he was about four the boy refused to go out of the house unless he were given pants, and his mother gave in; at five he defiantly cut off his curls. On both occasions he sensed that in some way his mother admired his rebellious spirit. He had felt as a child that his mother, who regarded women as weak and despicable, did not want him to act like a girl so much as to look like one. She never deprecated his genitals, even when she insisted on his covering them with a skirt.

This attitude is in contrast to what Stoller (1974) describes in the mother of a "transsexual boy" who developed "femaleness with no oedipal strivings" (p. 207). In his work on transsexuals, Stoller depicts parents whose fantasies and wishes assign their child the sex other than the one anatomy has decreed, and who impose these fantasies and wishes with a delusional intensity. This interferes with the establishment of what Stoller calls "core gender identity [which] seems fairly well formed by a year and a half or two years of age. It is almost irreversible by around age five or six" (1973, p. 314). This interference with "core gender identity" had not occurred for my patient, whose mother's wishes were more contradictory and perhaps more lightly held than those of the mother who cultivates the transsexual child.[3]

Certainly the boy found his mother's behavior very confusing. The stubborn refusals and rebelliousness that she could not tolerate in her

3. I feel that this mother definitely wanted her son to have a penis under his skirt and that she was using him to represent unconsciously what she herself wanted to be; her intense penis envy took the form of despising women and identifying with men sexually involved with other males. Consciously she despised male homosexuals as "feminine," but I speculate intuitively that on a deeper level she might have agreed with Jean Genêt that "a man who fucks a man is twice a man."

husband she frequently put up with in her son. She occasionally beat him, but not severely, and he was more afraid of her rage than of her beatings; in contrast he was terrified whenever she called on his father to spank him.

The aggressive surge that successfully won the boy the right to wear pants and have short hair was followed by an event that brought a climax to the anal and sadomasochistic overstimulation to which he had been subjected as a child. He was seduced or forced to passive anal intercourse by an adolescent male relative who was used as a baby-sitter. (In contrast to his memory of the incest once it had come out of repression, the "memory" of the sexual experience itself was vague and mostly secondhand—that is, derived in part from the stories of relatives. The aftermath of the sexual contact was however remembered clearly.) This apparently happened only once. There was anal damage and bleeding, which alerted the parents, and the baby-sitter was banished. It was only in analysis that the patient was able to realize his mother's implicit arrangement of this seduction. The baby-sitter's homosexual proclivities were common knowledge in the family—why had the mother left her son alone in his care? After it happened, the mother was most alarmed; she feared her son would become homosexual and was for a short time obsessed by this dread. But characteristically, after the anal tear had healed, she never mentioned the incident again.

The family's ability to blot out what was painful and frightening was contributed to by the father's frequent absence, but stemmed mainly from the mother. The boy early on felt that he had occasionally to rationalize for her and disguise from her the reactions of puzzled and hostile neighbors, who apparently regarded her as a precariously domesticated "crazy" lady best left alone. The mother did not feel any need for protection; she had little insight and could bring into use a blame-projecting righteousness that served to justify her rages.

The period of latency seemed to mark another predominant surge toward masculinity. The boy found a group of friends at school and cultivated athletic interests that kept him away from home. And his mother seemed willing to let him go, relaxing her hold even to the point of giving up the enemas and daily stool inspections. (Was this, I wondered, a reaction to some guilty awareness that she had wished to have the boy anally seduced?) She became a kind of bystander and shifted her interest to his younger siblings. As he grew toward puberty he excelled in athletics and began to dress, act, and walk in a somewhat exaggeratedly masculine way. He was polite and well behaved, and did well at school. His prowess in sports and his dark good looks began to attract the attention of girls in his class, who actively sought him out. He was both pleased and frightened by their attentions but assumed a cool, rejecting manner that enhanced his desirability. With puberty imminent there was an upsurge of sexual feeling, and masturbation without ejaculation, accompanied by vague fantasies about girls. He remembered no homosexual feeling or activity.

The boy's growth was precocious, and before he was twelve he was taller than his father. He was both proud and ashamed of his developing pubic hair, large genitals, and frequent erections. His mother again took an obsessive interest in his body and he became increasingly upset by her obtrusive curiosity. He tried to deny the unmistakable flow of sexual excitement between them. The mother would walk in on him in the bathroom (never locked); she would come into his room in the morning before her son awakened and he would "find himself" uncovered with an erection, exhibiting to her. I speculate that this mother must have been so afraid of her own incestuous wishes that she had to try, or half-try, to bring up her first son as a girl. Then, with his precocious growth toward puberty, those wishes became too much for her. Rangell (1970) wrote of parents being "stimulated both by the sense of declining power and, in contrast, by the lusty coming of age of [their] children" (p. 333). He also pointed out "the remobilization of the parents' repressed scoptophilic impulses" (p. 329) when their children reached puberty. In her excited curiosity and probably in the incest this mother was also expressing her castrating impulses toward her son (clearly present in her battles with her husband).

The boy began to develop anxiety and had disturbing dreams, and his work at school deteriorated. As he relived some of this time in analysis, what bothered him most was the intensity of the anger (accompanied by wishes for revenge) that was mixed with the anxiety and sexual excitement.

One day on coming home from school the boy found himself as usual alone with his mother. She had just emerged from a bath and left open the bathroom door. As he approached she bent over, as if to wipe her feet with a towel. She gave him a look of invitation and again bent over, presenting another open door. The boy was overwhelmed with excitement and, penis erect, advanced toward her "as if in a trance."[4] He penetrated her vagina. She had an orgasm. He was not yet capable of ejaculation, but there was a kind of orgasm. It was felt as a wonderful experience. This sequence was repeated several times over the next few weeks, always without words; and it was never mutually acknowledged. Then, not long after the incestuous contact began, the boy achieved ejaculation after penetrating his mother. She noted it, became violently disturbed and rushed away, shrieking, "No! No! No!" The incest was never repeated and never again mentioned; it was as if it had never happened. And the boy repressed it, which seems almost incredible in retrospect given that the recall was marked by such passionate and sensual intensity. The memory emerged only after several years of analysis.

From his memory the patient painted for me an unforgettable picture of his mother offering herself to him (which he had nonetheless forgotten), full of sensory and sensual detail: the steamy vapor of the room; the inviting, wet warmth of her flesh; the rosy pinkness of her hot skin and its moist, soft, peachlike texture; the rounded beauty of her buttocks; the mysterious, dark, and inviting cleft of her body—all was recalled in soft focus and suffused with an aesthetic glow (as in Louis Malle's film).[5] The mother was in some way deindividualized, transformed into a feminine goddess symbolizing all women. Gone was the terrifying, cold, murderous sphinx who threatened to eat up all those who dared stand against her. He said that his mother bending over for him meant her offering herself to him as "cunt": a word he found (in relation to his mother) charged with beauty and promise. At least in

4. This is simultaneous hypnotic evasion and facilitation (see chapter 8).

5. I have tried to reproduce something of the *feel* of the patient's description: a mixture of the poetic and the pornographic. His narrative also included many peripheral details that were "ultraclear" (see Freud 1937b, 266), such as the vivid memory of drops of water on a blue bathroom floor-tile. Freud adduces these peripheral particulars about furniture and rooms "recollected with abnormal sharpness" (p. 266) as confirmation *from memory* of the validity of constructions made by the analyst. I had supplied no construction of the incest. But I was initially unsure whether I was hearing fantasy or memory and felt that the specificity of these details confirmed the memory quality that it became clear the patient had no doubt about.

retrospective, idealizing fantasy, an affectionate or nourishing giving had distanced rage and castration and destruction.

The nonderogatory, honorific use of "cunt" is reminiscent of that of another oedipally bound son, the great writer D. H. Lawrence. In *Lady Chatterly's Lover*, the gamekeeper, Mellors, after a "lovely . . . beautiful" bout of intercourse, says to his mistress, Lady Chatterly: "Th'art good cunt . . . best bit o' cunt left on earth . . . Cunt! Ah, tha's the beauty o' thee, lass" (1928, pp. 212–213).

For my patient the experiences of penetration and the one time of ejaculation were recalled as "glorious"[6], wonderful, and beautiful. I believe there was in this aesthetic and idealized transformation something false and something genuine; the patient was both defending against and expressing what he had experienced. (I feel similarly about the quoted passage from Lawrence, and its mawkish dialect, and about Louis Malle's film.) My patient had a lifelong, intense feeling for beauty in nature and in art. An artistic transfiguration had helped him to disguise and defend against the aggression involved in the reduction of his mother to "cunt"—a reduction to a deindividualized part-object not only of the potentially beloved oedipal mother but of the preoedipal mother-witch-sphinx. The person was reduced to a body part that could then be transferred onto other women. In this sense the incest appeared (paradoxically) to have helped the adolescent fulfill his need for "progressive disengagement from primary love objects" (Blos 1965, 146). And he seemed by virtue of the incest to have modified somewhat the predominantly destructive, aggressive quality of his sexuality with a kind of fusion with libido (see Katan 1973). Yet these advances were made at the terrible price of grievously jeopardizing two precious attainments (which even in ordinary development are at least transiently compromised in the adolescent's dangerous but defended sexual world of "cunt" and "cock"): his individuality (dependent as that is in part on recognizing the individuality of others), and his ability to love.

The patient had recalled how angry he was with his mother's seductiveness before the incest, a feeling expressed by many adolescent boys. The mother's literal seduction of the boy is the exceptional element

6. Strachey used the same word to translate the Rat Man's "*grossartig*" in this famous patient's dramatic, triumphant soliloquy during his first intercourse: "This is *glorious*! One might murder one's father for this!" (Das is doch grossartig! Dafür könnte man seinen Vater ermordern!) (1910, p. 201; my italics)

here. Did this enable my patient to overcome some of the fear of his rage at the preoedipal mother and discharge it through intercourse? Was he not also pushed by the terror of his intense passivity? With the penetrative, active acceptance of his mother's offer, the boy accomplished a major reversal: instead of being the passive anal and oral victim of the phallic, invasive devouring mother (the parent as sphinx), he triumphed over her and made her subject to his phallic, penetrative power.[7] In two different ways he played the role of Oedipus: "[First, he] won the prize of an all-prosperous future; he slew the maiden with crooked talons who sang darkly [the Sphinx]; [Second,] he *arose* for our land *as a tower* against death" (Jebb, trans., p. 47; my italics). A speculation: did the experience of the boy and his penis rising "as a tower" against his mother save him from a lifelong subjection to the preoedipal mother, from homosexuality, and from other possible vicissitudes of bondage to passivity? (see Blos 1965).

Narcissistic Triumph

When I first thought of writing about this patient, the title that occurred to me was "Guilt-Ridden Arrogance Derived from Incest." Freud (1917) wrote: "If a man has been his mother's undisputed darling he retains throughout life the triumphant feeling, the confidence in success, which not seldom brings actual success along with it" (p. 156). What then of the man who has been his mother's sexual darling, who has had intercourse with her? Oedipus is the classic example. In an earlier chapter I quoted what I will now repeat. When Jocasta finally realizes in *Oedipus Rex* that she has married her son, she rushes off before the shepherd can reveal this terrible truth to Oedipus. He reacts to her desertion with a speech attributing it to fear of hearing that she has wed the son of a slave: "Yon woman [Jocasta] thinks shame of my base source. *But I who hold myself son of Fortune*, will not be dishonoured —*she* [Fortune] is the mother from whom I spring . . . such being my

---

7. It may be that this man stressed the aesthetic quality, the *beauty* of his triumph, to mask some of the fear of experiencing power, which has intimations of murdering both parents. For my patient (like the Rat Man), the "glory" was linked with the terrifying feeling that "one could kill one's father for this," yet served to defend against it.

lineage, never more can I prove false to it or spare to search out the secrets of my birth" (Jebb, trans., p. 42; my italics).

My patient had solved the riddle of the Sphinx in incestuous action, and then repressed it. But the arrogance continued for him, the narcissistic triumph derived from feeling himself the "son of Fortune."[8] During his analysis my patient remembered his secret pride at the age of twelve at having had intercourse with a grown woman when his friends were only daydreaming about sex. He consciously tried then to dissociate any thought of the "grown woman" from the concept of mother or even from the word *mother*, which inevitably connected with *father* (see Weich 1968 for a contrasting view of the use of the terms *mother* and *father* in relation to incest). In later adolescence (after repression), he habitually attracted attention by wearing a bright red, flannel "worker's shirt," which had Marxist connotations for him. This was "the flag of his disposition"; in analysis he called it the "costume of a humble coxcomb" (*coxcomb* can refer to both a fool and an exhibitionist—an apt mixture of shame and pride), and he associated the word and the image of a cock's comb to his mother's genitals and to his own red and far-from-humble erection. He was unknowingly draping himself in an incestuous revolutionary red banner. In later life, when there was competition for a particular post, or if he had to submit work in contention with that of peers, he confidently assumed he would win; true to Freud's prediction, he often did. He was both intelligent and gifted, and that helped him live up even to overweening pretensions. Although generally good-natured and even "humble" in manner, he had many arrogant traits. He never wore a watch, which certainly was an inconvenience in business; his attitude was a breezy "let the others wait." There was more than a touch in this of a concomitant strand in his superego: provoking punishment. (He was never late in his analysis, where he had to confront the deeper meanings of warring with Time.) His wife would frequently be stimulated to repeat to him: "You know, you are not of royal blood."[9]

8. Freud uses almost the same words, with no reference to Oedipus, in his construction of the thoughts of Goethe, one of Freud's alter egos: "I was a child of fortune" (1917, p. 156; my italics).
9. The regal glory of consummated incest is also present in the young man described by Margolis (1977), who was seduced by his mother into having intercourse with her when he was sixteen. He would later vent his anger toward her

But alongside the hubris and quasi-delusional pride, and completely unsynthesized with it, was an intense need to lose out and be chastised. One of the effects of the consummated incest was this split in my patient's conscience. A patchwork pattern seems to have been established, of achievement followed by the unconscious arrangement for failure and punishment. It was a dim awareness of this that had led him into analysis when he, like Oedipus, was blind to the reason for the "plague" in his life.

After bringing the memory out of repression, the patient felt relief and liberation. For a while the need for punishment seemed in abeyance. In contrast to the positive changes that began to occur in his life, he became increasingly resistant in his analysis. He did not doubt his memory—the recalling had been too vivid—but he seemed unable to consolidate it, to add to it, to connect it with what happened later on. There was a blank space after his mother's "No! No! No!" that was never filled in. He would remember the incest from the vantage point of his later, inhibited adolescence but would come up against a "hole" in his memory. And he would not or could not integrate his memory of incest in the presence of his analyst. It had happened; it had been remembered; now it was over. He seemed to have identified with his mother's "No! No! No!"[10] I interpreted this and he agreed with the interpretation, but no further work was done. There were again periods of silence and of autohypnosis (as if the "trance" in which he had advanced to take his mother sexually was now used to disguise and unconsciously preserve what he had done). After some months of stubborn resistance, the patient left analysis.

I feel that the preservation and isolation of the "hole" in the patient's memory also expressed a need to retain a feminine identification in defense against his oedipal triumph. An awareness of his passivity and femininity was in turn warded off by his leaving analysis with much

---

in sex and said that "after subduing her and having intercourse with her he felt like 'King of the World'" (p. 271).

10. A colleague wondered if the mother's "No! No! No!" might not have contributed to the patient's ability to bring the memory out of repression during his analysis. Although a negation, it was a verbalization. His mother may have influenced the "aural lobe" of the superego with words that signified that something had happened; perhaps this enhanced permission for registration and verbal communication for the son.

of the feeling of his oedipal victory intact (this had been restored by the amnesia removal). He was leaving while he still felt like the son of Fortune. The aura of active, powerful sexual and narcissistic triumph seemed to have had a predominantly strengthening and adaptive effect on his later life. But he felt that this fragile, defensive, potentially stabilizing current of emotion was threatened by further analytic work. Proceeding with the analysis probably would have meant facing up to the whole preoedipal and oedipal developmental range of dangers, involving his passivity and wish for annihilation, as well as his activity and wish to murder (see Loewald 1978 on a man with oedipal fixations: "In his case, as in so many others, preoedipal currents and those belonging to the positive and negative Oedipus complex were inextricably blended"; p. 388).)

The patient would have had to be able to bear and work with anxiety and depression, castration fear and guilt, intensified and focused onto his analyst in transference. Perhaps he preferred leaving when he could feel like his mother's "rapist" rather than like the murderer of his mother, father, and analyst.[11] In any case, he apparently needed to run away to preserve a precarious, predominantly defensive psychic equilibrium.

The Barrier against Incest

The key to the mystery of an abrogated incest taboo between mother and son is found by and large in the mind of the mother. Every parent is also the child of his or her own parents and in fantasy can play both the role of child and that of parent. In recorded instances of mother-son incest, the mother is invariably described as psychotic. This description is not necessarily an explanation. One would need a much greater number of cases than have been published to be comfortable with the generalization (which might still be true) that mothers who seduce their adolescent sons are psychotic, or even with the lesser conclusion that those who come to the attention of psychiatrists are psychotic. I did not directly observe my patient's mother, who was able to defy the in-

11. Richard Brinsley Sheridan is purported to have remarked of a notoriously brutal and arrogant womanizing military hero, "Rapes are the relaxations of murderers."

cest barrier but not the prohibition against the son's impregnating the mother. I studied the incestuous son who found his mother irresistible. I felt that the mother was probably psychotic.

Whether or not his mother felt responsibility or guilt, her son was subject to fears in relation to incest and especially to making his mother pregnant. These involved the whole gauntlet of psychic dangers spelled out by Freud (1926). The most terrifying of these is the danger of psychic annihilation: loss of the mental representations of the self and the mother. These fears connected with penetrating and impregnating the mother would be present in the childhood fantasy of both boys and girls; and the fears in relation to the mother will still be there when the little girl grows up and herself becomes a mother. The inhibiting effects of these fears of incest must operate with more force on the mothers of adolescent sons than on the fathers of adolescent daughters; otherwise, assuming the primary parental responsibility for incestuous action, we could not account for the difference in frequency between mother-son incest and father-daughter incest.

It has been suggested to me that the difference in frequency might also be due to some inherent access of castration anxiety in the boy, as distinct from that in the girl, because he has a penis to lose. This might seem at first glance like a corollary to Freud's unempathic early premise that girls cannot have castration anxiety because they have no phallus (an offense against Freud's own discovery of psychic reality; from my own clinical work I feel sure that castration anxiety is present in women, although it has different and often disguised forms). I have already mentioned my opinion that the heightened genital awareness during puberty probably makes for more castration anxiety in boys than in girls, because the potential for penetrating and impregnating the mother is experiential—something that the boy can feel with his penis. If this is true, feeling this forbidden potential would be part of the adolescent son's contribution to the infrequency of mother-son incest. More clinical observations are needed rather than assumptions based on theory.

In father-daughter incest the father is the stronger party and usually the one more responsible for the action. In such cases the penetration and thrust of the inseminating genital discharge (in fantasy a potentially destructive force) is at least in the action directed toward the future generation and away from the parents, especially from the mother whose place has been taken in *unconscious* fantasy by the daughter. For the daughter, the destructive component of her feelings is aimed at the father (again, at least in the action); in fantasy, however, the mother is injured and replaced.[12] In relative terms, father-daughter incest spares the mother—the primary parent, the indisputable source of one's own life and body. In mother-son incest, by contrast, the mother is directly involved in the deed and is central to the fantasies of both son and mother. (I am indebted to some ideas of Victor Calef for this line of speculative thought.)

These ideas of the mother as primary and primal parent relate to the question of the phylogenetic origin of the incest taboo. Studies of incest in primates other than man show that shunning incest is the rule in these related species too: "Incest avoidance appears to be universal among higher primates" (Demarest 1977, 330). As with humans, the taboo against mother-son incest makes for its rarer occurrence than sister-brother incest. The social structure and sexual habits of some primate groups (like monkeys) are such that although there may be a group leader who acts as an authority figure, there is no way of determining who any individual's father is, and therefore observers cannot study father-daughter incest (see Demarest 1977, 327). Whatever awareness these primates have of consanguinous ties can be felt only toward their mother. The mother is the only sure link to the past generations—a fact implicit in some human customs and laws (for example, the matrilineal definition of Jewishness by some Jews and by the state of Israel). In humans the precariousness of paternity is less spectacular, but it is still "a wise child who knows his own father." The phylogenetic impact of the mother would appear to be much more important.[13]

12. In a personal communication, Martin Grotjahn remarked that in father-daughter incest it is frequently if not regularly found that the mother has consciously or unconsciously offered the daughter to the father. When this is the case the destructive feelings toward the mother in the daughter's fantasies may also be tempered.

13. It is interesting that the only personal observation made by Sade (1968) of a mother-son mating among rhesus monkeys occurred in an exceptional situation in which the son had first challenged and fought with the mother for a period of months over dominance. When he finally triumphed over and beat up his mother (he mastered his aggression by aggressively mastering her), copulation ensued (p. 31). The reversal of power between son and mother evokes the Sphinx and Oedipus. Sade's account bears a certain resemblance to my case history and to that of Margolis (1977).

There are other social structures in primates that might reinforce the idea of fatherhood (that of couples who mate for life, for example); but here mother-son incest is just as rare. The unsureness of who one's father is increases with historical and phylogenetic perspective. Among primitive peoples today sexual intercourse is not always connected with childbirth. (I agree with Calef that this connection is a momentous intellectual achievement in man's history; it represents the coming to consciousness of impregnation wishes.) Freud's hypothetical Primal Father (from *Totem and Taboo*) is likely to have been the leader of the horde and sexual owner of the mother, and was not necessarily recognized by the child as the procreator.

The Fear of Making the Mother Pregnant

I feel that my patient, like his mother and in identification with her, was unable to face the implications of possibly impregnating her. It is in large part from this man that I have derived my impression that the fantasy of impregnating the mother is part of the "bedrock" of the fear of incest, in the sense used by Freud (1937a, p. 252) of having passed through all the psychological strata and reached the rock bottom of the biological. Although I am outlining only the male's development, in both sexes the forbidden wish to impregnate the mother evokes fears associated with all the psychic dangers. The wish can involve the pre-oedipal, cannibalistic fantasy of projecting oneself or part of oneself into the womb and into the mother, which means destroying self and mother (fusion and loss of self- and object-representations). Separation anxiety is obviously involved. There is a marshaling of intense castration anxiety, for the youth who dares to sleep with his mother and get her pregnant is literally taking his father's place and himself becoming a father. The wish to castrate and kill off the father in the face of the early adolescent's need for the father's strength to deal with the imago of the preoedipal mother (see Blos 1965) leads to the boy's negative oedipus complex and the impact of bisexuality, which Freud held to be the "bedrock" of the male's resistance to psychoanalysis.

With Freud I feel (I hesitate to say *think*) that there is a definite phylogenetic component to the incest taboo and that it involves impregnation. The incest taboo is necessary to make "a kind of remodelling of the biological conditions of mating and procreating" (Lévi-Strauss

1956, 258) in the service of decreasing inbreeding and preserving the species.

Ontogenetically and experientially, the thought of impregnating the mother brings out the feelings of the adolescent boy's active responsibility: the excitement, the erection, the ejaculation are his doing. In this case I have described the mother was clearly the seducer; but the son took the parental guilt onto himself (as daughters also do in relation to seductive, soul-murdering parents), even after he had again remembered how much the initiative was his mother's and how irresistible she was. He blamed her, but blamed himself much more. Oedipus had put the responsibility for his crimes onto a parent figure, the god Apollo, yet took it onto himself in action when he blinded himself:

> 'Tis Apollo; all is Apollo;
> 'Tis he long time hath planned
> These things upon me evilly, evilly.
> Dark things and full of blood.
> I knew not; I did but follow his way; but mine the hand
> and mine the anguish. What were eyes to me when naught
> to be seen was good? (Murray, trans., p. 204)

Sophocles put into his play all the levels of horror against impregnating the mother (including the fear of losing one's identity). Oedipus addresses his daughters:

> Is there any evil wanting? Your father killed his
> father; sowed the womb of her who bore him; engendered
> you at the fount of his own existence! (Fitts, trans., p. 75)

> Incestuous sin! Breeding where I was bred!
> Father, brother, and son;
> Bride, wife, and mother;
> Confounded in one monstrous matrimony!
> All human filthiness in one crime compounded!
> Unspeakable acts—I speak no more of them.
> Hide me away at once for god's love, hide me away,
> Away! Kill me! Drown me in the depths of the sea!
> *Take me*! (Watling, trans., p. 64; my italics)

By running away from his analysis, my patient seemed to be serving his need for punishment. He was banishing himself. I was unwittingly playing the role of Creon, who in Sophocles' play grants Oedipus's last wish: "Cast me from this land" (Murray, trans., p. 209).

The patient was not going to work through the fantasies of killing me and his father; nor of identifying with his mother and submitting to me sexually ("Take me!"). I had helped him and penetrated him with my interpretations, which culminated in the recovered memories. But this need not bear fruit, and the patient had to run away both to preserve the recovered feeling of triumphant power and to prevent it from recharging his fantasies. By leaving he was also avenging himself against me, in his view the godlike parent who permitted such evil in the world as feminization of sons and the seduction of children. He was robbing me of my power by not letting me help him further—an acting out of the anger and of the wish to castrate that he was afraid to feel and acknowledge. (I believe it was above all fear of the soul-murdered murderous rage that motivated him to run away.)

When the patient returned to see me for a short period many years later I gained more insight into this and into his adolescence after the incest, as well as into his life after the analysis. Consciously he was coming back for advice about family problems. But there was a deeper need to show me what the analysis had done for him, and to try to consolidate it. He allowed this only fleetingly; such was his ambivalence. During this brief period much anger was expressed. There was rage at his father for being too weak to protect him against his mother; and rage at his mother, whose rejection of him after the incest had again pushed him toward passivity and deprived him of the glory of his triumph, while loading him with the guilt for what had happened. There was rage at me for banishing him (this was how he remembered his running away) and thus repeating his mother's "No! No! No!" (He suddenly understood during this time why he always became enraged or depressed when a woman refused him intercourse.) There seemed to be too much rage for him to stay with me and become responsible for it.

During the short reanalysis the patient elaborated on his adolescence after the incest. The boy was increasingly afraid of his father, whose place he felt he had taken. He became subservient to him, bringing him his slippers every evening, which involved bending over for his father, as his mother had done for him. There was very little emotional communication with either parent. He lived the life of an inhibited adolescent seemingly under the sway of castration anxiety. He avoided his athletic friends and chose a new group of ascetic intellectuals who behaved in a predominantly asexual way. They shared leftist political interests; he began to wear his red "worker's shirt." His sexual feelings were intense, but he was extremely secretive about his masturbation, which was accomplished as quickly and with as little fantasy as possible; what he remembered of this showed a concentration on the part-object, the mysterious and exciting "cunt," now largely stripped of its connotations of beauty and regarded as somewhat degraded and cloacal. Homosexual pressures were manifested only in an intense dislike for the subject of perversion and for obviously effeminate men. He was still sought out by girls and in later adolescence had intercourse with a series of rather aggressive young women (he feared and avoided older women), one of whom he finally married.

Only in his analysis had the man become aware of how much dissatisfaction and sadomasochism were present in the relationship with his wife. He provoked her anger and withheld tenderness and sex; she belittled him and was usually frigid. But there was also some affection and mutual caring—their children were cared for and cared about by both parents (although he kept a defensive emotional distance). The relation to his wife was less than a loving one, but, as he said on his return, "As the world goes, it was not a bad marriage." Both his strong sexual drive and his intense ambition had been kept suppressed by an obsessive distancing and by reaction formation (anal narcissistic defense), with an occasional arrogant flash that I have already noted. He had done well at college and work but had never lived up to his full promise. After the heroic incestuous triumph, his life had become dull and disappointing. In retrospect his adolescent development appeared rather normal for a predominantly passive, somewhat masochistic, inhibited heterosexual man.

Loewald (1978) said of those who are not capable of "non-incestuous object-relations" that their "need for punishment tends to become inexhaustible" (p. 10). This seems not to be true for my patient (so far), even though the need for punishment is palpable. He appears to have attained some point of fragile balance between defense and impulse satisfaction, between punishment and gratification, which has allowed him until now to get beyond the horror and madness usually associated with mother-son incest. Indeed, this balance seems to have been achieved in part as a result of the incest—first by the experience of intercourse with his mother, later by the reinforcing memory of it. I feel he was able to reverse a predominantly passive, castrated psychological position to a predominantly active, castrating one that was not incompatible with some considerable ability to love. And somehow (it is necessary to be vague) the dangerous destructiveness involved in the parentocidal and suicidal impulses that are so much a part of preoedipal and preadolescent sexuality, especially after soul-murder experiences, seem to have been partly ameliorated and made more tolerable, more containable, by the incest itself. This man who had been raised by his mother to look like a girl (as were Oscar Wilde and Rilke) had perhaps avoided homosexuality or at least some grave deformation of his sexual life.

My last mystery: the incest consummated in adolescence appears to have undone some damage from early childhood; if this is so, and I believe it to have been so for this man, why is this kind of reversal by incest in adolescence not seen more often?[14] Instances of soul murder are alas not uncommon. Seduction and beating in childhood do affect the barrier to incest in the child, and obviously also in the soul-murdering parent, who is so often repeating his or her own victimization in childhood. And a daughter's seduction by her father in her childhood must be one of the factors making for father-daughter incest in adolescence. But what of mother-son incest? If its rarity is due to the strength of the incest taboo in relation to the mother, and if the soul murder (the preoedipal seductions and enforced transvestitism) weakened the taboo in this case, why is incest between mother and adolescent son not seen more often? I have done my inadequate best to address this last question, but a satisfying answer needs much more than I have to give, and as Freud wrote to Jung, "Anyone who gives more than he has is a rogue" (Freud and Jung 1900–1914, 40).

After the break with the first period of analysis, the patient had done much better than I would have expected. He had divorced his wife after some years, and with other women there had been a flowering of his

14. Rascovsky and Rascovsky (1950) have published a case of consummated father-daughter incest. They also comment on the "virtual lack of psychoanalytical and anthropological contributions to the subject" (p. 42). The nineteen-year-old daughter was induced to perform fellatio on her father and then had intercourse with him several years later. The authors feel that the consummated incestuous intercourse may have saved the daughter from psychosis. In my opinion, however, their conclusions are stated rather than demonstrated.

sexual feelings ("like a real adolescence") with much more pleasure and even joy in sex. He had married again, this time to a more loving and responsive woman. The sense of conviction about the occurrence of the incest had if anything strengthened (I perhaps showed my own wish to deny in asking him about this); he had in some measure come to terms with what had happened between him and his mother. It was a connected part of the past and had the full quality of memory. This partial synthesis had occurred in the years after the analysis, through the patient's own efforts, and in large part preconsciously. The upsurge of sexual desire and pleasure had been forthcoming about a year after he had stopped therapy, and had been maintained. In recent years he had become more aware of the rage at his parents and his analyst. He seemed to have lost something of his driving ambition, and I saw no signs of the old arrogance during his second series of visits. But the need for punishment was still seen in his behavior toward his superiors at work; and although he had permitted himself more material success and had more feeling of personal power and self-esteem, there had also been occasional periods of depression and a more constant expectation of catastrophe. He said ruefully that he still felt himself subject to "bad luck" and could still feel the black clouds charged with thunderbolts hovering over him. Despite this, considering what he had lived through, his story seems to me to have had a happy ending. But as the Sophoclean final chorus warns: "Behold, this is Oedipus, who knew the famed riddle, and was a man most mighty; on whose fortunes what citizen did not gaze with envy? Behold into what a stormy sea of dread trouble he hath come! Therefore, while our eyes wait to see the destined final day, we must call no one happy who is of mortal race, until he hath crossed life's border, free from pain" (Jebb, trans., p. 58).

10

Dickens, *Little Dorrit,* and Soul Murder

Murder and soul murder are recurrent motifs in Dickens's works. Humor and sentimentality are suddenly mixed with violence. There is a persistent repetition of murder in all his novels: from *The Pickwick Papers* (where it appears in the melodramatic, interpolated stories) to his last, unfinished *Mystery of Edwin Drood.* Edmund Wilson points out how acute Dickens can be in revealing the psychology of a murderer, like Jonas Chuzzlewit in *Martin Chuzzlewit:* "For example, after the murder when Jonas is 'not only fearful *for* himself but *of* himself' and half-expects, when he returns to his bedroom, to find himself asleep in the bed" (1941, p. 23).

The themes of abandoned and neglected children, and unfeeling and negligent parents and institutions, appear as obsessive interests during Dickens's life and recur throughout his fiction. The great novelist has created a gallery of monstrous parents and parental substitutes, as well as some who are good—more often unbelievably good.[1] Dickens portrays in so many of his novels a human characteristic that was called "the undeveloped heart" by E. M. Forster (who felt it was especially

---

1. There are more good fathers than good mothers. Even a good mother-substitute, like Betsy Trotwood in the autobiographical novel *David Copperfield,* is given the quality of masculine decisiveness (for Dickens), which both Copperfield's mother and Dickens's own lacked. On the other hand, David Copperfield's father is dead, and killing off fathers in his fiction is another of Dickens's obsessions.

applicable to the English).[2] Forster was describing the inability to care
enough about another person, a deficiency of the capacity for love, joy,
and empathy. This impoverishment of the soul is both the result and
the cause of soul murder; it can evoke in the deprived and frustrated
child a terrible intensity of rage that can burst out into actual murder
if it is not frozen by isolating defenses. And the parent's undeveloped
heart can of course be expressed not only by indifference to the child
but also by hatred and cruelty.

Nurses' Stories

Freud frequently wrote of the seductive and destructive effect on the
fantasy life of children of the ministration of servants, especially nurses.
He himself had had as a nurse an old Catholic woman who told him
stories about God and hell—and whom he accused of seducing him:
"She was my teacher in sexual matters . . . [and the] prime originator
[of my neurosis]" (1887–1904, p. 269). Dickens described the lasting
effect on his imagination of stories heard and read in childhood. He
wrote of these as providing places for the mind to go and people to
be revisited; in these recurrent psychic journeys, the wonderful and
terrible settings and characters retain something of their original, perfervid psychic reality: "Utterly impossible places and people, but none
the less *absolutely real*—that I found had been introduced to me by my
nurse *before I was six years old*, and used to be *forced* to go back to at
night without at all wanting to go. If we all knew our own minds . . .
I suspect we should find our nurses responsible for most of the dark
corners we are forced to go back to, against our wills" (1840b, p. 150;
my italics).

Dickens was reporting a compulsion to repeat early traumatic experiences—the horrible and the overwhelming being accompanied for
him by something exciting and fascinating. His essay "Nurses' Stories"
was inspired by his first return as an adult to Chatham (where he had
lived from the age of five to the age of nine), "revisiting the associations of my childhood" (1840b, p. 150). The years in Chatham before

2. In *The Longest Journey*, 1907. A parallel phrase with similar meaning is used
by Wassermann in the subtitle of his novel about Kaspar Hauser (1908): *Die
Trägheit des Herzens* (The Slothfulness of the Heart).

the family's descent into poverty were perhaps the happiest years of Dickens's life.

Dickens's nursemaid there was a young woman named Mary Weller (her name reappeared in *The Pickwick Papers*). She seems to have been kind as well as mischievous and frightening, and Dickens had strong, ambivalent feelings about her.[3] She was in the habit of taking him along to visit friends who had given birth: "In my very young days I was taken to so many lyings-in, that I wonder I escaped from becoming a professional martyr to them in after life" (1840a, p. 118). On one of these occasions Dickens remembered visiting a lady who had just been delivered of stillborn quadruplets or quintuplets, and seeing "how the four or five deceased young people lay, side by side, on a clean cloth on a chest of drawers; reminding me by a homely association, which I suspect their complexion to have assisted, of pigs' feet as they are usually displayed at a neat tripe-shop" (1840a, p. 119).[4] Despite Dickens's jocular tone, this indicates the association with death and cannibalism that the birth process acquired on these enforced visits. It was during these

3. See Kligerman 1970 on the importance of the many Marys in Dickens's life (but Kligerman leaves out Mary, mother of Christ). Kligerman also points to Dickens's fascination with an amateur pianist named *Christine Weller*, whom he met when he was giving a reading in 1844. Dickens, thirty-two and married at the time, was according to Johnson (1952) "amazed by his own interest in her and startled by his feelings" (p. 498). He went to see her and wrote some rhymes in her album: "I put in a book, once, by hook and by crook, / The whole race (as I thought) of a 'feller,' / Who happily pleased the town's taste, much diseas'd, / —And the name of this person was Weller. / I find to my cost that *One Weller* was lost— / Cruel Destiny so to arrange it! / I love her dear name, which has won me some fame, / But, Great Heaven! how gladly I'd change it" (quoted in Johnson 1952, 498).

4. This image from Dickens's childhood has a kind of parallel in Freud's memory of being seduced by his nurse as a young child (during a period when Freud's mother gave birth to two siblings, one of whom died after several months). The memory came from his associations to a dream, which he described to Fliess: "I saw the skull of a small animal and in the dream I thought 'pig'" (1887–1904, p. 269). I would speculate that for Freud and perhaps also for Dickens, the color of the flesh of the pig is confused with that of the female genitals (as well as of sexually excited flesh). Dickens wrote of attending the "lyings-in," and Freud remembered about his nurse: "Moreover, she washed me in reddish water in which she had previously washed herself . . . The interpretation [of this] is not difficult" (1887–1904, p. 269).

years that Dickens's own mother frequently had a "lying in." Dickens was born in 1812; three younger siblings were born by 1820, and eventually there were ten in all. A brother born when Charles was two died after a few months. I assume that Dickens's confounding of his mother with his nursemaid Mary (an obvious prototype for the horrid, dishonest nurse Sairey Gamp in *Martin Chuzzlewit*)[5] contributed to the child's fear of women, and later to the man's. But alongside the awful Mrs. Gamp is the beloved nurse Peggotty in *David Copperfield*, who probably also stemmed from Mary Weller; here the compounding of nurse with mother would have influenced Dickens's love of women.

Dickens gives lengthy accounts of two of Mary Weller's terrifying stories. Both involve murder and cannibalism, and one features rats.

5. Sairey and her friend Betsey Prig were two humorously presented, coarse, selfish, and sadistic nurses. Sairey was also both a midwife and a "layer out" of dead bodies. (She is depicted as straightening out the arms of one of her sleeping charges to see what a "beautiful" corpse he will make.) Sairey is wont to praise herself and make indirect demands for food, money, and gin by quoting constantly in endless circumstantial detail from a "friend," Mrs. Harris (who turns out to be a creation of Sairey's invention). Here is an example of Sairey's sadism as expressed toward the depressed and senile old clerk Mr. Chuffey, who is one of her patients. His hesitant, wandering phrases mentioning death have disquieted his listeners, and Sairey responds: " 'Why, highty tighty, sir!' cried Mrs. Gamp. 'is these your manners? You want a pitcher of cold water throw'd over you to bring you round; that's my belief; and if you was under Betsey Prig you'd have it, too, I do assure you, Mr. Chuffey. Spanish Flies is the only thing to draw this nonsense out of you; and if anybody wanted to do you a kindness, they'd clap a blister of 'em on your head, and put a mustard poultige on your back. Who's dead, indeed! It wouldn't be no grievous loss if some one was, I think!' . . . Mrs. Gamp took him by the collar of his coat, and gave him some dozen or two of hearty shakes backward and forward in his chair; that exercise being considered by the disciples of the Prig school of nursing (*who are very numerous among professional ladies*) as exceedingly conductive to repose, and highly beneficial to the performance of the nervous functions. Its effect in this instance was to render the patient so giddy and addle-headed that he could say nothing more; which Mrs. Gamp regarded as a triumph of her art . . . 'Now, I hope, you're easy in your mind. If you should turn at all faint, we can soon revive you, sir, I promige you. Bite a person's thumbs, or turn their fingers the wrong way,' said Mrs. Gamp, smiling with the consciousness of at once imparting pleasure and instruction to her auditors, 'and they comes to, wonderful, Lord bless you!' " (Dickens 1843, 676; my italics).

The first story, told to him "hundreds of times" (1860b, p. 153), concerns a certain Captain Murderer who was given to murdering his many wives. First he would insist that they make pie crust for a meat pie: "Then said the lovely bride, 'Dear Captain Murderer, I see no meat.' The Captain humorously retorted, 'Look in the glass.' . . . And the bride looked up at the glass, just in time to see the Captain cutting her head off; and he chopped her in pieces, and peppered her, and salted her, and put her in the pie and sent it to the baker's, and ate it all, and picked the bones" (p. 151). Captain Murderer's last wife was the dark-haired, twin sister of one of his victims; she had seen her sister's murder through the window. She poisoned the pie-crust before the captain was able to kill her: "And Captain Murderer had hardly picked her last bone, when he began to swell, and to turn blue, and to be all over spots, and to scream. And he went on . . . until he reached from floor to ceiling and from wall to wall; and then . . . he blew up with a loud explosion" (1840b, pp. 152–153).

Mary Weller loved to tell this story to the frightened but fascinated boy:

> Hundreds of times did I hear this legend of Captain Murderer, in my early youth, and added hundreds of times was there a mental compulsion upon me in bed, to peep in at his window as the dark twin peeped and to revisit his horrible house [Dickens was sharing a sexual curiosity that had led to the death of the "dark twin"], and look at him in his blue and spotty and screaming stage, as he reached from floor to ceiling and from wall to wall. The young woman who brought me acquainted with Captain Murderer had a fiendish enjoyment of my terrors, and used to begin, I remember —as a sort of introductory overture—by clawing the air with both hands, and uttering a long hollow groan. So acutely did I suffer from this ceremony in combination with this infernal Captain, that I sometimes used to plead I thought I was hardly strong and old enough to hear the story again just yet. *But she never spared me one word of it.*" (1840b, p. 153; my italics)

The cheerful tone runs in counterpoint to the frightening subject matter until the last sentence, where Dickens's bitterness toward the nurse takes over. It is a shade of feeling we will come across again in relation to his mother.

Then there was the story of Chips and the rats: Chips, like his father and grandfather, sold himself to the Devil for an iron pot, a bushel of nails, half a ton of copper, and a rat that could speak. He did not want the rat, but he had no choice. The rat could read Chips's mind. Chips tried to kill it by pouring boiling pitch on it, but the rat would not die. The rat said instead (as the Devil had said before him):

> A Lemon has pips
> And a Yard has ships,
> And I'll have Chips.
> (1840b, p. 155)

The rat then disappeared, but a terrible thing happened the next day: Chips found a rat in his pocket:

> And in his hat he found another; and in his pocket handkerchief, another, and in the sleeves of his coat, when he pulled it on to go to dinner, two more. And from that time he found himself so frightfully intimate with all the rats in the Yard, that they climbed up his legs when he was at work and sat on his tools while he used them. And they could all speak to one another, and he understood what they said. And they got into his lodging, and into his bed, and into his teapot, and into his beer, and into his boots. (1840b, p. 155)

By appearing to the prospective bride, the rats interfere with Chips's getting married. Dickens adds this aside: "By this time *a special cascade of rats was rolling down my back*, and the whole of my small listening person was overrun with them. At intervals since, I have been morbidly afraid of my own pocket, lest my exploring hand should find a specimen or two of those vermin in it" (1840b, p. 156; my italics).[6]

Chips tried to run off to be a sailor, but the rats infested the ship and started to eat the planks. When Chips told the captain that the rats were "nibbling a grave for every man on board" (1840b, p. 157), the Captain thought him mad. But the rats did sink the ship and drowned the crew: "And what the rats—being water rats—left of Chips at last

6. Compare Freud's Rat Man. "Rolling down my back" and the fear of "my own pocket" show the characteristic "rat fear," of losing control of the anal sphincter, that is central to Chips's story and is clearly connoted by the listening child's sympathetic identification bringing on the psychological "*cascade* of rats." (One of the dictionary's definitions of chips is "dried pieces of dung.")

floated to shore, and sitting on him was an immense overgrown rat, laughing" (1840b, p. 157). The invasive, murderous, and cannibalistic rat imago emerges fully in this story; these rat meanings psychically evoke the primal parent—the parent-as-sphinx who eats its children— and subjection to the parent.

Mary Weller, who summoned up the Devil and the ghoulish rats, had another characteristic of the primal parent—mendaciousness (although it appears here in a playful, pretended, but still frighteningly intimi- dating way): "This same female bard . . . made a standing pretense which greatly assisted in forcing me back to a number of hideous places that I would by all means have avoided. This pretense was, that all her ghost stories had occurred to her relations. Politeness towards a meritorious family, therefore, forbade my doubting them, and they ac- quired an authentication that impaired my digestive powers for life" (1840b, pp. 157–158). Dickens as a boy was subject to abdominal colic, especially when under stress. He had a series of these attacks when he was working at a blacking factory "infested with rats" (see Wilson 1941, 14), where to his lasting shame and rage he had to work when his father was put in debtors' prison. Dickens wrote of Mary's recitation of the story of Chips and the rats: "As it always recurs to me in a vague association with calomel pills, I believe it to have been reserved for dull nights when I was low with medicine" (1840b, p. 153).[7]

Dickens ends his essay with a discussion of brainwashing:

> There was another narrative describing the apparition of a young woman who came out of a glass-case and haunted another young woman until the other young woman questioned it and elicited that its bones (Lord! To think of its being so particular about its bones!) were buried under the glass-case, whereas she required them to be interred, with every Undertaking solemnity up to twenty-four pound ten, in another particular place. This narrative I considered I had a personal interest in disproving, because we had glass- cases at home, and how, otherwise, was I to be guaranteed from the intrusion of young women requiring *me* to bury them up to twenty-four pound ten, when I had only twopence a week? But my remorseless nurse cut the ground from under my tender feet, *by*

---

7. Calomel was used as a purgative, and Dickens's "association" shows another linkage between the rat imago and the bowels.

informing me that She was the other young woman; and I couldn't say "I don't believe you"; it was not possible. (1840b, p. 158; my italics)

Dickens's Parents and the Blacking Factory

As far as can be gathered by his biographers, Dickens's parents appear to have been weak rather than cruel. At crucial times, they did not care enough ("the undeveloped heart"). His mother, Elizabeth Barrow Dickens, and his father, John Dickens, were in their twenties and had been married three years when Charles, their first son and second child, was born. Charles may have been fond of his mother in his earliest years. He told his friend John Forster that she had taught him to read, and coached him in English and even in the beginnings of Latin. Mary Weller, interviewed in her old age, called Elizabeth Dickens "a dear good mother and a fine woman" (Johnson 1952, 13), but one wonders how objective the creator of Captain Murderer was.[8]

John Forster called Dickens "a very little and a very sickly boy subject to attacks of violent spasm which disabled him from any exertion . . . but he had great pleasure in watching other boys at [active] games, reading while they played" (1872–74, p. 3). The attacks are believed to have been either intestinal or kidney colic, and Dickens also had migraine —both conditions came on when he was under stress. It is not known if Dickens's mother tended to him when he was sick, although he did praise his father for sitting up nights with him when he was afflicted. Some of the fictional characterizations of his mother, and Dickens's re-corded bitterness about his mother's ineffectuality and irresponsibility, suggest that she might have left his care to others in times of real need. Dickens described himself in a letter to Washington Irving as having been a "not-over-particularly-taken-care-of-boy" (Forster 1872–74, 6). As a man, his writings show that at least in his memory he had been much more fond of his father, who was also irresponsible (he is the model for Mr. Micawber in *David Copperfield*). He particularly liked

8. Dickens produced a cruel and hilarious satirical picture of his mother as the silly and unempathic, although not unloving, Mrs. Nickleby in *Nicholas Nickleby*, written when Dickens was twenty-six. He was astonished and amused when his mother did not recognize her fictional portrait.

taking long walks and going on excursions with his father during his years in Chatham.

The Blacking Factory

In 1822, when Charles was ten, his father's debts were increasing with the size of his family. John Dickens was transferred to London; Charles stayed in Chatham to finish the school term and was separated from the rest of his family for several months. During this time the family fortunes sank further. John Dickens had to sell some of his furniture before leaving Chatham, and Mary Weller, leaving the family service and now about to be married, bought some of the chairs, so she too was lost to Charles. All together, it was a traumatic separation for a ten-year-old. When the boy rejoined his family in London the debts were getting worse; in four rooms with a little back garret he found what were now eight members of his family, in addition to an orphan girl from the workhouse taken on as servant.

Dickens was intensely resentful that neither parent seemed to have had any idea of sending him to continue his schooling; they were of course intensely taken up with how to make ends meet. When Dickens was in his mid-thirties, he wrote about this time in an autobiographical fragment sent to his friend John Forster:

> I know my father to be as kindhearted and generous a man as ever lived in the world. Everything that I can remember of his conduct to his wife, or children, or friends, in sickness or affliction is beyond all praise. By me, as a sick child, he has watched night and day, unweariedly and patiently, many nights and days . . . He was proud of me, in his way, and had a great admiration of [my] comic singing. But, in the ease of his temper, and the straitness of his means, he appeared to have utterly lost at this time the idea of educating me at all, and to have utterly put from him the notion that I had any claim upon him, in that regard, whatever. So I degenerated into cleaning his boots of a morning, and my own; and making myself useful in the work of the little house; and looking after my younger brothers and sisters (we were now six in all); and going on such poor errands as arose out of our poor way of living. (Forster 1872–74, 13)

It made things much worse for the boy during these almost two years of "degeneration" that he did not know what was going on—why was his father not making everything all right? He did not understand his parents' whispered references to financial matters: Johnson comments on Foster's account: "Charles began to hear of a mysterious and ominous something called 'The Deed,' which he tremblingly confounded with one of those satanic compacts in the tales with which Mary Weller had terrified him or with the dark deeds of the witches in Macbeth" (1952, p. 28). Forster simply says Dickens "confounded 'The Deed' with parchment of a much more demoniacal description": "What dreadful thing had his kind father done? What awful fate was about to descend upon him: The child's imagination shuddered with uncertainty and apprehension" (Forster 1872–74, 9).

"The Deed," of course, had to do with his father's debts, which were steadily growing. During this time the boy's abdominal spasms and fever recurred. But worse was to come. When Charles was twelve, a relative of his mother offered to give him a job at a blacking factory, which made paste-blacking for boots and fire grates; Charles's task was to wrap and put labels on the blacking pots. He was to work twelve hours a day in a rat-infested old warehouse. (This must have revived the story of Chips.) In fictional form this terrible episode in the blacking factory was assigned to David Copperfield. But David was cast away by his stepfather and his stepfather's sister, the awful Murdstones. The unbearable fact was that Charles's real parents had sent him, a small boy in precarious health, to do menial work—a "young gentleman" thrown among common, lower-class boys with no future who jeered him for his way of speaking and being. This is recalled in an autobiographical fragment written for Forster in 1846 and included in Forster's *Life of Dickens*:

> It is wonderful to me how I could have been so easily cast away at such an age. It is wonderful to me, that, even after my descent into the poor little drudge I had been since we came to London, no one had compassion enough on me—a child of singular abilities, quick, eager, delicate, and soon hurt, bodily or mentally—to suggest that something might have been spared, as certainly it might have been, to place me at any common school . . . My father and mother were quite satisfied. They could hardly have been more so, if I had been twenty years of age, distinguished at a grammar-school, and going to Cambridge. (Forster 1872–74, 21)

The adult is still feeling the child's pain and reproach. (It was not the least of the child's bitterness that while he was thus "cast away" with no thought of his further education, his older sister, Fanny, was allowed to stay at the Royal Academy of Music, where she had won a boarding scholarship.)

Soon after the humiliating drudgery began at the factory came the worst of all: John Dickens was put into debtors' prison, the Marshalsea (this was to figure prominently in Dickens's novel *Little Dorrit*). When he saw the doors close on his father as a prisoner, Dickens wrote many years later, "I really believed at the time that they had broken my heart" (Forster 1872–74, 15). Some weeks after this, all the family and the orphan servant went into the prison to stay with the father (a not uncommon practice then)—all, that is, except for Charles and Fanny. Charles's father arranged for him to be lodged near the factory but quite far from the family in the prison. Charles spent Sundays at the Marshalsea with the family, and had barely enough to eat for the rest of the week. He had to pay for his own food out of what he earned at the blacking factory:

> I know I do not exaggerate, unconsciously and unintentionally, the scantiness of my resources and the difficulties of my life. I know that if a shilling or so were given me by anyone, I spent it in a dinner or a tea. I know that I worked, from morning to night, with common men and boys, a shabby child. I know that I tried, but ineffectually, not to anticipate my money, and to make it last the week through . . . I know that I lounged about the streets, insufficiently and unsatisfactorily fed. I know that, but for the mercy of God, I might easily have been, *for any care that was taken of me*, a little robber or a little vagabond. (Forster 1872–74, 25; my italics)

Here again the lack of parental empathy is hardest of all to bear—harder than the separation, harder by far than the attacks of colic that kept occurring, even at the factory, where one of the boys tried to ease Charles's pain by filling some of the blacking bottles with hot water and applying them to his side.

After about three months in the Marshalsea, John Dickens's mother died and left him money, and he was suddenly able to pay his debts and leave prison; the family then moved to a small house. But nothing was done about taking Charles out of the blacking warehouse. By this time the boy had become so skilled at tying up the blacking pots that crowds

would gather to watch him at the window. When his father once came
to visit him, Dickens wrote later, "I saw my father coming in at the door
one day when we were very busy, and wondered how he could bear
it" (Forster 1872–74, 32). Perhaps this public display caused Charles's
father to quarrel with the relative who had hired him, James Lamert.
In reaction to an angry letter from John Dickens, Lamert dismissed the
boy. His mother was distressed by this—probably the extra money was
still needed—and arranged for the boy to be taken back. But his father
was now set on ending the boy's work and sending him to school.

Dickens's autobiographical fragment comes to an emotional climax
with the words he uses to record his mother's "undeveloped heart": "I
do not write resentfully or angrily for I know how all these things have
worked together to make me what I am: but I never afterwards forgot,
I never shall forget, I never can forget, that my mother was warm for
having me sent back" (Forster, 1872–74, 32). Dickens appears to have
excused his father (whose bad aspects do come out in *Little Dorrit*), but
not his mother. The residue of feelings about the blacking factory he
describes in what he sent to Forster:

> From that hour until this at which I write, no word of that part
> of my childhood which I have now gladly brought to a close, has
> passed my lips to any human being. I have no idea how long it
> lasted; whether for a year, or much more, or less. *From that hour,
> until this, my father and mother have been stricken dumb upon it. I
> have never heard the least allusion to it, however far off and remote,
> from either of them.* I have never, until I now impart it to this paper,
> in any burst of confidence with any one, my own wife not excepted,
> raised the curtain I then dropped, thank God. (Forster 1872–74,
> 32–33; my italics)

My italics emphasize what made this terrible time a soul-murdering
business for Dickens: the denial of what had happened. The soul murder was partial—Dickens did not entirely repudiate his feelings. Indeed, he could not forget what had happened to him, what he felt had
been done to him:

> The deep remembrance of the sense I had of being utterly ne-
> glected and hopeless; of the shame I felt in my position; of the
> misery it was to my young heart to believe that, day by day, what I
> had learned, and thought, and delighted in, and raised my fancy

and my emulation up by, was passing away from me, never to be brought back any more; cannot be written. My whole nature was so penetrated with the grief and humiliation of such considerations, that even now, famous and caressed and happy, *I often forget in my dreams that I have a dear wife and children; even that I am a man; and wander desolately back to that time of my life.* (Forster 1872–74, pp. 22–23; my italics)[9]

And yet Dickens followed his parents' unspoken commands and could not talk with them about this "trauma from which he suffered all his life" (Wilson 1941a, 15). He could not deal effectively with his hatred of them, and a large part of it must have turned to guilt and to self-hatred and self-destructiveness. There were also positive and strengthening results: Dickens became determined never again to suffer such helplessness and misery; the trauma fed an intense ambition. But he was left with terrible conflicts: he needed both to idealize his parents and to accuse them, which made for splits in his inner images of his parents and in his own identity that can be seen projected into his fiction, particularly in *Little Dorrit* (1855–57), written when Dickens was in his early forties.

Little Dorrit

Little Dorrit (1855–57) is perhaps the most profound transcription into his fiction of Dickens's experience in this terrible time,[10] but as a novel it transcends this genetic personal source. It is one of the most telling of Dickens's studies of the English social and economic conditions of his time. Although predominantly somber, it has much of Dickens's won-

9. Dickens describes himself here as being unmanned by the memory, and I think that beneath the obvious reference to regression to childhood helplessness he was dealing with feeling like a woman, a need to become the mother he could not forgive, to distance his murderous hatred toward her.
10. Real and terrible as these occurrences were, the time in the blacking factory still probably has the significance of a screen experience. Aside from what he has written about the effect of Mary Weller's stories (and even these start at the age of five), we know nothing about which earlier childhood instances of overstimulation and helplessness were relived, condensed and disguised, in the experiences and then the memories of the blacking factory.

derful humor—and it presents a picture of soul murder, as do most of Dickens's other books (*Dombey and Son* is a particularly apt example).

In *Little Dorrit*, Dickens examines several instances of emotional deprivation and demonstrates how the "undeveloped heart" can warp the character and inhibit the ability to love. It is a novel of terrible accusation—of parents, and of society, and of the capitalist system in mid-nineteenth-century England. According to George Bernard Shaw, "*Little Dorrit* is a more seditious book than *Das Kapital*. All over Europe men and women are in prison for pamphlets and speeches which are to *Little Dorrit* as red pepper to dynamite" (quoted in Johnson 1952, 883). *Little Dorrit* contains the great metaphor of the English governmental bureaucracy as the Circumlocution Office, the motto of which is "How Not to Do It." In a masterful sublimation to effective social criticism, Dickens generalizes his parents' "undeveloped heart" and ineffectuality and transfers these qualities onto those who rule England. Edmund Wilson noted: "In his novels from beginning to end, Dickens is making the same point always: that to the English governing classes the people they govern are not real" (1941, p. 30). This lack of empathy is portrayed in those who govern families and institutions as well as the nation. Dickens's novels provided for his readers the sensory details of what it was like to be dependent, to be poor, to be in prison, to be a neglected child or servant or clerk or workman.

Dickens's novels are marred by his defensive need for splitting and denial; the accusations are accompanied by reassurances and falsifications. There are the compulsively happy endings that threaten to violate verisimilitude (and sometimes do). The bleak realism of *Little Dorrit* is partly spoiled by sentimentality, one of Dickens's chronic weaknesses. (The use of sentimentality to further denial is not uncommon in soul-murder victims). Probably as a result of how it became necessary to regard his parents, Dickens characteristically needed to deny some of the effects of the evil he was also able to portray and hate—a split registration typical of soul murder.

In this novel Dickens has split himself into a male alter ego and a female one: Arthur Clennam and Little Dorrit, the two main sufferers from lack of love and empathy as children. They are depicted as too noble and good to be true (especially Little Dorrit), considering the parental neglect and abuse to which they have been subjected. In similar, monolithic fashion, the badness that they would also have had (as any human being would) is split off and projected onto other characters who are completely villainous (for example, the hypocritical murderer Rigaud and the rage-filled, quasi-lesbian, paranoid feminist, Miss Wade).[11] This kind of juxtaposition is used in as early a work as *The Pickwick Papers* (1836), where the predominantly cheerful and humorous adventures of Mr. Pickwick and his friends are interrupted by strikingly contrasting interpolated tales, the predominant melodramatic content of which is full of violence and murder (see Wilson 1941a). The influence clearly remains of Mary Weller's bedtime stories: her last name is used for Pickwick's servant, Sam, and her first for the girl whom Sam is to wed.

The central image of *Little Dorrit* is that of a prison: the Marshalsea, the debtors' jail in which Little Dorrit's father, William, is put and into which he takes his wife and family (paralleling the experiences of the Dickens family). Dickens had an obsessive interest in prisons. They appear throughout his oeuvre, beginning with his first book, *Sketches by Boz*; he visited prisons wherever he went (see Wilson 1941a, 22).

Little Dorrit begins in "a villainous prison" (p. 2) in Marseilles: "A prison taint was on everything there. The imprisoned air, the imprisoned light, the imprisoned damps, the imprisoned men, were all deteriorated by confinement. As the captive men were faded and haggard, so the iron was rusty, the stone was slimy, the wood was rotten, the

---

11. These are the "flat" character caricatures that E. M. Forster (1927) describes as typical of Dickens. Caricature can convey some of the severe obsessive-compulsive (anal) defensiveness so often evoked by the need to distance the torment of an abused childhood—as in the case of Kaspar Hauser. Some of Dickens's caricatures (such as Sairey Gamp) are full of life as well as larger than life. When there is no admixture of love and hate in making the "flat" character, the character often falls flat. A case in point is the hateful Miss Wade, whom Dickens clearly hated. I am indebted to Professor Rena Grant for pointing out to me that Miss Wade is most likely herself a victim of soul murder: there is a kernel of truth in her paranoid narrative. Professor Grant remarked that the chapter written by Miss Wade, "The History of a Self-Tormentor," stands out as the only one in the book written in the first person—a formal way for Dickens of showing that something is very important to him. I speculate that the character (who has a twin in Rosa Dartle in *David Copperfield*) represents a projection of Dickens's consciously repudiated, destructive feminine self-image: the image of a self-tormenting seeker of revenge and punishment derived from the author's identification with hated aspects of his mother and his nurse.

air was faint, the light was dim. Like a well, like a vault, like a tomb, the prison had no knowledge of the brightness outside" (p. 3). In the last sentence, the prison is fully anthropomorphized and characterized as denying what it cannot control. The whole passage alludes to the blacking factory, which could have been described in similar terms. The prison also evokes aspects of Dickens's childhood, symbolically depicted (with falsification and exaggeration) as all bad, and as having been dominated by emotionally restrictive, depriving parents. Perhaps its basic symbolic meaning stems from the body as the confining house of the soul. A specific body symbol of the prison, conceived of as a terrible, dirty, and destructive place, would be the anus—the organ which closes and holds, projected onto the environment.

The prison in Marseilles contains the murderer Rigaud. The novel's hero, Arthur Clennam, is outside the prison but also confined—in quarantine with the rest of the passengers from a vacation cruise ship that has stopped at a plague-ridden port in the East. He describes himself to an acquaintance from the cruise, Mr. Meagles, a paterfamilias whose doting behavior is so different from what Clennam has experienced:

> I'm the son, Mr. Meagles, of a hard father and mother. I am the only child of parents who weighed, measured, and priced everything; for whom what could not be weighed, measured, and priced, had no existence. Strict people as the phrase is, professors of a stern religion, their very religion was a gloomy sacrifice of tastes and sympathies that were never their own, offered up as a part of the bargain for the security of *their possessions*. Austere facts, inexorable discipline, penance in this world and terror in the next —nothing graceful or gentle anywhere, and *the void in my cowed heart everywhere*—this was my childhood, if I may so misuse the word as to apply it to such a beginning of life. (p. 20; my italics)

The child, like some of my soul-murdered patients, had been treated as his parents' possession. He is now a man of about forty, who feels that life offers him nothing to look forward to. The description of himself that follows shows his awareness of having been subject to soul murder:

> "I have no will. That is to say," he coloured a little, "next to none that I can put in action now. Trained by main force; broken, not bent; heavily ironed with an object on which I was never consulted and which was never mine; shipped away to the other end of the

world before I was of age, and exiled there until my father's death there, a year ago; always grinding in a mill I always hated; what is to be expected from *me* in middle life? Will, purpose, hope? All those lights were extinguished before I could sound the words." (p. 20; italics in original)

When Arthur Clennam returns to his mother's home after years of absence, he finds everything unchanged: the dark, bare, and grim, prisonlike interior of his childhood home evokes the poverty of his mother's heart. She turns out to be as hard and rejecting as ever:

'How weak am I,' said Arthur Clennam . . . 'that I could shed tears at this reception! I, who have never experienced anything else; who have never expected anything else.'

He not only could, but did. It was the momentary yielding of a nature that had been disappointed from the dawn of its perceptions, but had not quite given up all its hopeful yearnings yet. (p. 31)

The abused and rejected child cannot help hoping to be loved *the next time* by the mother, who will have changed. Waiting for her to appear, Arthur looks around the familiar room:

The old articles of furniture were in their old places; the Plagues of Egypt, much the dimmer for the fly and smoke plagues of London, were framed and glazed upon the walls. There was the old cellerat with nothing in it, lined with lead, like a sort of coffin in compartments; there was the old dark closet, also with nothing in it, of which he had been many a time the sole contents, in days of punishment, when he had regarded it as the veritable entrance to that bourne to which the [biblical] tract had found him galloping. (p. 32)[12]

Like his creator, Arthur had believed literally in the stories his religiose parents had forced on him: "There was the dreary Sunday of his childhood, when he sat with his hands before him, scared out of his senses by a horrible tract which commenced business with the poor child by asking him in its title, why he was going to Perdition?—a piece of curiosity that he really in a frock and drawers was not in a condition

12. The pictures of the Plagues of Egypt would of course have included the murder of the first-born sons. Arthur was an only child.

to satisfy" (p. 28). Arthur recalls his parents in words that could have been used by my incest patient described in chapter 9: "[His mother] and his father had been at variance from his earliest remembrance. To sit speechless himself in the midst of rigid silence, glancing in dread from the one averted face to the other, had been the peacefullest occupation of his childhood" (p. 32).

His mother proceeds with her compulsive routine despite the return of the son she had not seen for so many years. Her servants bring in her usual evening refreshment at precisely nine o'clock. Her manservant and partner, the sinister Flintwich

> filled a tumbler with a hot and odorous mixture, measured out and compounded with as much nicety as a physician's prescription. Into this mixture, Mrs. Clennam dipped certain of the rusks and ate them; while the [maidservant] buttered certain other of the rusks, which were to be eaten alone. When the invalid had eaten all the rusks and drunk all the mixture, the two trays were removed; and the books and the candle, watch, handkerchief, and spectacles were replaced upon the table. She then put on the spectacles and read certain passages aloud from a book—sternly, fiercely, wrathfully—praying that her enemies (she made them by her tone and manner expressly hers) might be put to the edge of the sword, consumed by fire, smitten by plagues and leprosy, that their bones might be ground to dust, and that they might be utterly exterminated. As she read on, years seemed to fall away from her son like the imaginings of a dream, and all the old dark horrors of his usual preparation for the sleep of an innocent child to overshadow him. (pp. 34–35)

Dickens wonderfully evokes the obsessive, oppressive, joyless atmosphere of a home in which the parents sadistically identify with the wrathful God of the Old Testament, to maintain and fortify themselves while they exclude and terrify their child.

Later, Arthur gently defies his mother by refusing to continue in the family business. It is an unaccustomed defiance: "[I] represent to you that I have lived the half of a long term of life, and have never before set my own will against yours." Although obeying her in action, his soul has not completely given in—but he has been robbed of joy: "I cannot say that I have been able to conform myself, in heart and spirit, to your rules. I cannot say that I believe my forty years have been profitable or pleasant to myself, or any one; but I have habitually submitted, and I only ask you to remember it" (Dickens 1855–57, 44).

Arthur tells his mother that she has always been stronger than his father, and that he has never understood why she sent first her husband and then her son to the Orient to take care of the family business there. He suspects that his father had some gnawing guilt, and this is part of the reason Arthur is renouncing his rights in the family business. "Is it possible," he asks his mother, "that he had unhappily wronged any one, and made no reparation?" (Dickens 1855–57, 46). His mother, enraged by the question, calls for a Bible, and for Flintwich to stand witness: "Reparation! . . . let him look at me, *in prison and in bonds* here. I endure without murmuring, because it is appointed that I shall so make reparation for my sins." She picks up the Bible and resumes:

> In the days of old, Arthur, treated of in this commentary, there were pious men, beloved of the Lord, who would have cursed their sons for less than this; who would have sent them forth, and sent whole nations forth if such had supported them, to be avoided of God and Man, and perish, *down to the baby at the breast*. But I only tell you that if you ever renew that theme with me, I will renounce you; I will so dismiss you through that doorway, that you had better have been motherless from your cradle. I will never see or know you more. *And if, after all, you were to come into this darkened room to look upon me lying dead, my body should bleed, if I could make it, when you came near me.* (Dickens 1855–57, 47–48; my italics)

According to legend, it is the murderer who causes the dead body of the victim to bleed, so the mother is accusing the son of killing her. Like Jocasta, she is prohibiting him from proceeding toward the truth of his origins. And here Dickens exhibits a mother the reader cannot help but want to get rid of: she is presented without any of the guilt-making love that accounted for part of the ambivalence the author had toward his own mother. But her son Arthur is incapable of hating her, just as Little Dorrit, who is introduced a page or two after the diatribe by Arthur's mother, is maddeningly incapable of resenting the domination of her selfish and insufferable father and his unacknowledged abuse of her.

Later in the novel, before Clennam himself loses his money, he wants to help his mother:

It was like the oppression of a dream, to believe that shame and exposure were impending over her and his father's memory, and to be shut out, as by a brazen wall, from the possibility of coming to their aid. . . . His advice, energy, activity, money, credit, all his resources whatsoever, were *all made useless. If she had been possessed of the old fabled influence, and had turned those who looked upon her into stone, she could not have rendered him more completely powerless* (so it seemed to him in his distress of mind) than she did, *when she turned her unyielding face to his, in her gloomy room.* (Dickens 1855–57, 648–649; my italics)

The imagery gives the mother the power of the Gorgon, of Medusa: the monster-mother whose exhibitionism is used to entrap, excite, and castrate the son.

Arthur himself ends up in the Marshalsea; the prison swallows him and he begins to decline; he is symbolically trapped with his invalid mother, by her, and as her. In this "unmanned" state, he is sought out and tended to by Little Dorrit.

The novel ends happily in that Little Dorrit and Arthur Clennam marry, but the ending is bad artistically: Dickens brings in too many melodramatic and unbelievable plot devices to punish the wicked and reward the good. Mrs. Clennam suddenly ends her hysterical paralysis and not only walks but runs; it is revealed that she is not Arthur's natural mother (though Arthur himself is not made aware of this). Arthur was an illegitimate child of Mrs. Clennam's husband and a young girl from whom the wronged wife took the child. She later had the younger woman put in an asylum and persecuted her to her grave. She also claims (not too convincingly) to have cared about Arthur in her own way, and to have wanted to be loved by him. I speculate that Dickens's conflicts about his own natural mother may have contributed to his problems with the novel's ending, which mixes the psychologically false with the true. As her "crimes" are being revealed, Mrs. Clennam offers this justification for her acts: she had been "brought up strictly and straitly. . . . Mine was no light youth of sinful gaiety and pleasure. Mine were days of *wholesome* repression, punishment, and fear. The corruption of our hearts, the evil of our ways, the curse that is upon us, the terrors that surround us—these were the themes of my childhood. They formed my character *and filled me with an abhorrence of evildoers* (Dickens 1855–57, 740; my italics).

Thus Mrs. Clennam justifies as "wholesome" the soul murder practiced on her by her parents. By becoming "righteous" while abusing and depriving her "son," she repeated her relationship with her parents, actively reproducing the enforced passivity of her own childhood. Her partial conversion at the last minute into a loving and caring person, her softness toward Little Dorrit, is simply not credible. Everything is tied up in the ending by Victorian plot contrivances (stolen documents, unknown twin brothers, sudden, miraculous changes of character, the timely, accidental death of the villain Rigaud, the suddenly rich, impossibly good Daniel Doyce, who functions as a deus ex machina in rescuing Arthur from the prison), and these are inconsistent with the realities of individual psychology. But they still leave Dickens the scope to serve the truth of the psychology of soul murder, at least unconsciously. Mrs. Clennam is portrayed at the end as the Sphinx. The motivation for her sudden conversion from hysterical paralysis to locomotion goes to the heart of soul murder; the child she has abused must not know the truth. This Jocasta had not been impelled to see or help her son when he was crippled by imprisonment for debt and lying ill in the Marshalsea. But like Jocasta and the Sphinx, the mother cannot bear to have her son solve her riddle. To keep Arthur from learning the truth, she literally runs off (after astounding her servants and Rigaud by first rising from her wheelchair and standing).[13] And she gets Little Dorrit to promise that while the mother lives, she will never reveal to Arthur the truth of his parentage—the Sphinx must keep the symbiosis intact. Finally, further paralleling the fate of Jocasta and the Sphinx, the mother is destroyed when her secret is revealed. As Mrs. Clennam is watching the unexpected and terrifying explosion of her house (like Captain Murderer's house!), symbol becomes what is symbolized when she has an inner explosion and is felled by a stroke. Thus Dickens punishes her with true paralysis—followed by some years of being an immobile, uncommunicating, living "statue" (p. 738)—before killing her off. The author is able to become the triumphant Oedipus, reversing the usual course of events by depriving the Sphinx of locomotion and life.

One feels that Dickens knows that he hates Mrs. Clennam, even

13. The destructive parent (here to keep her hold on the son who might otherwise walk away) goes through some of the changes in locomotion that are at the heart of the riddle of the Sphinx (see chapter 4).

though some denial compulsively forces itself through at the end. But more of Dickens's hatred of women peeks through in his revelation (of which he seems unaware) of the suppressed anger *of* Little Dorrit that simultaneously expresses Dickens's suppressed anger *toward* Little Dorrit. She seems only too delighted to be able to nurse the depressed and sick Arthur Clennam, as she once had her own father. The decline and imprisonment of Clennam at the end of the novel bring out Little Dorrit as the nurse: "[She] *nursed* him as lovingly, and *GOD* knows as *innocently*, as she had *nursed* her father in that room when she had been but a baby, needing all the care from others that she took of them" (Dickens 1855–57, 723; my italics). The capitalization of "GOD" is Dickens's. I speculate that an extraordinary amount of idealization in the service of denial might have been necessary here to make for Dickens's "innocently." Innocence is appropriate neither to the soul murder of Little Dorrit herself nor to her reappearance here as the nurse—bringing Dickens and us back to Mary Weller.

There is a compulsive, controlling masochism in Little Dorrit; she is trapped by her fixation on her father, and now turns to a man almost old enough to be her father, who had been wont to call her jestingly his daughter. Although now supposedly rich, she even dresses in her old prison clothes when she first goes to see the imprisoned Clennam. But her suppressed sadistic side is exposed (showing her own identification with the soul murderer) when she cooperates with Mrs. Clennam's disavowing purpose by agreeing never to tell Arthur about his real mother until his false mother is dead. Even after she marries Arthur, Little Dorrit does not reveal to him the truth of his lineage. She was similarly never able to face the evil in her father. Just before they marry, Little Dorrit even has Arthur unknowingly burn the documents that would have revealed Mrs. Clennam's secret:

> "My dear love," said Arthur. "Why does Maggy light the fire? We shall be gone directly."
> "I asked her to do it. I have taken such an odd fancy. I want you to burn something for me."
> "What?"
> "Only this folded paper. If you will put it in the fire with your own hand, just as it is, my fancy will be gratified."
> "Superstitious, darling Little Dorrit? Is it a charm?"
> "It is anything you like best, my own," she answered, laughing

with glistening eyes and standing on tiptoe to kiss him, "if you will only humour me when the fire burns up."

So they stood before the fire waiting: Clennam with his arm about her waist, and the fire shining, as the fire in that same place had often shone, in Little Dorrit's eyes. "Is it bright enough now?" said Arthur. "Quite bright enough now," said Little Dorrit. "Does the charm want any words to be said?" asked Arthur, as he held the paper over the flame. "You can say (if you don't mind) 'I love you!'" answered Little Dorrit. So he said it, and the paper burned away. (Dickens 1855–57, 787)

Little Dorrit obviously feels she is acting for Arthur's good in keeping the truth from him, as Mrs. Clennam felt she was, and Dickens goes along by clearly portraying this castrative and mendacious protectiveness as a loving act. Perhaps most apparent in this passage is the legacy of soul murder in Dickens, so closely associated for him with the feminine and his mother. This split in the registration of what is happening and has happened makes it possible to "love Big Brother" or "Bad Nurse" or "Bad Mother." Dickens himself is Little Dorrit and cannot tell himself the whole truth.[14]

I have not dealt adequately with Dickens's strengths: his generosity, kindness, and capacity for enjoyment, his talents as an actor, his amazing industry and marvelous imagination. Some of this imagination and some of his humor do come through in the excerpts I have quoted.[15] I have said nothing about the intensity of his attachment to his wife's sisters and his idealization of innocent young girls (see Kligerman 1970) and have not dealt with his marital troubles, his desertion of his wife,[16]

14. In relation to Dickens's feminine identification with "Bad Nurse": William Allingham, in his diary for 1850, reports being "at a performance given at the Hanover Square Rooms, in which Dickens played . . . Mrs. Gamp 'in brown bonnet and corkscrew curls'" (1907, p. 68).

15. It is interesting that although Dickens makes his mother the butt of humor in his transformation of her into Mrs. Nickleby, he leaves that character bereft of a sense of humor of her own, even though by all accounts Elizabeth Dickens definitely had one.

16. Dickens separated from his wife, Catherine, in 1858, after he had completed *Little Dorrit*. Among the charges he made in self-justifying letters to his friends was that she had never been a good mother to their nine children: "If the children loved her, or ever had loved her, this severance would have been

or his affair with the young actress Ellen Ternan, nor with his qualities as a father of his nine children. The picture I have drawn connecting Dickens with soul murder is not balanced. (If one had the facts, however, one might find his talents and strengths, as well as his subject matter, linked genetically to his early, traumatic experiences.)

After *Little Dorrit* Dickens had thirteen productive years. The obsession with murder and murderers continued to the end. It has frequently been observed that Dickens committed murder against himself by continuing with his public readings, against his doctors' advice, after heart disease had been diagnosed (see for example Wilson 1941). These readings, which ranged from the comic to the horrific, were wildly successful.

It was especially taxing for Dickens to read an excerpt from *Oliver Twist* that culminated in Nancy's murder by Bill Sikes and in Sikes's flight and death:

> He had indeed made something appalling. One warm afternoon [Dickens's son] Charley was working in the library with the windows open when he heard a sound of violent wrangling from outside. At first he dismissed it as some tramp beating his wife, but as the noise swelled into an alternation of brutal yells and dreadful screams Charley leaped to his feet, convinced that he must interfere. He dashed out of the door. There, at the other end of the meadow, was his father—murdering an imaginary Nancy with ferocious gestures. (Johnson 1952, 1102)

---

a far easier thing than it is. But she has *never* attached one of them to herself, *never* played with them in their infancy, *never* attracted their confidence as they have grown older, *never* presented herself before them in the aspect of a mother" (Dupee 1960, 235; my italics). "I will merely remark of her that the peculiarity of her character has thrown all the children on someone else" (Dupee 1960, 237). The repeated "nevers" evoke the terrible "I never afterwards forgot, I never shall forget, I never *can* forget" that Dickens applied to his mother in connection with the blacking factory. There were many and complex reasons for the separation, but in part it seems to have been based on Dickens's unconscious confounding of his wife with his mother. Toward both he became implacably hostile. Once he separated from his wife, he lived for twelve more years without ever seeing her again—and, as with his mother, he never forgave her (see Dupee 1960, 161).

Dickens added this frightening item to his repertory during the last year of his life. Already exhausted by the readings, he was entreated by family and friends not to include the excerpt from *Oliver Twist*; everyone agreed that he did it marvelously, but the vivid enactment took so much out of him. His pulse was routinely taken by his friend Dr. Frank Beard after such readings, and was at its highest after "Sikes and Nancy." During his last tour of Britain his manager, Dolby, was appalled to learn that Dickens intended to include the murder scene three nights out of every four, and tried to persuade him to reserve it for the larger towns:

> Dickens bounded up from his chair and threw his knife and fork so violently on his plate that it was smashed to pieces. "Dolby!" he shouted, "your infernal caution will be your ruin one of these days!" It was the only time Dolby had ever heard him address an angry word to anyone . . . Then [Dolby] saw that his Chief was crying. "Forgive me, Dolby!" he exclaimed between sobs, going toward him and embracing him affectionately. "I really didn't mean it; and I know you are right." (Johnson 1952, 1108)

But he continued to include "Sikes and Nancy" in his performances. It was his doctor's opinion that the repeated readings of this violent and melodramatic scene did hasten Dickens's death.

The prostitute Nancy (Dickens removed the word *prostitute* after the first edition) is the soul-murder victim of her lover, Bill Sikes, who treats her with a demeaning, terrifying, jealous possessiveness. In the novel, soul murder culminates in actual murder. Sikes brutally clubs Nancy to death after he learns that she has betrayed him and others in Fagin's gang. This is more than the primitive and ferocious Sikes can bear—the one person he is close to (in his own savage, narcissistic way) does not really care for him, can contemplate separating from him. This motivation is one Dickens could share, and killing Nancy provided a cathartic outlet for the author's suppressed murderous feelings.

Doing the readings brought on a kind of feverish, addictive arousal in Dickens that reached its height with Sikes's murder of Nancy. His reading and acting out of the scene (Wilson calls it "an obsessive hallucination"; see Wilson 1941, 85) involved him in a fascinated horror that made him his own Mary Weller. Despite knowing that it was destructive for him, Dickens felt compelled to repeat the excitement of the murderous encounter and its hysterical reception by the audiences; he was both participating in the killing and looking on at it. For Dickens this was like his empathizing again with the dark-haired twin looking on at Captain Murderer—a murderous primal scene in which he could play both roles.

Wilson believes that reading "Sikes and Nancy" enabled Dickens to reenact symbolically the banishment of his wife, Catherine. This is probably true, but it scants the terrible destructive intensity from the world of childhood nightmare that reading the scene allowed him to discharge in sublimation: the pent-up, cannibalistic hatred toward his betraying mother and all such "bad" (prostitute) women. At the same time, Dickens could become the murdered Nancy succumbing to a brutal man, and this feminine, masochistic identification both provided gratification and fulfilled a need to be punished (like the identification with Little Dorrit). Becoming the woman he both loved and hated meant that Dickens could turn the destructive rage on himself—being Sikes to his own Nancy. This was a suicidal course, and his compulsive, passionate commitment to it did contribute to his death. Three months after his last reading, at a time when there were many premonitory symptoms, he died at fifty-eight of a paralytic stroke—the same fate he had assigned to Mrs. Clennam.

God's Concentration Camps

In the Introduction I quoted Randall Jarrell's characterization of another English writer, Kipling, as "someone who [had] been for for some time the occupant of one of God's concentration camps" (1963, p. 146; this referred to the time that Kipling spent as a boy in what he called the "House of Desolation"—see chapter 12). In an article published after his tragic suicide, the writer Primo Levi discusses how after his book about being a prisoner in Auschwitz appeared, he was asked by an eight-year-old in a fifth-grade class he was addressing why he had not tried to escape. He explained to the children that the inmates had felt escape was impossible. The American and British prisoners of war, who were relatively well fed, had tried repeatedly to escape; they had been able to sustain themselves physically with packages from the Red Cross and to keep up their morale through a system of discipline that won respect from the Germans. In contrast, the inmates of the concentration camp were weak and starving, and covered with sores—especially on their feet. Their morale had been undermined by the implacable torture of the Nazis who guarded, fed, and despised them but on whose whim their very lives depended. (This dependence, we know, made the prisoners prone to some degree to identify with their torturers and turn the guilt on themselves. They had to love Big Brother; the very source of their torment was their only hope for rescue and survival. The incompatibility of this need for love and the inevitability of hate splits the soul, makes for brainwashing's break with reality.) The concentration camp's prisoners found it almost impossible to maintain any bond of mutuality; instead they had been divided by clever manipulation and forced to turn on one another in suspicion and betrayal. An attempt at escape was treated as the worst of crimes and punished with brutal torture leading to certain death. So escape was almost physically and psychologically impossible. Above all, there was no place an escaped prisoner could go. The Jews especially had no relatives or friends to provide refuge, for they were regarded after years of propaganda as evil and hated enemies of the state. No foreign border was open to them; they felt trapped like helpless children. The eight-year-old who had put the question to Levi then asked him to draw the concentration camp, the position of the fences, the guards, and so on:

> My interlocutor studied the drawings for a few instants . . . then he presented to me the plan he had worked out: here, at night, cut the throat of the sentinel; then, put on his clothes; immediately after this, run over there to the power station and cut off the electricity, so the search lights would go out and the high tension fence would be deactivated; after that I could leave without any trouble. He added seriously: "If it should happen to you again, do as I told you. You'll see that you'll be able to do it." (Levi 1987, 12)

It is not only an eight-year old who cannot bear to feel what it is like to be in a concentration camp, to be a child neglected and unprotected by benevolent God or Fate, in the complete power of tyrannical authority. The experience of overwhelming pain and torture cannot be kept in mind very long. And we can all regress to the time when it was insupportable to feel that we had a Bad Parent; this feeling evokes the possibility of having no parent, and the danger of losing the parent and parental love is one of the greatest resistances to change in the adult. Dickens's reading (perhaps an unconsciously motivated suicide, like Levi's and Jarrell's) can help us to achieve that terrible empathy with the victim of soul murder for whom Dickens struggled so manfully in his life and whom he projected so vividly in his writings.

11

Sanity and Paranoia
The Cases of Chekhov and Schreber

Anton Chekhov was regularly beaten as a young man by a sadistic, tyrannical father—an irrational persecutor of his wife and children. In many fictional and direct portraits his father, Pavel, is marvelously brought to life as a selfish, irrational, religiose, intermittently senti-mental and "loving," irascible, petty, miserly shopkeeper. Such a vivid evocation is not achieved for Anton himself. Although areas of uncer-tainty and mystery inevitably remain, good biographies of Dickens and Kipling give the reader a conviction of what they were like, or at least an illusion of what they were like. In contrast, the biographers' Chekhov, although at times vividly alive, is terra incognita in some areas essential to empathizing with his inner life, his soul (for example, the qualities of his ability to love others and of his sexual life). In his fiction and plays Chekhov is able to depict essential moments that marvelously bring out human character, but like some of his heroes and heroines, the author manages to present himself as an enigma. He is the "good doctor" who is able to observe and understand others, but who, despite disclosing so many specific, contradictory details about himself keeps his inner self hidden. (There is a similar, typical withdrawal in George Orwell; it is also present, more intermittently and less characterologically, in Dickens and Kipling, who like some of their characters frequently erupt into involved caricature. This elusiveness may be a defensive manifes-tation of soul murder. Schreber too fails to emerge convincingly from the many pages written by and about him—at least the healthier aspects of his character do, in contrast to the caricature imposed by his pathology; see H. Israels 1981.)

In 1892, when Anton Chekhov was thirty-two, he had a nightmare in which a black monk rushed at him out of a whirlwind. He worked this dream into one of his longer stories, *The Black Monk* (published in 1894).

At thirty-two Chekhov was already a famous author in Russia. He was also a physician, spending a part of every working day practicing medicine on his estate. He was unmarried but very popular with women. The details of his sexual life remain mysterious, but judging from his letters he seems to have slept with a variety of women. His brother Michael said that Anton had had many affairs with girls when he was a teenager, and Chekhov himself wrote in an autobiographical sketch of 1892: "I was initiated into the secret of love at the age of thirteen" (quoted in Magarshack 1952, 27). But he had some difficulty with sustained intimate relationships and repeatedly eluded marriage until after he was forty. He finally wed the young actress Olga Knipper in 1901, but lived apart from her for long periods during the few remaining years of his life. He died in 1904 at the age of forty-four.

In 1892 Chekhov was the head of a large household and the chief support of his parents and siblings. (He was the third of five brothers and had a younger sister.) From his eighteenth year he had had symptoms of the tuberculosis that would finally kill him, and in recent years he had been in worse health, suffering from severe coughing fits.[1] At the time his dream occurred, he had been summoned home from St. Petersburg because his father was gravely ill.

Chekhov's father, Pavel, was a freed serf who had made his way in life through hard and humiliating work, mostly as a small shopkeeper in Taganrog, a provincial town on the sea of Azov. After he went bankrupt Pavel sneaked away and the family moved to Moscow, leaving Anton, then sixteen, in Taganrog for several years to finish his schooling. During Anton's childhood, Pavel was a petty tyrant at home and in his shop, where the children were forced to work; selfish and inflexible, he beat his children savagely for real or fancied disobedience. In

---

1. Chekhov suffered many illnesses of the chest, with much spitting up of phlegm between the ages of seven and nine, and two later attacks of peritonitis. This suggests that Chekhov acquired the tuberculosis before he was eighteen (see Hingley 1976, 18).

an "autobiographical passage" (Magarshack 1952, 16) from his story *Three Years*, published a year after *The Black Monk*, Chekhov wrote: "[I was] born when mother was worn-out from being in a perpetual state of terror. I remember Father started giving me lessons—putting it bluntly, he started beating me—before I was five even. He birched me, boxed my ears, hit me on the head. The first thing I did when I woke up every morning was wonder whether I'd be beaten that day. [My brothers] and I were forbidden to play games or have any fun" (1895, p. 102).

The hero of *Three Years* writes to his brother: "For every step I take I'm scared of being flogged. I cringe before nonentities, idiots, swine who are immeasurably inferior to me both intellectually and morally. I'm afraid of house porters, janitors, city police. I'm scared of everyone because I was born of a persecuted mother—from childhood I've been beaten and bullied. We'd both do well not to have children. [Chekhov did not have any children.] Let's hope, God willing, that the distinguished merchant house comes to an end with us" (1895, p. 151). A biographer notes of Pavel Chekhov:

> One night he pinned a set of rules on the wall in which the duties of each member of the family were carefully enumerated. The first morning these "Rules and Regulation of the Domestic Duties of the Family of Pavel Chekhov, resident in Moscow" appeared, Michael got up later than he should have done and was given a whipping by his father. When he pointed out that he did not know anything about the rules as he was asleep when they were pinned up on the wall, Pavel replied: "You should have known about them." After Ivan, who was a boy of seventeen, joined his family in Moscow, he, too, committed some offense. Pavel took him out into the yard and whipped him so mercilessly that the neighbours came running at his cries and the landlord threatened to give them notice. (Magarshack 1952, 33)

Pavel Chekhov had an obsessive interest in church music and organized family religious services, insisting that Anton takes a place in his amateur church choir even when the boy desperately needed sleep. There was no Sunday or holiday rest for any of the children: "The tubercle bacillus, Chekhov's ultimate executioner, had a powerful ally in the regimen of his early days: the intensive shop-minding [for his father], the punitive ritual of church-going, involving much sleeplessness and braving the blizzards . . . in the small hours" (Hingley 1976, 18).

Chekhov studied to become a physician, and to supplement his income began to write and publish comic sketches (at first under the pseudonym Antosha Chekhonte, given him by a priest who was a favorite schoolteacher), and then the stories that made him famous. He displaced his father as the emotional head of the family, at nineteen organizing the family so efficiently in its tenement in Moscow that his older brother Alexander dubbed him "Papa Antosha" (Troyat 1984, 40). Although he has been described as characteristically kind and easygoing, Anton was capable of acting the stubborn tyrant, like his father, and sometimes insisted on having his own way in family matters. By the time he was twenty-one, he had become the family's financial mainstay.

The hero of *The Black Monk*, Andrey Kovrin, is an intellectual, a university lecturer on psychology and philosophy. He lives a "nervous . . . restless" (1894a, p. 318) and empty life. As the story opens he is in a state of nervous exhaustion. Advised by his doctor to spend spring and summer in the country, he accepts an invitation to stay with his former guardian, the celebrated horticulturist Yegor Pesotzsky, who had brought up Andrey after the boy's parents had died.[2] Pesotzsky lives with his daughter, Tanya, who helps him tend his experimental gardens. Kovrin's foster father, Yegor, is described as tall, broad-shouldered, and fat—suffering from shortness of breath, yet walking so rapidly that it is difficult to keep up with him.[3] Yegor is tyrannical,

2. Chekhov wrote *The Black Monk* at his newly purchased estate in Melikhovo, near Moscow. He became an amateur horticulturist, and for a while an obsessed one like Yegor, buying and planting hundreds of trees. The horticultural details from his story came from his personal experience (see Hingley 1976, 161).

3. Chekhov's paternal grandfather was named Yegor. It was he who had saved money to buy the family out of serfdom (Chekhov's father, Pavel, was born a serf). Anton was very much influenced by this old man, for the family used to spend the summer on the estates that Yegor managed. Like his son Pavel, Yegor was most religious and a stern taskmaster. Magarshack (1955) calls him "a very religious man, somewhat of an eccentric and, as Chekhov characterised him, 'a most rabid upholder of serfdom'" (p. 18). This Yegor most likely contributed unconsciously to the character of Yegor Pesotsky and to his representation as the Black Monk: "When I was a boy staying with Grandfather

selfish, and obsessed by his work, to which he is prepared to sacrifice his child's future welfare. He lives in dread of her marrying a stranger who will not care for his beloved gardens. He is depicted as impatient and blustering, quick to threats and anger, yet at other times sentimentally kind—in fact, not unlike Pavel Chekhov. Both Yegor and Tanya idealize Kovrin, and the old man (who has thought of him as a future son-in-law) is very happy to see him. When Andrey arrives, the father and daughter are worried about the effect of the frost on their gardens. Tanya and Andrey walk through the gardens and orchard, where "a dense, *black*, acrid smoke was spreading over the ground and enveloping the trees" (1894b, p. 193; my italics). They talk about the smoke, which is meant to protect the trees from the frost. Tanya tells Kovrin how much she wants him to treat her and her father as his family, and he says that he does. She says: "You must know Father idolizes you. At times I think he loves you more than me. He's proud of you" (1894b, p. 194).

Tanya speaks of how much it meant to her when Andrey would come back to visit them during his school holidays when she was a little girl. Her voice is full of feeling. "Suddenly Kovrin was struck by the idea that he might even conceive an affection for this small, fragile, loquacious creature . . . and fall in love . . . he leant down toward that dear, worried face and softly sang:

> Onegin I will not hide it
> I love Tatyana madly (1894b, p. 195)[4]

on Count Platov's estate I had to spend entire days from dawn to dusk noting the weight of the threshed grain. The whistles, the hissing, the deep whirring note of the threshing engine under full steam, creaking wheels, plodding oxen, *clouds of dust*, fifty-odd labourers with *black*, dusty faces: it all etched itself in my memory like the Lord's Prayer" (Chekhov, quoted in Hingley 1976, 17; my italics).

4. This is the beginning of an aria from Tchaikovsky's opera *Eugene Onegin*, the libretto of which is derived from Pushkin's great poem. It is sung by Tatyana's somewhat elderly husband, Count Gremin, to his friend Onegin, who had rejected Tatyana's love for him when she was a young girl. But now that she is married to Gremin and has become a beautiful, self-assured woman, Onegin is beginning to fall in love with her. It is an oedipal triangle: that she belongs to his friend Gremin and is now unavailable makes her more desirable to Onegin.

Tanya and Andrey return to the house, and Kovrin then goes back into the gardens with Yegor. The old man asks about Andrey's life at the university. "*But suddenly* he pricked up his ears, making a *terrible* face, ran to one side . . . and soon disappeared in the clouds of [black] smoke behind the trees (Chekhov 1894a, 317; 1894b, 196; my italics). One of Yegor's serfs had carted *manure* into the orchard and tied his horse to an apple tree, from which the tight reins rubbed off some bark. Yegor has a hysterical tantrum, crying out that "they" have ruined his garden, "*ruined, frozen, polluted, mucked everything up!*" (1894b, p. 196; my italics). "Hanging's too good for him" (p. 196), Yegor says.

This fit of paranoid temper (we are told it is characteristic) is stimulated by a small detail of disorder in the orchard filled with *black* smoke. Part of what I have underlined alludes to the anal connotations of the castrative effect on Yegor of the rubbing off of a bit of bark, in a scene witnessed by Andrey. Yegor's garden has been violated, and it is unconsciously an anal rape. The murderous hanging fantasy results. At the beginning of this incident, Chekhov supplies an instance of what I have frequently seen in former victims of soul murder, which I have called the "and suddenly phenomenon." A phrase such as this emerges in the associations of a patient who seems oversensitive to sudden changes in others (with a corresponding tendency to quick alterations in the patient's own mood and behavior). I have sometimes found this traceable to patients' experiences from childhood: sudden changes in the parent (often psychotic) prefigured an angry or sexual attack on the child. These attacks were usually interpreted by the victim as an abrupt rage in which the good parent was completely lost and transformed into a monster. The scene in the garden resembles what Anton Chekhov would have witnessed in his childhood as repetitive behavior of his father, Pavel. Yegor's sudden change from a friendly father figure into someone full of rage with a "terrible face" represents the transformation of the good, empathic parent into the cannibalistically impatient, destructive, humorless primal parent (Sphinx). The scene reveals Yegor's easily evoked violence, his outrage at a bit of disorder; and it gives a sense of what it must have been like to have been a child, serf, or servant under his care (or Pavel Chekhov's, or, as we shall see, Father Schreber's). The rest of the scene also evokes Pavel's contradictory character: "After he had calmed down [Yegor] put his arms round Kovrin and kissed him on the cheek. 'Well, God bless, God bless' . . . he muttered. 'I'm very pleased you came. I can't say how glad I am'" (1894b, p. 196). The sun rises—Kovrin anticipates a fine day and a long, fine summer ahead. There follows another "and suddenly": "And suddenly there welled up within him that feeling of radiant, joyous youth he had known in his childhood, when he had run around this garden. And he embraced the old man in turn and kissed him tenderly" (1894b, pp. 196–197). Andrey feels happy: the present and future seem full of splendor. He tries to work, to read a book. "It seemed every vein in his body was pulsating and throbbing with pleasure" (1894b, p. 197).

This joy does not last. Andrey is again sleepless and irritable. One evening he hears Tanya and some friends rehearse a song (Braga's *Serenade*) about a psychotic girl whose strange hallucinations transport her to heaven. After this he becomes obsessed with a legend the source of which he cannot remember. It concerns the image of a black monk first seen a thousand years ago in the Syrian wilderness. The monk's image moves through the earth's atmosphere and is reflected in it. After being seen all over the world, the image leaves the earth for the heavens. There is a prophecy that the black monk is to return after a thousand years. Thinking of the legend and wondering how he knows about it, Andrey walks to a deserted and exposed place by a river bank, where he feels alone and yet thinks: "It feels as if the whole world were watching me, hiding and waiting for me to understand it" (1894a, p. 320). The wind rustles through the rye, and he hears it disturb the trees *behind* him. Then Kovrin stands "motionless in astonishment" (1894b, p. 199) at what he sees ahead (here is another "sudden" event): "On the horizon a tall black column was rising up into the sky, like a whirlwind or tornado. Its outlines were blurred, but he could see at once that it was not standing still, but moving at terrifying speed straight towards him" (1894b, p. 199).

As it nears, the column becomes smaller and clearer. It is the black monk, smiling kindly yet slyly at Kovrin (who has to jump aside to avoid him). He passes by, and as he grows larger flies across the river and disappears. Although he feels the monk is probably a hallucination and that he will be thought mad if he talks about it, Kovrin has a sense of great joy.

After this Yegor tells Andrey of his greatest fear: that Tanya will marry and leave him, and that there will be no one to care for his beloved gardens after his death.[5] He suggests that Andrey marry Tanya

5. Here Chekhov projects himself onto Yegor. Twice when he was the head of the household (and during the years at his estate in Melikhovo, where he wrote *The Black Monk*) he impeded the marital prospects of his sister. Maria,

so that they can all stay together: "You're the only man I wouldn't mind marrying my daughter . . . but the main reason is—I love you like a son" (1894b, p. 202). This triangle of older man, young woman, and young man is an idealized variation on the scene involving Prince Gremin, Tatyana, and Onegin from Tchaikovsky and Pushkin[6]—here with a promise of all three sharing love.

Yegor leaves, and Andrey starts to read some of the old man's horticultural articles, which are full of petty, quarrelsome detail infused with pathological hatred and rivalry. There follows an argument between Yegor and Tanya, who accuses her father of tormenting her with his verbal abuse. She weeps bitterly, and Kovrin feels that Tanya and her father are the only people he has ever loved (he is an orphan whose mother died of consumption), that Tanya is like him: "This weeping, trembling girl's nerves were reacting to his own half-sick, overwrought nerves like iron to a magnet. He could never have loved a healthy, strong, rosy-cheeked woman, but that pale, weak, unhappy Tanya attracted him" (1894b, p. 205).

Father and daughter make up, and Andrey goes out for a walk. He thinks about the black monk and then sees him a second time; the monk again smiles at Andrey and talks to him. Andrey asks the monk why he is looking at him "so rapturously" and asks, "Do you like me?" The monk replies: "Yes. You're one of the few who are rightly called God's Chosen. You serve Eternal Truth. Your ideas, intentions, your amazing erudition, your whole life—all bear the divine, heavenly stamp" (1894b, p. 206). The monk says that Kovrin is one of the elect who will lead humanity toward a wonderful future. He affirms that he himself

---

three years younger than her famous brother, was devoted to him and closer to him emotionally than to anyone else in the family. She dedicated her life to her brother and was his literary executor after he died. She also tended to things for him as Tanya did for Yegor: for example, she helped oversee the frenzied tree planting that Chekhov started when he bought Melikhovo. Maria Chekhov was seriously interested in at least one of her two suitors, but she remained unmarried, serving her brother Anton during his lifetime and long after his death. Chekhov's biographer Hingley (1976) states that Chekhov's selfish coldness when Maria asked him whether she should marry "must rate as the unkindest single act in a life happily marked by few instances of comparable inconsiderateness" (p. 165).

6. Actually, Gremin is the name given to Tatyana's husband in the opera only. In the poem he is Prince N., not only an older friend of Onegin's but a relative, which enhances the incestuous nature of the triangle.

is an apparition, a product of Kovrin's imagination. He enjoins Andrey not to worry if this is madness: "Nowadays scientists say that genius is akin to madness . . . only the mediocre, the common herd, are healthy and normal . . . if you want to be healthy and normal, go join the herd" (1894b, p. 207). Andrey feels that the monk is expressing his own ideas. The monk disappears and Andrey is left in ecstasy. He meets Tanya, feels he loves her, and impulsively asks her to marry him. She agrees.

Tanya and Andrey are married; Yegor is delighted. The hallucinations and Kovrin's joy and sense of heightened powers continue. Then the black monk appears when Kovrin is in bed with his wife. Kovrin tells the monk he is so full of joy that he feels God will be angered. Tanya notices with horror her husband's talking to the air. She realizes he is "sick in [the] mind" (1894b, p. 214), and Andrey, seeing the situation through her eyes, suddenly knows he is really mad. He leaves the estate to go for treatment, recovers his health, no longer sees the black monk. When he returns to Tanya, his transcendent joy, the "megalomania" (p. 215), are gone. Andrey now feels he is an uninteresting mediocrity. He hates his father-in-law, is cold and rude to him, reviles him to Tanya and somehow holds the old man responsible for everything that is wrong. He hates his wife too—in some way she and her father have done all this to him. He longs for the ecstasy of his madness.

Andrey leaves Tanya for Barbara, an older woman who nurses him— he has developed consumption—and treats him like a child. Two years after leaving his wife, in bad health, he goes with his mistress to the Crimea. Tanya writes to him, and when he sees her letter he remembers with guilt how "once, when he wanted to hurt his wife, he told her that her father had played a most distasteful role in their romance, having asked him if he would marry her" (1894b, p. 219). Yegor had overheard this, and rushed into the room "speechless from despair; all he could do was stamp his feet and make a strange bellowing noise, as if he had lost the power of speech, while Tanya looked at her father, gave a heart-rending shriek, and fainted. It was an ugly scene" (1894b, p.218). It was a primal scene—a sadomasochistic primal scene transformed and reversed, the former child's sadistic attack being the active agent that causes the parent's loss of control and undoing.

From Tanya's letter Andrey learns that Yegor has died,[7] and that

7. Chekhov dreamed his own "awful dream" of the Black Monk (see Magarshack 1952, p. 264) when he was summoned to his estate from St. Petersburg by a message that his father was gravely ill. Chekhov's beloved sister Maria was

the old man's beloved gardens are being managed by strangers. Tanya blames Andrey and curses him: "I hate you with all my heart and hope you'll soon be dead . . . May you be damned! I took you for an outstanding man, for a genius, I loved you, but you turned out a madman" (1894b, p. 220; my italics). Andrey tears up the letter, but he feels guilty and in despair thinks again of his mediocrity. Once more he hears "two female voices" (according to Fliess, two categorically identical objects symbolize the mother), who sing Braga's *Serenade* about the mad girl transported to heaven. He sees again the huge black pillar coming toward him and the black monk appears. Blood begins to flow from Kovrin's throat, and as he dies the black monk whispers to him that he is a genius and is merely leaving his feeble mortal body. He dies with a frozen smile of joy.

Like Chekhov's later short story *Ward Number Six* (much admired by Lenin), *The Black Monk* expresses doubts about the difference between madness and ordinary, mediocre sanity. And like *Don Quixote*, Chekhov's story is both a study of madness and an exploration of the meaning of reality and illusion, and the relationship between them. Could the transcendent ecstasy of madness have empowered Kovrin to write, think, and be what his mediocre and prosaic self could never otherwise attain? Questions about the source of artistic and philosophic creativity are asked but not answered by this great story, to which my outline does an injustice. That injustice is partly sanctioned by my point of view, which complements one expressed by Chekhov when he wrote to a friend about this story: "The subject is a medical one, *historia morbis*, I deal with the mania of greatness in it" (quoted in Magarshack 1952, 264; italics in original). Chekhov is said to have been proud of the scientific accuracy of his pathological study, and rightly so. He not only described beautifully the paranoia that Freud made explicit in his study of Schreber in 1911, but also intuitively provided the dynamic background for it.

There are always superficial resemblances in the content of paranoid

---

also ill, and it was after Chekhov spent two sleepless nights at their bedsides (his ego weakened by exhaustion) that he had his dream. (Again the triangle from Pushkin recurs.) The relation of Maria to Pavel to Anton corresponds to that of Tanya to Yegor to Andrey. It is also noteworthy that when away from home Anton would send detailed instructions about the gardens and trees to Maria—as Yegor did to Tanya.

delusions. A redeemer fantasy is present for both Kovrin and Schreber. Schreber, like Andrey, believes he has a mission to redeem the world and restore it to its lost state of bliss. He "strives to make his way up to heaven" and hears "holy music," like the girl in Braga's *Serenade*. But it is the similarity of the circumstances and motives of the two men that is most fascinating. Andrey is already ill when the story begins. So too, Schreber is "nervous" on his second contact with Dr. Flechsig (this takes place during Schreber's prepsychotic stage), who is to become Schreber's paranoid object and "soul murderer". The original cordiality and gratitude in his feelings toward Flechsig only later turn to persecutory delusions about him. Chekhov outlines a similar relationship between Andrey and his foster father. Initially Andrey is happy to return to Yegor and Tanya. (Tanya is a bridge to Yegor, as Schreber's wife is to Dr. Flechsig.) For Schreber, Flechsig and later God represent his father (as primal parent); for Andrey, the Black Monk, whose celestial connotations connect him with God too, represents his foster father (also as primal parent).

Characterological harmonies resound in Schreber's father, in the fictional Yegor, and in Chekhov's own father. Freud (1912) wrote of Schreber's fixation on Flechsig: "It appears that the person to whom the patient ascribes so much power and influence . . . is either identical with someone who played an equally important part in the patient's emotional life before his illness, or is easily recognizable as a substitute for him" (p. 41). Freud is pointing toward Schreber's father. (Recall that the third chapter from Schreber's *Memoirs*, which deals with soul murder and was largely expurgated [see chapter 1, above], involves what Schreber calls "events concerning other members of my family"; see Schreber 1903, 61.) "Thus in the case of Schreber we find ourselves once again on the familiar ground of the father-complex. The patient's struggle with Flechsig became revealed to him as a conflict with God, and we must therefore construe it as an infantile conflict with the father whom he loved [and rebelled against]" (Freud 1912, 55).

It was after Yegor suddenly and impatiently ran away from Andrey to scream at his serf that Andrey felt a yearning for his childhood—suppressing his rebellious feelings. The two men then exchanged "tender" kisses, prefiguring the happy reunion with the father image that emerged in Kovrin's hallucination of the Black Monk in the megalomanic phase of his paranoia.

Freud (1911) wrote of paranoid people like Andrey and Schreber:

"It is in an attempt to master an unconsciously reinforced current of homosexuality that they . . . come to grief" (p. 59). Schreber, who had been thinking of Flechsig, expressed this dramatically: "One morning while still in bed . . . I had a feeling . . . the idea that it really must be rather pleasant to be a woman succumbing to intercourse" (Macalpine and Hunter 1955, 63). Andrey too expresses a feminine sexual longing for the father figure in his hallucination of the Black Monk. The homosexuality is unconscious and kept well disguised.[8] After the hallucination comes the marriage proposal by Yegor, with the idea of father, daughter, and son living together evoking the primal scene triangle and showing Yegor's active, seductive role in reinforcing the homosexual current (one can assume this had its counterpart in Andrey's childhood). That Father Schreber had a similar effect on Schreber as a boy can be traced in Niederland's writings (1959a,b). Andrey's identification with Tanya, who is her father's beloved, is made clear in thoughts that he has before carrying out Yegor's suggestion to propose marriage: he wants to marry a weak and nervous being like himself (see the quotation above).

When his mania of greatness passed, Andrey begins to feel persecuted by Yegor, whom he begins to hate. After receiving the letter from Tanya announcing Yegor's death, Andrey surrenders passively and ecstatically to the father-imago and is reunited with it. Andrey is staring at the sea (symbolically the mother), which is described, anthropomor-

8. One can see the wish depicted symbolically and allusively, as in dream, in the locale and events of the hallucination scene. Andrey goes to a river bank and crosses the river; before him lies a broad, open field covered with young rye. He looks across the open and deserted field toward "the unknown, mysterious place where the sun had just gone down" (that is, the primal scene; 1894a, p. 320). Then: "From the horizon there rose up to the sky, like a whirlwind or a waterspout, a tall black column. Its outline was indistinct, but from the first instant it could be seen that it was not standing still, but moving with fearful rapidity, moving straight toward Kovrin" (1894a, p. 320). The pillar decreases in size: "Kovrin leapt aside into the rye to make way—and he was only just in time" (1894b, p. 199). The black monk is recognized, the pillar passes on and again enlarges. Note the phallic symbolism, the evocation of erection with the rising up and changes in size of the pillar, the projection of the primal scene onto the environment, and Andrey's being rushed at and over (expressing the predominant identification with the passive partner), in a transformation of the previously described scene of Yegor rushing down upon his workman.

phically, as seductive: "The bay, which seemed to be alive, looked at him with its many sky-blue, dark-blue, turquoise and flame-coloured eyes and beckoned him. It was truly hot and humid, and a bathe would not have come amiss" (1894b, p. 221). This impulse to plunge into the symbol for the mother is immediately taken over by an identification with her. Again Andrey hears Braga's *Serenade* about the beautiful, psychotic girl who ascends to heaven (Braga's song figures throughout the story as a leitmotiv for Kovrin's feminine strivings and mother-identification), and again the huge black pillar appears on the opposite coast and sweeps toward him across the bay. Once more Kovrin believes that he is the elect of God and a genius. Blood flows from his throat. He wants to call Barbara for help, but instead:

> He called on Tanya, on the great garden with its gorgeous flowers sprinkled with dew, he called on the park, the pines with their shaggy roots, the rye-field, his wonderful learning, his youth, his daring, his joy; he called on life, which had been so beautiful. On the floor near his face, he saw a large pool of blood and was too weak now to say one word, but an ineffable, boundless happiness flooded his whole being. Beneath the balcony they were playing a serenade, and at the same time the black monk whispered to him that he was a genius and that he was dying only because his weak human body had lost its balance and could no longer serve to house a genius. (1894b, p. 22)

This is the state of bliss described by Schreber. For Kovrin it involves surrender to his father, in identification with his mother, who had also died of consumption.

The similarity between the character of Yegor Pesotzky and that of Pavel Chekhov has been noted. Niederland's work on Schreber's father evokes another such emotional atmosphere. The latter half of the nineteenth century was very much the era of the "heavy" father; the fictional father and the two real ones belong to that category. Anton's letters give many details about the kind of oppressive, tyrannical father he knew as a child. Several times he describes his father with the same word that is so inimical to Andrey: as "a *mediocrity*, a man of little ability." And yet Pavel was a man of many talents; it is clear that he could appear to his children when they were young as the wrathful, capricious, exacting, godlike figure that the elder Schreber was to his son. In many descriptions of his childhood in his letters and stories,

Chekhov repeatedly insists on the despotism of his father. In a letter to his older brother Alexander, taking him to task for his mistreatment of his common-law wife, Anton wrote: "Let me ask you to recall that it was despotism and lying that ruined your mother's youth. Despotism and lying [characteristics of the primal parent and the Sphinx] so mutilated our childhood that it's sickening and frightening to think about it. Remember the horror and disgust we felt at those times when Father threw a tantrum at dinner over too much salt in the soup and called Mother a fool . . . ? There is no way Father can forgive himself all that now. . . . Despotism is three times criminal" (Karlinsky and Heim 1973, 129).

Church music was the obsessive passion of Pavel Chekhov, corresponding to Yegor's preoccupation with his gardens and the elder Schreber's system of health rules and behavior modification devices; in each case the feelings and welfare of the children were sacrificed to the father's fanaticism. As I have noted, there is more than a suggestion that Anton's health was undermined because of his father's rules. His older brother Alexander wrote:

> Father was meticulously punctual, strict and exacting about every-
> thing that had to do with church services . . . Poor Anton, who was
> still a small boy with an undeveloped chest, a thin voice and a poor
> ear for music, had an awful time of it. He often cried bitterly dur-
> ing the choir practice which went on till the late hours and which
> deprived him of the sleep which was so necessary to his health . . .
> If his choir had to sing at morning mass during the high festivals,
> [Father] would wake his children at 2 or 3 o'clock in the morning
> and go to church with them regardless of the weather. His chil-
> dren had to work hard on Sundays and holidays as well as on the
> weekdays . . . Father was as hard as flint and it was quite useless
> to try to make him change his mind. (quoted in Magarshack 1952,
> 19–20)

Much of this is reflected in Yegor—relentlessly and continuously driving himself, his daughter, and his workmen for his beloved gardens, supervising every detail from morning to night. Niederland (1959b) wrote that the elder Schreber's writings on the health and training of children "far from being theoretical educational concepts were literally, meticulously, and often personally enforced in the upbringing of his own children" (p. 388). "[These concepts included] detailed rules for every action during almost every hour in the regular routine of the child's life, . . . the threat of immediate punishment, . . . no deviations allowed" (1959a, p. 159).

Dr. Schreber's system of rewards and punishments, like that of Chekhov's father, expressed sadistic violence mixed with seductive attention. Chekhov wrote to a friend in 1899: "I had so little kind treatment as a child that now that I'm an adult I look on it as something out of the ordinary, something that is still an new experience for me. That's why I would like to treat others kindly but I don't know how" (Karlinsky and Heim 1973, 130). This would suggest that Chekhov's characteristic kindness, lauded by so many who knew him, was an effort for him. He was physically punished so regularly as a child that he simply could not believe a schoolmate who claimed never to have been beaten. Magarshack quotes a friend of Chekhov as having said that the continual beatings of the child left "a scar on his *soul*" (1952, p. 17; my italics). Here is a continuation of the autobiographical passage quoted above from Chekhov's story *Three Years*: "I was forbidden to play games and romp. I had to attend the morning and evening church services, *kiss the hands of priests and monks,* read psalms at home . . . when I was eight years old . . . I worked as an ordinary errand boy, and that affected my health, for I was beaten almost every day" (quoted in Magarshack 1952, 16; my italics).

Pavel Chekhov's metamorphosis into the black monk is made more convincing by Chekhov's statement that he "had to kiss the hands of priests and monks," and more convincing still when we hear from Anton's younger brother Michael that "Father . . . at home played the part of a priest" [and actually dressed up as one, although] "in everything else [he] was as much an unbeliever as ourselves" (Magarshack 1952, 20). In the family estate that Chekhov bought at Melikhovo, where Anton had his "most awful dream [of being] visited by a black monk" (Troyat 1984, 168), Pavel "had a monastic cell complete with oversized church books and the pungent aroma of incense . . . With age he had grown even more pious, never missing a service, praying aloud in his room, intoning psalms, and, on holidays, swinging a censer through the house" (Troyat 1984, 153–154).

All three fathers make one agree with Niederland that "there was always castration in the air" (1959b, p. 401). In the story itself we get only an indirect glimpse into Andrey's childhood, but the grandiose and paranoid horticultural diatribes that Yegor gives Andrey to read are the equivalent of Father Schreber's hygienic works, and Andrey says of them: "What highly charged, almost pathological fervour . . . it's passion and warfare" (1894a, pp. 202–203).

One of Schreber's complaints against God, obviously aimed at his father, is that God does not understand living men and has no need to understand them because he deals only with corpses. And soul-murdering parents frequently do treat their children like completely submissive cadavers. It is characteristic of soul murder that the parent not only fails to respond to the child's identity, but attempts to stamp it out. Soul-murdering fathers frequently usurp the maternal role in their personal overconcern with every aspect of the child's behavior and every detail of the child's care (the mothers are in subjection, ineffectual, or just not there). When this is so, the child's sexual identity can easily become confused.

It is not hard to characterize the three fathers. They are grandiose and paranoid, with confused sexual identities. They have aspects of the psychotic about them, and yet superficially appear to have a predominantly obsessive-compulsive character of a particular kind. Every detail must be attended to: a detail out of place brings about not just anxiety but an overwhelming, cannibalistic rage, and the murderous, omnipotent *Urvater* emerges (as in Goya's *Uranus*). All three fathers also had periods of expansive, megalomanic benevolence during which a sticky, narcissistic, indulgent "love" emerged, or at least was professed;[9] this is reflected in the delusions of the two unquestionably psychotic sons, Andrey and Schreber. The "love" tends to be grandiose and generalized—it exists at the pleasure or whim of the parent and may have little to do with the child's needs. Each son pays tribute to the "goodness" of the father in a rather dutiful, half-hearted fashion (for example, in Chekhov's letters), which is appropriate to the abstract Goodness or Health or Duty or Religion that masked the father's gratification of his own impulses.[10]

9. In any specific case of soul murder it is possible for real parental love and caring also to be present—alongside the false show or alternating with it. Historical truth cannot be established from records alone; see the exhaustively documented book by Han Israels (1981) on the elder Schreber.

10. From a letter written by Chekhov at seventeen to his cousin Michael: "When you see my father, tell him that I have received his dear letter and that I am

Chekhov wrote a long letter about his nightmares that throws light on his dream of the Black Monk. It also allows us to trace the derivatives of a motivationally important detail of Anton's childhood experiences that is similar to one of Schreber's experiences: the cruel exposure of the child to severe cold (which Schreber takes into his delusions of "cold miracles"). Niederland quotes Schreber: "Miracles of heat and cold were and still are directed against me—always with the purpose of preventing the natural feeling of bodily well-being. During the cold miracles the blood is forced out of the extremities, so causing a subjective feeling of cold . . . from youth accustomed to enduring both heat and cold, these miracles troubled me little" (1959b, pp. 385–386). Niederland then quotes from the father's textbook on child care its detailed instructions for using cold water to toughen the child physically from the age of three months onward. As a child Chekhov was forced to get up in the middle of the night to "be hustled off to an unheated church in the miserable cold of a Russian winter." His brother Alexander described how as a schoolboy Anton was forced to work in his father's shop (like the boy in the story *Three Years*), which he loathed. He somehow managed to do his homework there, and there he froze during the bitterly cold winter nights (see Magarshack 1952, 25).

Magarshack (1952) quotes a letter to the novelist Grigorovich in which Chekhov wrote: "Whenever I feel cold, I always dream of a venerable and learned canon of a cathedral who insulted my mother when I was a boy" (p. 21). This statement gathers force when we recall that Pavel Chekhov used to quarrel violently with his wife, and that it was most frequently when he was angry with Anton's mother that Pavel dressed up as a priest.

The letter to Grigorovich was written in 1887, when Chekhov was twenty-seven. Grigorovich had written a fictional account of a dream in which cold apparently figured prominently, and Chekhov responded by connecting his own nightmares with cold. In the excerpts from the

---

very grateful to him. He and mother are the only people in the world for whom I shall never be sorry to do anything I can. If I ever achieve a great position in the world, I shall owe it entirely to them. They are good people and their great love for their children puts them above all praise, makes good all the faults they may have acquired in the course of a hard life" (Magarshack 1952, 17). The "scar on his soul" is completely covered here.

letter that follow, some of the details underline elements, qualities of the landscape, and feelings of Andrey's hallucination and delusion of the Black Monk.

To begin with, the feeling of cold you convey is wonderfully subtle. When my blanket falls off at night, in my dreams I begin to see enormous slippery boulders, cold autumnal water, bleak barren shores—all this is vague, misty, without a patch of blue in the sky; I am dejected and melancholy, as if I had gone astray or been deserted, and I gaze upon the stones and feel a sort of compulsion to cross a deep river . . . then as I run from the shore, I encounter on my way the crumbling gates of a cemetery, funeral processions, my high school teacher. And all the time I am utterly pervaded with that peculiar nightmarish cold which is impossible in reality and experienced only by sleepers [11] . . . When I feel cold in my dreams I always see people . . . the people one meets in dreams are bound to be unpleasant. During the sensations of cold, for example, I always dream of the good-looking and learned ecclesiastic who insulted my mother when I was a little boy; I dream of evil, persistently intriguing, maliciously smiling, vulgar people whom one never sees in one's waking hours . . . [you] feel the pressure of an evil will during your dream and the inevitable ruin caused by some power over whom you have no control . . . when my body gets accustomed to the cold, or when somebody in the family covers me up [here one catches a glimpse of the forbidden passive wish]—the sensation of cold, loneliness, and oppressive evil gradually vanishes. Along with the warmth I begin to feel as though I were treading on soft carpets or on green grass, I see the sun, women and children." (Koteliansky and Tomlinson, pp. 96–97)

"When someone in the family covered [him] up," the nightmare turned toward bliss. Is it too fanciful to see the counterpart to this magical transformation in the description of Andrey's death, when

11. In the story of the Black Monk, at one point when the monk is urging him to feel joy Kovrin suddenly and strangely responds with "bad expectations," distrust of "the Gods": "But supposing the Gods suddenly become angry?" Kovrin said and burst out laughing. "If they were to take my comforts away and make me *freeze* and starve I don't think I would like that" (1894a, p. 213; my italics—note that freezing comes before starving).

he ecstatically cries out to Nature, after being "covered" by the black monk? He is dead, but "a blissful smile was *frozen* on his face" (1894b, p. 222; my italics).

Freud dealt in various writings (1900, 1908, 1922) with the relation between dreams and delusions, stating that in cases where dreams precede an acute mental illness they are not its cause, but that dream and delusion are both manifestations of the same dynamic conflict. The same buried thoughts and feelings can be expressed in a dream, slip, neurotic symptom, delusion, or the like. He contrasted (1922) the case of a paranoid psychotic whose dreams were totally devoid of paranoid formations with that of a man not overtly paranoid whose delusions appeared only in his dreams. The latter man's dreams resemble Chekhov's dream of the Black Monk.[12] Freud's patient dreamed of "a pursuer, from whom he managed to escape only in terror, who was usually a powerful bull or some other male symbol which even in the dream itself he sometimes recognized as representing his father" (Freud 1922, 229). Freud said that such dreams may be regarded as forerunners or substitute formations of the delusional ideas.

Schreber had a series of dreams that coincided with the onset of his psychotic attack: "During this time I had several dreams to which I did not then attribute any particular significance . . . [but] my experiences in the meantime . . . made me think of the possibility of their being connected with the contact which had been made for me by divine nerves. I dreamt several times that my former nervous illness had returned" (Macalpine and Hunter 1955, 63). I would venture to interpret these dreams as meaning: "I want to see Flechsig (that is, father) again." It was after these dreams that Schreber speculated about how a woman feels in intercourse, (Kovrin's counterpart wish might have been ex-

12. Yarmolinsky (1973) gives an excerpt from Chekhov's letter of 1894 to his friend and publisher Suvorin; I include Yarmolinsky's footnote: "I think I am mentally fit. True, I am not especially eager to live, yet this is not, properly speaking, a disease, but something probably temporary and, indeed, a normal occurrence in everyday life. In any event, if an author depicts a person mentally ill, it does not mean that he himself is a mental case. I wrote 'The Black Monk' in a state of cold reflection and without any gloomy thoughts. I simply took it into my head to picture megalomania. ['If I had not become a writer,' Chekhov told a friend, 'I would probably have become a psychiatrist.'] As for the monk scudding along over the fields, I saw him in a dream, and after I woke up in the morning I told Misha about it" (pp. 243–244).

pressed in relation to his delusion as follows: "I want to see the Black Monk again." This came to pass at his death.)

Schreber and Chekhov each had dreams of longing for his father at a time when he had thoughts of his father being ill or dying. Niederland (1959) pointed out the correspondence between the accident and illness of the elder Schreber at fifty-one and his death at fifty-three, and the outbreaks of mental disturbance in his son at the same ages. Schreber's dreams occurred at a time approaching the anniversary of his father's death.

I emphasize that Anton Chekhov was not psychotic. On the contrary, he appears to have been singularly free from neurosis,[13] judging from his biographies and from descriptions by his friends. (See the quotation from his letter of 1888 given below.) He had a sense of judgment and a perspective on his life and work that were unusually clear and balanced, healthily sane. He could work prodigiously both as a physician and as a productive writer, and he could enjoy as well: "He liked pretty women, he liked wine and a party; he kept open house for his friends; he enjoyed music and fishing and bathing and gardening and money and fame" (L. Hellman in Chekhov 1885–1904, 5). Chekhov's work is full of common sense, of the most subtle, acute, sane observations and self-observations. What a contrast to the shrill sterile catalogue of obsessive, narcissistic details that make up Schreber's *Memoirs*!

One can say that the similarity of their fathers' characters and of the atmosphere of their childhoods made for a similar paranoid potentiality in Chekhov and Schreber. But there the similarity ceases. One of the enormous differences in the vicissitudes of that potentiality is due to Chekhov's artistic endowment: he was able to transform a bad dream into a short story; it did not become a delusion. As Freud (1928) noted specifically about the problem of artistic creativity, the ego differences between the "normal" (that is, the neurotic) and the psychotic, indeed between the "normal" and the creative artist, are still problems before

---

13. There were obvious inhibitions to loving one woman and marrying that did not seem to have prevented Chekhov from having a full sexual life. When he finally married, in his forties, he obviously cared for his much younger wife. That he was a sick man by then makes it hard to evaluate his need to distance his wife physically and emotionally. Although his inner life is enigmatic, the usual signs of having experienced soul murder are not obviously present in Chekhov.

which "analysis must, alas, lay down its arms" (p. 177). One can also ask, but not definitively answer, whether Chekhov's persecution by his father might not have contributed to his ego strengths and creativity. The effect of what is done to a child depends on what is already there in the child: "The true poet dreams being awake. He is not possessed by his subject but he has dominion over it" (Charles Lamb, quoted in Trilling 1940, 45).

How is that "dominion" to be analyzed? It derives from different powers and sensibilities in the ego and superego of the individual creative artist; those hypothetical controlling mental structures are based on inherited endowment (including the id, the intensity and quality of which will vary), as well as on the early experiences that influence the structural development of the mind. Yet all this jargon covers so much that we do not know. The controlling superstructure in Schreber became involved in abandoning reality in the service of certain drives. Yet at the same time, as Chekhov points out in *The Black Monk*, the grandiose paranoid psychotic like Schreber or Andrey can have a kind of transcendent vision and a sense of mastery that are elements needed for creative "dominion." But these are not enough. Creativity is not to be traced to pathology but to gifts and genius (Trilling 1940); the psychosis is not the source of the artistic ability, although it can become part of the material that is molded by the artist's powers and becomes part of the artist's works. Chekhov's story suggests how some psychotic symptoms might affect creative power favorably, giving a kind of transcendent perspective that a talented artist or a genius might make use of. Kovrin did not have a creative mind; he simply had the illusion of greatness.

Chekhov's neurosis cannot explain his artistic power (his "unanalyzable artistic gift," to use a phrase that Freud applied to Dostoyevsky; see Freud 1928, 179), although his neurosis can become the subject matter to be shaped and dominated. (It can of course also inhibit the "dominion.") Artistic creativity involves a change from passive suffering of childhood traumatic experiences to active manipulation and re-creation of these experiences, but this is unsatisfactory because it is equally true of Schreber's psychosis and Chekhov's art. Kris (1953) amplified the "flexibility of repression" seen in the artist by Freud, calling it "the capacity of gaining easy access to id material without being overwhelmed by it, of retaining control over the primary process and perhaps specifically, the capability of making rapid, or at least appropriately rapid, shifts in the level of psychic function" (p. 25). Certainly Chekhov could regress without losing his powers of self-observation, feel what Schreber felt, and objectify it, externalize it, in a story about a paranoid psychotic. But what makes it a great and meaningful story —a successful creative act, a story that can question disturbingly the nature of reality—is not "analyzable" by our methods.

Chekhov's controlled regression recalls the task of the analyst who works by what Fliess (1942) called "trial identification"—sampling what it is like to be in the patient's shoes. Like the analyst, Chekhov was never interested primarily in achieving any partisan, moralistic, or philosophic aim in his art (a transitory interest in Tolstoy's ethical tendentiousness was strongly and sanely repudiated). He strove for objectivity and truth in all its moral ambiguity. He wrote to a literary friend in 1888: "I look upon tags and labels as prejudices. My holy of holies is the human body, health, intelligence, talent, inspiration, love and the most absolute freedom imaginable, freedom from violence and lies, no matter what form the latter two take. Such is the program I would adhere to if I were a major artist" (Karlinsky and Heim 1973, 109). From another letter:

> You upbraid me about objectivity, styling it indifference to good and evil, absence of ideals and ideas, etc. You would have me say, in depicting horse thieves, that stealing horses is an evil. But then, that has been known for a long while, even without me. Let jurors judge them; for my business is only to show them as they are. I write: You are dealing with horse thieves—know, then, that these are no beggars, but men with full bellies, that these men belong to a cult, and that stealing horses is not simply stealing, but a passion [Here we see his empathic gift.] Of course it would be gratifying to couple art with sermonizing, but, personally, I find this exceedingly difficult and . . . all but impossible. Why, in order to depict horse thieves in seven hundred lines I must constantly speak and think as they do and feel in keeping with their spirit. (Yarmolinsky 1973, 133)

To be able to speak, think, and feel like a horse thief or a paranoid psychotic means that in some still unanalyzable way Chekhov can transcend and transform his neurosis—at least in his art. We are confronting a magnificent psychological gift and talent, not pathology; this is terra incognita for the psychoanalyst; another Freud is needed.

Another letter of 1888 contrasts with the apostolic tone of soul murder (of the Schrebers, Pavel Chekhov, Yegor, and Andrey). It incidentally evokes, although with some exaggeration, the desired "set" of the analyst's mind:

The artist is not meant to be judge of his characters and what they say; his only job is to be an impartial witness . . . Drawing conclusions is up to the jury, that is, the readers. My only job is to be talented, that is, to know how to distinguish important testimony from unimportant, to place my characters in the proper light and speak their language. Scheglov-Leontov criticizes me for finishing [my] story ["Lights"] with "You can't figure anything out in this world!" To his mind the artist who is a psychologist *must* figure things out because otherwise, why is he a psychologist? But I don't agree with him. It's about time that everyone who writes —especially genuine literary artists—admitted that in this world you can't figure anything out. Socrates admitted it once upon a time, and Voltaire was wont to admit it. The crowd thinks it knows and understands everything; the stupider it is, the broader it imagines its outlook. But if a writer whom the crowd believes takes it upon himself to declare he understands nothing of what he sees, that alone will constitute a major gain in the realm of thought and a major step forward. (Karlinsky and Heim 1973, 104; italics in original)

One can see from this passage how much Anton had repudiated the hypocritical absolutism of his father. Indeed, from his days as a student he became the real father of his family, and of his own father too. The effort to shed the identification with his father is described in the following passage from a letter of 1889:

A young man—the son of a serf, a former grocery boy, a choir singer, a high school pupil and university student, brought up to respect rank, to kiss the hands of priests, to truckle to the ideas of others—a young man who expressed thanks for every piece of bread, who was whipped many times . . . who used his fists, tortured animals, was fond of dining with rich relatives, was a hypocrite in his dealings with God and men, needlessly, solely out of a realization of his own insignificance—write how this young man squeezes the slave out of himself, drop by drop, and how, on awaking one fine morning, he feels that the blood coursing through his veins is no longer that of a slave but that of a real human being. (Yarmolinsky 1973, 107)

A biographer chillingly adds that Anton Chekhov had his first hemorrhage at twenty-four; the tuberculosis was a fatal flaw. In his story *The Black Monk*, about a young man dying of consumption, Chekhov prefigured his own end, and by 1894 some part of his mind knew what to expect. His dream came when his father was ill, and must have expressed the fears and wishes that would accompany his thoughts of that hated and loved old man dying. The former potential soul murderer was now a helpless dependent. But the longing for the Urvater reasserted itself. Chekhov too died of tuberculosis, which ran in the maternal side of his family. One can see in his dream and creative fantasy not only his need to punish himself for his vengeful rage at the attempted soul murder and for his parricidal wishes, but also his negative oedipal striving for union with the father. But then, the passive surrender to The Black Monk comes inevitably to us all.

12

An Attempt at Soul Murder
Kipling's Early Life and Work

Soul murder can be overwhelmingly or minimally effected; it can be partial, diluted, chronic, or subtle. Kipling's case involves his desertion by good parents and their replacement by bad, persecutory guardians. A child can frequently bear much pain and torment if his parents can share his misery, literally or empathically. To experience trauma alone, with no recourse to parents, means that in addition to the external insult, the absence of protection, and the possibility of rescue there exists a psychic threat to the identity-sustaining sense of narcissistic promise. The child's feelings of identity and self-esteem depend on an ability to maintain the image of an omnipotent parent who cares, who will cure illness and solve problems. Separation from this needed parental imago and the transformation of it originate as part of the image of the self and are necessary for maturation; but to be tolerable the differentiation should be gradual, and the result is always incomplete. No one ever loses completely the need for the "emotional re-fueling" (Mahler 1972), so obvious in the toddler who finally and triumphantly walks away from the mother, and yet still craves to return periodically and must do so.

Separation from Parents

A sudden, unprepared-for loss of parental care is one of the greatest human tragedies, even for adults. Such loss is inherent in brainwashing techniques, which alternate overstimulation and sensory deprivation, to increase the need for loving concern and yet destroy the hope of receiving it. These methods were used by Stalin to break down seasoned revolutionaries in the Moscow trials of the 1930s. It is much easier to destroy the souls, the psychic life, of children, especially if they are separated from their parents. Children have little ability to contain overwhelming stimulation and intense feelings of rage. Anna Freud reminded us that for children to tolerate hatred directed against their parents, who are also loved, the parents' "reassuring presence" is essential (1965, p. 113).

If there has been a period of good parental care before the attempt at soul murder, as there was with Kipling, the potential psychic destruction is lessened. Still, the fall from bliss to torment is a cruelly traumatic loss. Here is a comment on Kipling's parental desertion, from an autobiographical story (Kipling 1888b):

> When a matured man discovers that he has been deserted by Providence, deprived of his God, and cast, without help, comfort or sympathy, upon a world which is new and strange to him, his despair, which may find expression in evil-living, *the writing of his experiences,* or the more satisfactory diversion of suicide, is generally supposed to be impressive. A child, under exactly similar conditions *as far as its knowledge goes,* cannot very well curse God and die. It howls till its nose is red, its eyes are sore, and its head aches. (p. 290; my italics)

Kipling describes the child's helplessness, made so terrible by its lack of understanding. He also mentioned what was for himself a way toward transcendence: when grown, the child may be able to write of the earlier experiences. This means the child must know what happened; and the more that is known of what happened to soul as well as to body, the more free the child can become. The soul—the identity—can be preserved if like Whitman the adult can say, "I am the man, I suffered, I was there" (1855, p. 76). Rudyard Kipling used his mind to fight to preserve his soul.

Kipling was born in 1865 in Bombay to a young and presumably loving British couple. He was a wanted first child whose every wish was indulged by a self-effacing pair of substitute parents: his ayah (nurse) and his bearer. As the only son of an important sahib, he was the center of a world full of wonder. His domain was the garden of a bungalow in the compound of an art school presided over by his father. He was treated as a young prince.[1] Meeta, the Hindu bearer, talked to him in the native tongue that was the boy's predominant speech in his early years. Rudyard's first memory was of early morning walks to the fruit market in Bombay with his ayah, a Roman Catholic from Goa who sometimes took the child to her church. Death and castration were in the background of his idyllic existence. The family house was near the Towers of Silence, where the Parsee dead were exposed to be devoured by vultures. "I did not understand my mother's distress when she found 'a child's hand' in our garden, and said I was not to ask questions about it. I wanted to see that child's hand" (Kipling 1937, 356). Some of the boy's questions were answered by his ayah. She and Meeta often told stories to the children (a sister was born when Rudyard was two-and-a-half) at bedtime or before the afternoon nap. An example occurs at the beginning of the autobiographical short story "Baa, Baa, Black Sheep" (in which the children are given the sadomasochistically charged names of Punch and Judy):

> They were putting Punch to bed—the *ayah* and the *hamal* [bearer] and Meeta, the big *Surti* boy, with the red and gold turban. Judy, already tucked inside her mosquito-curtains, was nearly asleep.

1. From *His Majesty the King*, written when Kipling was in his twenties, comes this evocation of the imperiousness of a six-year-old Sahib at bedtime, expressed in a baby talk that is difficult to tolerate (Chimo is his dog): "Yeth! And Chimo to sleep at ve foot of ve bed, and ve pink pikky-book, and ve bwead—'cause I will be hungwy in ve night—and vat's all, Miss Biddums. And now give me one kiss and I'll go to sleep. So! Kite quiet. Ow! Ve pink pikky-book has slidded under ve pillow and ve bwead is cwumbling! Miss Biddums! Miss Biddums! I'm *so* uncomfy! Come and tuck me up, Miss Biddums!" (1888c, p. 319; italics in original).

Unlike Rudyard's parents, those of "His Majesty" are bitterly hostile to each other and indifferent to their child. The quoted passage illustrates the boy's partly compensatory narcissistic confidence, and his tyranny over his English governess, Miss Biddums. Rudyard was six when he was deserted by his parents. Apparently Rudyard himself had dogs as a young child, a Chang if not a Chimo. His father wrote about Rudyard when the child was two: "He gets into imminent peril with chairs and things daily. It's the quaintest thing in life to see him eating his supper, intently watched by three dogs to which he administers occasional blundering blows with a little whip and much shouting. His best playfellow is one 'Chang,' a small Chinese pup" (Green 1965, 21). The letter shows the family atmosphere of laissez-faire, and something of the child's sadism as well as his lordliness.

Punch had been allowed to stay up for dinner . . . He sat on the edge of his bed and swung his bare legs defiantly.

"Punch-*baba* going to bye-lo?" said the *ayah* suggestively.

"No," said Punch, "Punch-*baba* wants the story about the *Ranee* [princess] that was turned into a tiger. Meeta must tell it and the *hamal* shall hide behind the door and make tiger noises at the proper time." (Kipling 1888b, 283)

Most of these stories were told by the ayah or his mother, and Rudyard may occasionally have confounded the two. A theme from Kipling's description of his earliest years resounds through his fiction and poems: he is rescued from a bad mother figure (like the *Ranee*-tiger) by a good father figure: "Meeta unconsciously saved me from any night terrors or dread of the dark.[2] Our *ayah*, with a servant's curious mixture of deep affection and shallow device, had told me that a stuffed leopard's head on the nursery wall was there to see that I went to sleep. But Meeta spoke of it scornfully as 'the head of an animal,' and I took it off my mind as a fetish, good or bad, for it was only some unspecified 'animal'" (Kipling 1937, 356). Readers of the Mowgli stories might think of the bad tiger Shere Khan and the good panther Bagheera—the two expressing the boy's ambivalence, here split, toward parents and parent figures.

Rudyard had another bad, early experience with the feminine (about which he was consoled by a man) when he was attacked by a hen while crossing the garden:

I passed the edge of a huge ravine a foot deep where a winged monster as big as myself attacked me, and I fled and wept. [He was comforted by his father who] drew for me a picture of the tragedy with a *rhyme* beneath:

> There was a small boy in Bombay
> Who once from a hen ran away.
> When they said: 'You're a baby,'
> He replied: 'Well, I may be,
> But I don't like these hens of Bombay.'

2. This is the first of many references to Kipling's lifelong preoccupation with fear of the dark, and to the great significance of light and dark as metaphors in his work.

This consoled me. I have thought well of hens ever since. (1937, p. 357; my italics)

Kipling's light humor here expresses a characteristic minimizing of fear and hatred, and he ends with a denial. This may be an important memory—later in his life, when he was trying to elevate rhyme to the level of poetry, he could identify with his father, who set an example for transcending a trauma by "the writing of [one's] experiences."

Like so many other parents of the Victorian age, Kipling's were in the background of nursery life.[3] Rudyard was the favorite and lord in a nursery world dominated by maternal and maternalizing figures. He was strengthened by the grandiosity that comes with maternal favoritism against the threats of his own hostility and of the dangerous, fascinating world outside the nursery. As Freud (1917) said of Goethe: "If a man has been his mother's undisputable darling, he retains throughout life the triumphant feeling [*Eroberergefühl:* feelings of a conqueror], the confidence in success, which not seldom brings actual success with it" (p. 156). One thinks of the marvelous self-confidence of Kim, or the more cloying aplomb of Wee Willie Winkie.

There was a sharp break in Kipling's life when he was two-and-a-half. His mother was pregnant, and the family returned to England, where she would have the baby.[4] In old age Kipling wrote about this journey: "There was a train across the desert (the Suez Canal was not yet opened)—and a halt in it and a small girl wrapped in a shawl on the seat opposite me, whose face stands out still. There was next a *dark* land, and a *darker* room full of cold, in one wall of which a *white* woman made *naked fire*, and I cried aloud with dread, for I had never before seen a grate" (1937, p. 357; my italics). This might be a screen memory

3. After the children's afternoon naps, "We were sent into the dining room after we had been dressed, with the caution 'Speak English now to Papa and Mamma.' So one spoke 'English,' haltingly translated out of the vernacular idiom that one thought and dreamed in. [Part of Kipling's penchant for "the vernacular"—any vernacular—is perhaps explained here: as a boy in India the local vernacular was his true mother tongue.] The Mother sang wonderful songs at a black piano and would go out to Big Dinners" (1937, p. 356).
4. This could have conditioned the boy to associate sibling envy (the narcissistic blow of being displaced as the center of the family world) with separation from his parents and Indian servant-parents, with travel, and specifically with England.

—the frightening woman again appears. The visual stimulation of the dangerous "naked" fire against the "dark" background might well have been associated then or later with the child's fantasies of the primal scene, and of his mother's pregnancy.[5]

When the Kiplings arrived in England in 1868 they stayed with relatives of Rudyard's mother (Alice Kipling). The indulged Anglo-Indian child was quite uninhibited and rather aggressive; his behavior was not what was expected of an English child of those days.[6] He is remem-

5. Actually this memory, or at least the Egyptian part of it, came back to Kipling in 1913 when he was making a railroad trip across the isthmus of Suez. Again the imagery of the description seems full of scoptophilic excitement with light and fire, contrasted with darkness and desolation: "On one side our windows looked out on *darkness* of the *waste*; on the other at the *black* canal all spaced with *monstrous headlights* of the *night-running steamers*. Then came towns, *lighted with electricity* [this then evoked the memory of the trip at the age of two-and-a-half] . . . such a town, for instance, as Zagazig, last seen by a very small boy who was lifted out of a railway carriage and set down beneath a *whitewashed* wall under *naked stars in an illimitable emptiness* because they told him *the train was on fire*. Childlike this did not worry him. What stuck in his sleepy mind was the absurd name of the place and his father's prophecy that when he grew up he would '*come that way in a big steamer*.' So all his life the word "Zagazig" carried memories of a brick shed, *the flicker of an oil-lamp's floating wick, a skyful of eyes*, and *an engine coughing in a desert at the world's end*" (1913, p. 247; my italics—evoking the primal scene elements).

The unforgettable name "Zagazig" must at some time have become associated with the word "zigzig"; this army slang word, common in Arabic countries, according to Partridge means copulation and was used to proposition soldiers on the streets of Cairo as recently as the Second World War. To link this word with the name of the town would have reinforced the primal scene meaning of the early travel memory. Certainly Kipling had a lifelong intense curiosity: a need to see and know and almost become those around him, especially the possessors of secrets and inner knowledge. He would quiz comparative strangers ruthlessly, in compulsive research about the look, sound, and feel of their lives and occupations. In later life this habit made some of his naive neighbors in Vermont think he was crazy.

6. A pupil of his father, the Parsee artist Pestonjee Bomanjee, remembered the boy fondly in his old age and described him as "coming into a room where the students were modeling and proceeding to pelt them with clay. He was a real nuisance to the class until his father came in, took him by the scruff of the neck and pushed him out" (quoted in Green 1965, 24–25).

bered as charging down the streets of a country town, yelling: "Out of the way! Out of the way, there's an angry Ruddy coming" (Stewart 1966, 1). After the Kiplings left, Rudyard's Aunt Louisa wrote of the visit: "[Alice's] children turned the house into such a bear-garden, and Ruddy's screaming tempers made Papa so ill, we were thankful to see them on their way. The wretched disturbances one ill-ordered child can make is a lesson for all time to me" (Green 1965, 23).

The family returned to Bombay after the birth of Rudyard's sister Alice (usually called Trix); the mother's labor had been difficult. Two-and-a-half years later, when Rudyard was five, a third child was born and died in India. There is no direct evidence of the effects of these births on Rudyard, but they must have profoundly influenced the child, threatening and perhaps compensatorily increasing his narcissism and adding to his aggressiveness (and particularly to his hostility toward the betraying mother). But the boy remembered his first six years of indulgence as overwhelmingly wonderful and magical. The epigraph to the first chapter of his autobiographical fragment *Something of Myself* is a Jesuit maxim: "Give me the first six years of a child's life and you can have the rest" (1937, p. 350)—a proper Freudian sentiment.

Paradise was lost when Rudyard was almost six and his parents again took him to the "dark land." It was customary for members of the British ruling class in India to send their children to England to be educated. According to Carrington (1955), Kipling's admiring, "official" biographer, the timing of the separation in the Kipling family "came early by customary standards" (p. 14). This would appear to be an understatement: Trix was left in England with Ruddy, and she was not yet three! Mrs. Kipling had a large, distinguished, and seemingly devoted family in England. One sister, a lifelong favorite of Rudyard, was married to the successful pre-Raphaelite painter Edward Burne-Jones; another wed the painter Edward Poynter, who later became president of the Royal Academy; and a third married a wealthy ironmaster, Alfred Baldwin, and became the mother of the future prime minister Stanley Baldwin. It is a mystery to Kipling's biographers that the children were not left with anyone in the family. A friend of Alice Kipling said: "She had never thought of leaving her children with her own family, it led to complications" (Wilson 1941b, 45).

The children were put in the charge of complete strangers who had come to the parents' attention through a newspaper advertisement. Rudyard and Trix were abandoned suddenly, without any preparation or explanation—their parents simply disappeared and returned to India. Not knowing why they had lost their parents was an agony to the children. Rudyard's mother told him later that she had been advised to spare the children the torment of a goodbye. Whatever Alice Kipling's motives, the cruelty involved is not found in descriptions of her; but neither is the pain often ascribed in chronicles of childhood in Britain to parents who sent their children away to public schools. At the very least, Alice Kipling shared the lack of empathy for the child that seems to have been so prevalent in Victorian times and that was frequently passed down from one generation to the next as part of a compulsion to repeat the past, sowing misery even in the homes of the wealthy and privileged. The adult Kipling describes his mother as a loving and charming person, very devoted to her son. Yet after learning of Rudyard's suffering and breakdown under the care of the foster parents, and after removing him, she left her daughter Trix, a sensitive and nervous child, for several more years with the woman who had so mistreated Rudyard. How could she? It is a mind-boggling enigma.

Here is a description of Alice by her sister Edith: "The Irish blood which is pretty certainly in our family seemed to take effect in Alice; she had the ready wit and power of repartee, the sentiment, and I may say, the *unexpectedness* which one associated with that race. *It was impossible to predict how she would act at any given point. There was a certain fascination in this* and fascinating she certainly was . . . a cheerful and loving friend all my life through" (Green 1965, 17–18; my italics). The unexpectedness I connect with the capacity to impose those cannibalistically impatient "transformations" (the "and suddenly" phenomenon) that are so powerful and prevalent in the lives of those subjected to attempts at soul murder. Unexpectedness was a quality in Alice's puzzling character that fascinated and tormented her son. Secrecy and unpredictability are evident not only in her failure to say goodbye to the children:[7] when she returned to England six years later it was also

---

7. In *Something of Myself* (1935) Kipling poignantly covers over the failure to say goodbye, talking of a "parting in the dawn with Father and Mother, who said that I must learn quickly to read and write so that they might send me letters and books" (1937, pp. 4–5). This is apparently fiction, like the account given in his short story "Baa Baa, Black Sheep" (1888). Mason (1975) says flatly: "The parents slipped away secretly. The children had not been warned" (p. 31). At seventy he could not take the truth any better than he could as a youth in 1888: the "unexpectedness" still hurt too much.

without notice. Years afterward she had Rudyard's schoolboy poems privately printed without his knowledge or permission. (When Rudyard returned to India and found this out he was furious. What was published included early love poems, which could expose his "soul.") Her brother Frederick described Alice's verbal aggressiveness: "My sister had the quickest mind and readiest wit I have ever known. She saw things in a moment, and did not so much reason as pounce upon her conclusions . . . Her wit was for the most part humorous and genial, but on occasion it was a weapon of whose keenness of point there could be no doubt, and foolish or mischievous people were made to feel it" (Stewart 1966, 5).

Kipling apparently struggled to keep split mental images of his parents; a tendency to split was already present in relation to the ayah and the bearer. His real parents remained "good," the foster parents became "bad." The intensity of the overtly loving and dependent later relationship with his mother is implicit in Kipling's editorial comment in his short story "The Brushwood Boy." (This story, by the way, strongly influenced Strindberg, who made early, significant use of the term *soul murder*; see Burnham 1971.) When the Brushwood Boy returns as a man from India to his home in England, his mother, in some dread, asks if he plans to marry. She comes up to his bedroom to tuck in the grown man: "And she sat down on the bed, and they talked for a long hour, as mother and son should, *if there is to be any future for our Empire*" (1895b, p. 355). Beneath this cosmically significant harmony of mother and son lies all the intense antagonism and distrust of women that so pervade Kipling's poetry and prose.[8]

Kipling's father, Lockwood Kipling, was a distinguished artist, artisan, and teacher. His brother-in-law Frederick Macdonald wrote that he was "gentle and kindly in spirit, and companionship with him was a continual refreshing" (Carrington 1955, 33). In later years Rudyard certainly shared that opinion. Macdonald continued:

> [In comparison with his wife's] his mind moved more slowly and cautiously, but covered a wider range. His power of acquiring and retaining knowledge was extraordinary. His memory seemed to let

8. Alongside the mawkish blindness is insight: the tête-à-tête proceeds to an oedipal close. After the mother concludes she has no rival, she "blessed him and kissed him on the mouth, which is not always a mother's property" (p. 356; my italics).

nothing slip from its grasp. On what may be called his own subjects, those connected with the plastic arts, with sculpture, modelling and engraving, with craftmanship in metals, wood and clay, with industrial processes where they come into the domain of art, he was a great expert, learned in their history and skilful in their practice . . . His curiosity was alive and active . . . all things interested him. He seemed to know something about everything as well as everything about some things. (Green 1965, 18–19)

Rudyard's formidable intellectual equipment and memory, as well as his intense curiosity, came in part from his father, through inheritance, identification, or both.

The Kiplings left their children in the care of the Holloways: a retired sea captain whom Rudyard liked and who unfortunately died soon after, and his wife, called "Aunty Rosa" by the children. She was a tyrannical, narrow-minded, religiously obsessed woman. Aunty Rosa was the boy's prime persecutor, almost invariably called "the Woman" in his writings. The old captain had become entangled in a harpoon line in an accident while whaling and had been dragged down. Almost miraculously he had got free, "But the line had scarred his ankle for life—a dry, black scar, which I used to look at with horrified interest" (Kipling 1937, 5). The children usually referred to Lorne Lodge, the Holloways' house in Sussex, as the House of Desolation. They stayed there for six years without seeing their parents. Trix described their lodgings:

Down a short flight of stairs was the basement with the kitchen behind and the nursery in front . . . there was a rusty grate there but never a fire, or any means of heat, even in the depths of winter. This perhaps accounted for the severe broken chilblains that crippled me from December to February every year, until Mamma came. "Aunty" had an economical theory that if children played properly they kept beautifully warm, but our mushroom-smelling den, with wall cupboards where even a doll's china dinner-set grew blue mildew in two or three days, was too small for any active games. (Fleming 1937, 169)

It was not the physical discomfort that the children minded most, and they were adequately fed. But the atmosphere was full of sadism, disguised as religious righteousness. "It was an establishment run with the full vigour of the Evangelical as revealed to the Woman. I had never heard of Hell, so I was introduced to it in all its terrors—I and whatever luckless little slavey might be in the house, whom severe rationing had led to steal food. Once I saw the Woman beat such a girl who picked up the kitchen poker and threatened retaliation. Myself I was regularly beaten" (Kipling 1937, 6).

As long as the old captain was alive there was someone to intervene and protect Rudyard from the Woman; he occasionally gave Rudyard some kind words and, more important, rational explanations. (When Ruddy was being taught to read by Aunty Rosa the boy asked her, "Why does AB mean ab?" Her answer was, "Because I say it does.")

The Holloways had a son, Henry, who was six years older than Rudyard. "Aunty Rosa" was apparently jealous of the younger, brighter boy. She seems to have treated Trix well, but Rudyard was rejected as a black sheep (which is what he calls himself in his fictionalized account; see 1888b. Trix recalled:

> ["Aunty"] had long wanted a daughter, therefore she soon made a pet of me, and did her best to weaken the affection between the poor little people marooned on the desert island of her house and heart. From the beginning she took the line that I was always in the right and Ruddy invariably in the wrong: a very alienating position to thrust me into; but he, with his curious insight into human nature, said she was a jealous woman, and of such low caste as not to matter, and he never loved me less for her mischief-making . . . She never struck me, or threatened me with bodily punishment, and I am still grateful to her for some of her early teaching. But her cruelty to Ruddy poisoned everything. (Fleming 1937, 169)

The attempt to separate the children emotionally evokes the potentially brainwashing atmosphere of the prison and the concentration camp.

> From the first ["Aunty Rosa" punished] the children whose united ages did not amount to ten years, and who had no relations nearer than London, by forbidding them to speak to each other for twenty-four hours. This penalty, which meant solitary confinement, with Aunty as a very competent jailer, was imposed for such crimes as spilling a drop of gravy at dinner [or] forgetting to put a slate away. (Fleming 1937, 168)

The Woman's divisive attempts ultimately failed. Rudyard could almost always rely on his sister's devotion. The impact of her passionate loyalty in these years must have helped him in later life to fight off his hatred of women.

Harry cooperated with his mother in tyrannizing and punishing Rudyard. The two used the zealousness of religious conviction about original sin in children to justify their actions: "The Woman had an only son of twelve or thirteen as religious as she. I was a real joy to him, for when his mother had finished with me for the day, he (we slept in the same room) took me and roasted the other side" (1937, p. 6).

Mother and son cooperated in trying to brainwash the boy: "If you cross examine a child of seven or eight on his day's doings (specially when he wants to go to sleep), he will contradict himself very satisfactorily. If each contradiction be set down as a lie and retailed at breakfast, life is not easy. I have known a certain amount of bullying, but this was calculated torture—religious as well as scientific" (1937, p. 6). This righteous religiosity perhaps contributed to making Kipling a lifelong agnostic. The cross-examination was regularly followed by

> punishment and humiliation—above all humiliation. That alternation was quite regular. I can but admire the infernal laborious ingenuity of it all. *Exempli gratia.* Coming out of church one day I smiled. The Devil-Boy demanded why. I said I didn't know, which was child's truth. He replied that I must know. People don't laugh for nothing. Heaven knows the explanation I put forward; but it was duly reported to the Woman as a "lie" . . . The Son after three or four years went into a Bank and was generally too tired on his return to torture me, unless things had gone wrong with him. I learned to know what was coming from his step into the house. (1937, p. 11)

The driven, consuming, persecutory regimen (the Devil-Boy evokes O'Brien, with Aunty Rosa as Big Brother) deprived the children not only of joy but even of the opportunity for a simple, quiet existence—of the timelessness and contemplative relaxation so necessary for the child's soul. The boy was forced into an *adaptive* paranoid attitude: "Nor was my life an unsuitable preparation for my future, in that it demanded constant wariness, the habit of observation, and attendance on moods and tempers; the noting of discrepancies between speech and action; a certain reserve of demeanour; and automatic suspicion of sudden favours" (1937, p. 16).[9] To ward off the persecution, Kipling had to justify the repeated accusation—he was forced to lie. Kipling described this as having had some creative potential: "[The torment] made me give attention to the lies I soon found it necessary to tell; and this, I presume, is the foundation of literary effort" (1937, p. 6).[10]

Trix documented this obligatory need to deceive by divorcing action from feelings (anal control and defensiveness made into conscious policy). After their mother came to rescue the children, she "wrote to my father that the children . . . had . . . seemed delighted to see her, but she had been a little disappointed by the way we had both hung round [Aunty Rosa] in the evening. She did not know that well-trained animals watch their tamer's eye, and the familiar danger signals of 'Aunty's' rising temper had set us both fawning upon her" (Fleming 1937, 268).

Kipling felt that he had been able to survive because of the month he spent each year with his mother's relatives—especially his Aunt Georgina (Burne-Jones). There love and affection were not stinted, and

9. This paragraph could have been written by my patient M., described in the section on autohypnotic watchfulness (see chapter 8).

10. In his autobiographical book *Father and Son*, which is a story of soul murder, Edmund Gosse describes the effect of one of his father's attempts to take over his individuality. Like Kipling, Gosse was able to adapt, and this enhanced his attempts to become a writer. As a boy he "was still but a bird fluttering in the network of my Father's will, and incapable of the smallest independent action" (1907, p. 232). The boy had become fond of reading about words—a separating activity that upset his father: "He urged me to give up such idleness, and to make practical use of language. For this purpose, he conceived an exercise which he obliged me to adopt, although it was hateful to me. He sent me forth, it might be, up the lane to Watbury Hill and round home by the copses . . . and he desired me to put down, in language as full as I could, all that I had seen in each excursion. As I have said this practice was detestable and irksome to me, but, as I look back, I am inclined to believe it to have been the most salutary, the most practical piece of training which my Father ever gave me. [Gosse's father was a religious fanatic, an apostolic figure like Mrs. Holloway who believed in the imminent second coming of the Lord, and even after his father's death the son cannot help but capitalize "Father," as Kipling capitalizes "Woman"; see note 13, below.] It forced me to observe sharply and clearly, to form visual impressions, to retain them in the brain, and to clothe them in punctilious and accurate language" (1907, p. 221).

the boy had an important role in the large family's activities: "It was a jumble of delights and emotions culminating in being allowed to blow the big organ in the studio for the beloved Aunt, while the Uncle worked . . . and if the organ ran out in squeals the beloved Aunt would be sorry. Never, *never* angry!" (1937, pp. 13–14). This follows a passage that links fear of the dark and blackness, and conflicts about seeing and being seen, with the need for what was so lacking in the House of Desolation: protection from dark, bad monsters (mainly feminine, like the Sphinx), provided by the benevolent presence of men: "At bed-time one hastened along the passages, where unfinished cartoons lay against the walls. The Uncle often painted in *their eyes* first, leaving the rest in *charcoal*—a most effective presentation. Hence our speed to our own top landing, where we could hang over the stairs and listen to *the loveliest sound in the world—deep-voiced men laughing together over dinner*" (1937, p. 13; my italics).

Kipling's works, especially the stories about children (*The Jungle Books, Kim, Captains Courageous*), are full of the longing for fathers, fulfilled by a multitude of good father figures. The narrative about Aunt Georgina's house continues: "But on a certain day—one tried to fend off the thought of it—the delicious dream would end, and one would return to the House of Desolation and for the next two or three mornings there cry on waking up. Hence more punishments and cross examinations" (1937, p. 15). In some ways Aunty Rosa's brainwashing was effective—Rudyard never told on her. He provided this explanation: "Often and often afterwards, the beloved Aunt would ask me why I had never told anyone how I was being treated. Children tell little more than animals, *for what comes to them they accept as eternally established*. Also, badly treated children have a clear notion of what they are likely to get if they betray the secrets of a prison-house before they are clear of it" (1937, p. 15; my italics).

Whether children continue to accept what comes to them as eter-nally established depends largely on parental attitudes, and being in the power of a parent figure like Mrs. Holloway who claims to speak for God must inhibit the development of the child's own judgment and identity. But Kipling's deepest motivation for keeping silent probably related more to the parents who had betrayed him to the prison house than to Aunty Rosa. They whom he had so trusted had deserted him, and so even seemingly trustworthy people like Aunt Georgina could do this again. At the same time, he had to distance the anger and torment caused by his parents' betrayal. (The road to doublethink is clearly indicated by the painful nature of the contradiction and confusion.) The acute need to keep the memory of good parents made silence, minimization, and even denial necessary. How could his parents have done this to him? It was too unbearable to keep that question in mind very long. (One recalls Oedipus's comment on learning that his mother gave him up as an infant, feet shackled, to be abandoned on Mount Cithaeron, "And could a mother's heart be steeled to this?"; and Dostoyevski's "and it was her mother, her mother did this.")

Kipling gave three accounts of his time in the House of Desolation. The first, written when he was twenty-two, was the short story "Baa Baa, Black Sheep," a fairly straightforward narrative of the desertion, torment, and rescue of "Punch" and "Judy."[11] The second account, altered in many details, makes up the first chapter of *The Light That Failed*, a novel Kipling wrote in 1890 (at the age of twenty-five). It was not until the very end of his life, when he was more than seventy, that he wrote the autobiographical fragment *Something of Myself*.

"Baa Baa, Black Sheep" shows the child wrestling with the problem of evil, trying to keep from attributing to the parents the actions of the cruel parent-substitute. After being beaten for the first time the child thinks: "Aunty Rosa . . . had the power to beat him with many stripes. It was unjust and cruel, and Mamma and Papa would never have allowed it. Unless perhaps, as Aunty Rosa seemed to imply, they had sent secret orders. In which case he was abandoned indeed" (Kipling 1888b, 297–298). In her memoirs Trix expressed the children's feelings about the desertion:

> Looking back I think the real tragedy of our early days, apart from Aunty's bad temper and unkindness to my brother, sprang from our inability to understand why our parents had deserted us. We had had no preparation or explanation; it was like a double death, or rather, like an avalanche that had swept away everything happy and familiar . . . We felt we had been deserted, "almost as much as on a doorstep," and what was the reason? Of course Aunty used to say it was because we were so tiresome, and she had taken us out of pity, but in a desperate moment Ruddy appealed to Uncle

11. Ironically, in 1890 a reviewer of the collected stories in *Wee Willie Winkie* found them all commendable "except 'Baa Baa, Black Sheep' which was 'not true to life'" (Carrington 1955, 142).

Harrison, and he said it was only Aunty's fun and Papa had left us to be taken care of because India was too hot for little people. But we knew better than that because we had been to Nassick [a cool summer resort in the Indian Hills], so what was the real reason? Mama was not ill—Papa had not had to go to a war. They had not even lost their money—there was no excuse; they had gone happily back to our own lovely home, and had not taken us with them. There was no getting out of that, as we often said. Harry, who had all a crow's quickness in finding a wound to pick at, discovered our trouble and teased us unmercifully. He assured us we had been taken in out of charity and must do exactly as he told us—we were just like workhouse brats, and none of our toys really belonged to us. (Fleming 1937, 171)

The suddenness, the unexpectedness, of the desertion increased its traumatic effect by depriving the children of any chance to prepare for what they were to experience (that is, to work it out in thought *and with their parents*). This *not understanding* increased the brainwashing effect. But Rudyard *was* able to fight with his mind to keep Trix with him emotionally and to preserve the memory of the good parents, the ayah, and Meeta, evoking the good home as a populated place for psychic refuge from the persecutors. Trix said he "called Aunty Rosa a *Kutch-nay*, a Nothing-at-all, and that secret name was a great comfort to us, and useful too when Harry practised his talent for eavesdropping" (Fleming 1937, 169) . . . Ruddy remembered our lost kingdom vividly" (p. 171). Remembering the past was a torment to the children, but it also restored the promise of bliss and this strengthened them. Rudyard's gifts, his creative imagination, also helped: in his stories to Trix he conjured up an idealized world and wonderful parents. All this kept the children together so that the desertion did not mean complete isolation. (Contrast this to the forced separation and mutual betrayal of Winston and Julia in *1984*.) Usually in cases of soul murder, the child's intense need to deflect murderous rage away from the tormenting parent makes for a displacement onto the sibling of cannibalistic intensity; fortunately the attempt to turn the children against each other failed with the Kiplings.

Yet there was also much confusion, an agony of not knowing why, to whom they belonged, or what their place was in the order of things. No wonder Rudyard became an archconservative, a pillar of the established order. One can see how the law of the jungle in *The Jungle Books*, which assigns a place to everyone, making all relationships clear and enforcing ordinary "human" virtues, represents a wish fulfillment for Kipling. And so did Mowgli's parents: wolves, but wolves of outstanding decency and dependability, with Mother Wolf ready to fight a tiger to the death to keep Mowgli.

Another soul-saving factor during this time was the boy's absorption in reading. Rudyard could not read or write when left with the Holloways, and it was Aunty Rosa who taught him. At first he resisted learning, but he then discovered that books offered a means of escape into fantasy that could distance his torment. He called reading "a means that would make me happy. So that I read all that came within my reach. As soon as my pleasure in this was known, deprivation from reading was added to my punishment. I then read by stealth and the more earnestly (1937, p. 16). This sinning *with the eyes* was followed by retribution: "My eyes went wrong, and I could not well see to read. For which reason I read the more and in bad lights. [Kipling's masochism shows here.] My work at the terrible little dayschool where I had been sent suffered in consequence, and my monthly reports showed it. The loss of 'reading time' was the worst of my 'home' punishments for bad schoolwork" (1937, p. 16).

The eye trouble amounted to near blindness. Aunt Georgina noticed that Rudyard was walking into trees in her garden and wrote to her sister, which led Alice to return to England and deliver the boy from the House of Desolation. But before that there was a terrible, humiliating punishment that resembled one given by the cruel Murdstones to Dickens's alter ego, the fatherless and then completely orphaned David Copperfield: "[One school report] was so bad that I threw it away and said that I had never received it. But this is a hard world for the amateur liar. My web of deceit was swiftly exposed—the Son spared time after banking hours to help in the auto-da-fé—and I was well beaten and sent to school through the streets of Southsea with the placard 'Liar' between my shoulders" (Kipling 1937, 16). In *David Copperfield* the placard reads, "He bites"—a more direct evocation of cannibalistic impulse.

What Kipling calls "some sort of nervous breakdown" (1937, p. 17) followed this. The shadows provided by his failing vision were supplemented by shadowy hallucinations, making for a terrible darkness: "I imagined I saw shadows and things that were not there, and they worried me more than the Woman" (1937, p. 17). When a doctor sent by Aunt Georgina discovered that Rudyard was half-blind, "This too was supposed to be 'showing off' [according to 'Aunty Rosa'] and I was segregated from my sister—another punishment—as a sort of moral leper" (1937, p. 17). When Alice Kipling returned to England after hearing from Georgina of the doctor's report, there was more than a hint of direct reproach toward his mother in Kipling's dry statement: "I do not remember that I had any warning" (1937, p. 17); this sort of reproach was very rare for Kipling, as it would not have been for Dickens. Kipling later recalled being told by his mother that on the first evening of her visit to the children at Lorne Lodge, "When she first came up to my room to kiss me goodnight, I flung up an arm to guard off the cuff that I had been trained to expect" (1937, p. 17). The children were promptly taken away. They had been in the House of Desolation for six years.

For some months Rudyard was tended to by his mother in a small farmhouse near Epping Forest, where he was allowed to run wild: he felt "completely happy . . . except for my spectacles" (1937, p. 17). Although Rudyard was freed, Trix was later returned to Mrs. Holloway's care. It is not easy to understand this, even though Trix's experience had been different from her brother's. She had been treated as a favorite and had become

> a little Evangelical herself. At the same time she was obstinantly loyal to a brother who was constantly being exhibited to her not merely as the Black Sheep of his family, but veritably as among the damned. The strain upon Trix must have been very great, and leaving her with Mrs. Holloway was, upon any possible reading of the total situation, a grave error of judgement. It comes as no surprise when we learn that in later life Trix was subject to recurrent nervous illness. (Stewart 1966, 11)

In her memoirs Trix says that after removing the children from Lorne Lodge, her mother "wanted us to forget Aunty . . . as soon as possible" (1937, p. 168). She does not mention being sent back to the House of Desolation after the idyllic summer away from it.

Kipling makes two somewhat contradictory statements about the effect on his later life of the stay at Lorne Lodge. He ends the story written in 1888 with Punch telling Judy three months after they have been taken away from the House of Desolation by their mother: "Told you so . . . it's all different now, and we are just as much Mother's as if she had never gone. [But the narrator adds:] Not altogether, O Punch, for when your lips have drunk deep of the bitter waters of Hate, Suspicion, and Despair, all the Love in the world will not wholly take away that knowledge; though it may turn darkened eyes for a while to the light, and teach Faith where no Faith was" (1988b, p. 315).

In *Something of Myself* Kipling, now an old man, describes the torment and humiliation at Lorne Lodge: "In the long run these things, and many more of the like, drained me of any capacity for real, personal hate for the rest of my days. So close must any life-filling passion lie to its opposite. 'Who having known the Diamond will concern himself with glass?'" (1937, p. 16). This last sentence is rather cryptic: the metaphor of the Diamond, probably consciously ironic, still suggests masochistic idealization. Both statements show a realization of the lifelong effects of the House of Desolation, but the later one denies that the author could hate in a personal way, as if the hatred had been cathartically discharged once and for all. This was patently not so; what happened was that the conflict within his mind made it necessary to construct massive isolative defenses against hatred (these were anal narcissistic defenses—see Shengold 1985, 1988), but the hatred still broke through.

Kipling was a most complex man. Certainly his creativity was not destroyed by the years in the House of Desolation—it may even have been enhanced. He was not deprived of his ability to love, although it may have been damaged. His capacity for humor and laughter survived, though marked and sometimes marred by sadism. An intense and often cruel personal hatred that Kipling denied is nonetheless obvious to the most casual reader. It is not possible that this could have been confined only to his work. The terrible, destructive hatred of the tormented child who "cannot curse God and die" is perhaps the heaviest burden of soul murder. Where is the hatred to go? After the years in Lorne Lodge the free motor and verbal expression of the "angry Ruddy coming" was no longer possible. Part of the hatred was bound by identifying with the tormentor. But such intense hatred must be disclaimed, must not be felt, must be denied—and so it was with Kipling. Too many of Kipling's poems and stories are about revenge and sadistic practical jokes, revealing naked hatred.[12] Jarrell (1963) comments on the hatred toward

12. An example is "The Rhyme of the Three Captains," a poem about pirates written just after Kipling's work had been extensively pirated in America, to

authority that is hidden in Kipling's celebration and justification of it: "Kipling's morality is the one-sided, desperately protective, *sometimes vindictive* morality of someone who has been for some time the occupant of one of God's concentration camps, and has had to spend the rest of his life justifying or explaining out of existence what he cannot forget" (p. 146; my italics).

Kipling's close friend Mrs. Edmonia Hill wrote of Kipling when he was working on "Baa Baa, Black Sheep" while staying at her home in 1888:

> [Kipling has been writing] a true story of his early life when he was sent with his little sister to England to be educated . . . It was pitiful to see Kipling living over the experience, pouring out his soul in the story, as the drab life was worse than he could possibly describe it. His eyesight was permanently impaired, and as he had heretofore only known love and tenderness, his faith in people was sorely tried. When he was writing this he was a sorry guest, as he was in a towering rage at the recollection of those days. (Green 1965, 33; my italics)

So much for being deprived of the capacity for personal hatred!

---

his fury. In the poem a sea captain who had been robbed speaks of his wishes for revenge against the pirate chief:

> Had I guns (as I had goods) to work my Christian harm.
> I had run him up from the quarter deck to trade with his own
>   yard-arm;
> I had nailed his ears to my capstan-head, and ripped them off
>   with a saw,
> And soused them in the bilgewater, and served them to him raw;
> I had flung him blind in a rudderless boat to rot in the
>   rocking dark,
> I had towed him aft of his own craft, a bait for his brother shark;
> I had lapped him round with cocoa husk, and drenched him
>   with the oil,
> And lashed him fast to his own mast to blaze above my spoil;
> I had stripped his hide for my hammock-side, and tasseled his
>   beard in the mesh,
> And spitted his crew on the live bamboo that grows through the
>   gangrened flesh. (1890, pp. 256–257)

As the pathological, cannibalistic intensity mounts, the reader wants to cry "Enough!"

Trix's disclaimer about hatred was similar to her brother's. (She had probably read *Something of Myself* before she wrote her own account of the years at Lorne Lodge.) She wrote of the "odious Harry": "Perhaps hate is a disease, like measles, that it is well to recover from early, and up to the age of eleven I hated Harry so wholeheartedly that I have only disliked a few people, in a mild tepid way, ever since. [But] I am ashamed to say that only last year, when I found a scrap of his detested writing on the fly-leaf of an old book, I tore it out and burned it at once, and dark eyes, set near together, and black hair, plastered with pomatum, still make me shudder with dislike" (Fleming 1937, 169).

There was a short-lived repetition of the desertion and desolation at Lorne Lodge when the twelve-year-old Kipling was sent to a public school nine months after his removal from Aunty Rosa's. The school had to be inexpensive, and his parents settled on the United Services Colleges (also called Westward Ho!), a new institution designed mainly to prepare the sons of army officers for a military career. The head-master, Cormell Price, was a friend of the Kiplings, a man known and liked by Rudyard (who called him "Uncle Crom" outside of school). The school was made famous by Kipling's glorification of it in his *Stalky* stories. But that Kipling's first months at school meant a return to hell is concealed by these stories and belied by their comic tone. During this time Kipling's mother was still in England. In *Something of My-self* (1937) he calls the school "brutal enough . . . my first year and a half was not pleasant. The most persistent bullying comes less from the bigger boys, who merely kick and pass on, than from young devils of fourteen acting in concert against one boy" (p. 23). Here were new versions of that "Devil-Boy," Harry.

In *Stalky and Co.* (1899), Beetle (Kipling) rebukes a bully, whom he describes as one of those who claim to "never really bully . . . only knock 'em about a little bit. That's what [you] say. Only kick their souls out of 'em, and they go and blub in the box-rooms. Shove their heads into the ulsters and blub. Write home three times a day—yes, you brute, I've done that—askin' to be taken away" (p. 162). Kipling actually had. His sister later wrote: "For the first month or so, he wrote to us twice or thrice daily (and my mother cried bitterly over the letters) that he could neither eat nor sleep" (Stewart 1966, 22). Despite her tears, Alice Kipling left England before the Easter holidays, when her son could have told her firsthand what he had been going through. She may have had reassurances from the headmaster.

Eventually things did improve for Rudyard—markedly so after the first eighteen months. He was accepted by the others and ceased to be a victim: "After my strength came suddenly to me about my fourteenth year, there was no more bullying; and either my natural sloth or past experience did not tempt me to bully in my turn" (1937, p. 23). He found his special friends, Beresford and Dunstervill (M'Turk and Stalky in his stories), and they formed a little group that provided a feeling of shared, active, masculine identity. There was a glorious summer holiday when he was thirteen and "the Father" returned from India and took him to Paris for the Exposition of 1878 (this was followed by a lifelong fondness for things French).[13] At school he was under the benevolent eye of Uncle Crom. In this place the Woman held no sway; he lived with brothers who were mostly good, and the fathers were in power.

But the dark past still threatened. The boy was beaten by the masters (this was a regular part of English public school education). The prevailing aura of brutality, which continued life with Harry, if not with Aunty Rosa, is depicted in *Stalky and Co.* But now Kipling's creative imagination enabled the tables to be turned on the bullies. *Stalky* was described as follows by Edmund Wilson (not an Anglophile): "The book itself, of course, presents a hair-raising picture of the sadism of the English public school system. The older boys have fags to wait on them, and they sometimes torment these younger boys till they have reduced them almost to imbecility; the masters are constantly caning the boys in scenes that seem almost as bloody as the floggings in old English sea stories; and the boys revenge themselves on the masters with practical jokes as catastrophic as the Whams and Pows of the comic strip" (1941, p. 21). Lionel Trilling wrote of the book's "callousness, arrogance and brutality" (1943, p. 89). It demonstrates Kipling's mental splits—his being on both sides of the struggle between persecutor and victim. He shows contempt for the school's compulsory games. There is a general acceptance of the cruelty that is presented, and cruelty to animals is taken for granted. In one story a cat is shot by the boys in Kipling's group and its corpse left to stink on the rafters above the dormitory of offending enemies.[14] The sadistic masters are exposed and get tricked in successful revenge schemes, yet eventually their au-

13. Kipling's idealization of his parents took the revealing form of his referring to them in his memoirs as "the Father" and "the Mother," matching his reference to Mrs. Holloway as "the Woman".

14. To paraphrase Freud's well-known phrase, a cat is also a cat. But its symbolic meaning, like that of the Cigar in "The Betrothed" ("And a woman is

thority is justified. This is expressed in the poem "A School Song," with which Kipling prefaces the book:

> Western wind and open surge
>   Took us from our mothers;
> Flung us on a naked shore
> (Twelve bleak houses by the shore!
> Seven summers by the shore!)
>   'Mid two hundred brothers.
>
> There we met with famous men
>   Set in office o'er us
> And they beat on us with rods—
> Faithfully with many rods—
> Daily beat on us with rods,
>   For the love they bore us.

These ironic lines seem to express censure, and certainly Kipling does not deny the beatings. In his autobiography he was able to express anger toward the masters, especially toward his first housemaster, the school chaplain, an especially ferocious and sanctimonious man. Kipling saw through him as a schoolboy too. But characteristically his poem ends by glorifying the school system. He first portrays the microcosm of the school as preparing the boys to go out and rule the Empire. Then he praises Big Brother:

> This we learned from famous men,
>   Teaching in our borders,
> Who declarèd it was best,
> Safest, easiest and best—
> Expeditious, wise and best—
>   To obey your orders.
>
> This we learned from famous men,
>   Knowing not we learned it.
> Only, as the years went by—
> Lonely, as the years went by—
> Far from help as years went by,
>   Plainer we discerned it.

---

only a woman, but a good Cigar is a Smoke"; 1885, p. 49), is important too, here hostility toward the female genitalia ("pussy") in the predominantly anal sadistic, male homosexual context of these stories.

Bless and Praise we famous men—
  Men of little showing—
For their work continueth,
And their work continueth
Broad and deep continueth,
  Great beyond their knowing!

(1899, pp. xv–xvii)

Soul murder results in breaking the victim's identity into contradictory fragments that function independently, without effective synthesis. In psychoanalytic terms, the victim's mental images of the self and of the parents are vertically and irreconcilably split. After the abandonment by his good parents and the years with the bad, Kipling had contradictory and unresolvable views about authorities. He continually tried to portray them as good, but his rage and the need to attack broke through. And he did not permit himself to know it: in telling of his school years, Kipling described how he started to write, and he connected this with the personal hatred of which he claimed to have been drained. In the course of his studies at Westward Ho! he had discovered "a man called Dante who, living in a small Italian town at general issue with his neighbors, had invented for most of them lively torments in a nine-ringed Hell where he exhibited them to after ages . . . I bought a fat, American-cloth-bound notebook and set to work on an *Inferno*, into which I put, under appropriate tortures, all my friends and *most* of the masters" (Kipling 1937, 33–34; my italics).[15]

About a most important part of the young boy's experience Kipling wrote nothing and nothing is known: his sexual life. Was the memory of the intense wish to see the child's severed hand a screen for masturbation? We know that there was much early indulgence, that the ebullient boy was separated from his parents and from his beloved ayah and bearer at the height of his oedipal development. We gather from his writing the importance of primal scene fantasies, and his character and talents show his intense curiosity. Between the ages of six and twelve, the so-called period of sexual latency, he was dominated by a cruel mother figure whose weak husband soon died, and he shared a bedroom with a pubescent Big Brother who tormented him. It is not

15. After quoting the last lines Randall Jarrell adds: "Why only *most*? Two were spared, one for the Father and one for the Mother" (Jarrell 1962, 144).

known if anything sexual happened during the years of desolation, but it is not hard to imagine the Woman's attitude toward masturbation. One infers from his autobiography that puberty came at fourteen, with his spurt of physical growth. He developed a precocious mustache and at seventeen looked like a man, though a short one.

The conventions of Victorian literature dictated that sexual details be avoided in popular fiction; but in contrast to most of his contemporaries, Kipling showed in his stories his awareness of sexuality and its power. It is implicit in many of the *Plain Tales from the Hills* (1888a), which are full of predatory women. *The Light That Failed* (1890a) clearly though discreetly pictures a sexual liaison between Torpenhow and the streetwalker Bessie Broke and suggests the lesbian potential of "the red-haired girl" with whom the heroine lives.

Kipling's first direct reference to sex in his autobiography concerns his years at school—and it is a disclaimer: "Naturally, Westward Ho! was brutal enough, but, setting aside the foul speech that a boy ought to learn early and put behind him by his seventeenth year, it was clean with a cleanliness that I have never heard of in any other school. I remember no case of even suspected perversion, and am inclined to the theory that if masters did not suspect them, and show that they suspected, there would not be quite so many elsewhere" (1937, p. 23). Kipling seems to imply that if homosexuality is ignored, it ceases to be important—a typical denial on his part. Apparently, it was Cormell Price's policy to deter sexual activity by exhausting the boys through sports, but the purported absence of sexuality would make Westward Ho! singular indeed. Kipling's refutation is different from the ignoring of sex in school life by other Victorian writers of memoirs. For Kipling, minimizing homosexuality parallels his minimizing of anger.[16]

16. Something of Kipling's inner turmoil about homosexuality during the years at "Westward Ho!" can be inferred from Kipling's concerns about his son John at public school, as revealed in some of his letters to the boy from 1912. Sexuality is not referred to in direct language, which is of course not surprising between father and son and was consistent with the mores of the time, when homosexuality was "the love that dare not speak its name." But Kipling appears to be projecting an identification upon his fifteen-year-old son, feeling a terrible danger with him and perhaps as him. The father was externalizing a punitive superego as part of his inner conflict over sexual impulses, and expressing an intolerant, destructive hatred. We do not know who initiated the discussion about "beastliness" or what John confided to his father about some

He wrote of his being beaten by the prefect of games while at school: "One of the most difficult things to explain to some people is that a boy of seventeen or eighteen can thus beat a boy barely a year his junior, and on the heels of the punishment go for a walk with him; neither party bearing malice or pride" (1937, p. 80). One wants to respond to this, at best a partial truth; do the "parties" know, *can* they know, what they feel underneath?

In Kipling's early writings women are depicted as sexually attractive but destructive, or as cold and asexual. In his first novel, *The Light That Failed*, the only real affection is between men. At this time of his life, Kipling's ideal girl seems to have been one who could be called a "regular fellow." Miss Martyn of *William the Conqueror* (1895) has as a first name Bill or William, looks like a boy with her cropped hair, is "clever as a man . . . [and] likes men that do things . . . [and] doesn't understand poetry very much—it made her head ache" (p. 172). Kipling gives Miss Martyn his own feelings toward the literary men of London when he returned there in 1889 (at the age of twenty-four) after his years as a journalist in India. It was the time of Oscar Wilde, Aubrey Beardsley, and the "Yellow Book." Kipling expressed his aversion in verse:

> But I consort with long-haired things
> In velvet collar-rolls,

---

of his athletic friends, but this is Kipling's response: "What really bothered me most was not being able to have a last jaw with you. I wanted to tell you a lot of things about keeping clear of any chap who is even suspected of beastliness. There is no limit to the trouble possible if one goes about (however innocently) with swine of that type. Give them the widest of wide berths. Whatever their merits may be in the athletic line they are at heart only sweeps and scum and *all* friendship or acquaintance with them ends in sorrow and disgrace. More on this subject when we meet" (letter of May 1, 1912, quoted in Kipling 1983, 127; italics in original).

A month later, after a meeting: "I can't tell you what a joy it was to me to have that time with you. I hope I didn't bore you with good advice but it *is* good advice . . . I'd give a deal if some day I could see you head of your house. Remember my council. Keep your tongue between your teeth: don't criticize aloud (write it out all to me!) and flee from the contaminating swine!" (letter of June 5, 1912, quoted on pp. 131–132; italics in original). Superficially, the clear indication is that scandal will keep the boy from being appointed head of his dormitory. On a deeper level, "Keep your tongue between your teeth" is a proscription against an unconscious fantasy of fellatio; and "Write it out all to me" shows the father's identificatory possessiveness.

Who talk about the Aims of Art,
   And "theories" and "goals,"
And moo and coo with womenfolk
   About their blessed souls.

It's Oh to meet an Army man,
   Set up, and trimmed and taut,
Who does not spout hashed libraries
   Or think the next man's thought . . .
And walks as though he owned himself,
   And hogs his bristles short.

(1889, p. 173)

The Light That Failed was published in 1891. At twenty-six Kipling would seem to have shared the belief of Torpenhow, the friend and roommate of his hero Dick Heldar, who prophesied Dick's finish as an artist and man if he were to fall in love. This is expressed in dialogue that would fit in with the preadolescent, unconscious homosexual myth of the American West—one can almost hear it spoken by John Wayne: "She'll spoil his hand. She'll waste his time. She'll marry him, and ruin his work forever. He'll be a respectable married man before we stop him, and—he'll never go on to the long trail again" (p. 76).[17]

Maisie, the frigid and selfish heroine of *The Light That Failed*, has a direct prototype in Kipling's life—a girl he fell in love with when he was fourteen-and-a-half. She was associated with the House of Desolation.

Rudyard met Florence Garrard when he traveled to Mrs. Holloway's to bring Trix away for a holiday in 1880. Florence, a little older than Rudyard, was a paying guest at Aunty Rosa's; her parents were abroad. Like Maisie in the novel, Florence kept a pet goat, and the character of both could be described from Kipling's point of view as "self-centered

---

17. One wearer of the "velvet collar," Max Beerbohm, whose somewhat feminine sensibilities perhaps enabled him to spot those of Kipling (and motivated him to ridicule them), appreciated that Kipling was a genius but loathed his work. He wickedly pretended to believe that "Rudyard Kipling" was the pseudonym of a female author: "Should the name of Rudyard Kipling be put between inverted commas? Is it the veil of feminine identity? . . . Dick Heldar . . . doted on the military . . . strange that these heroes with their self-conscious blurting of oaths and slang, their cheap cynicism about the female sex, were not fondly created out of the inner consciousness of a lady novelist. *Who else would say, 'Oh to meet an Army man . . . ?'* " (quoted in Green 1965, 100; my italics).

and elusive, lacking in sympathy and affection" (Carrington 1955, 76). Rudyard felt that he was in love with her for five or six years. When he was sixteen and about to go back to India, he begged her to become engaged to him and felt she had agreed. He often mentioned her in his letters from India to his aunts, but it is still difficult to judge the depth of his feelings: Florence sounds like an official girlfriend whom Kipling mentions to give himself status as a grown man. But it seems that at least initially he was strongly involved,[18] and he was again affected when he met Florence many years later.

This second encounter came just before Kipling wrote his novel, and no doubt the meeting influenced his decision to use Florence for his heroine Maisie, who like the Flo of that time was studying to be a painter. Seeing Florence made him recall Lorne Lodge; substituting her for Trix, he wrote a first chapter about the time the two children stayed there. The boy and girl are depicted playing with a forbidden loaded pistol, and Maisie temporarily blinds Dick by shooting it. The incident prefigures the novel's theme of the effect on a man of the castrating and blinding woman (destructive of physical and mental creative power). Because Maisie is an amalgam of Florence and Trix, the forbidden pistol play can be taken to refer symbolically to masturbatory (but incestuous!) contact between Trix and Rudyard. We can feel certain about fantasy, but actuality rests on speculation. Ironically enough, if any such thing actually occurred, it may well have helped to save the boy's masculinity.

Rudyard was nearly seventeen when he left England to rejoin his parents in India after graduating from Westward Ho!:

> That was a joyous homecoming. For—consider!—I had returned to a Father and Mother of whom I had seen but little since my sixth year . . . *The Mother* proved more delightful than all my imaginings or memories. *My father* was not only a mine of knowledge and help,[19] but a humourous, tolerant and expert fellow-craftsman . . . I do not remember the smallest friction in any detail of our

18. Kipling's Aunt Edith "recalled how impressed she had been by the alarming force of his feelings as he gave her an account of his love for Flo Garrard, the girl who took his heart when he was still a schoolboy and did it no good before she tossed it back to him" (Stewart 1966, 32).

19. Interestingly, in this description of the reconstituted oedipal triangle, the idealized reference to "the Mother" is succeeded by the ordinary "my father."

lives. We delighted more in each other's society than in that of strangers; and when my sister came out, a little later, our cup was filled to the brim. Not only were we happy, but we knew it. (1937, pp. 39–40; my italics)

It was paradise regained. Rudyard's mother began the habit, adopted by them all, of calling the four contented Kiplings "The Family Square."[20]

In his autobiography (1937) Kipling called the period he spent in India "Seven Years Hard." During this time he worked as a journalist and began to write the poems and stories of India that made him famous as a young man. He learned about Indian life from the inside, getting to know the Indians and especially the Anglo-Indians (a term that in Kipling's time meant the English living in India). As a reporter he traveled over the entire subcontinent, exploring the rigid castes of both cultures: from the native underworld of Lahore and the barracks of "Tommy Atkins" to the Maharajahs and the generals and political leaders of Delhi and Simla. He looked and listened and quizzed, picking up characters for his stories and verses. Kipling's parents became friends of the viceroy, Lord Dufferin, providing Rudyard with a view of governmental politics from the top, of which he made good use in his newspaper fiction (collected later in *Plain Tales From the Hills*, 1888a). Many of these stories are told in a tone that promises to reveal secret knowledge, that knowing, grown-up tone so frequent in Kipling's writing (and sometimes so irritating). The tone denies the child within who must not know. One expects it from adolescents (and the young journalist in India was scarcely more than that), but it stayed on with Kipling. Perhaps in part because of the reader's shared feeling of being "in the know," Kipling's stories were eagerly read by the Anglo-Indians, and the young man found himself famous in his provincial world. He had the gratification of being asked about the opinions of the enlisted men in the barracks by the commander-in-chief himself, General Roberts.

Some of the early stories are about the influential, fascinating Mrs. Hauksbee, of whom it was said in *The Education of Otis Yeere* that a man's scalp was "generally drying at [her] wigwam door" (1888a, p. 6). "At the end of 1887, Kipling was so much in thrall to Mrs. F. C. Burton, the 'original' of Mrs. Hauksbee, that he dedicated *Plain Tales from the*

---

20. It is in a *square* formed defensively by British soldiers that Dick Heldar in *The Light That Failed* gets the wound that eventually blinds him.

Hills to her as 'The Wittiest Woman in India'" (Green 1965, 78). Mrs. Burton was old enough to be Kipling's mother, another great wit. To be in thrall to the Woman continued to be a pattern, as we shall see.

Kipling's non-neurotic and creative attributes during these years are worthy of mention. Kay Robinson, an editor for whom Kipling worked, described the young man's unprepossessing appearance and added: "The charm of his manner, however, made you forget what he looked like in half a minute . . . Kipling, shaking all over with laughter and wiping his spectacles at the same time with his handerchief, always comes to mind as most characteristic of him in the old days when our hardest work on "The Rag"—for fate soon took me to Lahore to be his editor—was as full of jokes as a pomegranate of pips" (Green 1965, 81). Contemporaries also noted Kipling's intense love for children, and his extraordinary ability to communicate with them. He had the gift of empathy. And above all, these years in India brought forth creative work that despite mixed quality and jejune defects is marvelous in its variety, quantity, brilliance, and force. Several short stories are masterpieces.

Kipling's work meant loneliness at times, however, and even solitude. For years Kipling was left in charge of the newspaper during the sweltering hot season when his family and most of the British community left for the cooler hill country. One year during this abandonment, Kipling had what he called a "pivot experience." At twenty, he was the only Englishman left to do all the editorial and supervisory work. It was too much: "It happened one hot-weather evening, in '86 or thereabouts, when I felt that I had come to the edge of all endurance. As I entered my *empty house in the dusk* there was no more in me except the *horror of a great darkness,* that I must have been fighting for some days. I came through that *darkness* alive, but how I do not know" (1937, p. 65; my italics). The desertion and darkness must have evoked the House of Desolation and its threat of the hallucinated "shadows and things that were not there," and the incipient blindness. Being alone at night may have brought with it forbidden sexual and masturbatory temptations.

We know from the imagery of his writings that darkness meant for Kipling the occasion for soul murder: for too-muchness (perhaps connected with primal scene fantasies); for desolation of spirit; the blackness of depression; the hatred and self-hatred mixed with fear of castration and death of the abandoned child who "cannot very well curse

God and die." Kipling's first memories of England were of a dreadful place of darkness: "a dark land, and a darker room full of cold, in one wall of which a white woman made naked fire" (1937, p. 4). His bearer, Meeta, was credited with saving the child Kipling "from any night terrors or dread of the dark," but we have seen how ineffective this was when there was no Meeta to give reassurance. Dobrée (1967) shows the horror of darkness and desolation to have been a recurrent theme in Kipling's work, usually associated with what Kipling calls "breaking strain," the unbearable overstimulation that is the essence of trauma. "Breaking strain" is applicable both to what Kipling suffered at twenty from overwork in the intolerable heat, and to the time at Lorne Lodge. He uses the term in one of his last poems, "Hymn of Breaking Strain":

> But in our daily dealing
>   With stone and steel, we find
> The Gods have no such feeling
>   Of Justice toward mankind;
> To no set gauge they make us,—
>   For no laid course prepare—
> And presently o'ertake us
>   With loads we cannot bear:
> Too merciless to bear. (1935, p. 298)

The agnostic Kipling charged the gods with responsibility for the unbearable load, and he included the specific accusation, so relevant to his parents, that they did not prepare human beings for the "breaking strain." But predictably, the condemnation of parent-gods ends in their justification—they are needed:

> Oh veiled and secret Power
>   Whose paths we seek in vain,
> *Be with us in our hour*
>   *Of overthrow and pain;*
> That we—by which sure token
>   We know Thy ways are true—
> In spite of being broken
>   *Because of being Broken,*
>   May rise and build anew.
>   Stand up and build anew!
>   (1935, p. 299; my italics)

For the children Ruddy and Trix, the protective power of parents was not "with us in our hour of overthrow and pain." The undoing of the accusation in the line "Because of being Broken" surely approaches loving Big Brother (here again "the cut worm forgives the plough").

The engineer Hummil dies from great fear and shock in "At the End of the Passage" (1890c; the title describes the condition of Hummil's soul under the stress of overwork in India, such as that which brought on Kipling's "pivot experience"). He has seen something horrible, and his doctor attempts to photograph his retinas to see what it was. The reader is not told the result of this dubious scientific attempt. In the nightmare delirium that precedes his death Hummil sees "A blind face that cries and can't wipe its eyes, a blind face that chases him down corridors!" (p. 188). Hummil's Indian servant says: "In my poor opinion, this that was my master has descended into the Dark Places, and there has been caught because he was not able to escape with sufficient speed" (p. 192). Kipling continued periodically to descend into Dark Places. In 1907 he addressed a group of students at McGill University: "Some of you here know—*and I remember*—that youth can be a season of great depression, despondencies, doubts, waverings. The worse because they seem to be peculiar to ourselves and incommunicable to our fellows. There is a certain *darkness* into which the *soul* of the young man sometimes *descends*—a horror of desolation, abandonment and realized worthlessness, which is one of the most real of hells in which we are compelled to walk" (1907, p. 21; my italics).

Kipling describes experiencing in 1896 "a Spirit of deep despondency" (1937, p. 134) in the first house he and his wife rented after they returned to England after living for some years in Vermont. (This return too meant an enforced exile: Kipling was running away from what he expected would be a permanent home in the United States because of persecution by his American brother-in-law.) Kipling calls what they felt in the rented house: "a gathering *blackness* of mind and sorrow of the heart, that each put down to the new, soft climate and, without telling the other, fought against for long weeks. It was the Feng-sui—the Spirit of the house itself—that *darkened the sunshine* and fell upon us every time we entered, checking the very words on our lips" (1937, p. 134; my italics). This was worked over in a story about a haunted house, "The House Surgeon," written years later, in 1909. In this story the narrator has a terrible experience, which starts with something reminiscent of Rudyard's boyhood hallucinations: "And it was just then that I was aware of a *little grey shadow*, as it might have been a snowflake seen *against the light*, floating at an immense distance in the background of my brain. [This leads to a climax.] . . . My amazed and angry soul dropped gulf by gulf into that horror of great darkness which is spoken of in the Bible[21] . . . despair upon despair, misery upon misery, fear after fear. (p. 539; my italics)

In one of his last stories, a fable called "Uncovenanted Mercies" (1927), Kipling makes Satan, the Prince of Darkness, afraid of the dark, and again uses the same phrase: "The glare of the halo he wore in His Own Place fought against the *Horror of Great Darkness*" (1927, p. 331; my italics). For Kipling, Hell was a dark place, blindness (the punishment of Oedipus) a constant threat, and light a promise of salvation —but in a vicious cycle, the promise could lead by way of the fires of sexuality and anger back to Hell.

Eighteen months after Kipling returned to India at the age of seventeen, Florence Garrard wrote to him to end their engagement. He commented on this in his verse. A poem of 1884, "Failure," prefigured his novel *The Light That Failed*, written in 1890. Again a fascinating but frightening woman appears who is linked with darkness, fire, and light, and she extinguishes the light:

> One brought her Fire from a distant place.
> And She—what should She know of it?—She took
> His offering with the same untroubled look
> Of peace upon her face.

21. The italicized words are the very ones Kipling used to describe his "pivot experience." It is worth quoting the biblical passage, from the Book of Job: "There are those who rebel *against the light*, who are not acquainted with its ways, and do not stay in its paths. The murderer rises *in the dark*, that he may kill the poor and needy; and *in the night* he is as a thief. The *eye* of the adulterer also waits for *the twilight*, saying 'No *eye* will see me'; and he disguises his face. *In the dark they dig through houses; by day they shut themselves up; they do not know the light. For deep darkness is morning to all of them; for they are friends with the terror of deep darkness*" (Job 24: 13–18; my italics). The passage shows the attraction of darkness, which is light to the murderers, thieves, adulterers, and those who "dig through houses." Kipling consciously rejected this identification with the criminals (soul murderers), yet he constantly sought the darkness that he fled. Note that the offending eye in the passage belongs to the adulterer, evoking both the voyeur at the primal scene and the blindness of Oedipus.

"And I have brought it of my best," quoth he,
By barren deserts and a frozen land.
What recompense?" She could not understand,
  But let the bright light be.

"A kindly gift," the answer broke at length.
"A kindly gift. We thank you. What is this
That fiercer than all house-hold fires is,
  And gathereth in strength?"

"Strange fires! Take them hence with you, O sir!
Presage of coming woe we dimly feel."
Sudden She crushed the embers 'neath Her Heel,—
  And all light went with Her. (1884, p. 101)

The capitalization of *She* and *Her* shows that Kipling is still dealing with the Woman.

Wilson (1977) connects Kipling's difficulty in sleeping and his night prowling to the time at Lorne Lodge, pointing out what he calls Kipling's "typically splendid frightening phrase" about the results of Aunty Rosa's regime: "the night got into his head" (p. 62). The phrase is frightening in multifarious ways connoting not only the effect of insomnia but sexual penetration, identification with the "dark" penetrator, and mental and emotional disturbance.

There is another implication of darkness: ignorance, the not knowing that both contributes to soul murder and is a result of it. Trix too uses darkness as a metaphor when writing of her parents' not defining the children's situation and exposing them to desolation: "We missed Papa and Mamma far more than these kind parents ever realised. They doubtless wanted to save us, and themselves, suffering by not telling us clearly beforehand that we were to be left behind, but by doing so they left us, as it were, *in the dark*, and with *nothing* to look forward to" (Fleming 1937, 171; my italics).

Toward the end of his "seven years" in India (between the ages of sixteen and twenty-three), Kipling broke away from the "Family Square" by taking a job on a newspaper in Allahabad. He transferred some of his familial dependence onto Mr. and Mrs. Edgar Hill, with whom he stayed for some time. He was especially devoted to Mrs. Edmonia "Ted" Hill, seven years his senior, although the relationship does not seem to have been sexual or romantic. As with Mrs. Burton, Rudyard was "in thrall" to an older, managing woman. Accompanied by the Hills, Kipling left India and his family shortly after Trix became engaged to an army man, one of those doers whom Kipling so admired. The Hills were going back to Ted's family in the United States, Kipling decided to accompany them for a roundabout journey on his way to London to further his literary career. He spent several months with Mrs. Hill's family, was attracted to her younger sister, Caroline Taylor, and then continued to London with the Hills. His Indian stories and poems had already attracted some critical attention in England, but his first year in London, 1890, was a year of marvelous success—very like the success that he gives Dick Heldar, the painter who is the hero of *The Light That Failed* (1891). Each man took London by storm with his art.

When the Hills returned to India, Kipling was again left alone, although his uncles and aunts were in the background as they had been during the years in the House of Desolation. He was working intensely: most of the famous *Barrack-Room Ballads* (published in 1892) were written in London. It must have helped him banish the painful past by again experiencing those feelings of his very first years of being a conqueror: like Goethe and Freud, he was conquering with his pen.

The Light That Failed begins with a near autobiographical chapter about two orphan children under the care of an Aunty Rosa in the House of Desolation. The first scene, in which the two pubescent children Maisie and Dick are playing with a forbidden, loaded target pistol, is an unconscious allusion to "dangerous" masturbation, as I have mentioned. Stewart (1966) calls the novel a work of genius but "a very young sick man's book. Its power comes from the irruption, for a time, of something always latent in Kipling: an almost magical fear and hatred of women—of women who are not good chaps, answering to nicknames like William and 'Ted'" (pp. 93–94). And, one might add, of women who desert one in one's need.

Most ironic is the dedication poem of the book, and the irony is certainly unconscious. On the surface it is a tribute to a loving mother, a mother who would never abandon her son—maternal love can follow the son anywhere:

> If I were hanged on the highest hill,
> *Mother o'mine, O mother o'mine.*
> I know whose love would follow me still,
> *Mother o'mine, O mother o'mine!*

If I were drowned in the deepest sea,
  Mother o'mine, O mother o'mine!
I know whose tears would come down to me,
  Mother o'mine, O mother o'mine!

If I were damned of body and soul,
I know whose prayers would make me whole,
  Mother o'mine, O mother o'mine.
                              (1891, Dedication)[22]

The poem presents the fantasy from childhood that the son will die and the mother will be sorry, love him, and follow him. Despite this wishful tribute to his mother, Kipling portrays himself in *The Light That Failed* as an orphan. Perhaps he makes Dick an orphan to keep from writing a direct attack on his mother. (Dickens may have orphaned David Copperfield for the same reason.)

Heldar's blindness begins as the child Kipling's had, with the appearance of a grey haze at the periphery of his vision. And blindness was the fate that the child at Lorne Lodge expected for himself. The theme is introduced in the first chapter, when the child Maisie (the transformed Flo Garrard) almost blinds Dick by accidentally shooting a revolver past his face. Heldar's eyes are especially precious, because he needs them for his art.

Dick Heldar's masterpiece, which he frantically finishes as he begins to go blind, is called "Melancolia"—again blackness is involved. The portrait represents the head of a woman who has suffered terribly but insolently laughs at fate. Dick obviously fears and admires this woman defying black depression; the novel covertly shows his identification

22. Eugene O'Neill, unlike Kipling fully conscious of the irony, makes use of this poem in his autobiographical play *Long Day's Journey into Night.* In Act 4 Jamie, who represents O'Neill's older brother in the play and frequently quotes Kipling, has just returned drunk from a whorehouse. He extols the comfort a whore can bring, then thinks of his mother, an addict who has just resumed taking drugs: "What's the use of coming home to get the blues over what can't be helped? All over—finished now—not a hope!" (He stops, his head nodding drunkenly, his eyes closing, then suddenly he looks up, his face hard, and quotes jeeringly) "If I were hanged on the highest hill, / Mother o'mine, O mother o'mine! / I know whose love would follow me still" (1956, p. 161). The terrible ambivalence of the first-born son, deserted by the mother, was there for both Rudyard and Jamie.

with her. The portrait's features are taken from cold, selfish Maisie and the model-prostitute Bessie Broke. Bessie destroys the painting to avenge the scornful way Dick treats her (as if she were a thing with no feelings) when he breaks up her affair with his friend Torpenhow. The female head he painted is apparently malign; Torpenhow says, "Dick, there's a sort of murderous, viperine suggestion in the poise of the head that I don't understand" (p. 142). The novel portrays women as vampires who cannot love and who destroy men and their art. Only masculine love sustains and can be relied on.

The intensity of Kipling's sadism shows in the novel's brutality. Kincaid-Weeks has made a distinction between Kipling's objective treatment of a brutal subject or situation "and a brutal attitude or satisfaction felt toward it" (1964, p. 198). He gives as an example the fine description of the brutal attack of three thousand Sudanese on a square of British soldiers, in contrast to an incident at the end of the attack that expresses the brutality of Kipling's sadism. The gouging out of an eye, the oedipal self-punishment, is here directed against an enemy, which prefigures the hero's fate: "Torpenhow had gone down under an Arab whom he had tried to 'collar low,' and was turning over and over with his captive, feeling for the man's eyes . . . [he] had shaken himself clear of his enemy, and rose, wiping his thumb on his trousers. The Arab, both hands to his forehead, screaming aloud, then snatched up his spear and rushed at Torpenhow, who was panting under the shelter of Dick's revolver. Dick fired twice, and the man dropped limply. His upturned face lacked one eye" (1890a, pp. 27–28). Later, when blind, Dick asks Torpenhow: "D'you remember that nigger you gouged in the square? Pity you didn't keep the odd eye. It would have been useful" (p. 148). Presumably his irony is intended to show ability to laugh at fate, as in his "Melancolia".

At the end of the novel, blind and abandoned by his friends (who think Maisie is taking care of him), Dick leaves England to seek out his beloved big brother Torpenhow, the eye gouger. Earlier, when Dick's blindness becomes manifest, a scene between the two men conveys homosexual contact, although Kipling obviously does not know this: "[Dick] made as if to leap from the bed, but Torpenhow's arms were round him, and Torpenhow's chin was on his shoulder, and his breath was squeezed out of him . . . the grip could draw no closer. Both men were breathing heavily. Dick threw his head from side to side and groaned. [Dick then falls asleep after asking to hold Torpenhow's hand,

and the scene ends with Torpenhow kissing him] light on the forehead, as men do sometimes kiss a wounded comrade in the hour of death, to ease his departure" (1890, pp. 145–146). Torpenhow's attentions to Dick are maternal (as Meeta's had been to Ruddy), protecting him from the horror of great darkness.

Dick returns to Egypt to die. He has an ecstatic response to arriving in time to take part in a battle, or at least to hear one. Just before finding Torpenhow, Dick again invokes mother: " 'What luck! What stupendous and imperial luck!' said Dick. 'It's just before the battle, *mother*. Oh, God has been most good to me!' " (p. 219; my italics). The blinded child can share in the sadistic primal scene.[23] Dick then meets Torpenhow and dies in his arms; it is a *Liebestod*.

In contrast to his hero's death in Egypt, Kipling's success in London made him feel like a conqueror of Egypt. After *The Light That Failed* was published, he sent to his parents a telegram that read, "Genesis 14:9." The passage referred to reads as follows: "Make haste to go to my father and say to him, 'Thus says your son Joseph, God has made me lord of all Egypt; come down to me; do not tarry.' " Here Kipling identifies with his namesake (his full given name was Joseph Rudyard), the biblical prototype of parental favorites. Apart from the reference in this telegram, Kipling rarely used his given first name. Joseph, son of Jacob, of course also suffered separation from his parents. But Rudyard's ambition and success had taken him, the "lord of all Egypt," far from the Egypt of darkness and fire that he saw on his first train journey to England as a small child, and far from the "depression [and] realized worthlessness" that he recalled to his student audience at McGill in 1907.

In addition to his presumably platonic ties to two older, forceful, married women, Mrs. Burton and "Ted" Hill, Kipling had emotional involvements (including plans for marriage) with two women before his "lordly" year of 1891: Caroline Taylor, the sister of Mrs. Hill, and Florence Garrard, whom he used for the sister figure Maisie in his novel. He went on to marry another sister, the sister of a man with whom he developed the deepest friendship of his life, Wolcott Balestier. Kipling met him just after he had been writing about the reliable emotional closeness between Dick Heldar and Torpenhow, and although

23. I have postulated a primal scene fantasy in relation to the memory from the age of two-and-a-half of the train fire in Egypt, land of the Sphinx (see above).

not literally an army man, Balestier may well be thought of as Kipling's embodied Torpenhow. Balestier was a twenty-nine-year-old American of great charm and considerable talent who had made himself influential as a publisher's agent in literary London. In his middle age Henry James was "captivated" by his young compatriot (Edel 1962, 283). Balestier was in London trying to sign up English writers; his employers realized that the impending international copyright agreement would end the literary piracy in America that so infuriated Kipling. Despite Kipling's great distrust of publishers and their agents, he immediately became a close friend of the American, and they soon embarked on a collaborative novel set in America and India, *The Naulahka*. Kipling must have been impressed by Balestier's ability to get what he was after, the quality of an "army man" that always attracted him. (Alice James characterized Balestier after his death as "the effective and indispensable"; (See Edel 1962, 299.) According to Carrington, "No other man ever exercised so dominating an influence over Rudyard Kipling as did Wolcott Balestier during the eighteen months of their intimacy" (1955, p. 225). Kipling soon met the whole Balestier family. An understanding seems to have been quickly reached between Rudyard and the elder of Wolcott's two sisters, Caroline. Like Flo Garrard, Carrie Balestier was older than Rudyard (by three years). She had taken over a leading role in the family (the father had died) and was looking after her beloved brother Wolcott and managing his household affairs.

It is said that when Kipling's mother first saw the rather aggressive Carrie Balestier, she declared with scant enthusiasm: "That woman is going to marry our Ruddy" (Carrington 1955, 229). Kipling's father commented "Carrie Balestier is a good man spoiled" (Carrington 1955, 229). Little is recorded about the progress of the love affair. Motivated partly by his doctors' advice to travel, Kipling set off by himself for America, South Africa, Australia, New Zealand, and India; it seems a strange venture for a recently engaged man. During this time he wrote some of his first imperialist poems, identifying with the Empire and becoming its spokesman. In December 1891, Kipling heard that Wolcott had contracted typhoid fever in Germany. When Wolcott died Carrie sent Rudyard a cable asking him to come home. Henry James, also summoned (from London), arrived to find Carrie in charge of everything. He wrote of her in a letter: "The three [Balestier] ladies came insistently to the grave . . . by far the most interesting is poor little concentrated Carrie . . . remarkable in her *force, acuteness, capacity, and*

courage—and in the intense, *almost manly nature* of her emotion . . .
she can do and face . . . for all three of them, anything and everything
that they will have to meet now" (quoted in Carrington 1955, 239; my
italics).

Rudyard married Carrie eight days after he joined the family in London. Henry James, who gave the bride away, wrote that she was "a
hard devoted capable little person whom I don't in the least understand
[Kipling] marrying" (Carrington 1955, 241). "The reason why Rudyard
hurried halfway round the world to marry Wolcott's sister is bound up
with his devotion to Wolcott. There is little doubt that Wolcott himself
fostered the match, that Wolcott on his death bed commended the care
of his family to his friend Rudyard, that Wolcott's wishes were accepted
by Rudyard as obligations" (Carrington 1955, 242). Wolcott's death
was one of the great blows of Kipling's life. Sharing Carrie's feeling for
a beloved brother figure was part of Rudyard's motivation in marrying
her.[24] Carrie was in the role of his own worshipful sister, Trix.

Aunty Rosa used to say that Trix would grow up to marry Harry, and
she seemed to Trix seriously to expect this. The "manly" Carrie would
seem to have had some of the significance for Rudyard of both Aunty
Rosa and Harry (whose name rhymes with Carrie), with their qualities as Woman and Big Brother transformed from bad to good. Carrie
laid down the law in the family, kept Kipling's accounts, watched over
his every move. She protected him and kept him from distractions and
intruders. She had looked after her brother Wolcott with her "concentrated," intense devotion, and she transferred her management and her
feelings to Kipling: "Until Rudyard's death, forty-four years later, the
two were inseparable and her services to him were indispensable . . .
[She] gave Rudyard her life's endeavour and grudged him, perhaps,
his faculty for withdrawing into a world of the imagination where she
could not follow him" (Carrington 1955, 242–243). Here was someone
"whose love would follow me still . . . if I were hanged on the highest
hill." It was security, but not without ambivalence.

After the wedding the couple traveled to Vermont, where they stayed
with Carrie's younger brother Beatty (with whom Kipling quarreled

24. There is a "cryptic reference to his love for Carrie and his friendship for
Wolcott in Chapter VII [of The Naulahka]: 'He was to Tarvin more than a
brother; that is to say, the brother of one's beloved' " (Green 1965, 105). Carrie
was the sister "of one's beloved."

violently in later years). Their first child, Josephine, was born in Vermont. Kipling had fallen in love with Brattleboro, and the family decided to settle there. They built a house, called Naulakha and so evoking Wolcott, but with a curious, enigmatic change in the spelling of the novel's title. The house, says Stewart, "had one notable feature, to be reduplicated in essentials wherever the Kiplings subsequently lived. Kipling's study had only one entrance, through a room occupied by his wife. There Carrie would sit at a desk ordering her domestic affairs, and guarding her husband against all possibility of intrusion. He could remain undisturbed for as long as he liked; sometimes, perhaps, for rather longer" (1965, p. 104). Here are connotations of the Sphinx guarding the road to Thebes. Kipling had chosen a female, potentially malevolent "watcher" (Sophocles, trans. Jebb, p. 17) to keep strangers from disturbing his solitude.

Here the narrative of Kipling's life may be ended; my biography is intended to illustrate his partial soul murder and so mainly concerns his early years. Ahead lies his time as the official poet of imperialism, of political conservatism, of hatred against the Boers and Boches, of friendship with Cecil Rhodes and George V. So does so much intensely creative work—his masterpiece, *Kim,* and the wonderful short stories written late in his life that bring him closest to being a major artist.

Kipling was scarred by soul murder. His intense hatred was a burden adversely affecting his art as well as his life. His marvelous talent for seeing and knowing (he is one of the greatest describers in English literature) was often inhibited by the need to attack and simultaneously justify the established order. He escaped overt homosexuality but married a domineering, masculine woman. In some ways this was a narcissistic choice, for he too had identified with Aunty Rosa, with a lifelong bent for the Harrys—the doers and bullies of this world. But the relationship with his wife was close and contained much happiness. Kipling was a loving father to his children and suffered terribly when two of them died. He was subject to moods of depression and irritability, but he could also laugh, occasionally even at himself, and make others laugh. He became a great success, a public figure, the most widely read author in English since Shakespeare. After the First World War his critical reputation plunged. The intellectual generation that grew up in the twenties was uninterested in the poet of patriotism and imperialism, even hostile toward him. Except for his books for children, he had become the "Kipling that nobody read" (Wilson 1941b).

There was a group of devoted readers he never lost, but the artistry of his late short stories went largely unrecognized until after his death in 1936, when critical interest in his work revived in the 1940s.

The psychoanalyst who approaches a subject through reading has no special source of insight; whatever the analyst's theoretical knowledge of depth psychology, any view of an author's childhood derived from books is of necessity superficial. What is done with the patchwork surface must in large part be based on conjecture and generalization, as with any other biography. On the surface, Kipling's childhood is portrayed as six years of bliss followed by six years of hell. The crucial first six years of his life must have provided Kipling with the strength to survive the soul murder in the House of Desolation; he says so himself. How much did these early years also provide the seeds of his self-destructive tendencies and weaknesses? The reader can only speculate, reconstructing from what Kipling wrote and basing a shaky structure on a general knowledge of human development. The boy would seem to have experienced an overwhelming acceptance of his importance. He was a wanted child, perhaps too much wanted. There was little curbing of his aggression, which was freely displayed in the nursery world. (This usually results in anxiety in later development.) Although his parents may have been distant at times, his ayah and bearer were physically close and very indulgent. In his memoirs and stories Kipling depicts the narcissistic vulnerability that can accompany the grandiosity of the overindulged child. (It should be clear from some of the clinical material in this book that overindulgence plays its considerable role in soul murder alongside deprivation.) It would be helpful to know more about the specific details of Kipling's relationship with his parents, especially with his enigmatic mother. It must be meaningful that Trix wrote of herself in Lorne Lodge as having had "no least recollection of" her mother (Fleming 1937, 168), while "remember[ing] that dear *ayah* known and loved all my short life in India" (p. 170).

The births of his sister and stillborn sibling must have evoked Rudyard's anxiety in relation to his anger and his sexual feelings. These births were probably linked to fantasies about parental intercourse and the first trip to the "dark land," England. The lifelong, obsessive preoccupation with metaphors of light and darkness, vision and blindness, suggests a considerable impact on Kipling of primal scene fantasies, which had exciting, terrifying connotations. Further, implicit evidence of his primal scene fixation is his lifelong, intense curiosity and need to be "in the know"; these tendencies were mysteriously transmuted into Kipling's artistic gifts as an observer, describer, and evoker of realistic physical and psychological detail.[25]

During the time of the attempted soul murder (between the ages of six and twelve), Kipling had to face three major situations of psychological danger and their concomitant anxieties. These intermixed and overlapped, but can be placed in an oversimplified, approximate chronological order: the loss of his parents and separation anxiety; the overstimulation of the soul murder itself and traumatic anxiety; the threat of castration and castration anxiety. At six Rudyard was at the height of his oedipal development. At Lorne Lodge he was in a situation perhaps repeating in some ways his first years in India, dominated by a cruel, all-powerful woman, with the much-needed protective father at a distance.

The trauma of desertion was made more terrible by the boy's being completely unprepared for it.[26] Suddenly the children were in Hell. Their fate resembles that of the children cared for and studied by Anna Freud during the emergency evacuations from London in the blitz of the Second World War—they were suddenly separated from their parents:

> The child experiences shock when he is suddenly and without preparation exposed to dangers which he cannot cope with emotionally. In the case of evacuation the danger is represented by the sudden disappearance of all the people he knows and loves. Un-

25. Randall Jarrell quotes a wonderful description of a drugstore from Kipling's short story "Wireless" and adds, "One feels after reading this: well, no one ever again will have to describe a drugstore; many of Kipling's descriptive sentences have this feeling of finality" (1963, p. 269). Elsewhere he writes: "Knowing what the peoples, animals, plants, weathers of the world look like, sound like, smell like, was Kipling's métier, and so was knowing the words that could make someone else know" (1962, p. 137).

26. I am grateful to Dr. Charlotte Lichtenberg and Dr. Joseph Lichtenberg for pointing out to me the instance of soul murder in Kipling's short story "Lisbeth" (from Plain Tales from the Hills, 1888a). The story shows the destructive effect of not saying goodbye and lying about a desertion (seemingly with good motive) at the instigation of a bad woman. It certainly reflects Kipling's childhood experiences.

satisfied longing produces in him a state of tension which is felt as shock . . . In reality it is the very quickness of the child's break with the mother which contains all the dangers of abnormal consequences. Long drawn-out separation may bring more visible pain but it is less harmful because it gives the child time to accompany the events with his reactions, to work through his own feelings over and over again, to find outward expressions for his state of mind, i.e., to abreact slowly. Reactions which do not even reach the child's consciousness do incalculable harm to his normality. (A. Freud 1939–45, 208–209)

At six, Rudyard was better able to face the loss than was the three-year-old Trix, for images of both parents and of the predominantly loving servants were firmly fixed as part of the structure of his mind. He had achieved "object constancy."[27] As long as he could remember and think, his parents could not be completely lost. He could use his mind, his creative imagination, to fight against that part of himself that turned toward Aunty Rosa and Harry, gave into them, identified with them. Trix wrote that "Ruddy at six always understood the realness of things, and his parents knew that his frequent phrase, when three years old, 'Don't disturv me, I'm finking,' had a very real meaning" (Fleming 1937, 170). The power of the six-year-old to know and remember was specifically attacked by the brainwashing techniques of the Holloways (as it is so regularly in soul murder). Reading and writing were

27. Anna Freud says about the crucial attainment of object constancy (the ability to retain images of the parents in the mind even when the parents are physically absent): "It is only after object constancy . . . has been reached that the external absence of the object is substituted for, at least in part, by the presence of an internal image which remains stable; on the strength of this achievement temporary separation can be lengthened, commensurate with the advances in object constancy" (1965, p. 65). Of a child of Trix's age (three-and-a-half years) in whom object constancy has not been firmly established, she writes: Distress and *desolation* are inevitable [in the young child who needs to separate from the mother on going to nursery school] . . . only if developmental considerations are neglected . . . if the child has reached object constancy at least . . . separation from the mother is less upsetting. *Even then, the change has to be introduced gradually, in small doses, the periods of independence must not be too long, and, in the beginning, return to the mother should be open to choice*" (1965, 89–90; my italics).

crucial skills, and reading, so tied to the forbidden seeing, became the subject of conflict and symptoms. Apparently there were occasional letters from the parents that must have helped reinforce the children's memories.[28] Rudyard could fight his passive entrapment in fantasies and memories by actively ordering the bad reality and playing with it (Trix was his eager listener and participant). Rudyard's father had consoled him with a nursery rhyme after the attack by a hen, and later the boy could identify with his protective father's humor and creativity to ward off the attacks by the Woman. He became a writer and poet, and his poems were based on a mastery of rhyme. The ambition to become a writer crystallized in adolescence, when there must have been a renewal of intrapsychic conflict over aggression and masturbation. He used the writer's hand to keep away the child's severed hand (to use the metaphor from his childhood memories). In his struggle over castration, he needed to identify with his father to conquer the bad Woman —to conquer her both in himself and outside himself.

When Rudyard was in the middle of his oedipal development he was subject to intense, shifting ambivalence toward both parents. The desertion and later sadomasochistic overstimulation made for libidinal regression and a terrifying access of rage. This enhanced his parricidal impulses (especially his patricidal ones) at a time when the boy desperately needed good parents to help fight off his bad internal images

28. One would like to know more about these letters. They could have meant a lifeline for Rudyard's identity, and therefore provided motivation for his own drive to be a writer. In his memoirs, Kipling described his writing as specifically motivated toward having his parents as an audience: "I think I can with truth say that those two made for me the only public for whom then I had any regard whatever till their deaths, in my forty-fifth year" (1937, p. 89). How often did the parents write? What did they say? Were the children allowed to read the letters and to answer them? We do not know. In *Something of Myself*, Kipling tells of the (apparently fictional) "parting in the dawn with Father and Mother, who said that I must learn quickly to read and write so that they might send me letters and books" (1937, pp. 4–5). The books sent by his father are mentioned by Kipling, but at six he had not yet been taught by his parents to read. Indeed, he resisted learning from Aunty Rosa, and this could have involved spite against his parents. Trix tells of Aunty Rosa treating as a crime the children's "crying like 'silly babies' when she read us letters from Bombay" (Fleming 1937, 165). So there certainly were letters, but neither Rudyard nor Trix has more to say about them or their impact.

of destructive ones. (The abandoned child must face alone the wish to murder the parents and what is felt as their wish to murder the child.) Anna Freud describes children about six years old (the age of Ruddy at Lorne Lodge) when she writes of the desertion involved in school phobias: "The distress experienced at separation from mother, parents or home is due to an excessive ambivalence towards them. The conflict between love and hate of the parents can be tolerated by the child only in their reassuring presence. In their absence, the hostile side of the ambivalence assumes frightening proportions, and the ambivalently loved figures of the parents are clung to so as to save them from the child's own death wishes, aggressive fantasies, etc." (1965, p. 113). This need to preserve the internal images of good parents, so intense for the wartime evacuees at the Hampstead Nursery where the parental substitutes were good and understanding, becomes desperate under conditions of soul murder, where hatred is often deliberately cultivated. It is devastating when the parental substitutes, with the fanaticism of the religiously righteous and the power of commandants in concentration camps, suppress rather than understand the child's thoughts and feelings. But most destructive of all of the soul is the brainwashing operation that aims at preventing the child from registering what has happened.

The subjection to Aunty Rosa as the Woman, with Harry as her phallic extension, threatened Rudyard's masculinity. He needed a strong father to take her away. Kipling continued to seek for fathers and older brothers in his work and life. The fear of the Woman, the need to submit to the phallic parent, to deny his parricidal urges, made homosexuality a continuing temptation. The good external relationship with his father in later life must have helped stave off his strong latent homosexuality. One can see in his life and work a conflict-ridden range of wishes: wanting both to be and to have a man, a phallic woman (the ranee-tiger from childhood), and a woman.

The presence of his sister at Lorne Lodge helped strengthen Kipling's masculinity and his identity. Toward her he was able to feel and act like the protective parent that both needed so much. Trix was grateful for his care and craved it. She was the living link to his home, his parents, and his past. His memory and gift for storytelling allowed him to become the author of a family romance based on real events, with Trix his primal audience. He could identify with mother and father and the ayah and Meeta, and this enabled both children to hold on to them.

The sharing of the past in the House of Desolation is reflected in Kipling's two collections of historical tales for children, *Puck of Pook's Hill* (1906) and *Rewards and Fairies* (1910). In these stories exciting scenes from the history of England and America are told to the brother and sister, Dan and Una. Under the magic guidance of Puck, they meet people from the past who observed and participated in the events. So brother and sister travel through history together and control it by knowing about it, denying their alienation and exile from the great figures and happenings of long ago. With the aid of a good, magical parent figure, they right history's wrongs together, mastering the "primal scenes": the frightening, fascinating doings of the historical and narrative past.

The devotion of Trix continued a love from a female, and for a female, that was not swept away by Rudyard's hatred toward the Woman. Together the two children could retreat from the desolation and persecution of their daily life to a sanctuary created by the boy's imagination. To create a wonderful and sometimes terrible world for abandoned children made Rudyard a god who need not fear abandonment. He could know and order what was what, reward the deserving, and punish the wicked. Throughout his long writing career he was obsessed with the family romance, and the enchanted telling of tales that began with Trix continued in his books: "To Kipling the world was a dark forest full of families; so that when your father and mother leave you in the forest to die, the wolves that come to eat you are Father Wolf and Mother Wolf, your real father and mother; and you are—as not even the little wolves ever quite are—their real son. The family romance, the two families of the Hero, have so predominant a place in no other writer" (Jarrell 1962, 145). And fantasies of family romance were enhanced for Rudyard by the constant parental care of the ayah and Meeta during his first six years. (This resembles what develops in so many other children from diverse cultures who are reared largely by servants.)

I have speculated that there may have been sexual play between Trix and Rudyard that had some saving effect on his masculinity. He did manage a heterosexual life, despite the strength of his aversion to women (part of his ambivalence). There is no real loving, sexual woman in Kipling's early fiction. Sex is never treated as joyous; at best it is a guilt-ridden pleasure followed by punishment: "For the sin ye do two by two / ye must pay for one by one" (1891, p. 361).

The pathological effects of soul murder on Kipling's later life were intermittently present, and complicated by his defensive and sporadically successful struggle against them. There was a need to repeat the sadomasochistic experiences of the House of Desolation. Kipling's predominant position as a victim had enforced an identification with the persecutors, presumably out of the abandoned child's need for "dear kind God" (Dostoyevski). The destructive hatred had to be turned toward others. He required and found enemies: strangers, Boers, Boches, "the lesser breeds outside the law." (For a review of the theme of "revenge and retribution" in Kipling's work see Mason 1975, 214–227.) But he could also remember what it was like to have been the victim, and in some of his best work his empathy and identification with the underdog catches the reader's emotions. He is successful in bringing to sympathetic life the Indians and the Lama in *Kim*, the natives in many of the early stories, the British privates and noncommissioned officers in his prose and verse, and, above all, the abandoned and neglected children.

But the persecutor raged against the victim within Kipling's mind, making him subject to attacks of depression. Just as he split the images of himself, he needed to split the mental pictures of his parents into good and bad. With intolerable rage against those he loved and needed, he was forced to deny his hatred. The denial, the need not to know, existed alongside his driving curiosity. The denial made the split registration possible: contradictory images and ideas could exist side by side in his mind without blending, as with Orwell's doublethink. As I have tried to show in my clinical material, this compartmentalization is a way of dealing with overwhelming and contradictory feeling, but it is paid for by sacrificing the power of synthesis that is needed for joy, love, and the feeling of identity. The ease with which this splitting was possible was not due entirely to the defensive need to ward off hatred and fear from the mental images of good parents. Even before the bad Holloways assumed the role of parents, as a child in India Kipling had lived through the intense experiences of having two sets of parents—white and black, light and dark. The existence of the complicated split mental representations of self and parents does not automatically make for pathology.[29] That depends on how the splits are used. The crucial

29. A "creative" example of splitting can be seen in Kipling's attribution of responsibility for his writing not to himself but to his "Daemon": "My Daemon was with me in the Jungle Books, Kim, and both Puck books, and good care I

questions are whether the contradictory mental representations can be integrated if necessary, and whether they can be brought together and taken apart again so that they can be worked with in a flow of thought and feeling. If not, they must exist for most or all of the time frozen and isolated, beyond criticism and modification, as with the soul-murdered. For Kipling, beneath the fragile seeming clarity of the bad Aunty Rosa and Harry and the good mother and father was a terrible, ambivalent fragmentation and confusion. This is beautifully described by Jarrell: "As it was, his world had been torn in two and he himself torn in two: for under the part of him that extenuated everything, blamed for nothing, there was certainly a part that extenuated nothing, blamed for everything—a part he never admitted, most especially not to himself" (1962, p. 144).

There is a depiction of being "torn in two" in madness, or at least in a dream of madness, in a poem called "The Mother's Son" (1928). The narrator is in an asylum and looking into a mirror, that metaphor for split images:

> I have a dream—a dreadful dream—
>   A dream that is never done.
> I watch a man go out of his mind,
>   And he is My Mother's Son.
>
> And it was *not* disease or crime
>   Which got him landed there,
> But because They laid on My Mother's Son
>   More than any man could bear.
>
> .   .   .   .
>
> They broke his body and his mind
>   And yet They made him live,

took to walk delicately lest he should withdraw" (1937, p. 210). Jarrell (1963) describes Kipling as possessed "by both the Daemon he tells you about, who writes some of the stories for him, and the demons he doesn't tell you about, who wrote some others" (p. 140). Kipling wrote of having a "contract" with his Daemon (which evokes soul murder in the style of Schreber) and gave this advice to writers: "*Note here.* When your Daemon is in charge, do not try to think consciously. Drift, wait and obey" (1937, p. 210). Kipling here describes the creative benefits of passive subjection to his Daemon: his talents helped him split off what it meant to be in subjection to that "Devil-boy" Harry.

And They asked more of My Mother's Son
 Than any man could give.
.   .   .   .

And no one knows when he'll get well
 So there he'll have to be.
And, 'spite of his beard in the looking-glass,
 I know that man is me!
                (1928, pp. 398–399; italics in original)

Here the blaming of the mother is not conscious; it appears in the repeated, split-off characterization of the self as "My Mother's Son" (with Kipling's characteristic capitalization both accusing and idealizing). The too-muchness is attributed to an impersonal, bad "They," a projection of the bad self and a transference of the bad parents—as in the familiar "they" of the paranoid. For Kipling, "they" means not me, and not the mother or father, but the Holloways and the Shere Khans. The poem's last line, " 'spite of his beard in the looking glass" (vile phrase!), implies that the bearded man is looking in the glass for a beardless self. Kipling developed facial hair very early. The adult victim of unbearable strain is surely expecting to see the image of himself as a boy in the House of Desolation.

Kipling was most comfortable when the separation of mental images operated to suppress hatred. This could happen when he was active and in control, at one with his demon so that his creative energy could flow, and when in life he felt he had achieved that perfect ordering of things, that discipline that ruled out abrupt desolation so that the good could not suddenly become bad. In *The Jungle Books*, where the rules are dominated by "the Law" (they had begun with Mowgli abandoned to the mercy of the tiger), the final image is of animals and men taking part in a magnificent review before the viceroy, and a native officer responding to a stranger's asking how it was done: "The animals obey, as the men do. Mule, horse, elephant, or bullock, he obeys his driver, and the driver his sergeant, and the sergeant his lieutenant, and the lieutenant his captain, and the captain his major, and the major his colonel, and the colonel his brigadier commanding three regiments, and the brigadier his general, who obeys the Viceroy, who is servant of the Empress. Thus it is done" (1894, p. 421). In such a well-regulated world the empress, the great mother, watches over all. The Jungle seems to have lost its terror. And yet, as any reader of *The Jungle Books* can see, a main principle of "the Law" is the right to revenge.

I have described an attempt at soul murder directed against Rudyard Kipling as a child. His years in the House of Desolation had effects that continued to inhibit Kipling's ability to feel joy and to love, and that sometimes flawed his art. Yet the soul murder was far from completely effected: Kipling's identity was preserved as was some ability to love others,[30] and he became a great artist. The struggle to fight off the soul murder and its consequences strengthened him and may even have enhanced his creativity in some ways; it gave him motive and subject matter for his writing. I have connected those terrible years of his childhood to his flaws and to his greatness. Kipling's story touches on the mysteries of the origin of mental sickness and creativity. The explorer must be prepared for contradiction and complexity.

30. Kipling's affection for his children is displayed in his letters to them (see Kipling 1983). These are full of an uneasy, lumpish playfulness; under a humorous, often mocking and self-mocking surface, there is a perceptible presence of the Victorian "heavy" father about to pounce with disapproval. Sometimes the children are obviously addressed as extensions of Kipling himself, especially where his anxiety and hostility threaten some loss of control (the hostility is usually projected and predominantly self-directed). There is also a real fondness and appropriate concern (rather than an overappropriate concern). In these letters to his two surviving children one sees the dynamic identity of parenthood that shifts between narcissism and an ability to care about a separate person. All is not well when a child threatens to offend and disturb the existing order. Then empathy dissolves and hatred can burst out; Kipling can be cruelly derisive of physical failings (for example, in the joking allusions to his daughter Elsie's overweight). But one feels convinced that Kipling could also love his children, especially his son.

13

Insight as Metaphor

Psychoanalysts try to get their patients to remember rather than repeat the past. They do this by taking part in the formation of a relationship in which the patient inevitably relives the traumata and central fantasies of childhood, as distorted by defenses, by time, and by the innate limitations of one's connection to one's own history. History is said to be a series of messes. Only a feeling of personal identity (more or less continuing) can bring to the mess of one's past an impression of unity. The psychoanalyst tries to enhance the patient's sense of self in relation to the perspective of time by bringing into consciousness what the patient has forgotten or perhaps has never been able to remember: this is attempted by making verbal connections (interpretations). The patient remembers; the analyst reconstructs. The patient in analysis works on these connections between past and present, distorts them, corrects them, feels them; ideally they become the patient's own. If this happens, the patient can know with more conviction than before that there is a history for which the patient has become responsible: the patient *owns* this past. Insofar as the soul of the brainwashed victim of child abuse has been murdered, the victim cannot be responsible for what must not be remembered or felt. For this person insight, the making of connections, is the road to restoring identity and even humanity.

"Only connect!" is E. M. Forster's prescription for England in *How-ard's End* (1910)—"only connect the prose and the passion!" (p. 187). That is to say, connect with the emotions the ideas and the facts and the will and ability to act. This insight has been expressed in psychoanalytic language by Valenstein (1962): "Mutative or dynamic insight

... amounts to ... extended self-knowledge, combining ... affective-conative and intellectual cognitive components" (p. 323).

I will connect insight with metaphor by using one of my own papers, a minor commentary on some of the metaphors in Freud's *Interpretation of Dreams* (Shengold 1966). In these days, when psychoanalytic concepts and language have been attacked for their (inevitable) reliance on metaphor, I want to stand beside Arlow (1979) as its champion. To paraphrase Forster, psychoanalytic prose should be full of passion and its conveyer, metaphor. Trilling (1940) wrote that Freud pictured the mind as a poetry-making organ. Metaphor is inherent to human thought, and it follows that it is essential to psychoanalytic work: "The communication and interpretation of unconscious meaning is made possible largely through the use of metaphor" (Arlow 1979, 363). One must be aware of the limitations and defensive uses of metaphor and still be able to employ and translate it. (The ability to act with an awareness of limitations is part of the power granted by insight.) The word *insight* is itself a metaphor: it originally meant seeing "with the eyes of the mind or understanding" (*Oxford English Dictionary*). Arlow (1979) links the functions of metaphor and of insight: "In my view metaphor is an inherent quality of language in general and of how the human mind integrates the experiences of the individual. Metaphor typifies how perception and memory are integrated in terms of similarity and difference" (p. 373). Here metaphor performs, as does insight, by connecting, by integrating, by granting perspective.

Freud's use of metaphor stuck in my mind when I investigated his use of the word *insight*. It was no surprise that Blum (1979) and Abrams (1981) had also begun their research on insight by combing through the *Collected Works*; it is what an analyst should do. Abrams had learned from Guttman (1979) that the words Strachey translated from Freud's German as *insight* were used 195 times, but the only helpful application I had been able to find was the one that everyone knows, from the preface to the third English edition (1931) of *The Interpretation of Dreams*: "Insight such as this comes to one's lot but once in a lifetime" (1900, p. xxii).[1] What does this famous statement, expressing both pride and humility, imply about insight?

1. Anna Freud (1981, pp. 241f.) says that in German there are only two instances in which Freud used the word *insight (Einsicht)* in the sense of revelation (as in the quotation, which Freud wrote in English): the many other uses of

In my paper on Freud's use of metaphor I examined some implications of a few of the images that Freud intertwined with his central metaphoric plan in the dream book—that plan being a journey through a landscape. I indicated what I feel is a crucial place in the journey of that book: a turning point at the beginning of chapter 7, where Freud (1900, p. 509) changes direction to plunge into the depths of the wishes of the unconscious (a "veritable hell"—see Freud 1916–17, 143—like Dante, Freud undertakes a cosmic exploration involving the mind and the universe). That turning point is marked by the dream of the burning child. The speech in that dream is, "Father, don't you see I'm burning?" The dream and therefore the dream question are not Freud's own, but they can be linked with the exhibitionistic urination of the child Freud in his parents' bedroom (which brought on his father's unforgettable comment "That boy will come to nothing"), and with his own dream after the death of his father: "You are requested to close the eyes" (1900, p. 317). Both dreams refer to sight, to the metaphor of sight as understanding; and both dreams are to be connected with the mature and measured assessment of Freud's achievement, addressed to the fathers of this world, to heed or ignore at their peril: "Insight such as this comes to one's lot but once in a lifetime." By 1931 the child's burning had been tempered to a cool glance backward at the white heat of inspiration that marked the years following the death of his father.

The metaphors that interconnect with that of the journey include views and prospects, locomotion, ascents and descents to heights and depths, explorations, demonstrations, light and fire, darkness. They are all involved with the map of the world within and the world outside the mind—with how the world outside is registered within. The metaphors are aspects of the journey that lead to insight and outlook, to use Arthur Koestler's phrase.

Freud's statement of 1931 about insight pertained to a display of dynamic knowledge that revolutionized our concepts of the inner world (involving the self, the view within, and insight), but that also threatened the outer world of the authorities (outlook), as the man who likened himself to Copernicus and Darwin reminded us. The insights in the dream book were gained from Freud's "journey" of self-analysis, from

---

Einsicht or *Einblick* simply denote "knowledge of" or "insight into" illness (that is, awareness of being ill).

his exploration of the minds of his patients, and from contrasting the two: from a looking inside correlated with a looking outside.

The distinctions between insight and outlook and between inside and outside are confusing and ambiguous, and lead in psychology to the metaphysical and the moot. What is inside the mind, and what is outside? I know that the world outside my mind is represented within my mind. I know that I can observe myself and make discoveries about my inner world. I know that insight and outlook are inextricable in my mind, as its representational world, to use the metaphor of Sandler and Rosenblatt (1962). I know that at some early point in development mental representations of states of feeling that arise from the body and its functioning get linked with representations of things outside the mind; these primal mental connections are basic to metaphor and the process of insight, indeed are basic to thought. Despite this iteration of "I know" I must face the philosophic challenge of Montaigne's "What do I know?" Putting aside as we must the expectation of ever completing successfully our search for the "real" structure of the inner and outer worlds, we are left with sharpening our metaphors, left with the shadows on the wall in Plato's cave, which we sometimes choose to regard as two caves—the cave of the word and the cave of the mind. Experientially we feel that we know what inside and outside mean, and that the two are related; that the look within cannot be dissociated from the look without, and vice versa.

Analytic work repeats not only Freud's discoveries but also his way of integrating them. To explore the mental world of their patients, analysts empathize and listen; what they find must be correlated with their knowledge of their own inner world. In my usage here, the insights of analysts into the minds of their patients are really *outlook*; their view into their own minds involves insight. The work of analysts connects insight and outlook (in the above senses); they try to remove resistances and interpret transferences, and hope that their patients will learn to connect and correlate for themselves. When patients merely borrow the "outlook" of their analysts (the analysts' views into the patients' minds), it is not insight and there is no integration (Kris 1956a). The patients must slowly and painfully make their own the mental contents and finally the correlative power.

To return to its relevance for the metaphor of the journey, insight would refer first to an ability to see, and second to an ability to proceed and stop freely in the inner world that contains both changing and relatively stable representations of our selves and of our human and other environmental objects. The comparative freedom of this mental locomotion assumes that there is an optimal, flexible relation to and between those structural elements of our minds that register the inner pictures of the world inside and the world outside our bodies—those two environments of our psychic apparatus that Freud (1940) speaks of in the *Outline*. When Valenstein (1962) describes insight as mutative and dynamic, we can connect this with qualities that pertain to a "good" metaphoric traveler: command over action, locomotion, flexibility, choice. To speak less metaphorically and more experientially, we should be able to see and know what we are and were, whom we are with and have been with, where we are and where we have been. And we should know the limits of what we know and what we do not, as to both contents and qualities of our knowing. Who we are involves how we feel. Interpsychic travel (the flow, the stops, the reversals) requires the available interplay of the "affective-conative and intellectual": feelings, desire and will, and ideas. And implicit—even in acquiring mental representations for that matter—is gaining the power to coordinate, to synthesize, to put it all together so that one can say "Look!" to the parent, or "Eureka!" to oneself. And this look should involve not only integration, but an integration that furnishes perspective, balance, and proportion.

A journey includes at the least a going from place A to place B, or to put it in terms of one of Freud's favorite Jewish jokes, from here to Karlsbad. The relevant story (Freud called it "the constitution story") is worth recounting. It concerns a Schnorrer: "An impecunious Jew had stowed himself away without a ticket in the fast train to Karlsbad. He was caught, and each time tickets were inspected he was taken out of the train and treated more and more severely. At one of the stations on his *via dolorosa* he met an acquaintance, who asked him where he was traveling to. 'To Karlsbad,' was his reply, 'if my constitution can stand it'" (1900, p. 195).

Only distance and the traversal of distance can provide perspective, and one must be able to endure them emotionally. Insight is not a simple linear journey: it is full of stops and forks in the road (including the one at Thebes). The journey leads to all sorts of connections along different planes and in different dimensions, including the dimension of time. For integration and perspective, time travel as well as internal space travel is needed. The development of the ego involves locomotion; and this is more than metaphor: an emotional separation from the mother is necessary, and this is enhanced greatly when the child can first crawl and then finally walk away. Only with the mastery of locomotion is the child able to attain the idea of distance (if correlated psychic development permits), to compare sizes and shapes, and to explore and contrast in its own mind the sensory qualities of the objects in the external world. To gain perspective about external space, one must form after physical exploration internalized pictures of what is out there: "It is not in space that I must seek my dignity, but in the ordering of my thought . . . By space the universe comprehends me, swallows me like a speck; by thought, I comprehend it" (Blaise Pascal, 1670).

With the development and maturation of the powers of memory and language, the child's outward journeys can be registered and a traveling within the mind becomes possible; repetition eventually results also in a perspective in time. But many repetitions are required: one must go from here to Karlsbad many times to remember and correlate the journey with other journeys and then make maps and schedules. And as with Freud's Karlsbad Schnorrer (to connect the prose with the passion), one's "constitution" must be able to stand the trip. Too much feeling, the effects of too many traumas, and the journey of insight can suddenly be interrupted, or can continue aimlessly. It is to be expected that achieving and keeping insight will be especially difficult and dangerous for the victim of child abuse (the concomitant brainwashing effect of which limits the development of "locomotion" within the mind).

The sense of perspective that begins with the ability to go from one place to another demands an integration of various points with different kinds of connections, including contradictions, contrasts, and simultaneities. To shift to our theoretical metaphor, secondary process should be optimally enriched by primary process (Noy 1978). This complex development culminates in the attainment of emotional and moral perspective; these imply the ability to distance without dissociation or denial, and the power to modulate affect and values. To attain this kind of insight requires the full maturation and use of the mental apparatus (Kennedy 1979) and its mastery over the drives, implying the proper developmental unfolding of defense mechanisms (A. Freud 1979, 6; see also Shengold 1988). A mature and predominantly benevolent superego must have evolved, and there must have been enough luck with external reality to permit at least the transient coexistence of the philosophic yet active mind ("thought is trial action") with a free range of emotions: the prose connected with the passion. If an individual does not have the "constitution" to reach Karlsbad independently, we can help this person along the via dolorosa with psychoanalysis. "During analysis, insight fluctuates topographically and structurally. But at the end of the treatment we expect a new structural stability" (Neubauer 1979, 34). As Neubauer makes clear, he would agree that for all of us, especially those who like the Schnorrer have been beaten too much, reaching or at least approaching Karlsbad requires structural *flexibility* as well as structural stability.

One crucial, currently challenged point of view about insight is implicit in what I have stated (and in the metaphor of what one encounters on the journey): insight involves the patient's seeing and engaging with intrapsychic conflict; this is part of the via dolorosa of analysis. Many psychic healers seek to obviate the journey and the conflict by promising salvation through caring and love, which they and their patients feel the patients lacked (both may be right). But false promise fosters brainwashing, and this is especially pertinent to the victims of soul murder. Like Rome, Karlsbad meant to Freud a place one may never quite reach. We should not foster by delusion the goal of reaching the unattainable.

Patient O.: If My Constitution Can Bear It

O. came for treatment in his twenties, mainly because he was aware that he had a pattern of starting projects and commitments with great promise only to end up courting and achieving failure. He saw that he had a need to fail (and even saw a little how he managed it), but characteristically he did not *feel* it. He was another of those provocative but predominantly passive and masochistic people who deserve Samuel Butler's " 'Tis better to have loved and lost, than never to have lost at all." The passion that went into his losing was very far from the young man's responsible awareness. A compulsive, defensive emotional isolation and intellectualization barred the way to resonsibility and a true feeling of identity. O. acted the role of a bystander, an observer of his own life. Despite a surface of charm, wit, and even brilliance, O. possessed what E. M. Forster called "the undeveloped heart" (see chapter 12), functioning for the most part like a marionette (although with a kind of desperation in his search for someone to pull the strings). His emotional aridity was not complete; there was some anxiety, some ability to care about other people, and I could dimly sense the tip of an iceberg of congealed rage.

During his first hour O. told me of an obviously important early memory: "You Freudians will like this, "he said (deindividualizing me), "I'm going to tell you how my mother showed me her bush." When he was five he had asked to see his mother's genitals, and she had responded by taking him into the bathroom and "providing a display in three-dimensional depth" (a typical example of the patient's ironic and elliptical speaking style). This short journey, reported as prose without any passion, was often mentioned again, almost always with the original tag of metaphoric slang, "the time she showed me her bush," the affect frozen by the reduction to cliché. Moreover, the metaphor referred to the blur of the mother's pubic hair and avoided the mysterious, unfathomable, yet fully exposed genital abyss. (He stated several times, at first without giving details, "She showed me *everything*.")

After O. revealed this memory in the first hour, I wondered what he was going to remember later. But my reaction underestimated his isolation. It was reassuring to find several months later that it was a long torment for O. to tell me that he had the habit of picking his nose; that was something he really felt. The incestuous exhibition, in contrast, seemed freely available and often came into his associations; but it was not filled in emotionally, no details were added, and O. never connected it with his current sexual life or his feelings about his mother.

During the first session O. also said, "I'm very bright, I know, but the people I work under tell me that I sometimes act as if I can't add one and one to make two." I noted the metaphor "working under," with its passive connotations; and also the primal scene implications of the inhibition against putting one and one together. I wondered how much the first hour had indicated the analytic path; I could sense the defenses of isolation and of avoiding responsibility, and I sketched out the analytic task, in an outlook that was premature but as it turned out not inaccurate: the patient needed to make meaningful connections with his unconscious fantasy life that were implicit in his metaphors: *seeing the bush, working under people,* watching *one and one make two.*

After about three years, during which the voyeuristic memory and the momentary image that accompanied it had appeared in O.'s associations many times, disconnected except for witticisms that he refused to analyze, more resistance appeared. O. became unable to talk about the confrontation with his mother humorously or without anxiety. He was remembering more about what he had seen and how he had reacted. He "associated" with characteristic motions of his hands whenever he talked about the "bush." After this had been pointed out, O. said that he felt he was reproducing his mother's movements when spreading her labia. He started to react to the memory of the sight of her pubic hairs as if these were now detailed in a naturalistic painting, rather than the black impressionist smudge of the "bush." His emotions and body feelings began to flow in accompaniment to the memory: excitement, then feelings of inferiority about his penis, then the too-muchness, the overstimulation and terrible intimations of fear and rage. These feelings were sampled, as it were, as he began to transfer them from his mental pictures of his parents onto the analyst and thus to relive in the present the past event. His passive sexual feelings became part of the struggle, and so did the painful beginning of reawakened, intense fear of castration. O.'s terror of his aggressive impulses took the characteristic form of erotizing his pain. The analyst was assigned the role of the conductor on the train to Karlsbad, administering an emotional beating. In the course of attempting to analyze all this, the patient appeared to be more responsible for understanding what he had felt his mother and father were like and how he had reacted to them as a child, and he even seemed able to contrast this with what they might "really" have been like. The promise that was there in so many of his enterprises was appearing in his analysis. Alas, this turned out to be the usual harbinger of trouble.

The flow that connected the prose and the passion was too much for O. He could not bear the intensity of the excitement, rage, and anxiety—especially because his passive sexual and murderous impulses focused on the analyst and onto passionate impressions of his parents. He felt he would explode; he would harm himself; he would harm me; he would harm his parents. He hated his mother for what she had exposed him to. In perceptibly intense, emotional ways and clamorous, sensory ways he was again preoccupied with his own body and that of his mother. He was in effect saying to me, "Father, don't you see I'm burning?" O. was aflame with passions he felt he could not master, and he demanded a father who would magically keep mother's behavior in control and take all his bad feelings away. And the old pattern won out: all the promise, now meaningfully connected with his mother's seductive exhibition, led to the need to fail—a spiteful mixture of self-punishment, masochism, and revenge (just as the initial prospective excitement of seeing his mother's genitals had led to overstimulation and rage).

O. manipulated his realistic situation to get an excuse to leave the analysis. He did this before it could become clear whether his past could fairly be characterized as containing soul murder. There was the clear memory of only one instance of incestuous visual sexual contact. What had gone on earlier and later was lost in repression, isolation, and denial. A soul-murder scenario is suggested by the massive defenses involved, the intensity of the compulsion to repeat and be punished, and the centrality of the guilt-ridden fantasy life based on the memory. This remains speculative. More analytic work would be needed for O. to approximate the actuality of what had happened to him and in him as a child, to balance wishes and fantasies against reality, to determine the borders and the blending of narrative and historical truth. It is possible that O. will return to continue his journey, and discover what lies behind the screen of his mother's "bush." Or he may be one of the many whose constitution cannot stand the insight that psychoanalysis offers: an integration and a conviction that threaten to bring back to life a traumatic past.

The child who says, "Father, don't you see I'm burning?" has ultimately to be able to stand the searing impulses, preoedipal and oedipal, that lead to overstimulation and rage, incest and parricide. And insight also means giving up the promise of the much-needed, magically omnipotent, good parent. We must accept the sad truth that only those whose egos are strong or capable of being strengthened will be able to face the hell of the unconscious and the realization of one's peripheral and precarious place in an indifferent universe. This was a truth well known to Dostoyevski's Grand Inquisitor, who rebuked (and at first intended to *burn*) the returned Christ for having expected too much of men, for having asked them to accept truth and free choice rather than "mystery, miracle and authority": "Thou didst choose all that is exceptional, vague and enigmatic; Thou didst choose what was utterly beyond the strength of men . . . Didst Thou forget that man prefers peace, and even death, to freedom of choice in the knowledge of good and evil?" (1880, p. 302).

O. had approached and then run away from the threshold of freedom of choice—a place in the journey of his analysis that had been reached when metaphor, slowly stripped of its defensive function, had led to memory and the revival of body experience.

The Case of P.:
Integration and Establishing Perspective

P., a successful businessman, married and a father, had for several years warded off responsible awareness of his passivity with a rather stubborn and provocative resistance to his analysis, which he seemed to regard as a wrestling match with the analyst. Whenever he allowed his feelings to appear, anger toward me predominated, sometimes rationalized by fancied slights. He did his best to maintain that he had no deep feelings for me; he felt more comfortable with anger than with love. His emotions could intensify suddenly, which frightened him, and then he characteristically disowned them by a kind of dramatic projection: he would provoke people around him, cause them to react, and then proceed to aggravate or placate them while he felt he was observing it all from an emotional distance. (This relatively uninvolved action was what he meant by "wrestling.") Although his work had nothing to do with the theater, he lived his life as if he were an actor on stage. Only at rare moments was he responsible for his feelings. His marriage seemed based in part on a mutual need for emotional isolation. Shortly before the session that I will describe, he had begun to realize that beneath the surface of acting *as if* his analysis did not matter to him, he cared intensely. I had always known this from his faithful attendance, his passionate provocativeness, and his intermittent ability to engage in free association and emotionally meaningful analytic work.

One day P. started the session in a philosophic, transcendental mood, very unusual for him; his customary show of stormy affect was absent and he sounded calm: "You are of course not my enemy. You seem to me to be really a good, even a kind, person. You have been dependable and just, not like my father. And yet I hate you as I hated my father and I see that I expect that you will hate me as my father hated me."

P. had convincingly presented his father as an insensitive and even brutal man married to a frightened, passive, yet seductive woman who had turned to her son for comfort and rescue. It was not at all evident that the father had consistently hated his son, any more than that the son had consistently hated the father, but the latter had responded violently to the son's persistent provocations. (Later in the analysis, the instances of unprovoked cruelty that had been lightly mentioned deepened with the release from repression and emotional isolation into a history of a childhood that was full of torment; as P. became able to experience and contain his excitement and hatred toward his father, there could remain no doubt that soul murder was an appropriate metaphor for P.'s childhood.)

P. continued: "I know that I hate others with the terrible kind of hate my father always showed when he was crossed. What is different today is that when I *say* you are good, and yet I *know* I still hate you, I feel alright about it." The emotional balance was tentative and preliminary. Emotional change comes slowly, and this hour marked a beginning. The loving "good" (denoting a feeling which left P. so vulnerable and was therefore dangerous) is *said*, the more familiar hate is *known*. The patient went on to recollect a theme of recent sessions: fantasies about a woman at his office with whom he was tempted to have an affair, and their mutual employer, who reminded P. of his analyst. He had in effect been outlining a scenario for a sexual triangle:

> All that talking I have been doing about triangles, I have not felt involved in it. It has been like a shadow play, even though I really could have put it into action. but today, somehow, I feel that triangle and how it relates to my father and mother; I feel it in three dimensions. [This is said with excitement and involvement.] I feel the good feelings, and the bad feelings; the sex, and the jealousy. It's all mixed up, but it's real. It's not bad or good, it's bad-and-good. I hate my father and I love my father. You know this sounds like fancy intellectual stuff, but today it is different. It is all real and palpable; it's like a bowel movement!

I was aware of some intellectualizing defense at work, but also felt convinced that P.'s feelings did have a different and more authentic quality—convinced in part by the patient's excitement and involvement as he brought out his homely metaphor. It had marked a kind of epiphany and he had been close to tears.

With this overdetermined association to his anal erogeneity, P. was also unconsciously bringing in the perspective of time: the "wrestling matches" over his bowel training and subsequent anal overstimulation; and the more distant past, when that bowel movement meant representation of me and not me, inside and outside, self and object. These regressive paths were for future exploration, as was the reverse direction and the road to Thebes, Laius, and Jocasta that he had touched on in his associations. But in the remainder of the session, P. continued to show that he had temporarily made and integrated connections that established a sense of perspective, differentiation, and modulated affect —while holding on to the feeling of psychic reality as "palpable" reality. Primary process was felicitously intertwined with secondary process. The physical grasp of the bowel movement by his anal sphincter that had emerged from the unconscious to supply an experiential component of memory was facilitating the grasp of the ego. (This is the heart of my idea of "defensive anality," according to which the anal sphincter is the somatic, prototypical counterpart to the mind's defensive functions —see Shengold 1988.) The session ended with weeping, with expressions of gratitude from P. for the "feeling of wholeness" it had brought him. He was for the time being not an overwhelmed child but a man feeling what he was like as well as what his father was like; he felt able to deal with this analysis and his life. Of course, he quickly descended from this plateau of insight to more conflict and suffering in the depths; but the heights were there to be scaled again.

It is obvious that this good hour was the result of many small accretions of insight achieved in the course of "working through," to use our metaphor. I emphasize, however, that what seemed to announce and convey conviction in this hour was the association to the bowel movement as a metaphor for the real and the palpable. The patient had brought into consciousness as a nodal affective point a piece of the "pleasure-physiological body ego" (Fliess 1961, 246–254).[2] The association brought on an intense flow of affect involving erogeneity—one might call it "body affect." (The body ego had been evoked—that "first and foremost" psychic ego precursor.) This emotional phenomenon, which in this session seemed to break through the defensive wrappings of *as if,* can itself be viewed *as if* (I am in a labyrinth of metaphor) the word-presentation "bowel movement" suddenly approached the intensity of consciousness of a thing-presentation—another Karlsbad never

2. I am reminded of the effect of the official announcement that President Eisenhower had a "healthy bowel movement" after his myocardial infarct (a most unusual instance of official frankness at the time). This communicated both the vulnerable mortality and reassuring vitality of a public (father) figure.

to be arrived at.[3] The sensory intensity, combining affect and body sensation, furnished an ingredient that somehow made a connection allowing full dimensionality and conviction. Although one must beware of false conviction, which can range from quasi-delusion to hallucination (Kris 1956b), attaining conviction (consistent with being able to know when conviction is not appropriate and being able to operate without it) is part of what should follow from insight, from connecting the prose with the passion. Conviction is necessary to test reality and makes possible the firm setting of limits, the responsible awareness of doubts: this I know, this I don't know, this I think I know. Conviction contributes to a feeling of identity. With the evocation of the anal sensation (as part of the concatenation of metaphor), there seemed to follow an integration of a grasp of reality, a sense of conviction, and a feeling of identity, and this integration marked the full operation of insight as a process. There had been years of preparatory work with specific "insights." Metaphor evoking the experiential was later able so to transform memory that the full working through of the soul murder could be said to have begun with this session.

The metaphor *insight* refers to the coming to consciousness of the power that metaphor itself possesses to make psychic connections of force and meaning. Insight is a "condition, catalyst and consequence" (Blum 1979, 66) of the psychoanalytic process in Blum's elaboration of what Kris (1956a) called the "circularity" of the insight process (p. 261). Analysis can be conceived of in terms of a concentration on the characteristic metaphors of a patient: what and how they connect; how they are coordinated; what prevents or arrests the connective flow; how metaphor can be used for defensive purposes; the need to evoke the patient's awareness and responsibility for metaphors, and especially for the passions attached to them or contained in them. "Psychoanalysis is essentially a metaphorical exercise. The patient addresses the analyst metaphorically, the analyst listens and understands in a corresponding manner" (Arlow 1979, 373).

Using metaphor defensively as well as expressively can be traced back to what Fliess calls the symbolic equation of elements from the world of objects outside the mind. According to Freud these become symbols: registered within the mind are basic, instinct-laden aspects of

3. I am using the terms for the registration of objects that Freud supplied in one of his metapsychological papers (see Freud 1915).

infantile experience (mainly body parts, states of feeling, parents, and siblings), which in his additions of 1911 and 1914 to the dream book Freud conceived of as *that which is symbolized* (for example, a long stick, essentially a nonsexual object, is equated to the penis as its symbol, a part of what Fliess calls "the pleasure-physiological body ego"; see Fliess 1973, 43–49).

The symbolic equation is a developmental base for the ego functions of registering objects, using language, and testing reality. To Peto (1959), discussing symbolism, "Finding and evaluating external reality is to a great extent determined by refinding one's own body in the environment. *Thus the body image is of decisive importance in grasping the world around us*" (p. 230; my italics). These primal metaphorical links of the "pleasure-physiological body ego" with representations of the external world are at first so full of sensory perception and intense affect, combining the affective-conative and intellectual, and they are the first steps toward our thought, language, memory, and insight. Metaphor in this sense marks the beginning and the continuing road of the journey of our lives.

Metaphor leads to memory and the experiential: this is the first phase of the process of insight. A genetic principle is at work in relation to attaining the feelings of conviction and of "the real." When we use metaphor freely and creatively, we resuscitate something of that period of wonder of the second year of life, when we establish both a sense of self and a registration of the external world by laying down mental representations, equating as well as differentiating the inner and outer worlds. Mahler (1974) calls this the time of psychological birth. The sensory intensity stemming from the drives and body feelings matches and blends with the great excitement of the wish to explore and possess the universe (and especially the parents); the universe and the parents are being separated from the previously inchoate, undelineated self. This wish to know has all the intensity of a separate drive (it is of course made up of drive derivatives). The child is exploring and discovering, and developing what Piaget (1937) call evocative memory. It is a time of elation over the power to make inner journeys, and with the achievement of locomotion to make outer journeys. (The child can feel, "Father, don't you see I'm burning?" during this time of incandescence.) There will eventually be the painful discovery of limitations and dangers (the "rapprochement" phase of Mahler), a sort of developmental via dolorosa.[4] Metaphor provides a repetition of the earliest connections and differentiations between the inner and outer worlds, connections laden with body affect, and evokes the earliest experiential feelings of inside and outside, the awareness of the existence of self and others (people and things). When these connections approach some of their primal, fervid quality in our consciousness without jeopardizing our integrative powers, we can speak of insight. Metaphor that leads to insight supplies a conviction of real experience about the past. Metaphor leads to memory.

In its function of supplying and evoking the earliest experiential feelings of inside and outside, metaphor is "transitional" in Winnicott's sense: "It is assumed that the task of reality-acceptance is never completed, that no human being is free from the strain of relating inner and outer reality" (1953, p. 240). Winnicott goes on to speak of the strain being relieved by "transitional phenomena": transitional objects, child's play, artistic creativity. In a sense, metaphor and language are the basic transitional phenomena, mediating and providing links in both directions between the inner and outer worlds.

Perhaps what stands for the approach to Karlsbad of the metaphorical journey of insight is the access to the ego's responsible, conscious, integrating awareness of these early sensory and affect-charged representational connections between the "pleasure-physiological body ego" and the external world. Freud (1916–17) told us that our exploratory psychoanalytic work is directed neither toward the drives nor toward the actual causal beginnings of symptoms, but at some place above "the roots of the phenomena . . . at a point which has been made *accessible* to us by some very remarkable circumstances" (p. 436; my italics). Analysts try to make accessible to the ego for its work of synthesis these registrable beginnings of metaphor, these early, experientially charged connections of representational psychic structure, the actual first roots of which cannot ever quite be reached. Similarly, we can never quite recover the "actual" past or ascertain the "true" external reality. We

4. The via dolorosa, the road of suffering from Pilate's court to Golgotha, has at its end an equivalent of "Father, don't you see I'm burning?": "And at the ninth hour Jesus cried with a loud voice, 'Eloi, Eloi, lama sabachthani?' which means, 'My God, My God, why hast thou forsaken me?'" (Mark 15:34).

try to get as close as possible, and perhaps the journey matters more than the attainment of the goal.

Putting aside the centrality of metaphor for psychic events and change in everyone, the therapeutic challenge of attaining and preserving insight is even greater for those victims of child abuse and deprivation who have experienced too much. For them, to know with feeling and conviction means that they must again bear the unbearable, and their "constitution" may not be up to it. The analyst can only help the patient decide whether to pay the emotional price of losing the defenses that preserve the promise of the good parent whose magical powers were so desperately wanted. It is a price that many victims of soul murder cannot afford to pay, or do not choose to risk paying. At the least the analyst can help the patient make this seeming inability a conscious decision rather than an automatic reaction. Knowing where one is emotionally, even if it is a place that cannot or will not be abandoned, at least grants some mental perspective and some control. It provides some connection and therefore some insight.

We must not be deterred by the defensive powers of metaphor to distance the experiential. For insight is the seeing, the awareness of the journey we have embarked on, and the best linking we can make of the life of psychic fantasy with the memory of what was experienced. Only connect, we ask of ourselves and our patients: insight and outlook, past and present, memory and fantasy, prose and passion.

14

Two Clinical Sidelights

Quasi-Delusions and
the Enforcement of Isolation

Every normal person, in fact, is only normal on the average. His ego approximates to that of the psychotic in some part or other and to a greater or lesser extent. (Freud 1937, 235)

Quasi-delusions are one instance of manifestations in the "normal" that resemble those of psychosis. Patient M. illustrates one instance of this.

This rather masochistic young woman, in analysis for several years, was in mid-pregnancy. On this day she had arrived in the waiting room just as I opened the door to my office. She strode in past me with an unusual air of determination and proceeded to the couch:

Patient. I am really pissed. [silence] I have to go to the obstetrician after this session. Again I've forgotten to bring a fasting urine. I've forgotten it the past three times. I knew I would forget it. I don't want to talk about this. I'm going to change the subject. I was angry because I wanted to go to the bathroom before the session. But your door was open, there you were, and I was embarrassed. It doesn't really matter though—unless someone steps on my bladder.

Analyst. The "change of subject" sounds more like a continuation.

Patient. I want to keep away from why I keep forgetting the urine sample. I am furious at *his* nurse. I know that test itself isn't important—I had a blood sugar done recently. *She* keeps talking about albumen. I always will forget. I guess I'm so angry because *she* gave me this short narrow medical bottle to bring a sample in. It's impossible—no one could urinate into that bottle—at least no woman could. I'm furious with *her* [these are the patient's emphases] and I'm damned if I am going to do it unless *she* gives me another kind of bottle. It's just impossible to use that little thing.

Analyst. It sounds as if a few minutes of communication with the nurse could clear up the realistic part of the difficulty—is there some need to be angry with the nurse and keep the feeling that she has done something to you?

Patient. The "impossibility" of using the bottle could be gotten over by using another—or I could use a funnel or a plastic cup and pour it into the bottle. But I just won't. It makes me so mad. If *she* wants that sample, *she* is going to have to solve that problem. [Sheepishly] I know how irrational all this is. The nurse is really a very nice person. I could easily talk to her about this, and/or just bring in my own container. But I am really so furious about it that I put all my logic and knowledge aside and I feel stubborn —I just won't do it. *She* [back to the emphasis] can't make me use that bottle. *She* gave it to me and it's up to *her* to solve the problem.

Here a rational attitude toward what M. was feeling and thinking about the nurse was present alongside what seemed to be almost a delusional conviction about being forced and cheated by someone hateful. This was a typical, "stubborn" attitude (her own self-characterization), a kind of paranoid insistence, which intermittently emerged from this predominantly passive, cooperative, and agreeable young woman, *suddenly* giving her almost a different persona. She became hostile and provocative, angry and resistant, stubborn and spiteful, with obvious masochistic aim and a disregard of consequences. She seemed without responsibly knowing it to be courting punishment and a repetition of her traumatic past—the analyst would "step on [her] bladder." *Responsible* is the key word. It was obvious that in some real way she knew what was going on, but this kind of knowledge was provisionally not given access to her emotions and sense of conviction. Alongside this ineffective and distanced "knowing" there was a much more powerful, unsynthesized, and stronger "knowing"—a passionate, insisted on conviction that approached the delusional. The knowledge that M. was breaking with reality by the "delusion" was there, but it was compartmentalized and transiently "sterile," as Freud (1909) said of the Rat Man in a similar situation (see chapter 6).

These quasi-delusions are often overlooked and minimized, and not only by patients. We neurotics all have them. They can represent what Freud calls that "part" or "extent" of the ego of the "normal" (by which he means the neurotic) "which resembles the psychotic" (1937; see above).

In an earlier pregnancy, M. had had a similar conviction that she was growing a penis in her womb, alongside a critically sterile knowledge that she was not. Yes, this was a fantasy; and she certainly could have said that she "knew" this: "Look, I knew perfectly well I was going to have a baby and that I was not growing a penis—but I still somehow believed it all the same, if you know what I mean." I felt I did know what she meant, and some provisional yet fixed superstitious or magical belief is common enough: many women have quasi-delusions about having penises (see Calef and Weinshel 1981). A diagnostically trendy critic of this presentation might say that M. is "borderline." I would rejoin that if she is borderline, so are we all, in the specific sense that Freud described in 1937: "to a greater or lesser extent." Of course psychotics too have quasi-delusions as well as delusions. There is a range in intensity and flexibility, and varieties of dynamic flow, that make for crucial diversities in every individual. When we are not dealing with obvious extremes, these borderline phenomena are not easily differentiated.

The symbolism of the implement that is "too small" associated with urination and given by "*she . . . her*" (the deindividualized nurse-mother) is obvious, as is the evocation of the complexes (preoedipal as well as oedipal) involving castration anxiety and penis envy. These complexes stem from the body, from the early body-ego; so does the basic, near primal, metaphor involved in Freudian symbolization (see chapter 13). The regressive emotional intensity that characterizes quasi-delusion, granting it a stubborn, reductive, insistent, perfervid quality, marks the return to the earliest phase of development, when the body and those parts and functions of others that are at first regarded as parts of one's own body are the universe. This early combination of paradise and hell provides the motive power for our symbolization (in the Freudian sense), as well as the material for "that which is symbolized." This is basic to the power of our metaphor, the power of our minds. Whether we are "normal" or not, quasi-delusions mark a regression to a part of the unconscious mind that is differentiated early and remains in the grip of body ego predominance, and they also mark a perceptible getting stuck in this part of the mind that is at least transient. Quasi-delusions are fragments of our primal fantasies, and retain the power of those early bodily and drive-derived basic motivators to stretch and even break with later representations of external and internal reality. They are ubiquitous, but are used especially by victims of child abuse like M. who need to deny. It follows of course that these quasi-delusions are very difficult to analyze and make for stubborn resistances. But to begin to deal with these, the analyst must recognize the near delusional quality and convey this to the patient, who has to struggle (sometimes) to see the subtle break with reality and (always) to own it. I may be saying what everyone knows, but it is my impression that for many the fashion for "borderline" diagnosis has distanced the acceptance of Freud's cautionary insight of 1937 with which I began this chapter and I would like to see more about quasi-delusions in the psychoanalytic literature.

The Enforcement of Isolation and the Assault on a Child's Identity by a Seductive Parent

R., a young woman in analysis, told of her mother's having handed her over at birth to be brought up by a nurse, whom she remembered as kind and loving. Her mother had a career, which she abandoned when the child was four. The girl's life was suddenly and radically changed. Without warning, the good nurse was dismissed and the devastated child was then cared for by a series of maids directed by the mother. The mother, who had rarely appeared in the nursery while she was working, was remembered as omnipresent. (Actually, she turned out to have been often distracted or away.) Whenever a loving relationship between a maid and the girl appeared likely, the maid would be fired. The first nurse, who had found work nearby, tried to visit her former charge but was not allowed to speak to her. R. remembered hating the nurse for her weakness. Between the age of four and six the girl was brought up according to a strict time schedule that minimized human contact and included a daily nap lasting from mid-afternoon to early evening. The nap was especially onerous because it prevented the child from seeing her beloved father at dinner. Under pressure from the father, the mother gave up the rigid agenda—except for the nap, which was required until puberty. Other children were not allowed to visit or play with R.

The father cared about his daughter but seldom interfered with the mother; he was often gone for long periods. Whenever he left, the mother's attitude toward the child changed dramatically: the maid was banished and the tyrannical mother would insist on the child's presence. R. was taught to comb her mother's long hair "for hours" before bedtime, another interminable assignment full of erotic tension. R. was brought into the bathroom to watch her mother bathe and often shared the bath. She watched her mother defecate and urinate. The mother took the girl into her bed, and physical contact was encouraged. With all this seductive closeness, there was no expression of love or even affection. The child was treated as a thing that must be present to fulfill needs. She was characteristically hushed when she tried to communicate and deprecated as stupid and ugly. (Her photographs as a child showed her as quite pretty, but R. remembered how ugly she always felt.) The periods of intimacy would end suddenly and capriciously, with a peremptory dismissal back to the maid and the isolatory regimen. (During her analysis R. remembered that the sudden and shocking banishment sometimes occurred after her mother had achieved orgasm when masturbating.)

R. was kept from going to kindergarten and had to start school in the first grade, a neophyte among classmates accustomed to school. At first she was terrified to leave her mother and home and felt isolated from the other children. Gradually she became used to school and even fond of it, and she liked her kind and sympathetic teacher. R. remembered thinking that her teacher was the smartest and most beautiful person in the world; she grew to adore her and spoke at home of her. During this time her father was at home and her mother preoccupied with him. There was a happy period of many months during which the girl learned to read and became a good student, even surpassing her classmates. She no longer felt stupid and ugly. In the terms used by Kohut (1971), R. began to mirror her idealized teacher; her father had previously recognized and encouraged her brightness. The comparatively benign indifference of R.'s mother changed when her father left for a long European business trip. The mother began to interfere with R.'s going to school, insisting that the child was ill. When the mother was called to school for a conference with the teacher, R. became both hopeful and anxious. With tears and bitterness, she recalled in the analysis how much she wanted her mother to love her teacher and become like her. After the conference she ran up to her mother and asked, "Oh Mother, isn't my teacher beautiful?" Her mother responded in a voice full of hatred, "I've never seen such ugliness—she's ugly as sin. What a dog!" The girl was crushed. The precocious achievements at school stopped. A pattern emerged in which she turned away from all authorities as sources of good feelings and became involved alternately in zombielike indifference and spiteful, masochistic provocation often marked by pseudostupidity and "ugly" behavior. She alienated her schoolmates, submitted to and identified with her mother.

The incident at the age of six that crushed R.'s hope and joy left her feeling that her mother had the power to get rid of anyone the child cared for and needed. She remembered thinking when her father was away that she would always belong to her mother and that it was better not to feel any longing for anyone else. It was better not to feel anything. The rage she should have felt toward her mother was suppressed and sometimes displaced onto others, like the maids—but for the most part it was turned against herself. She saw the world and herself through her mother's eyes. "The most awful thing," she told the analyst, "was that my teacher really stopped looking beautiful to me. I couldn't tell if she was ugly or not. I became indifferent to her and I went back to not caring about myself." Cognition and feeling were both blocked; the ability to know had been interfered with.

R. convincingly described her mother as cruel, selfish, and "crazy"

(I use the word in the popular, descriptive sense rather than in a diagnostic sense). She acted out of her own intermittent need for symbiosis, treating her child as a need-fulfilling extension of her self. A typical remark to her daughter was, "I'm cold, put on a sweater!" She abandoned her use of the child for her masturbatory needs as casually and unempathically as she had begun it.

The mother did her best to interfere with models for identification other than herself. Her hold on the child led her to induce and maintain a mutual delusion of her own goodness and rightness. The child was forced to share the mother's distorted, narcissistic view of the world. (It was fortunate for R. that her mother's symbiotic parasitic needs were somewhat intermittent, so that she made only periodic destructive forays against the child's individuation.) R.'s mother apparently sensed that the saner and kinder nurse, father, and teacher might give the girl the power to see her mother's disturbance and cruelty, so she tried to isolate or banish them: The child could not be allowed a view from outside her mother's dominion. Efficient dictators appreciate the importance of propaganda and brainwashing. Physical isolation, especially that separating the victim from loving and caring people, is part of the brainwashing technique used in concentration camps (see Orwell's *1984*).

The development by the parent of a closed system for the child is the symbiotic container for soul murder. Entry to another family, sometimes effected by such simple means as frequent visits to a friend's home, has an eye-opening potential for change that is analogous to a visit to another culture by someone brought up under a totalitarian regime. Soul-murdering parents of this kind rarely grant visas or visitation rights. (R.'s mother, when she bothered to care, regularly found the girl's friends "ugly" and "stupid" and "dogs.")

Of course brainwashing cannot be undone suddenly. To fight denial requires a relationship that can fulfill basic psychological needs and permit the modification of basic identifications. The long and hard analytic work that partly restored R.'s capacity to feel and know was a continuation of the soul-saving direction initiated for her by the affectionate empathy toward R. of her first nurse and her father and by the girl's consequent absorption of their points of view. I speculate that it was especially the nurse's early loving care that helped make the damage done to R.'s soul partly reversible, and I know that the father's intermittent but eventually reliable approval had a similar effect. But for many years before her psychiatric treatment, R. lived a life without authenticity or passion, robbed of the sense of identity and of the vitality and joy that can lend grace to the human condition.

CHAPTER

15

Perspective and
Technical Considerations

I return to a statement made at the beginning of this book: in considering the effects of child abuse one must be prepared for the unexpected.
Human events are immensely complicated, and we know relatively
little about the resiliency of some individuals in the face of terrible and
tragic events. How frequent are the seduction and abuse of children?
They are certainly more common than had been realized for decades.
Now that people are increasingly aware of the fact of child abuse, accounts fill our newspapers, magazines, and even television (as well as
the psychiatric literature). It makes no sense to me that all neurotics
(and this means everyone) have been traumatically abused and seduced
in their childhood, as Freud first assumed and as Fliess and Masson
assert.[1] Soul murder has certainly not happened to everyone, but this
book is evidence of my conviction that overt, substantial parental seduction and deprivation are frequent. We know that there is an inevitable
(and usually preponderant), health-giving degree of seduction provided
by the mothering figure's bodily care; this is reflected in the universal fantasies of having been seduced. Correspondingly, in relation to
childhood deprivation, there is in every upbringing a range of experi-

1. The assertion that such specific pathogenic "craziness" is ubiquitous in parents reminds me of the little old lady on the witness stand in the film *Mr. Deeds
Comes to Town* who calls Gary Cooper "pixilated" (crazy). Her response to a
question from the judge is that "everyone is pixilated, except thee and me—
and I am not so sure about thee."

enced frustration and neglect: without any frustration no development is possible, and there is almost always a measure of ego-weakening overindulgence. With so many variables qualifying traumata and their effects, only the extreme degrees of too-muchness allow for much predictability, and even here there are surprises. But generally, too much emotional and physical neglect of a child can eventuate in psychic and even actual death. Similarly, the result can be an actual killing of the spirit, a consummated soul murder, if overstimulation is too prolonged and repetitive, if it occurs too early, or if it occurs without any tempering, empathic care that can be internalized as sustaining structure for the child's mind (this would include the parents' transmittable ability to say no to the child's demands). I have mentioned that the brother of one of my patients was singled out as the special object of persecution by the psychotic mother, who tried repeatedly to poison the scapegoated son. I know nothing of this child's inherent endowment, but it was not surprising to hear that he was regarded as feeble-minded and was institutionalized at an early age, according to my patient by a protective social worker. That child's soul was murdered, as his body very nearly was. But most of the people I have treated were able to survive their childhood experiences with considerable intactness, and even with what seems to be some psychic strengths brought out by the need to deal with and transcend the early overstimulations and deprivations (as is evident in the cases of the literary artists I have described). But my patients are a few individuals, not only healthy enough but successful and wealthy enough to sustain a psychoanalysis. Aside from an occasional contact in a clinic, how much can one psychoanalyst learn about individuals from the great mass of the devastated poor? What about the unmotivated, who are not that discontented with their "as-it-were" existence? And those who have become righteous soul murderers themselves? And the psychotic and psychopathic and "feebleminded"? More research is needed: more publication of specific cases,[2] and especially of descriptive statistics derived from clinical

2. For example: Weinshel (1986) on the effects of subtle forms of sexual abuse; Calef and Weinshel on "gaslighting" (1981); several papers by Kramer (1974, 1983); the description by Paul Dewald (1987) of a seemingly successful, short analytic treatment of a woman who was sexually assaulted by her father (I refer the reader to this paper even though the analysis sounds so easy in contrast to my long and laborious work with soul-murder victims, or perhaps because it

practice, like those of Vann Spruiell (1986). I have tried to describe what I have seen, and have emphasized the defensive and crippling scarring that many different human beings seemed to have in common. These scars appear to me to have stemmed from overwhelming experiences that the child was unable or forbidden to register and react to. We must not oversimplify pathogenesis by reducing everything to what has happened to us and ignore what we bring into the world when we are born, and the complicated mysteries involved in our development. But neither should we deny or attenuate the effects of actual traumatic events and situations.

General Considerations about Therapy

All depends on the patient's ability and willingness to change the way emotion is experienced. For soul-murdered people, emotional involvement involves terrible danger. Can the patient's feelings be acknowledged and modified? The key for the therapist in treating a soul-murder victim is understanding and empathizing with the patient's basic struggle about feelings. The patients have experienced too much and are easily subject to feeling too much: the automatic anxiety "belong[ing] to the traumatic situation of helplessness" (Freud 1926, 166) that underlies all situations of psychological danger. For traumatized people, fearing their intense feelings means fearing the fantasies that express these feelings, and the memories linked to those fantasies. (This is of course true of "ordinary" neurotics too, for there is no development free from trauma. But soul murder implies an economic difference: a too-muchness contributed to by the actuality of terrible experiences.) To repeat: soul-murder victims are afraid of feeling emotion, because emotion is the beginning of feeling more than is bearable. They do not always know this. With varying success and in varying ways, they have had to distance and discount their emotions. All this must become manifest in the analytic treatment.

Those who have been subjected to attempts at soul murder require one quality from the therapist or analyst above all others: patience. It is

---

sounds so easy); and Owen Renik's work (1987a, b) on adult children of disturbed and tormenting parents who manifested negative therapeutic reaction' to deny their past traumatic reality.

not hard to understand why change must be slow: there is so much distrust. The emotional connecting necessary for insight is initially more than soul-murdered people can bear. They learned as children that to be emotionally open, to want something passionately, was the beginning of frustrating torment. The deeply ingrained bad expectations are felt toward parents and all "grown-ups." The distrust is based not only on the projection of "bad" feelings (derived from the aggressive drives and the inevitable frustration of wishes), which give rise to intimations of losing control and a terror of being overwhelmed by feeling. Such fears beset every child in the course of development; they also lurk in our subsequent fantasy life (although their intensity varies with the individual). In addition to this, the distrust of parents and the entire affectively charged environment is based for soul-murder victims on *experienced* reality. They have been abused and neglected and have learned a lesson: if you cannot trust mother and father, whom can you trust? So a really meaningful alliance with the analyst takes a long time to develop, although at first it may appear that one exists; these people are likely to behave in "as if" fashion, to possess a façade of relatedness that combines compliance to what is usually expected with a provocative defiance that has a gamelike quality for them. People around them must not matter too much.

These patients may want consciously, even desperately, to love and trust the therapist, to whom they bring all the need for magical rescue of the helpless, traumatized child. In one of her first sessions on the couch, a previously bland and emotionally distant patient who had made more than one unsuccessful attempt at analysis surprised me with an uncharacteristically direct, deadly serious utterance: "In spite of my resolve not to let myself feel this way, I can't keep myself from hoping that *this* analysis will change me and bring me some happiness. If this hope gets frustrated—if this is just another of the many fruitless teases my life has consisted of—I will kill you. I mean it!" This address to the analyst was delivered after a routinely indifferent, subtly mocking and "resistant" recital of the previous day's events; it was marked by a sudden change of tone into a passionate minor key. (Analysts must be aware of the music as well as of the words of the patient's associations.) This kind of vehemence then disappeared from the analysis for many months, and it was not worked with for many years. The murderous rage was covered over, but the patient really did "mean it." For the most part, the early years of the analysis involved a patient who only seemed to trust and like her analyst.

Of course the distrust can also appear at the psychic surface in the soul-murdered, but it exists with such depth and intensity that the resistance to which it leads, if a therapeutic engagement turns out to be allowed at all, has to be experienced to be believed; it has to be experienced not only by the therapist (which is not very difficult) but by the patient. Because the formerly abused child has covered over passionate wanting by massive denial, he or she usually does not fully know, has not fully accepted, having the worst expectations about meaningful attachments. Such people are frequently unable to be responsible for the difficulty they have in really caring about others to whom they want to be close. Even those whose actions and thoughts convey a conscious wariness need to become responsibly cognizant of how much they distrust. (To love Big Brother means that the tortuous past has effectively been erased.)

To accept the analyst as a separate person and then as a predominantly benevolent one takes years of seemingly endless repetition and testing. One must never assume that the analyst will be felt by the patient as working for the patient's welfare; even with the "average expectable" patient, these anticipations of benevolence are at best intermittent. The analyst and the patient must be able to last it out. Given enough time, the near delusion that only the worst is to be expected, sometimes initially unconscious, can be modified by the reliability of the analytic situation: a time and place that can be counted on, the dependable, continuing presence of a generally accepting, nonpunitive parental figure, the persistent attempt to empathize and understand. Even with patients who cannot accept their past, cannot go much beyond giving provisional credence to the traumatic events and catastrophic reactions ("I know that I have remembered these things but I just won't believe them," said one patient at the end of a long attempt at analysis), the very existence of a long relationship with the analyst that has not resulted in a repetition of being harmed can in itself be of considerable benefit in softening the urgency of the effects of the past. For these patients, as well as for those who can accomplish more integration and "owning", that the analyst continues to be there, undestroyed and undestroying despite the murderous pitch of the patient's feelings, is a kind of miracle that has considerable ameliorative power.

But with life having had such a traumatic beginning (if it was too traumatic too early no change may be possible), one expects and finds a compulsion to repeat the overwhelming psychic and real events of the past. It follows that analysis that does not grant insight is not necessarily without potential harm. For some the commanding need to repeat the trauma can be enhanced in transference onto the therapist and can eventuate in destructive action or augmented masochistic self-punishment—and this may mean that the analysis cannot continue without hurting the patient. In such cases the relationship does harm and should be discontinued; one hopes that some insight will be imparted of why it should be discontinued. This has happened infrequently in my practice.

Those compelled to relive the traumatic past evoke the crippling, soul-shrinking (if not destroying) defenses that the traumatic anxiety has mobilized. Massive emotional isolation, psychical splits, and denial will have been necessary to contain and distance the child's terror and rage. "Anal narcissism" will have been enhanced, which diminishes human emotional qualities (see Shengold 1988): it is a narcissistic regression that makes difficult any commitment to other people, and even to interests and causes, and reinforces "anal" obsessive compulsive symptomatology and character. All this will reappear in the analysis: the obsessiveness means stubborn repetition in the transference onto the analyst; symptoms, memories, symptomatic actions, reenactment of past events, and defensive maneuvers in resistance will recur repeatedly. In response to the patient's stubborn repetitiveness, the analyst must iterate clarifications and interpretations with equal stubbornness and patience. "Working through" will require from the patient the ability to tolerate working on the edge of too-muchness, an ability that comes only with repetition, time, and eventually a sharing of the analyst's patience, if things go well.

One can expect at best a very slow acceptance of the analyst's benevolent neutrality, humanity, and empathy. The delusion of having had good parents (a loving Big Brother), which usually overlies the hatred and distrust, is transferred onto the analyst. Transference delusions are never easy to dissolve, and for those who were abused and deprived as children these idealized distortions remain desperately needed. If the patient presents with a further superficial covering of distrust (distrust overlaying delusional "trust" overlaying distrust), this too must be cleared away by interpretation before the pseudotrust is dealt with.

There is difficult resistance all along this complicated path. To see the analyst or therapist as different from the distorted, projected parental imagos is to begin to look truly and therefore critically at the parents, and this is the first step toward giving up an identification with them. Experientially, the patient feels the terrible danger of losing the parents psychologically. (To see the parent is not to be the parent.) This imminence of loss revives something at the heart of the child's traumatic anxiety (and the terrified child is very much alive within the adult): to be alone and beside oneself with distress and overstimulation, helpless in a terrible and destructive, or indifferent, world.

> I, a stranger and afraid
> In a world I never made.
> (Housman 1900, 111)

Without the inner picture of caring parents, how can one survive? The analyst must be able to feel first, how much the patient needs to hold on to the representations in the mind (delusional or not) of parents who care and who cared, inner pictures of the parents that if insight is possible are felt to be part of the image of one's self; and second, how reluctantly the patient can be expected to modify these representations, let alone give them up. Every soul-murder victim will be wracked by the question "Is there life without father and mother?" That is the central issue of these therapies.

The desperate attempt to hold on to the parents is usually concentrated on some kind of masochistic bondage. Frequently this is an extension of the chief historical, emotional tie to the sadistic, maltreating parent. With the indifferent or neglecting parent ("the undeveloped heart"), there is often a pattern of masochistic provocation aimed at obtaining some kind of recognition and attention. I have described several instances of partial soul murder, which as far as could be ascertained by memory and psychoanalytic work involved not sexual or aggressive abuse, or neglect of physical care, but indifference or rejection on the part of a parent. A parent's complete lack of love of a child, or what the child in fantasy can distort and interpret as this, can be as devastating as positive destructive hatred, sometimes more so. And the inevitable awareness by the child of the parental "undeveloped heart" means the arousal of the child's destructive hatred toward the parent. Lifelong conflicts can eventuate that have a sadomasochistic bent, and these inevitably keep a tie to the rejecting parent within the child's mind (despite evolution or even dissolution of the external, realistic relationship). There is always some degree of brainwashing and denial present for the child who needs parental caring and will try to make do with whatever exists. This can be expressed by varying combinations of idealizing subservience and provocative hostility, motivated by the child's trying to matter to the parent. These attitudes become subject to transference upon anyone who evokes emotional dependency, and these as well as the defenses against them become focused in the analysis.

Frequently other aspects of the relationship between parent and child are suppressed. Loving aspects that were "not enough" or that led to sexual traumata can be compulsively forgotten and denied. Or they can be transformed into the child's stubborn retention of his or her masochistic bind: in memory, by the compulsion to repeat in the present, or both. Sometimes the masochistic trap is malignant and even suicidal, leading to murder of the self in an effort to hold on to or rejoin the parent. The analyst's investigation of the masochistic bond implicitly threatens to modify the tie to the sadistic parent, and faces the soul-murder victim with the terrifying intensity of rageful wishes; these are felt capable of effecting a murder that will bring unbearable loss and aloneness. What is usually not conscious is the idealized fantasy that at the next sadomasochistic encounter the parent will this time emerge as the loving nurturer and rescuer who will magically erase the past, remove the murderous hatred, and make everything all right—in short, who will restore the prospect of paradise. This is an unconscious delusion that must be brought into awareness by the therapist and worked through emotionally by the patient.

I have found that the greatest burden borne by most of the patients who have made me think in terms of soul murder is the murderous intensity of their hatred. This invades all their meaningful relationships, and feeling it fully threatens to destroy every contemporary human tie, including that to the analyst. The need to retreat from their aggression and deny it (never accomplished completely, nor without paying an enormous price) is basically in the service of preserving the inner pictures of benevolent parents, which were once imperatively needed. Each patient has an individual way of defending against the cannibalistic intensity of his or her aggression, and this way is almost always massive and crippling.

It is the analyst's difficult task to interpret that aggression over and over again; to make it come alive means that the unbearable must eventually become bearable. The analyst should be aware of the dangers of getting mired in an inevitable sadomasochistic reenactment, with the analyst repeatedly interpreting the patient's anger at the analyst, and the patient either aggressively denying it to sustain a fighting contact, or masochistically provoking more interpretations that are experienced as verbal beatings. These are ways of holding on to the parent, and should be interpreted as such. In his work with those who manifest negative therapeutic reactions, Renik (1987b) persuasively points out the difficulties that ensue with interpretations of the patient's aggression toward the analyst. He quotes T. Jacobs tellingly: "Of course, if an analyst's interpretation of aggression perseveres 'like a hammer striking on an iron door' (Jacobs 1986), it can create a kind of specious self-confirmation by eliciting hostility in the patient" (Renik 1987b, 21). Renik counsels the analyst to convey to the patient "the subtle and complex ways that libidinal and defensive aims can be served" (p. 21) by the patient's resistances.

Interpreting aggression toward the analyst in such a way that the patient can make use of it requires great skill, perseverance, and (again) patience. Usually the patient begins with feelings about the analyst's malignity and rage that represent primarily a projection of the patient's own murderous feelings onto the analyst. Projection means delusion, which is ubiquitous in neurotics, though qualitatively different from psychotic delusion. The patient usually has only a sterile awareness that it is inappropriate to attribute the rage to the analyst, and acknowledges this through an intellectual lip service at best. It follows that projecting rage onto the analyst must in the course of the treatment be largely transformed into nondelusional transference of rage from the parent of the past onto the analyst.[3]

To accomplish this transformation of parentocidal impulses, the patient must become capable of tolerating the simultaneous consciousness that the analyst is intensely needed and cared about, and that there is intense destructive hatred toward the analyst. Repetitions over a long

3. Projection is almost always delusional; transference is sometimes so. The use of the word *delusion* in relation to neurotics raises hackles: some may prefer *quasi-delusions*. I feel that the delusions are true delusions—not amenable to reason. But they are more transient (although not necessarily less persistent) and more available to consciousness than the fixed delusions of the psychotic (see chapter 14).

time can make it possible for the patient to feel both hatred and love: the intense, conflicting feelings felt all at once and not in "separate compartments." This healing of splits in the sense of self does not of course undo the conflicts inherent to ambivalence, but it robs them of unbearable urgency: the feelings can be acknowledged and ameliorated. Love can at least partially neutralize hate when the patient experiences the identity-enhancing awareness that "I" can love and hate without the hate destroying the beloved.[4] For those healthy enough to sustain an analysis, there is usually some capacity to begin with for simultaneously tolerating these feelings, usually under special protective circumstances. If some ability to care about others has survived, this is a hopeful sign. Sometimes one sees this ability to love present toward children, so that making responsibly conscious the wish to hurt them in the way the patient was hurt as a child causes such distress that it becomes a strong motivating force toward change.

Dealing with Psychological Reality through Transference and Countertransference Phenomena

In emphasizing the importance of both the patient's life of fantasy and the memory of what actually occurred, I discussed the ideas of Spence (1982) about historical and narrative truth (see chapter 3): the reality of the past as distinguished from the analyst's putting together for the patient a consistent view of the patient's imperfect memories. In my experience, the analyst must almost always help reconstruct the past when the patient joins memories that have been retained with those that have been recovered, and then works over the amalgam (optimally

---

4. The victims of child abuse are stuck with a preponderant mixture of murderous and anxiety-laden instinctual drives, and the massive, regressive, and primitive defenses needed to contain them. In analysis there will then be a constant dealing with preoedipal conflicts, and at some point with oedipal impulses that have been influenced and colored by the earlier traumatic struggles. Sometimes years of work are needed before the libidinal and loving aspects of the sexual attachments to the parents can emerge as flexibly and reversibly separable from the murderous oedipal impulses (in contrast to the original, fixed, nonmodifiable, compartmentalized disjunction). Again, mingled love and hate must become experiential.

with much attention paid to the limits and boundaries of certainty and uncertainty). But this creation of "narrative" means working with the patient to construct using material that the patient has brought to the analysis. This involves concentrating not on the analyst's expectations derived from theory or the analyst's own conscious and unconscious desires, but on the patient's fantasies and memories as they appear in the course of the analysis as "associations"—ideas and feelings focused on the analyst. Analytic work centers on attending to the transference of the past as concentrated and distorted in the patient's current, unconscious wishes towards the analyst. In the course of examining these endlessly repetitious phenomena, the patient and analyst can determine what is currently available emotionally in the "space," in the transactions, between them. This determination aims at establishing the patient's psychological reality: how what has happened to the patient has been registered, and what the patient is compelled from within to repeat. The picture of the past as mirrored in these transference phenomena may be expected to be different and distorted from the relatively unrecoverable reality of the past. And both patient and analyst must remain aware that there has been an actual past, and that actual events and the reactions to them have helped form the patient's inner world and inner life. This inner life comprehends the fantasies that center on the analyst as parental figure, as the patient's projected past and present self, or as both; and these "transferred" representations appear as protagonists of the two-character and then three-character (and then more populated) scenarios that represent current manifestations of the patient's early development. Psychic reality, the registration of the past within, supplies at best a palimpsest as a historical document; yet compared with the irrecoverable "what actually happened" and the completely unreliable "what I think happened or want to have happened," it is a relatively recoverable, cognitively accessible palimpsest. This makes it possible to establish boundaries between what a patient feels certain of and what the patient feels uncertain of in the course of repeatedly enacting his or her dynamic unconscious repertory. To use Freud's metaphor, this repertory is full of ghosts, like those in the *Odyssey* who come to life by drinking the blood of the transference, and these ghosts are so impellingly registered that they have inevitably influenced thought, impulse, and action, taking over characteristics of the self. So the analyst must help the patient to discover the complex, various, and changing ways in which the chief actors (parents, siblings, self) and scenes have been registered in the theater of the patient's mind. Transcendent power is provided especially by capturing in responsible awareness those aspects of the present from the past that have remained out of consciousness, or if conscious have been disavowed and disowned.[5] Distinctions about past and present, about what "certainly" happened and what remains doubtful, about distortions of the present derived from the past—all these need the blood provided by feeling responsibly about the person of the analyst for the patient to be empowered with conviction about the reality of his or her inner life. And these newly found and at first tentative convictions that transform the personas and scenes of present and past psychical reality require that the patient be able to give up the repertory company of the past. The past is psychically engraved in registrations of others (chiefly parents) and self, which have been felt as a structure necessary to sustain a sense of self, of security and identity. The patient must be able to bear this psychologically real loss of psychic structure, of contents of the mind that are felt or unconsciously assumed to be precious and indispensable. Here is the patient's "journey to Karlsbad" (see chap-

5. Freud made several puzzling yet also helpful comments about the patient's recall of memories from the distant past: that memories might be regarded by the analyst as relatively certain historical truth. Of the Wolf Man (1918) he wrote, "So far as my experience hitherto goes, these scenes from infancy [represented by current regressive fantasies] are not reproduced during the treatment as recollections. They are the products of construction" (pp. 50–51). Freud went on to say that such "scenes" that are "recollected" can be based on true memories, frequently "distorted from the truth, and interspersed with imaginary elements" (p. 51). In his paper "Constructions in Analysis" (1937b), Freud considered as confirmatory evidence of constructions based on actual events the patient's "lively recollections . . . which they themselves have described as 'ultra-clear'—but what they have recollected has not been the event that was the subject of the construction but details relating to that subject . . . [recollecting] with abnormal sharpness the faces of people . . . or furniture in such rooms—on the subject of which the construction had naturally no possibility of any knowledge (p. 266)." Most of my patients' memories seemed to have the quality of true recollection when they were recalled with many of these "ultra-clear" peripheral details. I have often found in the later course of the analysis a confirmatory lifting of the repression of memories related to recollections and constructions (in addition to dreams and fantasies). But the analyst can never be certain about the patient's historical past.

ter 13), a terrible challenge to anyone's psychic "constitution." But the challenge is especially difficult for the victim of soul murder, who has lived out and experienced the feeling that it is impossible to exist without the inner presence of the aggressor, the soul murderer with whom the victim has identified. When in the course of early development there has been too much trauma or deficiency, there is a terrible intensification of the omnipresent psychological trap of wanting to kill the parent without whom one cannot live. Denial preserves this murderous and self-destructive vicious cycle, which demands that the destructive parent be submitted to and identified with. The need for the parental tie constitutes the core of resistance to change, and of the preservation of the abused child's commitment to soul murder.

REFERENCES

In addition to standard abbreviations, the following bibliographical abbreviations are used in this list:

CW *The Writings of Anna Freud.* 8 vols. New York: International Universities Press, 1974–81.

SE *The Complete Psychological Works of Sigmund Freud.* Standard ed. Ed. and trans. J. Strachey. New York: W. W. Norton, 1976.

RK *Complete Works of Rudyard Kipling.* 28 vols. New York: Doubleday and Doran, 1941.

Abraham, K. 1907. The experiencing of sexual trauma as a form of sexual activity. In *Selected Papers*. London: Hogarth, 1942.
———. 1922. The spider as dream symbol. In *Selected Papers*, 326–332. London: Hogarth, 1949.
———. 1924. The influence of oral erotism on character formation. In *Selected Papers*, 393–406. London: Hogarth, 1949.
Abrams, S. 1977. The genetic point of view: antecedents and transformations. *J. Am. Psychoanal. Assn.* 25: 417–425.
———. 1978. The teaching and learning of psychoanalytic developmental psychology. *J. Am. Psychoanal. Assn.* 26: 387–406.
———. 1981. Insight: the Teiresian gift. *Psychoanal. Study Child* 36: 251–270.
Allingham, W. 1907. *A Diary, 1824–1889*. Ed. H. Allingham and D. Radford. London: Penguin, 1985.
Arlow, J. 1979. Metaphor and the psychoanalytic situation. *Psychoanal. Q.* 48: 363–385.
Balzac, H. 1832. The venial sin. In *Droll Stories*, vol. 1, trans. A. Brown. London: Elek, 1958.
Barker, W. 1951. *Familiar Animals of America*. New York: Harper.
Bate, W. J. 1975. *Samuel Johnson*. New York: Harcourt Brace Jovanovich.
Baudelaire, C. 1861. *Poems*. Ed. F. Scarfe. Baltimore: Penguin, 1961.
Bender, T. and Blau, T. 1977. Incest and the sexual abuse of children. *J. Am. Acad. Child Psychiat.* 16: 334–346.

Berliner, B. 1940. Libido and reality in masochism. *Psychoanal. Q.* 9: 322–333.

Blake, W. 1793. The marriage of heaven and hell. In *Blake,* 93–108. Baltimore: Penguin, 1958.

Blos, P. 1962. *On Adolescence.* Toronto: Collier-Macmillan.

———. 1965. The initial stage of male adolescence. *Psychoanal. Study Child* 20: 145–164.

Blum, H. 1979. The curative and creative aspects of insight. *J. Am. Psychanal. Assn. Suppl.* 27: 41–70.

Boston, L. M. 1979. *Perverse and Foolish: A Memoir of Childhood and Youth.* New York: Atheneum.

Bowlby, J., Robertson, J., and Rosenbluth, D. 1952. A two-year-old goes to the hospital. *Psychoanal. Study Child* 7: 82–94.

Brunswick, R. 1940. The preoedipal phase of libido development. In *The Psychoanalytic Reader,* ed. R. Fliess, 261–284. New York: Inter. Univ. Press, 1948.

Buddicom, J. 1974. *Eric and Us.* London: Frewin.

Burnham, D. 1971. August Strindberg's need-fear dilemma. Unpublished.

Butler, S. 1885. *The Way of All Flesh.* New York: Macmillan, 1925.

Calef, V. and Weinshel, E. 1981. Some clinical consequences of introjection: gaslighting. *Psychoanal. Q.* 50: 44–66.

Carrington, C. 1955. *Rudyard Kipling.* London: Penguin, 1970.

Chekhov, A. 1885–1904. *The Selected Letters of Anton Chekhov,* ed. L. Hellman, trans. S. Lederer. New York: Farrar, Straus, 1955.

———. 1894a. The black monk. In *Select Tales of Chekhov,* vol. 2., trans. C. Garnett, 318–344. London: Chatto and Windus, 1965.

———. 1894b. The black monk. In *The Duel and Other Stories,* trans. R. Wilks, 192–222. London: Penguin, 1984.

Crick, B. 1980. *George Orwell: A Life.* New York: Penguin.

Daldin, H. 1988. The fate of the sexually abused child. *Clinical Social Work Journal* 16: 22–32.

Demarest, W. 1977. Incest avoidance among human and nonhuman primates. In *Primate Bio-Social Development,* ed. C. Chevalier-Skolnikoff and F. E. Poirier. New York: Garland.

Dewald, P. 1987. Effects in an adult of incest in childhood. Paper delivered at meeting of the American Psychoanalytic Association, December 1987.

Dickens, C. 1840a. Dullborough town. In *The Uncommercial Traveller and Reprinted Pieces etc.* 116–129. London: Oxford Univ. Press, 1958.

———. 1840b. Nurse's stories. In *The Uncommercial Traveller and Reprinted Pieces etc.* 116–129. London: Oxford Univ. Press, 1958.

———. 1843. *The Life and Adventures of Martin Chuzzlewit.* London: Macmillan, 1892.

————. 1857. *Little Dorrit*. Clinton, Mass.: Colonial Press, n.d.

Dickes, R. 1965. The defensive function of an altered state of consciousness, a hypnoid state. *J. Am. Psychoanal. Assn.* 13: 356–403.

Dobrée, B. 1967. *Rudyard Kipling*. London: Oxford Univ. Press.

Dostoyevski, F. 1864. Notes from underground. In *Short Novels of Dostoyevski*, trans. C. Garnett. New York: Dial, 1945.

————. 1880. *The Brothers Karamazov*. New York: Modern Library, n.d.

Dupee, F. W., ed. 1960. *The Selected Letters of Charles Dickens*. New York: Farrar, Straus and Giroux.

Edel, L. 1962. *Henry James. The Middle Years, 1882–1895*. New York: Lippincott.

Eliot, T. S. 1925. The Hollow Men. In *The Complete Poems and Plays, 1909–1950*, 56–59. New York: Harcourt, Brace, 1952.

Fenichel, O. 1945. *The Psychoanalytic Theory of Neurosis*. New York: W. W. Norton.

Ferenczi, S. 1909. Introjection and transference. In *Contributions to Psychoanalysis*. New York: Basic Books, 1950.

————. 1915. Micturition as a sedative. In *Further Contributions to the Theory and Technique of Psychoanalysis*, 317. New York: Basic Books, 1952.

————. 1921a. The symbolism of the bridge. In *Further Contributions to Psychoanalysis*, 352–356. New York: Basic Books, 1950.

————. 1921b. Bridge symbolism and the Don Juan legend. In *Further Contributions to Psychoanalysis*, 356–358. New York: Basic Books, 1950.

————. 1925. Psycho-analysis of sexual habits. In *Further Contributions to the Theory and Technique of Psycho-Analysis*, 259–297. London: Hogarth.

————. 1933a. *The Clinical Diary of Sandor Ferenczi*, ed. J. Dupont. Cambridge: Harvard Univ. Press, 1988.

————. 1933b. On the confusion of tongues between adults and the child. In *Final Contributions to the Problems and Methods of Psychoanalysis*, 155–167. New York: Basic Books, 1955.

Fergusson, F. 1953. *The Idea of a Theater*. New York: Doubleday.

Fleming, A. 1937. Some childhood memories of Rudyard Kipling. *Chambers J.* (March), 168–173.

Fliess, R. 1953. The hypnotic evasion. *Psychoanal. Q.* 22: 497–511.

————. 1956. *Erogeneity and Libido*. New York: Inter. Univ. Press.

————. 1961. *Ego and Body Ego*. New York: Inter. Univ. Press.

————. 1973. *Symbol, Dream and Psychosis*. New York: Inter. Univ. Press.

Forster, E. M. 1907. *The Longest Journey*. New York: Alfred A. Knopf, 1922.

————. 1910. *Howard's End*. New York: Vintage, 1954.

Forster, J. 1872–74. *The Life of Charles Dickens*, vol. 1. London: J. M. Dent & Sons for Everyman Library, 1966.

Frazer, J. G. 1890. *The New Golden Bough*, ed. T. Gaster. New York: Criterion, 1959.

Freedman, D. 1969. The role of early mother/child relations: The etiology of some cases of mental retardation. In *Advances in Mental Science*. Vol. 1, *Congenital Mental Retardation*, ed. G. Farrell, 245–261. Austin: Univ. of Texas Press.

———. 1971. Congenital and perinatal sensory deprivation: Some studies in early development. *J. Psychiat.* 127: 1537–1545.

———. 1975. Congenital and perinatal sensory deprivations: Their effect on the capacity to experience affect. *Psychoanal. Q.* 44: 62–80.

Freedman, D., and Brown, S. 1968. On the role of coenesthetic stimulation in the development of psychic structure. *Psychoanal. Q.* 37: 418–438.

Freud, A. 1939–45. Infants without families. *CW*, vol. 3: 543–664.

———. 1958. Adolescence. *CW*, vol. 5: 136–156.

———. 1965. *Normality and Pathology in Childhood*. New York: Inter. Univ. Press.

———. 1979. The role of insight in psychoanalysis and psychotherapy. *J. Am. Psychoanal. Assn. Suppl.* 27: 3–8.

Freud, S. 1887–1902. *The Origins of Psychoanalysis: Letters, Drafts and Notes to Wilhelm Fliess*. New York: Basic Books, 1954.

———. 1887–1904. *The Complete Letters of Sigmund Freud to Wilhelm Fliess*, ed. J. Masson. Cambridge: Harvard Univ. Press, 1986.

———. 1892–99. Extracts from the Fliess papers. *SE*, vol. 1: 177–282.

———. 1899. Letter to Wilhelm Fliess, January 16, 1899. *SE*, vol. 1.

———. 1899. Letter to Wilhelm Fliess, January 24, 1899. *SE*, vol. 1.

———. 1900. The interpretation of dreams. *SE*, vols. 4, 5.

———. 1901. Psychopathology in everyday life. *SE*, vol. 6.

———. 1905. Three essays on sexuality. *SE*, vol. 7.

———. 1909. Notes upon a case of obsessional neurosis. *SE*, vol. 10.

———. 1911. Psycho-analytic notes on an autobiographical account of a case of paranoia (dementia paranoides). *SE*, vol. 12.

———. 1913. Totem and taboo. *SE*, vol. 13.

———. 1916–17. Introductory lectures on psycho-analysis. *SE*, vols. 15, 16.

———. 1915. The unconscious. *SE*, vol. 14.

———. 1917. A childhood recollection from "Dichtung und Wahrheit." *SE*, vol. 17.

———. 1918. From the history of an infantile neurosis. *SE*, vol. 17.

———. 1920. Beyond the pleasure principle. *SE*, vol. 18.

———. 1921. Group psychology and the analysis of the ego. *SE*, vol. 18.

———. 1923. The ego and the id. *SE*, vol. 19.

———. 1926. Inhibitions, symptoms and anxiety. *SE*, vol. 20.

———. 1928. Dostoyevsky and parricide. *SE*, vol. 21.

———. 1930. Civilization and its discontents. *SE*, vol. 21.

———. 1931. Female sexuality. *SE*, vol. 21.

———. 1933. New introductory lectures. *SE*, vol. 22.

———. 1937a. Analysis terminable and interminable. *SE*, vol. 23.

———. 1937b. Constructions in analysis. *SE*, vol. 23.

———. 1938. Findings, ideas, problems. *SE*, vol. 23.

———. 1939. Moses and monotheism. *SE*, vol. 23.

———. 1940. An outline of psycho-analysis. *SE*, vol. 23.

Freud, S., and Breuer, J. 1893–95. Studies on hysteria. *SE*, vol. 2.

Freud, S., and Jung, C. 1900–1914. *The Freud-Jung Letters*, ed. W. McGuire. Princeton: Princeton Univ. Press, 1974.

Fyvel, T. 1981. *George Orwell*. London: Hutchinson, 1983.

Gill, M. and Brenman, M. 1959. *Hypnosis and Related States*. New York: Inter. Univ. Press.

Graves, R. 1955. *The Greek Myths*, Vol. 2. Baltimore: Penguin.

Green, R. 1965. *Kipling and the Children*. London: Elek.

Greenacre, P. 1960. Regression and fixation. *J. Am. Psychoanal. Assn.* 8: 703–723.

———. 1968. Regression and fixation. In *Emotional Growth*, 300–314. New York: Inter. Univ. Press.

Guttman, S., et al. eds. 1979. *The Concordance to the Standard Edition of the Complete Psychological Works of Sigmund Freud*. Boston: G. K. Hall.

Hanly, C. 1987. Review of *The Assault on Truth: Freud's Suppression of the Seduction Theory*, by J. Masson. *Inter. J. Psychoanal.* 67: 517–521.

Hegner, R. 1942. A Parade of Familiar Animals. New York: Macmillan.

Hingley, R. 1976. *A New Life of Anton Chekhov*. New York: Alfred A. Knopf.

Hoffer, W. 1950. Oral aggressiveness and ego development. *Inter. J. Psychoanal.* 31: 156–160.

Housman, A. E. 1900. Poem 12 of *Last Poems*. In *The Collected Poems*, 111. New York: Henry Holt, 1940.

Ibsen, H. 1894. *Little Eyolf*, trans. W. Archer In *Last Plays of Henrik Ibsen*, 1–70. New York: Bantam, 1962.

———. 1896. *John Gabriel Borkman*, trans. W. Archer. In *Collected Works*, vol. 11: 179–353. New York: Scribner's, 1926; trans. M. Meyer. In *When We Dead Awaken and Three Other Plays*, 215–302. Garden City, N.Y.: Anchor-Doubleday, 1960; trans. A. Paulsen. In *Last Plays of Henrik Ibsen*, 293–375. New York: Bantam, 1962.

Isay, R. 1975. The influence of the primal scene on the sexual behavior of an early adolescent. *J. Am. Psychoanal. Assn.* 23: 535–554.

Israels, H. 1981. *Schreber: Father and Son*. Amsterdam: privately printed.

Jacobs, B. 1969. "Psychic murder" and characterization in Strindberg's "The Father." *Scandinavica* 8: 19–34.

Jarrell, R. 1962. On preparing to read Kipling. In *Kipling and the Critics*, ed. E. Gilbert, 133–149. New York: New York Univ. Press, 1965.

————. 1963. The English in England. In *The Third Book of Criticism*, 279–294. New York: Farrar, Straus and Giroux, 1969.

————. 1965. An unread novel. Introduction to *The Man Who Loved Children* by Christina Stead (1940), pp. v–xli. New York: Holt, Rinehart and Winston.

Johnson, E. 1952. *Charles Dickens: His Tragedy and Triumph*. New York: Simon and Schuster.

Johnson, P., ed. 1906. *The Oxford Book of Political Anecdotes*. New York: Oxford Univ. Press.

Jung, C. 1938. Wandlungen und Symbole der Libido. Leipzig and Vienna: Deuticke.

Kanzer, M. 1950. The oedipus trilogy. *Psychoanal. Q.* 19: 561–571.

————. 1952. The transference neurosis of the rat man. *Psychoanal. Q.* 21: 181–189.

Katan, A. 1973. Children who were raped. *Psychoanal. Study Child* 28: 208–224.

Karlinsky, S., and Heim, M. 1973. *Letters of Anton Chekhov*, trans. M. Heim. New York: Harper and Row.

Keiser, S. 1954. Orality displaced to the urethra. *J. Am. Psychoanal. Assn.* 2: 263–279.

————. 1962. Disturbances of ego function of speech and abstract thinking. *J. Am. Psychoanal. Assn.* 10: 50–73.

Kennedy, H. 1979. The role of insight in psychoanalysis. *J. Am. Psychoanal. Assn. Suppl.* 27: 9–28.

Kincaid-Weeks, R. 1964. Vision in Kipling's Novels. In *Kipling's Mind and Art*. ed. A. Rutherford, 197–234. London: Oliver and Boyd.

Kipling, R. 1884. Failure. *RK*, vol. 28: 101–102.

————. 1885. The betrothal. *RK*, vol. 25: 97–99.

————. 1888a. Plain tales from the hills. *RK*, vol. 1.

————. 1888b. Baa baa, black sheep. *RK*, vol. 3: 281–316.

————. 1888c. His Majesty the King. *RK*, vol. 3: 317–322.

————. 1889. In partibus. *RK*, vol. 28: 171–174.

————. 1890a. The light that failed. *RK*, vol. 15: 1–244.

————. 1890b. The rhyme of the three captains. *RK*, vol. 25: 255–260.

————. 1891. Tomlinson. In *Rudyard Kipling's Verse: Definitive Edition*, 358–363. Garden City, N.Y.: Doubleday, 1940.

————. 1892. Barrack room ballads. *RK*, vol. 25: 163–214.

————. 1894. The jungle books. *RK*, vol. 11.

————. 1895a. William the conqueror. *RK*, vol. 6: 165–206.

————. 1895b. The brushwood boy. *RK*, vol. 6: 329–370.

————. 1897. Captains courageous. *RK*, vol. 16: 1–175.

————. 1899. Stalky & co. *RK*, vol. 14: 1–377.

————. 1901. Kim. *RK*, vol. 16: 181–525.

————. 1906. Puck of Pook's Hill. *RK*, vol. 13: 1–238.

————. 1907. Values in life. *RK*, vol. 24: 17–22.

————. 1910. Rewards and fairies. *RK*, vol. 13: 239–544.

————. 1929. Uncovenanted mercies. *RK*, vol. 10: 325–348.

————. 1935. Hymn of breaking strain. *RK*, vol. 28: 298–299.

————. 1937. Something of myself. *RK*, vol. 24: 349–518.

————. 1983. *O Beloved Kids: Rudyard Kipling's Letters to His Children*, ed. E. Gilbert. New York: Harcourt Brace Jovanovich.

Kitto, H. 1955. *Greek Tragedy*. New York: Doubleday.

Klein, M. 1933. Early development of the conscience in the child. In *Contributions to Psycho-Analysis*, 267–278. London: Hogarth.

Kligerman, C. 1970. The Dream of Charles Dickens. *J. Amer. Psychoanal. Assn.* 4: 783–799.

Kohut, H. 1971. *The Analysis of the Self: A Systematic Approach to the Psychoanalytic Treatment of Narcissistic Personality Disorder*. New York: Inter. Univ. Press.

Koteliansky, S. and Tomlinson, P. (n.d.). *The Life and Letters of Anton Tchekhov*. New York: George H. Doran.

Koestler, A. 1949. *Insight and Outlook*. New York: Macmillan.

Kouretas, D. 1963. L'homosexualité du père d'Œdipe et ses conséquences. Athens: privately printed reprint from *Annales médicales*, 1963.

Kramer, P. 1954. Early capacity for orgastic discharge and character formation. *Psychoanal. Study Child* 9: 128–141.

Kramer, S. 1974. Episodes of severe ego regression in the course of adolescent analysis. In *The Analyst and the Adolescent at Work*, ed. M. Harley. New York: Quadrangle.

————. 1983. Object-coercive doubting: A pathological defensive response to maternal incest. *J. Am. Psychoanal. Assn.* 31: 325–351.

Kris, E. 1953. *Psychoanalytic Explorations in Art*. London: George Allen and Unwin.

————. 1956a. Some vicissitudes of insight. In *Selected Papers of Ernst Kris*, 252–271. New Haven and London: Yale Univ. Press, 1975.

————. 1956b. The personal myth. In *Selected Papers of Ernst Kris*, 272–300. New Haven and London: Yale Univ. Press, 1975.

Kucera, O. 1959. On teething. *J. Am. Psychoanal. Assn.* 7: 284–291.

Lamb, C. 1799. Letter to Robert Southey. In *The Selected Letters of Charles Lamb*, ed. T. S. Matthews, 40–42. New York: Farrar, Straus and Cudahy, 1956.

————. 1833. Sanity of True Genius. In *Essays of Elia and Last Essays of Elia*. London: J. M. Dent and Sons, 1929.

Lawrence, D. H. 1913. The virgin mother. In *Complete Poems*, vol. 1. London: Heinemann, 1957.

———. 1928. *Lady Chatterley's Lover*. New York: Grove, 1957.

Levi, P. 1987. Beyond judgement. *New York Review of Books* 30, no. 20: 10–14.

Lévi-Strauss, C. 1956. The family. In *Culture and Society*, ed. H. Shapiro. London: Oxford Univ. Press.

Lewin, B. 1950. *The Psychoanalysis of Elation*. New York: W. W. Norton.

———. 1955. Dream psychology and the analytic situation. *Psychoanal. Q.* 24: 169–189.

Lewis, H. 1958. The effect of shedding the first deciduous tooth upon the passing of the oedipus complex. *J. Am. Psychoanal. Assn.* 6: 5–37.

Loewald, H. 1978. The waning of the oedipus complex. In *Papers on Psychoanalysis*, 384–404. New Haven and London: Yale Univ. Press.

Lorenz, K. 1963. *On Aggression*. New York: Harcourt, Brace.

McLaughlin, J. 1975. The sleepy analyst: some observations on states of consciousness in the analyst at work. *J. Am. Psychoanal. Assn.* 23: 363–382.

Mackenzie, H., and Mackenzie, J. 1979. *Dickens: A Life*. London: Oxford Univ. Press.

Magarshack, D. 1952. *Chekhov. A Life*. New York: Grove.

Mahler, M. 1952. On child psychosis and schizophrenia. *Psychoanal. Study Child* 7: 286–303.

———. 1972. On the first three subphases of the separation-individuation process. *Int. J. Psychoanal.* 53: 333–338.

———. 1974. Symbiosis and Individuation. *Psychoanal. Study Child* 29: 89–106.

Mahler, M., and Elkisch, P. 1959. On infantile precursors of the "influencing machine". *Psychoanal. Study Child* 14: 219–234.

Mahler, M., and Furer, M. 1968. *On Human Symbiosis and the Vicissitudes of Individuation*. New York: Inter. Univ. Press.

Mahler, M., and Gosliner, B. 1955. On symbiotic child psychosis. *Psychoanal. Study Child* 10: 195–214.

Mahler, M., Pine, F., and Bergman, A. 1975. *The Psychological Birth of the Human Infant*. New York: Basic Books.

Malcom, J. 1984. *In the Freud Archives*. New York: Alfred A. Knopf.

Malson, L. 1964. *Wolf Children*. London: NLB Press, 1972.

Margolis, M. 1977. A preliminary report of a case of consummated mother/son incest. *Annual of Psychoanal.* 5: 267–294.

Mason, P. 1975. *Kipling, the Glass, the Shadow and the Fire*. New York: Harper and Row.

Masson, J. 1984. *The Assault on Truth: Freud's Suppression of the Seduction Theory*. New York: Farrar, Straus and Giroux.

Masson, J., and Masson, T. 1978. The navel of neurosis: trauma, memory and denial. Unpublished manuscript.

Mills, E. 1959. Rats: Let's get rid of them. U.S. Dept. of the Interior, circular no. 22. Washington: GPO.

Mirbeau, O. 1899. *Torture Garden*. New York: Citadel, 1948.

Neubauer, P. B. 1979. The role of insight in psychoanalysis. *J. Am. Psychoanal. Assn. Suppl.* 27: 29–40.

Niederland, W. 1951. Three notes on the Schreber case. *Psychoanal. Q.* 21: 579–591.

———. 1959a. Schreber: father and son. *Psychoanal. Q.* 28: 151–169.

———. 1959b. The "miracled-up" world of Schreber's childhood. *Psychoanal. Study Child* 14: 383–413.

———. 1960. Schreber's father. *J. Am. Psychoanal. Assn.* 8: 492–499.

———. 1963. Further data and memorabilia pertaining to the Schreber case. *Inter. J. Psychoanal.* 44: 201–207.

Nietzsche, F. 1886. Beyond Good and Evil. In *The Philosophy of Nietzsche*. New York: Modern Library, n.d.

Noy, P. 1978. Insight and creativity. *J. Am. Psychoanal. Assn.* 26: 717–748.

O'Neill, E. 1956. *Long Day's Journey into Night*. New Haven and London: Yale Univ. Press.

Orgel, S., and Shengold, L. 1968. The gifts of Medea. *Inter. J. Psychoanal.* 49: 379–385.

Orwell, G. 1933. *Down and Out in Paris and London*. New York: Harcourt, Brace.

———. 1937. *The Road to Wigan Pier*. London: Secker and Warburg, 1950.

———. 1938. *Homage to Catalonia*. Boston: Beacon, 1955.

———. 1946. Why I write. In *A Collection of Essays*, 309–316. San Diego and New York: Harcourt Brace Jovanovich.

———. 1947. Such, such were the joys. In *A Collection of Essays*, 1–47. San Diego and New York: Harcourt Brace Jovanovich.

———. 1948. Letter to Julian Symons. In *The Collected Essays, Journalism and Letters of George Orwell*, vol. 4. *In Front Of Your Nose, 1945–1950*, ed. S. Orwell and I. Angus, 415–417. New York: Harcourt, Brace and World, 1968.

———. 1949. *Nineteen Eighty-four*. New York: Harcourt, Brace, 1949.

Partridge, E. 1961. *A Dictionary of Slang and Unexpurgated English*, vol. 2. London: Routledge and Kegan Paul.

Pascal, B. 1670. Pensées. In: *Blaise Pascal*, ed. and trans. J. Bishop, 163–256. New York: Dell, 1961.

Peto, A. 1959. Body image and archaic thinking. *Int. J. Psychoanal.* 40: 223–231.

Piaget, J. 1937. *The Construction of Reality in the Child*. New York: Basic Books, 1954.

Protheroe, E. 1940. *New Illustrated Natural History of the World*. New York: Garden City Press.

Rangell, L. 1955. The role of the parent in the oedipus complex. *Bull. Menninger Clinic* 19: 9–15.

———. 1970. The return of the repressed "oedipus." In *Parenthood*, ed. E. Anthony and T. Benedek. Boston: Little, Brown, 1970.

———. 1971. The decision-making process: A contribution from psychoanalysis. *Psychoanal. Study Child* 26: 425–452.

———. 1974. A psychoanalytic perspective leading currently to the syndrome of the compromise of integrity. *Int. J. Psychoanal.* 55: 3–12.

———. 1976. Lessons from Watergate: A derivation for psychoanalysis. *Psychoanal. Q.* 45: 37–61.

———. 1980. *The Mind of Watergate: An Exploration of the Compromise of Integrity*. New York: W. W. Norton.

———. 1987. A core process in psychoanalytic treatment. *Psychoanal. Q.* 56: 222–249.

Rank, O. 1912. *Das Incest-Motiv in Dichtung und Sage*. Leipzig and Vienna: Deuticke.

Rascovsky, M., and Rascovsky, A. 1950. On consummated incest. *Inter. J. Psychoanal.* 31: 42–47.

Reik, T. 1951. *Dogma and Compulsion*. New York: Inter. Univ. Press.

Renik, O. 1987a. A footnote to Victor Calef's observations on the hostility of parents to children. *Dialogue*, Spring 1987.

———. 1987b. One kind of negative therapeutic reaction. Unpublished manuscript.

Roheim, G. 1934. *The Riddle of the Sphinx*. London: Hogarth.

Rosenfeld, A., Nadelson, C., Kreiger, M., and Backman, J. 1977. Incest and the sexual abuse of children. *J. Am. Acad. Child Psych.* 16: 334–346.

Sade, D. 1968. Inhibition of son/mother mating among free-ranging rhesus monkeys. *Science and Psychoanalysis* 12: 18–38.

Sandler, J., and Rosenblatt, B. 1962. The concept of the representational world. *Psychoanal. Study Child* 8: 128–145.

Schatzman, M. 1973. *Soul Murder: Persecution in the Family*. New York: Random House.

Schour, I., and Masser, M. 1949. The teeth. In *The Rat in Laboratory Investigation*, ed. E. J. Farris and J. Q. Griffith. Philadelphia: Lippincott.

Schreber, D. P. 1903. *Memoirs of My Nervous Illness*. Ed. J. McAlpine and R. Hunter. London: Dawson, 1955.

Shakespeare, W. 1604. *Othello*. In *Shakespeare*, ed. T. Parrott. New York: Scribners, 1936.

———. 1623. *Macbeth*. In *The Arden Shakespeare*, ed. K. Muir. Cambridge: Harvard Univ. Press, 1957.

Shengold, L. 1963. The parent as sphinx. *J. Am. Psychoanal. Assn.* 11: 725–751.

———. 1966. The metaphor of the journey in *The Interpretation of Dreams*. *Am. Imago* 23: 316–331.

———. 1967. The effects of overstimulation: rat people. *Inter. J. Psychoanal.* 48: 403–415.

———. 1971. More about rats and rat people. *Inter. J. Psychoanal.* 52: 277–288.

———. 1974. The metaphor of the mirror. *J. Am. Psychoanal. Assn.* 22: 97–115.

———. 1975. Soul murder. *Inter. J. Psychoanal. Psychother.* 3: 366–373.

———. 1979. Child abuse and deprivation: soul murder. *J. Am. Psychoanal. Assn.* 27: 533–559.

———. 1985. Defensive anality and anal narcissism. *Inter. J. Psychoanal.* 66: 47–73.

———. 1988. *Halo in the Sky*. New York: Guilford.

Shuren, I. 1967. A contribution to the metapsychology of the preanalytic patient. *Psychoanal. Study Child* 22: 103–138.

Silber, A. 1974. Rationale for the technique of psychotherapy with alcoholics. *Inter. J. Psychotherapy* 3: 28–47.

———. 1977. The alcohol-induced hypnoid state and its analytic corollary. *Inter. J. Psychotherapy* 6: 253–264.

Simmel, E. 1944. Self preservation and the death instinct. *Psychoanal. Q.* 13: 160–185.

———. 1946. Alcoholism and addiction. *Psychoanal. Q.* 17: 6–32.

Sophocles. Oedipus Rex, trans. D. Fitts and R. Fitzgerald. In *The Oedipus Cycle*. New York: Harcourt, Brace, 1949; trans. R. Jebb. In *Tragedies*, London: Cambridge Univ. Press, 1928; trans. G. Murray. In *Fifteen Greek Plays*, ed. L. Cooper. New York: Oxford Univ. Press, 1963; trans. E. Watling. In *The Theban Plays*. Baltimore: Penguin, 1947.

Spence, D. 1982. *Narrative Truth and Historical Truth*. New York: W. W. Norton.

Spitz, R. 1945. Hospitalism: An inquiry into the genesis of psychiatric conditions in early childhood. *Psychoanal. Study Child* 1: 53–74.

———. 1946a. Hospitalism: A follow-up report. *Psychoanal. Study Child* 2: 113–117.

———. 1946b. Anaclitic depression. *Psychoanal. Study Child* 2: 313–342.

———. 1950. Anxiety in infancy. *Inter. J. Psychoanal.* 31: 128–143.

———. 1964. The derailment of dialogue: Stimulus overload and the completion gradient. *J. Am. Psychoanal. Assn.* 12: 752–775.

Spock, B. 1957. *Baby and Child Care*. New York: Duell, Sloan.

Spruiell, V. 1986. Trying to understand the consequences or lack of

consequences of overt sexuality between adults and children. Panel
presentation, American Psychoanalytic Association, December 21, 1986.

Stansky, P., and Abrahams, W. 1980. *Orwell: The Transformation*. New York:
Alfred A. Knopf.

Steele, B. 1970. Parental abuse of infants and small children. In *Parenthood*,
ed. J. Anthony and T. Benedek, 449–477. New York: Little, Brown.

——. 1976. Violence within the family. In *Child Abuse and Neglect*, ed.
R. Helfer and C. Kempe. Cambridge, Mass.: Ballinger.

——. 1977. Psychoanalytic observations on attachment and development of
absued children. Presented at Annual Meeting of the American
Psychoanalytic Association at Quebec City, April 1977.

Steele, B., Kempe, C., et al. 1962. The battered-child syndrome. *JAMA* 181:
17–24.

Steele, B., and Pollock, C. 1968. A psychiatric study of parents who abuse
infants and small children. In *The Battered Child*, ed. R. Helfer and
C. Kempe. Chicago: Univ. of Chicago Press.

Stein, M. 1965. States of consciousness in the analytic situation. In *Drives,
Affects, Behavior*, vol 2., ed. M. Schur. New York: Inter. Univ. Press, 1965.

Stewart, J. I. M. 1966. *Rudyard Kipling*. New York: Dodd and Mead.

Stoller, R. 1974. The creation of illusion: Extreme femininity. *Annual of
Psychoanal.* 2: 197–212.

——. 1973. *Splitting: A Case of Female Homosexuality*. New York:
Quadrangle.

Strindberg, A. 1887. Soul Murder. *Drama rev.* 13 (1968): 113–118.

Trilling, L. 1940. Freud and literature. In *The Liberal Imagination*, 34–57.
New York: Viking, 1950.

——. 1943. Kipling. In *Kipling's Mind and Art*, ed. A. Rutherford, 85–96.
London: Oliver and Boyd, 1964.

——. 1955a. George Orwell and the politics of truth. In *Orwell's Nineteen
Eighty-four: Text, Sources, Criticism*, ed. I. Howe, 217–226. New York:
Harcourt, Brace and World, 1963.

——. 1955b. Freud, within and beyond culture. In *Beyond Culture*, 89–118.
New York: Viking, 1965.

——. 1967. *The Experience of Literature: Drama*. New York: Holt, Rinehart
and Winston.

Troyat, H. 1984. *Chekhov*, trans. M. H. Heim. New York: E. P. Dutton, 1986.

Turnbull, C. M. 1972. *The Mountain People*. New York: Simon and Shuster.

Valenstein, A. F. 1962. The psychoanalytic situation. *Inter. J. Psychoanal.* 43:
315–324.

Van Der Sterren, H. 1952. The King Oedipus of Sophocles. *Inter. J.
Psychoanal.* 33: 343–351.

Von Feuerbach, A. 1832. *Kaspar Hauser: Beispiel eines Verbrecherens am
Seelenleben des Menschen*. Anspach.

———. 1832. *Caspar Hauser: An Account of an Individual Kept in a Dungeon, Separated from All Communication with the World, from Early Childhood to about the Age of Seventeen*, trans. H. Linberg. London: Simpkin and Marshall, 1833.

Wahl, C. 1960. The psychodynamics of consummated maternal incest. *Archs. Gen. Psychiat.* 3: 96–101.

Wallerstein, R. 1973. Psychoanalytic perspectives on the problem of reality. *J. Am. Psychoanal. Assn.* 21: 5–33.

Wasserman, J. 1928. *Caspar Hauser*. New York: Liveright, 1956.

Weich, M. 1968. The terms "mother" and "father" as a defense against incest. *J. Am. Psychoanal. Assn.* 16: 783–791.

Weinshel, E. 1986. Perceptual distortions during analysis: Some observations on the role of the superego in reality testing. In *Psychoanalysis: The Science of Mental Conflict: Essays in Honor of Charles Brenner*, ed. A. Richards and M. Willick. Hillsdale, N.J.: Analytic Press.

———. 1986. The effects of sexual abuse in childhood as observed in the psychoanalysis of adults. Panel presentation, American Psychoanalytic Association, December 21, 1986.

West, A. 1958. George Orwell. In *Principles and Persuasions*, 150–159. London: Eyre and Spottiswoode.

Whitman, W. 1855. *Leaves of Grass*. New York: Modern Library, 1921.

Wilde, O. 1893. *Salomé*. In *Plays of Oscar Wilde*. New York: Modern Library.

———. 1895. *The importance of being Earnest*. In *Plays, Prose Writings and Poems*, pp. 347–402. London: J. M. Dent for Everyman Library, 1975.

Wilson, A. 1977. *The Strange Ride of Rudyard Kipling*. London: Granada.

Wilson, E. 1941a. Dickens and the two Scrooges. In *Eight Essays*, 11–91. New York: Doubleday Anchor, 1954.

———. 1941b. The Kipling that nobody read. In *Kipling's Mind and Art*, ed. A. Rutherford, 17–69. London: Oliver and Boyd, 1964.

———. 1950. In memory of Octave Mirbeau. In *Classics and Commercials*, 471–485. New York: Farrar, Straus.

Winnicott, D. W. 1953. Transitional object and transitional phenomena. In *Collected Papers*, 229–242. New York: Basic Books, 1958.

Yarmolinsky, A., ed. 1973. *Letters of Anton Chekhov*. New York: Viking.

Yazmajian, R. 1966. Verbal and symbolic processes in slips of the tongue. *J. Am. Psychoanal. Assn.* 14: 443–461.

Zinsser, H. 1935. *Rats, Lice and History*. New York: Little, Brown.

INDEX